D0205716

HUME'S "Inexplicable Mystery"

*H*UME'S
*"I*nexplicable
*M*ystery*"*

His Views on Religion

*K*EITH *E. Y*ANDELL

TEMPLE UNIVERSITY PRESS
PHILADELPHIA

Temple University Press, Philadelphia 19122
Copyright © 1990 by Temple University. All rights reserved
Published 1990
Printed in the United States of America

The paper used in this publication meets the minimum
requirements of American National Standard for Information
Sciences—Permanence of Paper for Printed Library Materials,
ANSI Z39.48-1984

Library of Congress Cataloging-in-Publication Data

Yandell, Keith E., 1938–
    Hume's "inexplicable mystery" : his views on religion / Keith E.
    Yandell.
      p.   cm.
    Includes bibliographical references.
    ISBN 0-87722-643-1 (alk. paper)
    1. Hume, David, 1711–1776—Religion.   I. Title.
B1499.R45Y36   1990
210'.92—dc20
                                                        89-37202
                                                        CIP

To Professor Julius R. Weinberg, who I know would have disagreed with most of my assessments, and to Professor Marvin Fox, who I hope will not. Whatever is sound and right in my interpretation, or my work elsewhere, owes much to their scholarship and example.

CONTENTS

PREFACE

Along with much else, Hume's writings contain a philosophy of religion. *The Natural History of Religion,* a comparatively and unjustly neglected work, provides one of our earliest examples of a psychological explanation of religious belief. Its sophistication, even psychologically, compares favorably with such later attempts as the Freudian to account for religious belief by reference only to psychological factors. It differs from the Freudian account in that it is not a presupposition of its success that the belief it explains be unreasonable or false. The *Natural History* discussion, though explicitly framed to deal with polytheism and monotheism, easily extrapolates to non-theistic religious beliefs.

The *Dialogues Concerning Natural Religion,* in Parts One through Eight, provides one of the most sophisticated discussions ever of the argument from design. The discussion contains an orderly and insightful consideration of a series of axioms of inductive reasoning. This same discussion, recast along lines suggested by Hume's theory of meaning in Part One of *A Treatise of Human Nature,* relates to the issue of the conditions of intelligibility for religious discourse. Demea, who sponsors negative theology earlier in the *Dialogues,* defends *a priori* arguments for God's existence, and these form the focus of Part Nine. Parts Ten and Eleven deal in some detail with varieties of the problem of evil. That despair of commentators, Part Twelve of the *Dialogues,* returns to the theme of the *Natural History.* Nor should one forget the *Enquiry Concerning Human Understanding* concerning miracles and providence, or Hume on the immortality of the soul, suicide, and superstition and enthusiasm.

Hume's intention in developing a philosophy of religion of course was to understand and explain, to dispel all mystery concerning the issues that fall within its rubric. By his own appraisal, he met with limited success. *The Natural History of Religion* closes with these words:

> The whole is a riddle, an enigma, an inexplicable mystery. Doubt, uncertainty, suspense of judgment appear the only result of our most accurate scrutiny, concerning this subject. But such is the frailty of human reason, and such the irresistible contagion of opinion, that even this deliberate doubt could scarcely be upheld; did we not enlarge our view, and opposing one species of super-stition to another, set them a quarrelling: while we ourselves, during their fury and contention, happily make our escape into the calm, though obscure, regions of philosophy. [*N*, 98]

One can suggest that these remarks are but a closing flourish, an ironic nod in the direction of a piety that finds mystery where Humean natu-ralism finds mainly misery. But given the content of Hume's views on religion—their foundation in his theory of human nature and his very partial success in making that theory coherent—the remarks (which express a very Humean skepticism) offer a not inaccurate assessment.

As their titles suggest, *The Natural History of Religion* and the *Dia-logues Concerning Natural Religion* form a pair; they are, in effect, Vol-umes One and Two of *Hume's Philosophy of Religion*. A careful reader of the *Treatise* would expect the *Natural History* to be the more funda-mental work, and one who comes to the *Dialogues* with the *Natural History* in mind will note that the *Dialogues* return, in their final part, to the basic themes of the *Natural History*. To the considerable extent to which the *Natural History* has been neglected, and the *Dialogues* read alone, Hume's philosophy of religion has been only partially understood. In the work that follows, I will treat the *Natural History* as the key to Hume's philosophy of religion, as (I shall argue) does Hume himself. The major themes and arguments of the *Natural His-tory* will be critically presented, and then the major themes and argu-ments of the *Dialogues*, with the relevant portions of the *Treatise* al-ways in mind.

I owe, of course, an enormous debt to commentators on Hume, from Thomas Reid through Donald Livingston, and including Kant and Laird, Hendel and Kemp Smith, Penelhum and Flew, Norton and Noxon, and so on. But no one can have taken courses in Hume with

Marvin Fox, and spent countless hours discussing Hume with Julius Weinberg, and not feel a particularly deep debt to them for an astoundingly rich scholarship shared so warmly and freely.

Chapter 15, "Miracles," originally appeared with some changes as "Miracles, Epistemology and Hume's Barrier" in the *International Journal for Philosophy of Religion* 7, no. 3 (1976): 391–417. © Associates for Philosophy of Religion, Inc., Box 828, Mocksville, N.C., U.S.A. *Reprinted by permission of Kluwer Academic Publishers.*

ABBREVIATIONS

D   *Dialogues Concerning Natural Religion,* edited and with an introduction by Norman Kemp Smith (1779; reprinted Indianapolis: Bobbs-Merrill, 1962).

E   *Enquiries Concerning Human Understanding and Concerning the Principles of Morals,* with introduction and analytical index by L. A. Selby-Bigge, and revised text and notes by P. H. Nidditch (1748; reprinted Oxford: Clarendon Press, 1975).

N   *Hume on Religion,* edited by Richard Wollheim, containing *The Natural History of Religion,* the *Dialogues,* and *My Own Life* (New York: Meridian Books, 1963). Compare Hume's *The Natural History of Religion,* edited by H. E. Root (1757; reprinted 1957; reprinted Stanford: Stanford University Press, 1981).

O   *Of the Standard of Taste and Other Essays,* edited by John W. Lentz (Indianapolis: Bobbs-Merrill, 1965). "Of Superstition and Enthusiasm" originally published in 1741 in Hume's *Essays Moral and Political,* vol. 1. "On Suicide" and "On the Immortality of the Soul" first published in English in 1777.

T   *A Treatise of Human Nature,* 2d ed. Analytical index by L. A. Selby-Bigge with revised text and notes by P. H. Nidditch (1739–1740; reprinted 1888; reprinted Oxford: Clarendon Press, 1978).

HUME'S "Inexplicable Mystery"

INTRODUCTION

Hume's philosophy of religion is best understood as predicated on two assumptions: that it is unreasonable to accept any belief unless it is either appropriately basic or something for which we have evidence; that no religious belief is appropriately basic. It follows from these assumptions that no religious belief is reasonably accepted by anyone who lacks evidence for it.

Hume thinks that beliefs are appropriately basic only if one's having them can be explained by reference to what Hume calls "original" propensities of human nature. An original propensity of human nature is a propensity with these features: it produces the same belief in everyone in whom it operates, and it operates in everyone. Such propensities are activated by a sort of experience that everyone has. Hume's contention is that no religious belief is produced by an original propensity. Hence his view is that no religious belief is appropriately basic. *So one is unreasonable in accepting a religious belief unless one has evidence for it.*

It is also Hume's view that there is no evidence for any religious belief. Hence he holds that no one is ever reasonable in accepting a religious belief. Still, one's accepting a religious belief has an explanation. In one way, Hume's preferred explanation here is like his explanation of one's holding an appropriately basic belief. It refers to propensities that give rise to beliefs when they are activated by experiences. In another way, it is different. The propensities that give rise to religious beliefs are not original; they do not operate in everyone, and they do not produce the same beliefs in everyone in whom they do operate. Thus it is less natural to have religious beliefs than to have beliefs that arise from original propensities. Indeed, Hume's position seems to be that, in a way we shall explore, having religious beliefs threatens the unity and stability of human nature.

The Natural History of Religion explores propensity-activated-by-experiences explanations of religious beliefs. In Chapter 1, the focus is on a descriptive account of these explanations of religious belief. Chapters 2 and 3 recount Hume's doctrines concerning propensity-explanations of non-religious beliefs and his suggestion that the formation and possession of religious beliefs threatens havoc to human nature. Part Twelve of the *Dialogues* receives its proper consideration here. Chapter 4 considers Hume's theory of what a person is—of what constitutes a mind or self—and how this relates to his view of persons as propensity-bearers. Chapter 5 considers the rationale and implications of Hume's actual non-epistemic explanation of religious belief and by extrapolation, his non-epistemic explanation of religious experience. These discussions of topics that arise from *The Natural History* comprise Part I.

Part II relates to the *Dialogues Concerning Natural Religion*. Chapter 6 expounds Hume's evidentialism concerning religious belief, placing it in context and contrast to the Deism of such authors as Herbert of Cherbury and the natural theology of Bishop Joseph Butler. Chapter 7 considers changes in Hume's theory of meaning and its application to religious language. Chapters 8 through 10 trace the fortunes of the argument from design in the *Dialogues*. In Chapter 11, Hume's discussion of the ontological and cosmological arguments receives attention. Hume's treatment of the problem of evil serves as the subject of Chapters 12 and 13, which conclude Part II.

Other writings besides the *Natural Religion* and the *Dialogues* are relevant to Hume's philosophy of religion. His *Enquiry Concerning Human Understanding* contains the infamous essay on miracles and the misleadingly entitled article on providence and a future state, which is a sort of pre-*Dialogues* dialogue. Hume's "On Immortality" contains a treatment of arguments concerning the immortality of the soul, his essay "On Suicide" discusses monotheism and the duty not to commit suicide, and "Of Enthusiasm and Superstition" describes the title phenomena as "corruptions of true religion." Chapter 14 discusses the Humean essays just mentioned other than that on miracles, and Chapter 15 is devoted to this remaining essay. These two chapters comprise Part III; a final Conclusion completes the volume.

Hume's philosophy of religion is a sophisticated and sustained treatment of the topic. This being a philosophical analysis of Hume's views, the various chapters assess as well as describe. J. C. A. Gaskin's *Hume's Philosophy of Religion* finds the terrible David's perspective correct in starting point, method, and conclusion. I argue that it is skewed, mistaken, and often indefensible. But it bears the feature of good philosophical work, whether or not that work enjoys truth's smile: even its mistakes are instructive. If it errs, it errs intelligently, and so it richly repays careful study. Respect for work in philosophy does not require agreement with that work's conclusion. I confess to being glad that this is so.

PART ONE

The Natural History of Religion

CHAPTER 1

The Content of the Natural History

Hume's Theory of Religious Belief

HUME TELLS US that the more humans consider the causes of human ills, and "the uncertainty of their operation, the less satisfaction do they meet with in their researches; and, however unwilling, they must at last have abandoned so arduous an attempt, were it not for a propensity in human nature, which leads into a system, that gives them some satisfaction" (*N,* 40). He plausibly suggests that seeking "a system, that gives . . . some satisfaction"—no explanation is given of exactly what sort of satisfaction is in question—is inescapable. But what system should one accept? In fact, people accept different and various explanatory systems, and even if we consider only all-embracing worldviews the same person may accept different systems during a lifetime. It is a distinctive (though not unique) feature of Hume's philosophy of religion that within it there is, strictly speaking, no rational decision procedure for deciding between competing systems. It is more natural, but not therefore more in accord with evidence, to accept some systems of explanation rather than others. No appeal to the rational against the natural is possible. Further, the philosophy of religion that has this negative consequence is held to be itself rationally justifiable. Hume's skepticism, in religion as elsewhere, is restrained and rationally defended. He uses the standard skeptical strategy of balancing opposing arguments and opinions that would produce a justified suspense of judgment were having grounds for belief a condition of believing. But he also endeavors to explain the presence of belief in a manner consistent with restrained skepticism—consistent, that is, with psychologically firm, shared convictions being nonetheless rationally unfounded. Hume's skepticism scouts evidence, not belief. He holds that "nature, by an absolute and uncontrollable necessity, has determined us to judge as well as to breathe or feel" (*T*, 183). Belief is "more properly an act of the sensitive than the cognitive part of our nature" (*T*, 183). His general skepticism, and his skeptical philosophy of religion, rest on a theory of human nature that itself requires immunity from skeptical infection. The intent of the *Natural History of Religion* is to trace religious beliefs (and, by implication, experiences, rituals and institutions) to their origin in human nature. Hume writes:

> As every inquiry, which regards religion, is of the utmost importance, there are two questions in particular which challenge our attention, to wit, that concerning its foundation in human reason, and that concerning its origin in human nature. Happily, the first question, which is the most important, admits of the most obvious, at least, the clearest, solution. The whole frame of nature bespeaks an intelligent author; and no rational enquirer can, after serious reflection, suspend his belief a moment with regard to the primary principles of genuine Theism and Religion. But the other question, concerning the origin of religion in human nature, is exposed to some more difficulty. [*N*, 31]

Set aside, for now, Hume's answer to the first question, and note that it is the other, more difficult, question that occupies Hume in the *Natural History*. Referring to belief in an "invisible, intelligent power" that is the author of order in nature as "the original belief," Hume tells us: "What those principles are, which give rise to the original belief, and what those accidents and causes are, which direct its operation, is the subject of our present inquiry" (*N*, 31). Since he goes on to claim that polytheism, not the 'original belief,' is *historically* earlier than monotheism (of which the 'original belief' is in fact but a pale reflection), it is presumably a psychological sense of "original" Hume has in mind.

Nor does Hume forget this subject as the actual inquiry progresses. On the contrary, he refers constantly to human nature as the source of religious belief; the examples are legion. He contends that there is "a natural propensity" that is also a "natural frailty" for humans "to conceive all beings like themselves, and to transfer to every object those qualities with which they are familiarly acquainted, and of which they are familiarly conscious" (*N*, 41). He speaks of "the general principles of polytheism, founded in human nature" (*N*, 54) and repeats that "it is chiefly our present business to consider the gross polytheism of the vulgar, and to trace all its various appearances, in the principles of human nature, whence they are derived" (*N*, 51). He claims to find a natural human "propensity to adulation" (*N*, 59) and a "natural tendency to rise from idolatry to theism, and to sink again from theism into idolatry" (*N*, 62). He asserts that religious assent "is some unaccountable operation of the mind between disbelief and conviction" (*N*, 79). He says that he finds "a kind of contradiction between the different principles of human nature, which enter into religion" (*N*, 86). He notes a fact "which may be worth the attention of such as make human nature the object of their inquiry," namely that however high the morality of a religious tradition, its followers "will still seek the divine favour . . . either by frivolous observances, by intemperate zeal, by rapturous extasies, or by the belief of mysterious and absurd opinions" (*N*, 91). He posits a "universal propensity to believe in invisible, intelligent power" (*N*, 97), and says that religious beliefs are such that "their root strikes deeper into the human mind [than merely to the passions], and springs from the essential and universal properties of human nature" (*N*, 95). Whatever justice there is to G. E. Moore's remark that when a philosopher says that he or she is going to do so-and-so, that is a good reason for supposing that he or she will not do so-and-so, this does not apply to the Hume of the *Natural History.*

What, then, is religion's "origin in human nature"? Hume's answer comes largely in terms of the description of propensities. First, all persons have certain natural first-order propensities or share certain principles of human nature, many of which are relevant to religious belief. In particular, there is a propensity to believe in an invisible, intelligent power; there is a propensity to project human attributes onto natural objects and to attribute "human capacities and infirmities to the deity" (*N*, 41); there is a propensity to "rest attention on sensible, visible objects" (*N*, 51); and there is a "propensity to adulation" (*N*, 59) or to pile "epithets of praise" upon a deity. We might summarize these as propensities to *posit intelligent power,* to *anthropomorphize,* to *attend to observables,* and to *offer endless adulation.*

Second, there are other propensities—second-order propensities, perhaps—such as "a propensity in human nature which leads into a system which gives them some satisfaction," since the "imagination, perpetually employed on the same subject (the causes of human woe and weal), must labor to form some particular and distinct idea of them" (N, 40). There is a "natural tendency to rise from idolatry to theism" (N, 62) but also "a propensity, in this alternate revolution of human sentiments, to return back to idolatry." We might call these propensities to *understand* and to *fluctuate* (N, 63). The propensity to understand, under appropriate circumstances, often gives rise to, and is instantiated in, the operation of one or more of the set of first-order propensities mentioned above, in the way that the capacity to perform motor skills, under appropriate circumstances, gives rise to, and is instantiated in, walking across a room. For Hume, we *need* not accept a religious system of explanation, but most of us in fact do so. The propensity to fluctuate, presumably, is more latent. It presupposes a propensity to theism and a propensity to idolatry, and is a propensity to alternate between a state in which the one propensity is the more efficacious to a state in which the other is, rather as the tendency to be manic-depressive presupposes an activated tendency toward mania and an activated tendency toward depression and is a tendency to alternate from a state in which one tendency dominates to a state in which the other dominates. Thus one of the two new propensities is presupposed by the old ones; its activation yields them. The other of the two new propensities presupposes (some at least of) the old ones; their activation elicits its activity.

Third, there are facets of human nature that are not described as propensities, but that nonetheless affect the operation of the propensities that we have described. Hume tells us that "polytheism or idolatry was, and necessarily must have been, the first and most ancient religion of mankind" (N, 32). Why "necessarily must have been"? Because to Hume:

> It seems certain, that, according to the natural progress of human thought, the ignorant multitude must first entertain some groveling notion of superior powers before they stretch their conception to that perfect Being who bestowed order on the whole frame of nature. . . . The mind rises gradually, from inferior to superior: By abstraction from what is imperfect, it forms an idea of perfection: And slowly distinguishing the nobler parts of its own frame from the grosser, it learns to transform only the former, much elevated and refined, to its divinity. Nothing could disturb this progress of thought, but some obvious and invincible argument . . . yet I can never think that this consideration could have an influence on mankind, when they formed their first rude notions of religion. [N, 34]

It is not lucid what Hume's view here is, but its rough contours appear to be these: as an individual progresses in his or her ability to formulate increasingly sophisticated concepts, so does the race as a whole. Polytheism is not, and theism is, a sophisticated view; so polytheism is historically earlier than theism. The argument begins with a thesis about individual concept formation (and *perhaps* about concepts *per se*), and extrapolates to a thesis about the history of religion. Theses about how individuals form concepts are theses about one sort of human capacity—about part of what is included in human nature. Also, Hume suggests, doubt is inextricably linked with religious belief.

> Men dare not avow, even to their own hearts, the doubts which they entertain on such [religious] subjects. . . . But nature is too hard for all their endeavors, and suffers not the obscure, glimmering light, afforded in these shadowy regions, to equal the strong impressions made by common sense and by experience . . . their assent in these matters is some unaccountable operation of the mind between disbelief and conviction, but approaching much nearer to the former than to the latter. [*N*, 79]

The effect of sensory experience (and the propensities to belief that it elicits), given the overall composition of human nature, is stronger than that of the causes of religious belief—stronger in the sense that the beliefs associated with it are held with more constancy and conviction than are religious beliefs.

In these two general ways, then, Hume tells us, human nature is relevant to religious belief: it has affected the historical development of religious belief so that such belief had an evolution from polytheism to theism, and it produces non-religious beliefs (those associated with sensory experience) that have more durability than do religious beliefs (of whatever sort).

Fourth, Hume contends that:

> It must necessarily, indeed, be allowed, that, in order to carry men's intention beyond the present course of things, or lead them into any inference concerning invisible intelligent power, they must be activated by some passion, which prompts their thought and reflection; some motive, which urges their first inquiry. [*N*, 39]

While Hume refers to "motive," it is clear the emphasis falls on "passion"; the passions in question, he contends, are "the anxious concern for happiness, the dread of future misery, the terror of death, the thirst of revenge" (N, 39), and the like. Lest the point be in doubt, Hume writes:

> Any of the human affections may lead us into the notion of invisible, intelligent power; hope as well as fear, gratitude as well as affliction: But if we examine our own hearts, or observe what passes around us, we shall find, that men are much oftener thrown on their knees by the melancholy than by the agreeable passions . . . every disastrous accident alarms us, and sets us on inquiries concerning the principles whence it arose: Apprehensions spring up with regard to futurity: And the mind, sunk into diffidence, terror, and melancholy, has recourse to every method of appeasing those secret intelligent powers, on whom our fortune is supposed entirely to depend. [N, 43]

The same perspective is repeated when Hume remarks:

> The primary religion of mankind arises chiefly from an anxious fear of future events; and what ideas will naturally be entertained of invisible, unknown powers, while men lie under dismal apprehensions of any kind, may easily be conceived. [N, 85]

In Hume's view, passions must be present in order for the religion-relevant propensities to be activated, and he thinks that the darker passions are the ones that usually play this role. Further, these passions on the whole are caused by events that threaten our well-being.

> This . . . is obvious, that the empire of all religious faith over the understanding is wavering and uncertain, subject to every variety of humour, and dependent on the present incidents, which strike the imagination. [N, 81]

> We may conclude, therefore, that, in all nations, which have embraced polytheism, the first ideas of religion arose not from a contemplation of the works of nature, but from a concern with regard to the events of life, and from the incessant hopes and fears, which actuate the human mind. [N, 38]

Hume's overall perspective, then, goes something as follows: "mankind, in ancient times, appear universally to have been polytheists" (N, 33). Their acceptance of polytheistic beliefs is to be explained by their possessing the second-order propensity to form some particular and distinct idea of the causes that determine their condition. Afflicted by events they find threatening, people experience such emotions as hope and fear that together with these events activate this propensity to seek a satisfactory explanation, which in turn is instantiated by the operation of propensities to anthropomorphize, to attend to observables, and to offer endless adulation. The propensity to seek a satisfactory system is not instantiated, at this stage, by the operation of the propensity to posit an invisible, intelligent power because human cognitive processes are not yet sophisticated enough. Nonetheless, at some stage in the process this latter propensity is activated and people come to believe in an invisible, intelligent author of order in nature. Even when this occurs, the other propensities do not cease to operate; rather, their operation blends with that of the propensity to posit an invisible, intelligent power so that human qualities (including and especially the least elegant among them), and even physical attributes are attributed to the power due to the operations, respectively, of the propensities to anthropomorphize and to attend to observables. Due to the operation of this last propensity, one also gets idolatry. The propensity to offer endless adulation also continues to operate. One result is that the intelligent power is conceived to be, as it were, so special as not to be satisfied by moral behavior, but to require or to take pleasure in rituals and practices not required by morality, and not infrequently outrageously contradictory to it. Another result is so-called negative theology.

> In proportion as men's fears or desires become more urgent, they still invent new strains of adulation; and even he who outdoes his predecessor in swelling up the titles of his divinity, is sure to be outdone by his successor in newer and more pompous epithets of praise. Thus they proceed; till at last they arrive at infinity itself, beyond which there is no further progress: And it is well if, in striving to get farther, and to represent a magnificent simplicity, they run not [as does Demea in the *Dialogues*] into inexplicable mystery, and destroy the intelligent nature of their deity, on which alone any rational worship or adoration can be founded. [*N*, 57, 58]

Thus the propensity to posit an invisible, intelligent power seldom holds the field alone.

Further, as we noted, once the full range of religion-relevant propensities have been awakened, there is a second-order propensity in the one in whom they operate to fluctuate between belief in a single invisible, intelligent power and polytheism.

> The feeble apprehensions of men cannot be satisfied with con-
> ceiving their deity as a pure spirit and perfect intelligence; and
> yet their natural tenors keep them from imputing to him the least
> shadow of limitation and imperfection. They fluctuate between
> these opposite sentiments. The same infirmity still drags them
> downward, from an omnipotent and spiritual deity, to a limited
> and corporeal one, and from a corporeal and limited deity to a
> state of visible representation. The same endeavor at elevation
> still pushes them upwards, from the statue or material image of
> the invisible power; and from the invisible power to an infinitely
> perfect deity, the creator and sovereign of the universe. [N,
> 63–64]

Thus assent, so to say, is pushed by horizontal forces toward, and
then away from, each of Hume's permitted religious poles, theism
and polytheism.

Assent is also pulled downward by what Hume calls "nature" so
that steady assent is given to propositions associated with "the strong
impressions made by common sense and (sensory) experience," and
drained from propositions associated with religion. This, then, or
something much like it, seems to be a significant part of Hume's por-
trayal of the connection between human nature and religious belief;
but it is not all.

Hume's Apparent Approval of the Design Argument

In several passages in the *Natural History*, Hume at least seems to
speak kindly of the argument from design. These remarks, I suggest,
must be seen in a wide Humean context. What I mean by a "wide Humean context" is simply a combination of what is known about the
writing of the *Natural History* and related texts and what Hume says
elsewhere relevant to the topic at hand. The biographical evidence is
that Hume revised the *Dialogues* over the course of his life which
ended in 1776. Probably written in 1749 through 1751, the *Natural History* belongs to the same period as the original form of the *Dialogues*.
The *Dialogues* then were revised around 1761 and again (with substantial additions) in 1776. They were published posthumously in
1779. The *Natural History* was published in 1757. The *Treatise* was published in 1739, and its simplified version, the *Enquiry Concerning Human Understanding*, was published in 1748. As we shall see, the *Natural History* explanations of religious belief share many features with

the *Treatise* explanations of our beliefs in physical objects, causal connections, and an enduring self—so much so that it is hard indeed to suppose that the structure of the *Treatise* explanations are not the pattern for those of the *Natural History*. The *Treatise*, then, pre-dates the *Natural History;* it is published about a decade before the writing, and almost two decades before the publication, of the *Natural History*. But many of the *Treatise* themes are carried on in the *Enquiry Concerning Human Understanding* and what are for Hume the deepest and most fundamental themes find their way into the *Natural History*, as we shall see. The *Dialogues* found their origin in the same context of Humean activity as the *Natural History*. So there is considerable biographical basis for supposing that the philosophical activity that produced the *Enquiry, Natural History,* and *Dialogues* to a significant degree occurred together. The biographical evidence is supported by the overlap of the content of these works and the fact that the doctrines of each document are deeply influenced by the positions expressed in the *Treatise*.

Certain doctrines of the *Treatise* are relevant to the success or failure of the design argument as a piece of natural theology. One such doctrine is expressed in the explanations (to be discussed below) of our belief that there are enduring physical objects and causal connections. The *Treatise* argues against our having evidence or grounds for these beliefs and then offers a non-epistemic explanation of the fact that, in the absence of any epistemological basis favorable to their truth, we have these beliefs anyway. The premises of the argument from design are reasonably believed to be true only if we have reason to believe that there are physical objects, and that these objects enter into causal connections. Unless Hume has abandoned the *Treatise* position on these matters, his view is that we do not have reason to believe these things. Neither the *Enquiry Concerning Human Understanding* nor the *Natural History* retracts the *Treatise* position on these matters.

Another highly relevant doctrine of the *Treatise* is Hume's view that reason is "but a wonderful instinct in the soul" and that "reason" names a faculty or capacity that is much less basic to human nature than is the faculty called "imagination." "Imagination" has two senses in the *Treatise*, one in which it contrasts to "memory" and is the ability to reproduce ideas in an order and of a content not simply reproductive of past experience, and another sense continuous with but more important than the former in which "imagination" refers to the locus of our basic propensities to form beliefs and is tantamount to "human nature." The same view of the structure of human nature as appeared in the *Treatise* is introduced again in the *Natural History*, where it is refined and sophisticated, and where again "reason" designates a less fundamental set of propensities than those referred to the imagination.

If the premises of the design argument—premises that are false if there are no physical objects or if those objects bear no causal connections to other objects or to anything else—are no more reasonably believed than not, then however tightly they are related to its conclusion they do not lend that conclusion any increase in rational status. Hume accepts the presuppositions of the premises of the argument from design, but he also believes that there is no better reason—on his part, or anyone's—for believing them to be true rather than false. This rather diminishes any probative force that a Humean sanction of the argument from design might have. His famous contention that inductive reasoning requires a rational justification that it utterly lacks completes the case that Hume cannot consistently contend that the argument from design proves its point.

Were the argument from design, on Hume's own view, to prove its conclusion, and to do so in a widely recognized way, the effort to provide a psychological and non-evidential explanation of the acceptance of its conclusion would be bootless. At best, it would provide explanatory overkill. This point would not apply, of course, were Hume to except the conclusion of the argument from design from those propositions whose acceptance is propensity-based; but he does not. There are, then, strong reasons against Hume's being so read as to make him a proponent of at least the argument from design as successful natural theology. It is, then, in this wide Humean context that the following remarks are to be seen.

Hume refers often to the conclusion of the design argument in a variety of *Natural History* contexts. We had best have them before us all at once, though this necessitates some extensive quotations.

> (1) Happily, the first question [concerning religion's foundation in reason], which is the most important, admits of the most obvious, at least, the clearest, solution. The whole frame of nature bespeaks an intelligent author; and no rational enquirer can, after serious reflection, suspend his belief a moment with regard to the primary principles of genuine Theism and Religion. [*N*, 31]

> (2) Nothing could disturb this natural progress of thought, but some obvious and invincible argument, which might immediately lead the mind into the pure principles of theism, and make it

overleap, at one bound, the vast interval which is interposed between the human and the divine nature. But though I allow, that the order and frame of the universe, when accurately examined, affords such an argument, yet I can never think that this consideration could have an influence on mankind, when they formed their first rude notions of religion. [*N*, 34]

(3) Were men led into the apprehension of invisible, intelligent power by a contemplation of the works of nature, they could never possibly entertain any conception but of one single being, who bestowed existence and order on this vast machine, and adjusted all its parts, according to one regular plan or connected system. For though, to persons of a certain turn of mind, it may not appear altogether absurd, that several independent beings, endowed with superior wisdom, might conspire in the contrivance and execution of one regular plan; yet this is a merely arbitrary supposition, which, even if allowed possible, must be confessed neither to be supported by probability nor necessity. All things in the universe are evidently of a piece. Everything is adjusted to everything. One design prevails throughout the whole. And this uniformity leads the mind to acknowledge one author; because the conception of different authors, without any distinction of attributes or operations, serves only to give perplexity to the imagination, without bestowing any satisfaction on the understanding. [*N*, 37]

(4) Whoever learns by argument, the existence of invisible intelligent power, must reason from the admirable contrivance of natural objects, and must suppose the world to be the workmanship of that divine being, the original cause of all things. [*N*, 51]

(5) While they (persons in an idolatrous nation) confine themselves to the notion of a perfect being, the creator of the world, they coincide, by chance, with the principles of reason and true philosophy; though they are guided to that notion, not by reason, of which they are in a great measure incapable, but by the adulation and fears of the most vulgar superstition. [*N*, 58]

(6) Where theism forms the fundamental principle of any popular religion, that tenet is so conformable to sound reason, that philosophy is apt to incorporate itself with such a system of theology. [*N*, 70]

(7) Though the stupidity of men, barbarous and uninstructed, be so great, that they may not see a sovereign author in the more obvious works of nature, to which they are so much familiarized; yet it scarcely seems possible, that any one of good understanding reject that idea, when once it is suggested to him. A purpose, an intention, a design, is evident in every thing; and when our comprehension is so far enlarged as to contemplate the first use of this visible system, we must adopt, with the strongest conviction, the idea of some intelligent cause or author; the uniform maxims, too, which prevail throughout the whole frame of the universe, naturally, if not necessarily, lead us to conceive this intelligence as single and undivided, when the prejudices of education oppose not so reasonable a theory. Even the contrarieties of nature, by discovering themselves every where, become proofs of some consistent plan, and establish one single purpose or intention, however inexplicable and incomprehensible. [*N*, 96]

Briefly, these passages assert the following:

(1) and (4) Natural order so clearly "bespeaks an intelligent author" that no rational enquirer can suspend belief on this matter.

(2) Natural order affords an "obvious and invincible" argument for the existence of an intelligent author of this order.

(3) One sort of order is manifested throughout all of nature, and while it is logically possible that this order is to be explained by reference to a committee of intelligent beings working in consort, this explanation gives less satisfaction than does explanation by reference to a single intelligence.

(5) The notion of a perfect being, creator of the world, conforms to the principles of reason and true philosophy, and may be arrived at by "the adulation and fears of the most vulgar superstition."

(6) Philosophy is likely to "incorporate itself with" belief in an intelligent author of natural order, and belief in such an author is the "fundamental principle of any popular religion."

(7) Natural order establishes belief in an intelligent author of such order in any one of "good understanding."

Not all of these passages conflict with, or raise any question about, the view that all religious beliefs, including that in an intelligent author of natural order, are caused by propensities and arise in the absence of confirming evidence. Indeed, (5) says that this belief may be caused by "adulation and fears" and one needs only to add Hume's view that these emotions trigger a propensity to have the belief in question, and (7) is easily read along these lines. So is (6), which makes the belief in question the core of popular religion.

Passage (5), by itself, says too much for us to suppose that Hume accepted all of it. Nothing in his other remarks ascribes *perfection* to an intelligent author of natural order, and Hume was well aware of (and evidently accepted) both the principle that a cause inferred from an effect may not be supposed to have greater powers than those needed to produce the effect and that perfection in knowledge or power is not needed to produce natural order. *Creation,* as opposed to merely *design,* is not sanctioned elsewhere, and inferring to a creator rather than merely a designer is blocked by the same considerations as exclude inference to perfection. Shorn of these extravagances that Hume elsewhere challenges, passage (5) fits nicely into Hume's propensity-explanations-of-religious-belief perspective.

Passage (1) says that belief in an intelligent author of nature's order is something that no "rational enquirer" can "suspend belief" concerning, and passage (7) says that such order establishes this belief. But that we cannot suspend judgment regarding a proposition does not entail, or for Hume even suggest, that we have any reason or evidence or grounds in favor of its truth, and a belief can be established in the sense of its being psychologically in place as well as by its being shown to be true. So far, one can make a case, at least, for reading the comments in question along the lines already discussed.

Passage (2) says that natural order affords an obvious and invincible argument that an intelligent author causes natural order, and (3) says that explaining this order by reference to a *single* author gives more satisfaction than explaining it by reference to multiple intelligences. Passage (4) refers to "learning by argument that" natural order has an intelligent cause.

In the works of William Paley or Bishop Butler, such passages as (2), (3), and (4), and indeed (1–7), would not be surprising and their obvious import would be that the argument from design succeeded. In the context of Hume's writings, however, caution is needed and several things should be noted.

A careful reading of even passages (2), (3), and (4) reveals at least two things. One is that in them, in contrast to the *Dialogues,* Hume never offers any careful version of the argument from design; they include no detailed variety of this (or any other) argument for theism. In fact, the *Natural History* as a whole contains no such argument. Nor are any of the many objections to the argument considered. Second, for all their apparent enthusiasm about the conclusion of a design argument, they contain a reticent diversity about how that conclusion is reached. "No rational enquirer can suspend belief" after serious reflection on the proposition that there is an invisible, intelligent author of the frame of nature. I assume that this proposition—or at least one very like it—expresses what Hume means by "the primary principles of genuine Theism and Religion." Perhaps no rational enquirer can suspend such belief. But, as we noted, particularly given Hume's theory of human nature and his views about when we are unable to suspend belief, while that is compatible even with the proposition being self-evident, it is also compatible with the proposition being false. "The whole frame of nature bespeaks an intelligent author." This is what produces the assent of any rational inquirer—an assent that Hume contends is balanced by a tendency to polytheism and that he later says pales in contrast to the assent given to propositions associated with sensory perception. Other passages speak of "being led into the apprehensions of invisible, intelligent power by a contemplation of the works of nature" and of a natural order that "leads the mind to acknowledge one author." All this as much suggests propensities being elicited by experience as it does inferences being sanctioned by evidence. The same holds for "a purpose is evident in everything" and "we must adopt, with the strongest conviction, the idea of some intelligent cause or author."

The claim that "the order and frame of the universe, when accurately examined" provides "some obvious and invincible argument, which might lead the mind into the pure principles of theism" at least seems different in force and tone. There is, of course, the fact that Hume—for all his talent for such matters—does not state any carefully crafted version of the argument from design nor does he consider any of the myriad of objections one can make to that argument. One would think that it was not exactly the argument, as a piece of natural theology, that most interested him, but rather the argument's *effects*. There is the further fact that the difference is not great between one who, in the presence of a particularly striking instance of natural order, 'sees that' there is an invisible, intelligent agency and one who claims that the argument "there is natural order; if there is natural order, that order is intelligently caused; so natural order is intelligently caused" is sound and valid. The former has an intuition that the latter unpacks into a demonstration. As Descartes noted, one person can intuitively grasp what another requires a series of reflections to encompass, and his *Rules for the Direction of the Understanding* were intended to teach one to move from having to see the entailment-connections in complex chains of reasoning bit by bit in distinct inferences to a degree of intellectual accomplishment in which one could grasp the whole chain of inference at one fell swoop.

Hume is not the only author whose remarks on such matters can be, and have been, variously read. Saint Paul's remarks in Romans 1:18–21 have been seen as sanctioning some natural-theology argument at least similar to the design argument but also as simply saying that God has implanted in us all a tendency to recognize the divine origin of the power and intelligence that it is natural for us to see nature as manifesting. Hume himself writes that a universal propensity to believe in invisible, intelligent power "may be considered as a kind of mark or stamp which the divine workman has set upon his work" (*N*, 97) and Calvin did so consider it. In the long run, of course, the question must be faced as to whether the long discussion in the *Dialogues* in which the argument from design is stated and criticized and restated and recriticized in a very extended discussion yields the result that the argument is triumphant, and whether Hume thought that it triumphs. I will argue that it does not, and that Hume did not think that it did.

In any case, it is at least possible to read even the apparently most enthusiastic of the design argument passages as saying that an argument leads to conviction in the absence of providing proof or justification of its conclusion. Perhaps this reading will be justified only if one's choices are to adopt it, or to reject what Hume says more plainly in the *Natural History* and elsewhere. For the reasons noted, I think that is precisely the case.

The Secondary Status of the Propensities to Religious Belief

What else has Hume to say relevant to our topic?

> The belief of invisible, intelligent power has been very generally diffused over the human race, in all places and in all ages; but it has neither perhaps been so universal as to admit of no exception, nor has it been, in any degree, uniform in the ideas, which it has suggested. Some nations have been discovered, who entertained no sentiments of Religion, if travellers and historians may be credited; and no two nations, and scarce any two men, have ever agreed precisely in the same sentiments. [*N*, 31]

Not every person believes that there is an intelligent invisible power. Among the many who do, there is a great variety of conceptions of this power. Hence:

> It would appear, therefore, that this preconception springs, not from an original instinct or primary impression of nature, such as gives rise to self-love, affection between the sexes, love of progeny, gratitude, resentment; since every instinct of this kind has been found absolutely universal in all nations and ages, and has always a precise determinate object, which it inflexibly pursues. The first religious principles must be secondary; such as may easily be perverted by various accidents and causes, and whose operation too, in some cases, by an extraordinary concurrence of circumstances, may be altogether prevented. [N, 31, 32]

So there are original or primary instincts or impressions, and secondary ones. An original or primary one is possessed by all, is efficacious in all, and yields the same results in all. A secondary instinct or impression is possessed by all, but is not efficacious in all, and does not always yield the same results.

> The only point of theology, in which we shall find a consent of mankind almost universal, is, that there is invisible, intelligent power in the world: But whether this power be supreme or subordinate, whether confined to one being or distributed among several, what attributes, qualities, connections, or principles of action ought to be ascribed to those beings; concerning all these points, there is the widest difference in the popular systems of theology. [N, 44]

Not even, then, the propensity to posit intelligent power as the cause of natural order is original or primary. It is neither perfectly universal nor uniform in its results.

Toward the end of the *Natural History* Hume returns to this theme:

> The universal propensity to believe in invisible, intelligent power, if not an original instinct, being at least a general attendant of human nature, may be considered as a kind of mark or stamp, which the divine workman has set upon his work; and nothing surely can more dignify mankind, than to be thus selected from all other parts of the creation, and to bear the image or impressions of the universal Creator. But consult this image, as it appears in the popular religions of the world. How is the deity dis-

figured in our representations of him! How much is he degraded even below the character, which we should naturally, in common life, ascribe to a man of sense and virtue! [*N*, 97]

In these passages, Hume ascribes belief in invisible, intelligent power as cause of natural order to a propensity which he describes as "universal" but "secondary." It is efficacious—called into effect by experience of natural order—in almost everyone. In some, it leads to polytheism, in others to monotheism, in each case in a variety of formulations and versions.

It is clear that the so-called theism to which a secondary propensity is said to lead is a very *thin* theism. Omniscience, omnipotence, and omnibenevolence are not in view; neither is creation or providence. The 'power' is not Judge or Savior. No revelation, and no action in history, is ascribed to this power. Morality is not based on appeal to this power's nature or to its will. Even a deist deity who creates a world and leaves it alone is religiously 'thicker' than the power this propensity posits. So the use of "theism" for the view in question is clearly challengeable, though I shall retain it for sheer convenience.

Hume on Religion and Morality

Hume clearly favors his diaphanous version of what we are joining him in continuing to call theism. One reason for this he early makes evident. Theism does not, and polytheism does, pervert morality. This comes out, though not altogether without qualification, in Hume's comparisons of theism and polytheism.

> To any one, who considers justly of the matter, it will appear, that the gods of all polytheists are not better than the elves or fairies of our ancestors, and merit as little any pious worship or veneration. [*N*, 45] . . . These gross representations of the deities . . . if taken literally, contain a true atheism. [*N*, 46] To ascribe the origin and fabric of the universe to these imperfect beings never enters into the imagination of any polytheist or idolater. [*N*, 47] The difference between . . . [a polytheist] and a genuine theist is infinitely greater than that . . . between him and one that absolutely excludes all invisible, intelligent power. [*N*, 45]

But while Hume at times compares theism and polytheism in ways that favor the former, he yet makes plain that he thinks that the advantages cut both ways:

> Polytheism . . . is liable to this great inconvenience, that any
> practice or opinion, however barbarous or corrupted, may be
> authorized by it; and full scope is given, for knavery to impose
> on credulity, till morals and humanity be expelled from the reli-
> gious systems of mankind. At the same time, idolatry is attended
> with this evident advantage, that, by limiting the powers and
> functions of its deities, it naturally admits the gods of other sects
> and nations to a share of divinity, and renders all the various
> deities . . . compatible with each other. [N, 64]

So polytheism is capable of expelling "morals and humanity" from religion, but also fosters tolerance of competing perspectives. But:

> Theism is opposite both in its advantages and disadvantages. As
> that system supposes one sole deity, the perfection of reason and
> goodness, it should, if justly prosecuted, banish everything frivo-
> lous, unreasonable, or inhuman from religious worship, and set
> before men the most illustrious example, as well as the most
> commanding motives, or justice and benevolence. These mighty
> advantages are not indeed over-balanced (for that is not possible)
> but somewhat diminished, by inconveniences, which arise from
> the vices and prejudices of mankind. While one sole object of
> worship is acknowledged, the worship of other deities is re-
> garded as absurd and impious . . . the several sects fall naturally
> into animosity, mutually discharge on each other that sacred zeal
> and rancour, the most furious and implacable of all human pas-
> sions. [N, 65]

Still, Hume suggests, this ascription of perfection to the invisible, intelligent power has (besides any reference to intolerance) its darker
side.

> As men exalt their idea of their divinity [not their own apotheo-
> sis, but the deity they believe in]; it is their notion of his power
> and knowledge only, not of his goodness, which is improved. On
> the contrary, in proportion to the supposed extent of his science
> and authority, their terrors naturally augment. . . . All must be
> applause . . . And while their gloomy apprehensions make them
> ascribe to him measures of conduct, which, in human creatures,
> would be highly blamed, they must still affect to praise and ad-
> mire that conduct in the object of their devotional addresses.
> Thus it may safely be affirmed that popular religions are really, in

the conception of their more vulgar votaries, a species of dae-monism. [N, 87]

In proportion to the multiplied terrors of these religions, the barbarous conceptions of the divinity are multiplied upon us. Nothing can preserve untainted the genuine principles of morals in our judgment of human conduct, but the absolute necessity of these principles to the existence of society. [N, 88–89]

The greatest crimes have been found, in many instances, com-patible with a superstitious piety and devotion . . . to which we may add, that, after the commission of crimes, there arise re-morses and secret horrors, which give no rest to the mind, but make it have recourse to religious rites and ceremonies, as expia-tions of its offenses. [N, 94–95]

This (not especially balanced) association of religion with immo-rality is also made in others of Hume's works, and leads him to praise only that rare theism that arises only from the single propensity to posit invisible, intelligent power, unfestooned by contributions from the other religion-relevant propensities.

The task of evaluating a religious tradition in moral terms can take either of two forms. One is philosophical from beginning to end. Along this route, one derives a moral theory from the religious tradition's own theological and ethical claims and then assesses that theory. Assuming that one can tell what shape the ethical theory (or theories) will take when it (or they) are derived from the tradition's resources, and that ethical theories can be rationally assessed, one relevant consideration in assessing a religious tradition will be the ra-tional quality of the ethical theory or theories that follow from it. To the degree that it cannot be determined what the systematic moral im-plications of a tradition are, or how they are to be assessed, this strat-egy will fail, but it seems perfectly sensible to try it. On the whole, this purely philosophical approach is not Hume's.

The other approach, which on the whole is Hume's, is this. One endeavors to judge what historical consequences a religious tradition has yielded, morally speaking. This requires that one judge a reli-gious tradition on the basis of the morally relevant behavior of its de-votees *insofar as this behavior results from their embracing the religion in question rather than from some other source.* Otherwise it is not the *tradi-tion's* moral impact that is being considered. The morally relevant be-havior of a religious individual or group is likely to stem from a variety of sources, and it is enormously difficult to show (as opposed to merely *claiming*) that some particular behavior arises from religious as opposed to other sources.

Insofar as one can identify someone's religious beliefs as the source of their moral conduct, the same belief may cause one sort of behavior in one context and a very different sort of behavior in another. Suppose that both John and Jane believe that God has commanded that we honor our parents. John believes that if one becomes senile in this life then one will be senile in the afterlife. As his father shows significant signs of impending senility, John—with his mother's firm support and at his father's request—sends his father off to the open seas on an ice floe, which is his society's kindest version of euthanasia. Jane, who lacks the belief that senility now induces senility ever after, allows her father to descend into senility, and with her mother's full support and as much assent as her father can still give, arranges for a nursing home environment for her father where he is looked after and his life prolonged. Their frequent visits are saddened by his increasing senility.

Suppose that the belief that there is an afterlife is, in both cultures, a religious belief but the belief that senility here causes permanent senility there is part of John's general culture, with no particular attachment to any religious tradition, and that the same is true regarding Jane's rejection of this belief. The relevant religious belief, then, is shared by John and Jane. Yet in the light of their non-religious beliefs, they act in opposite ways. Presumably each would be shocked by the behavior of the other, particularly if they were aware of each other's shared belief that God commands that one honor one's parents and were unaware of their disagreement about the consequences of current senility. How, then, are we to judge the religious belief that God commands us to honor our parents? Or the belief that there is an after-life?

The second procedure—the one that Hume embraces—requires that one accept some morality for the purpose of evaluating the behavior of the devotees. One can embrace the morality of the religious tradition, at least for the sake of the argument. But then the most that one could show would be that the devotees were hypocrites; but nothing would follow about the truth or falsity of their beliefs. Or one could adopt some different and incompatible morality (a perfectly compatible moral theory would lead those who actually followed it to no different actions than those the devotees actually perform, insofar as they act on their religious beliefs—that is, on the moral theory those beliefs entail). If one has established the truth of the different and incompatible theory, then one also will have shown the religious tradition in question to be false, for *ex hypothesi* the ethical theory the tradition entails is incompatible with an *ex hypothesi* true theory; and whatever entails a falsehood is itself false. But then there is no need to offer a conduct-based critique. If one has not established that the ethical theory not derived from the religion in question is true, then what of any relevance follows from the devotees flouting it?

A religious tradition might support an ethical theory in some fashion short of entailment. An ethical theory can be supported by considerations that do not suffice to establish it. But such refinements can be matched by corresponding refinements in the statement of what would follow.

One might interpret Hume's remarks on religion and morality minimally. On this account, he is saying that some religious views lead their adherents to violate moral rules that we can easily see to be justified, and that this claim needs no complex defense. The idea, then, is that we can identify cases of religious beliefs the acceptance of which clearly leads people to act in morally deplorable ways. This is a more intellectualist account of moral motivation than Hume generally embraces; it ill accords with the Humean dogma that "reason is, and ought to be, the slave of the passions." Setting that aside, Hume seems clearly right, though of course the same thing can be said of a variety of non-religious beliefs—*their* acceptance leads people to do wicked things. In particular, this is so regarding various beliefs about what is right or wrong, but Hume sensibly does not thereby conclude that all of morality should be rejected. Similarly, no global conclusions regarding religion will follow from this minimal interpretation of Hume on religion and morality.

The basic Humean concern is with the real possibility that religion *add* something to ethics: that religious *motives* be added to moral motives and that religious *duties* be added to moral duties. Religious traditions typically do contain motives and duties not contained in non-religious moral traditions, whether these moral traditions are Humean or not. Hume assumes not merely that this sort of addition is negative in some of its instances but that it is inherently negative. Thuggee, on most accounts of what a religion is, counts as a religion; its ritual includes robbery and murder as duties performed to please the evil goddess Kali. Not many will defend these particular religious additions to a moral system. But as we noted, Hume's claim is general: *any* religious additions are unnecessary and dangerous. 'Pure theism' (a view with almost no content) is praiseworthy because it has no consequences for morality. One thing relevant to this dispute is whether any religious belief is true, and whether we have any reason to suppose that any religious belief is true. Another has to do with whether any true moral claims are entailed by any religious doctrines we have any reason to accept, and whether these moral claims have any sufficient rationale outside of appeal to religious doctrine. These issues seem to me more complex than they do to many philosophers. Certainly Hume has not shown that the answers required by his own perspective are the correct ones. While he makes clear what his view is, concerning the importance of separating morality from any influence by religion, it is hard to see that he shows that such separation is always good or necessary for morality's sake. Arguably, that depends on what religious beliefs one has in mind.

Religion and Human Nature

Not all of Hume's disfavor toward religion has to do with its effect on morality. While this topic is relevant to what sort of assessment Hume can make of religious belief that ostensibly falls within his own skepticism, and will be more fully discussed later in that regard, his views on religious belief and human nature are also relevant to the topics of this chapter and hence merit brief discussion here. He contends that religion tends to subvert human nature. He contends that there

> is a kind of contradiction between the different principles of human nature, which enter into religion. Our natural terrors present the notion of a devilish and malicious deity: Our propensity to adulation leads us to acknowledge an excellent and divine. And the influence of these opposite principles are various, according to the different situation of the human understanding. [*N*, 86]

In this important passage, Hume adds to his remarks about the propensity to waver between theism and polytheism. Feelings (terrors) push belief in one direction, a propensity (to offer adulation) pushes belief in another. The former tends to create belief in a malevolent deity, and the latter tends to create belief in an "excellent" one. Hume contends that: "Such rude, imperfect ideas of the Divinity adhere long to all idolators" (*N*, 86). Thus the terrors noted reinforce the propensity to polytheism, and in that way they oppose the propensity to believe in a single invisible, intelligent power. The propensity that leads to polytheism leads, of course, to a belief that is logically contrary to belief in a single intelligence. In that sense, the propensities conflict.

Hume views this conflict as unfortunate. In some way, it weakens human nature. Exactly how is not clear; perhaps what is involved is this. Hume contends that "the empire of all religious faith over the understanding is wavering and uncertain, subject to every variety of humour, and dependent on the present incidents, which strike the imagination" (*N*, 81). Late in the *Natural History*, he remarks:

> Whatever weakens or disorders the internal frame promotes the interests of superstition: And nothing is more destructive to them than a manly, steady virtue, which either preserves us from disastrous, melancholy accidents, or teaches us to bear them. . . . The more tremendous the divinity is represented, the more tame and submissive do men become (who are) his ministers: And the more unaccountable the measures of acceptance required by him, the more necessary does it become to abandon our natural reason, and yield to their ghostly guidance and direction. Thus it may be allowed, that the artifices of men aggravate our natural infirmities and follies of this kind, but never originally beget them. Their root strikes deeper into the mind, and springs from the essential and universal properties of human nature. [*N*, 95]

Part of what concerns Hume here is obviously the previously noted claim that religion can pervert morals. Even this older theme, however, is set in a new light in this passage: since morality itself for Hume stems from "natural reason" its perversion by a religious perspective that also arises from human nature provides a new conflict between the constituents of that nature. Contrary moral perspectives, and correspondingly competing modalities of conduct, are sanctioned by diverse propensities within a single human nature. In this way, propensities can conflict. Further, propensities toward holding a belief, and toward holding a contrary belief, activated at the same time within one person's nature, again will conflict. All of this may serve to weaken or disorder the efficacious operations of propensities to belief that (in part) comprise human nature. Too many conflicting propensities, or too much conflict among propensities, within a single system of human nature may reduce, or even abolish, its capacity for belief altogether. That, I suggest, is the worry that lies just beneath the surface of this passage. A steady virtue will prevent such conflict from arising in moral affairs (but how many have a steady virtue?). And it will not do to ascribe tendencies to having beliefs that further immoral conduct, or to have beliefs that conflict with one another, merely to "our natural infirmities and follies"; instead their root is deep in the mind in "the essential and universal properties of human nature."

The results of these new considerations for our question of how to relate the *argument* line of reasoning to the *propensity* line of reasoning are these. Hume, we have seen, both offers various propensities that he says serve, upon our having the appropriate eliciting experiences, to yield certain religious beliefs and he speaks with apparent favor toward the argument from design, though there is no detailed or careful statement of that argument that receives his approval. He adds that not everyone accepts the conclusion of the argument from design, and that often when someone does accept it she so festoons the alleged intelligent cause of natural order with properties besides intelligence that she is led to perform morally questionable activities in order to propitiate that intelligence. He also claims that forming beliefs in accordance with the propensity that leads one to belief in an intelligent cause of natural order may serve to weaken human nature, and insists that *all* of the religion-relevant propensities are secondary in the sense of being less fundamental to human nature than are other propensities that are ascribed to the imagination. All of this is independent of the fact that he neither supposes us to have reasons or evidence or grounds for acceptance of the presuppositions of the premises of the argument from design (the existence of mind-independent objects and causal connections) or for accepting the inductive inference that the argument requires. Further, insofar as the propensities to religious belief operate within us, they tend to introduce breaking points in the fragile web of belief. They weaken the gentle network of natural forces that produce belief that there is an external world of causally connected objects and an internal world of enduring minds whose impressions and ideas manifest a regularity of their own.

In the light of all this, I suggest the following. Hume's claim is that there is a rational propensity—a propensity in part constitutive of the faculty of reason—of this sort: upon observing natural order, to ascribe that order to an intelligent cause. The sorts of experiences that trigger this propensity are often described in the premises of standard versions of the argument from design. Hume's claim is that we have a propensity to believe that an intelligent cause is the source of order in nature, and this propensity is a propensity of reason, not of imagination. This, from Hume, is not a compliment; rational propensities are less basic than propensities of the imagination, and following them may lead to morally undesirable actions and to beliefs the possession of which in some manner 'weakens' human nature.

The *argument* passages, in effect, stress that it is a propensity *of reason* that leads to theism; the *propensity* passages, in effect, that it is a *propensity* of reason that leads to theism. In Chapter 2, I will develop Hume's general explanation of our having the religious beliefs that we do have in such a way as to set these merely suggestive remarks in the overall context of an explicitly defended reading of Hume's texts, and my success or failure in this interpretation of Hume will rest on whether that reading is defensible.

One more remark is in order here. Hume says that it is the question of religion's foundation in human reason, not the question of its origin in human nature, that is "most important," and my reading of Hume seems to suggest the reverse order of importance.

It may well be that Hume held the question about religion's foundation in human reason to be the important question; after all, he says that it is and I do not see any reason to think that this remark is ironic. Historically, it has seemed the more important. Both critics and supporters of natural theology have assumed that the important question was whether religious belief has any rational credentials and they have often not even asked what its status might be, other than as sheer superstition, if it has no solid foundation in reason.

Any view of Hume's own role in natural theology, as supporter or as critic, must rest on a detailed interpretation of the *Dialogues* as well as the *Natural History*, and must deal as well with the relevant themes in the *Treatise* and *Enquiry*. I will later defend the not unusual view that Hume is a critic of natural theology and believes that we have no reason whatever to think that theism is true. His arguments in the *Dialogues* and the essay on miracles, to go no further, seem to me plainly to cast him in this role. So he wrote copiously on natural theology, and if, in spite of his contentions there, there is good reason to be a theist, then his explanations of religious belief in the *Natural History* are otiose. They explain in a complicated way beliefs that can be explained much more simply by referring to the evidence that we have in their favor, provided only that this evidence is widely enough accessible for us to use it to explain widespread belief. Even if these reasons are not widely accessible, the overall impact of Hume's account of religious belief will be importantly different if there are good reasons to think that theism is true. So not only may it be Hume's own opinion that the question regarding religion's, and particularly theism's, foundation in reason is more important than the question of its origin in human nature; he may be exactly right about that. In any case, his being right in what he thinks the answer to the 'foundation in reason' question is provides an important background to his overall account of its origin in human nature.

For all that, its origin in human nature, according to Hume, is explanatory in a way that its (non-existent) foundation in human reason is not; better, its foundation in human reason is really only its origin in propensities of reason that are less fundamental to human nature than are the propensities of the imagination. That answers concerning origins are explanatory in a way or to a degree that answers concerning foundations are not does not entail that questions concerning foundations are less important than are questions concerning origins. The importance of a question may well depend on what follows if its answer is different than what it seems to be; even an atheist may think the question as to whether there are snails is less important than the question as to whether there is a God, even though he will be willing to explain some phenomena by reference to the behavior of snails but not be willing to explain any phenomena by reference to the existence of God.

This, then, is not all, but only a substantial portion, of Hume's philosophy of religion.[1] As we have seen, it contains an account, not free from a generous dose of *a priorism*, of how the history of religion went, because of how it must have gone. His data is gleaned from Greek and Roman sources. His use of those sources, and indeed his general treatment of the history of religion, and the issue of how his conclusions fare when compared with studies based on more generous and diverse data, are not my concern here. But simply his account of human nature, with its references to propensities and eliciting experiences and background conditions, is complex all by itself, and to offer it is to claim to have a rather sizeable chunk of information about Homo sapiens. One might wonder how, exactly, within a Humean epistemology all this knowledge is to be obtained. We will consider this question in due time.

It might seem that Hume is natural theologian of sorts—a natural atheologian who argues against religious belief, if one prefers—after all. He does offer an argument of sorts against having religious belief. He casts the religion-relevant propensities in the role of opponents to the original propensities that must operate in order for us to be human. These necessary propensities elicit belief in a public physical and personal world that is sufficiently orderly to make science and daily life possible. If any religion-relevant propensity is not involved in this conflict, it is the propensity to view the cause or causes of natural order as bearing some remote analogy to human intelligence. Otherwise, the religion-relevant propensities constitute some danger to our fragile personal unity. Thus there is a negative pragmatic natural theology at least implicit in Hume's writings.

Obviously, in this bald and undeveloped a form, it has little promise. Jewish and Christian monotheists, to go no further, have managed to contribute to science and technology, travel, enter public life, and plan for the future; their belief in a public, mind-independent world has flourished. Characteristically, they have been 'normal.' They also have believed that God is Creator of and Providence over a public world, belief in the existence of which is no rationalization. Whether, in the long run, monotheism is more plausibly construed as a mere rationalization than are the theories themselves on which those who claim that it is a rationalization rest their claim is a complex question. But such matters take us far beyond the task of discussing Hume's philosophy of religion.

Part Twelve of the *Dialogues*

The final section of the *Dialogues* has been something of a commentator's despair. T. E. Jessop is especially eloquent in this regard, writing that "the conclusion [that is, *Dialogue* Twelve] being disconnected from the argued content of the *Dialogues*, I shall ignore it." James Noxon writes about "the complete reversal of standpoint made by Philo in the twelfth and final dialogue." Richard Wollheim suggests that it would "be a mistake to look for any way of removing or resolving all the inconsistencies that appear in Hume's writings on religion, and of abstracting from them a rigorous and unified doctrine"—a mistake (if it *is* one) that the present volume is devoted to making. Further, commentators disagree about what overall perspective the *Dialogues* represent. Norman Kemp Smith says that "Philo, from start to finish, represents Hume"; Antony Flew agrees. A. Seth Pringle-Pattison regards Cleanthes as Hume's spokesman; Charles Hendel concurs. Only Demea (so far as I know) has not been forwarded as Hume's real voice in the *Dialogues*.

Pamphilus is represented as writing the *Dialogues* down for the sake of his friend Hermippus, who never appears as other than the one for whom the *Dialogues* are transcribed. To Pamphilus we are indebted for the concluding paragraph of the work, which reads as follows:

> Cleanthes and Philo pursued not this conversation much farther; and as nothing ever made greater impression on me, than all the reasonings of that day, so I confess that, upon a serious review of the whole, I cannot but think that Philo's principles are more probable than Demea's, but that those of Cleanthes approach still nearer to the truth. [*D*, 204]

It is from Pamphilus that we receive the explanation as to why the dialogue form fits the topics under discussion: the being and nature of deity. That explanation fits the *Dialogues* that follow and nicely chimes in with the remainder of Hume's discussion of religion. Why, then, not just take Pamphilus as Hume's own voice, in which his role then by his own testimony passes on to Cleanthes?

One reason is that Pamphilus says, "My youth rendered me a mere auditor of their disputes" and he presents himself, because his "curiosity, natural to the early season of life, has so deeply imprinted in my memory the whole chain and connection of their arguments," as having the hope that he "shall not omit or confound any considerable part of them in the recital" (*D*, 100, 101). He is a recorder of philosophizing, not a philosopher. There is no reason to suppose that Hume intends us to see the Pamphilus who now writes to Hermippus as no longer a mere auditor. Quite the contrary; Pamphilus says that he "had *lately* occasion to observe, while I passed, as usual, part of the summer season with Cleanthes, and was present at those conversations of his with Philo and Demea" (*D*, 101, my italics). To follow the fiction, Pamphilus is a mere auditor when he hears the *Dialogues* and when he offers his final paragraph comment on them.

Further, part of what very little we have from Pamphilus by way of philosophical opinion is claim that the being of a deity is "the surest foundation of morality, the firmest support of society, and the only principle which ought never to be a moment absent from our thoughts and meditations" (*D*, 128). Hume's own variety of morality is secular and has no religious foundations. There is no adequate textual basis for concluding that Pamphilus's remarks express Hume's considered opinion. We shall have to determine what Hume's own perspective is by other means than taking the word of Pamphilus.

None of the actual participants in the *Dialogues*—Cleanthes, Philo, and Demea—*always* represents Hume. *All* of them sometimes represent him. At least, this is so if our criterion is what Hume says elsewhere under his own name. Philo, for example, holds both that suspense of religious belief is possible (*D*, 135, 136) and that it is not (*D*, 216). Hume's view is that while such suspense is rare, it is not impossible (*N*, 75, 76). Explicitly, Philo closes *Dialogue* Eight with the assertion that "A total suspense of judgment is here [concerning all religious systems] our only reasonable recourse" (*D*, 160). Early in *Dialogue* Twelve, Philo tells Cleanthes that "notwithstanding the freedom of my conversation, and my love of singular arguments, no one has a deeper sense of the divine being, as he discovers himself to reason, in the inexplicable contrivance and artifice of nature" (*D*, 189). Philo there tells Cleanthes that he need not be "cautious on the subject of natural religion." For one thing, on that subject, he knows that he "can never, on that head, corrupt the principles of any man of common sense." For another, no one "in whose eyes I appear a man of common sense will ever mistake my intentions" (*D*, 189). He also holds that all religion corrupts "except the philosophical and rational kind" (*D*, 220), and our discussion of Hume's view of the connection between religion and morality makes it clear that Hume agrees. Cleanthes, however, holds that:

> Religion, however corrupted, is still better than no religion at all. The doctrine of a future state is so strong and necessary a security to morals, that we never ought to abandon or neglect it. For if finite and temporary rewards and punishments have so great an effect, as we daily find: How much greater must be expected from such as are infinite and external. [*D*, 119, 120]

This obviously is not the view of morality that Hume expresses in the *Treatise*, Book One, Part Three, or the *Enquiry Concerning the Principles of Morals*, nor is it compatible with the moral doctrines that these works teach. Neither is it the perspective that Hume expresses in the *Natural History* (*N*, 70–73). So in this respect Cleanthes does not speak for Hume. But when Cleanthes asserts that "there is an evident absurdity in pretending to demonstrate a matter of fact" (*D*, 162) he expresses a Humean position. Demea's claim that "*Chance* is but a word without meaning" (*D*, 162) expresses Hume's own position. But his claim that the ontological argument (or the cosmological argument) is sound and valid is non-Humean. At the severe risk of saying the obvious, it is the *Dialogues* that "speak for Hume." What *their* position is cannot be determined by slavishly following the lead of any one of its fictional participants.

Nonetheless, as we noted, Philo does change positions concerning whether complete suspense of religious is possible. The change of position, it can be argued, corresponds to a change in perspective. In *Dialogue* Twelve, Philo speaks from a commonsense perspective. What this amounts to is that the second-order religious propensities operate upon him, elicited by experience of order in nature and enlivened by passions. In the earlier context, he speaks as critical philosopher in whom the first-order propensities may act with full power but in whom the acid of skepticism has eaten away the power of the second-order propensities. So his overall position on this matter can be rendered consistent.

Nonetheless, the Philo of *Dialogue* Twelve does not quite represent Hume's own position on these matters. There is in Philo's remarks in *Dialogue* Twelve none of the concern about beliefs caused by second-order propensities weakening human nature. Nor is there, in Philo's fervent embracing of religious devotion, Hume's own apparent personal detachment from religious matters.

In *Dialogue* Twelve, then, Philo offers a litany in praise of the argument from design. In later chapters, the *Dialogues'* discussion of that argument will be thoroughly analyzed. To momentarily anticipate the results of that analysis, Philo manages to refute each variety of the argument that Cleanthes offers. Multiply reformulated, the argument is multiply rebutted until no further reformulation is forthcoming. Thus the Cleanthean sort of argument from design is laid to rest by Philonic criticism. Yet, after a discussion of the ontological argument in *Dialogue* Nine and the problems of evil in *Dialogues* Ten and Eleven, Philo is found waxing as eloquent in the argument's behalf as Paley or Butler.

The reason, of course, is that the topic has changed. In *Dialogues* One through Eight, the question was: is the design argument a successful piece of natural theology? Does it render it probable that the proposition *God exists* is true? In sum, the topic was *religion's foundation in human reason*.

In *Dialogue* Twelve, the topic has become *religion's origin in human nature*. Demea has departed. The discussion of natural theology is over. Cleanthes has defended the design argument and Philo has attacked it; they have argued about the problem of evil. Demea has joined in on these discussions, and Cleanthes and Philo have joined one another in arguing against Demea's acceptance of *a priori* arguments in favor of theism. The one Demean theme still relevant is his championing of divine ineffability, and Philo too is sympathetic to this line so there is no need for Demea to be there to champion it. Thus Philo relaxes with Cleanthes; the philosophical skeptic retires and the person of common sense re-enters. In a reversal of the dictum that there are no atheists in foxholes, it is after doing battle that Philo's religious belief, thin as it is, returns. The picture is just as one who has read carefully the *Natural History* would expect it to be: religion's lack of secure foundation in human reason does not affect its continuing presence in human affairs because religious belief has its origin in secondary propensities of human nature—propensities that operate in an evidence-irrelevant manner. Religious belief, not being based on natural theology, survives the collapse of natural theology. This theme of the *Natural History* is illustrated in the *Dialogues* in the person of Philo.

It is *not* surprising, then, to find that talented and savage critic Philo, having laid his sword aside, speaking not as skepticism's soldier but as common sense's representative, advocating that *Nature does nothing in vain* and *Nature acts by the simplest methods* and hearing with pleasure "Galen reasons concerning the structure of the human body" (*D*, 190). His *propensities* are like Cleanthes'; it is their *philosophies* that differ. In both cases, in Hume's view, imagination cheats reason to pay belief. When the beliefs are produced by the original propensities, the believer wins. When the beliefs are produced by the secondary propensities, the believer risks losing the game—risks reasonableness or sanity. Everyone wins. Most take the risk. Some lose what they had won.

Along these lines, then, *Dialogue* Twelve returns to, and exhibits, the themes of the *Natural History.* Professor Noxon is right to see a difference between what precedes *Dialogue* Twelve and that *Dialogue* itself; he speaks of a "complete reversal of standpoint" where there is a complete shift of perspective. Professor Jessop sees *Dialogue* Twelve as "disconnected from the argued content" of the *Dialogues,* and so it is. The "argued content" disputed design, dependent existence, and evil; it canvassed natural theology. *Dialogue* Twelve concerns natural religion. I have tried to show that what we are offered is not sheer inconsistency that cannot yield, in Professor Wollheim's terms, "a rigorous and unified doctrine." What Hume offers is precisely a fairly rigorous and highly unified doctrine in his writings on religion.

Verbal Dispute in *Dialogue* Twelve

Besides his declaration of allegiance to common sense, with its enthusiasm about design, Philo discourses on verbal disputes. Cleanthes has said:

> A false, absurd system, human nature, from the force of prejudice, is capable of adhering to, with obstinacy and perseverance. But no system at all, in opposition to theory, supported by strong and obvious reason, by natural propensity, and by early education, I think it absolutely impossible to maintain or defend. [*D*, 192]

Philo responds:

> So little do I esteem this suspense of judgment in the present case to be possible, that I am apt to suspect there enters somewhat of a dispute of words into this controversy, more than is usually imagined. . . . All men of sound reason are disgusted with verbal disputes [*D*, 192–193]

Nature bears "a great analogy to the productions of art"—to artifacts. "But as there are also considerable differences, we have reason to suppose a proportional difference in the causes" (*D*, 192). Nature, that is, is analogous, and it is disanalogous, to an artifact. One cannot *quantify* how analogous or disanalogous, and the qualitative issues of whether the analogies are evidentially more significant than the disanalogies, Philo suggests, is the sort of question that upon scrutiny vanishes into the mists. Thus dispute concerning the truth or falsehood of the crucial *premise* of the argument from design is verbal.

Philo thinks that the same holds for its conclusion. Concerning degrees of greatness or beauty, he claims:

> The degrees of these qualities are not, like quantity or number, susceptible of any exact mensuration, which may be the standard of the controversy. That the dispute concerning theism is of this nature, and consequently is merely verbal, or perhaps, if possible, still more incurably ambiguous, will appear upon the slightest enquiry. I ask the Theist, if he does not allow that there is a great and immeasurable, because incomprehensible, difference between the *human* and the *divine* mind: The more pious he is, the more readily will he assent to the difference: He will even assert that the difference is of a nature which cannot be too much magnified. [*D*, 193]

So the pious theist is left asserting only that there is an incomprehensible mind that is immeasurably different from the human mind. (What content there is to such theism that justifies any piety is open to doubt.)

Philo next turns "to the Atheist who, I assert, is only nominally so, and can never possibly be in earnest" (*D*, 193), and asks whether "the rotting of a turnip, the generation of an animal, and the structure of human thought be not energies that probably bear some remote analogy to each other: It is impossible he can deny it" (*D*, 194). Philo comes to what he sees as the sum of the matter in these words:

> The Theist allows that the original intelligence is very different from human reason: The Atheist allows, that the original principle of order bears some remote analogy to it. Will you quarrel, Gentlemen, about the degrees, and enter into a controversy which admits not of any precise meaning, nor consequently of any determination. [*D*, 194]

On the face of things, Philo's perspective is implausible. A monotheist of Jewish, Christian, or Islamic sort believes in an omnicompetent Creator and Providence. They are joined in this belief by the monotheists of the Vsistadvaita and Dvaita Vedanta traditions in (South Asian) Indian thought. Atheists, in European or American or Indian cultural contexts, deny the existence of a Creator and Providence.

"Omnicompetent" means "omnipotent, omniscient, and morally perfect." These terms can be defined with a fair degree of precision. God is omnipotent if and only if, for any proposition P such that neither P nor *God makes P true* is a contradiction, God can make P true. An omnipotent God thus can do anything that it is not logically impossible that God do. This contrasts sharply with the case of an ordinary human being; *no* matter how powerful a person may be, there are an indefinitely large number of things that it is logically possible or non-contradictory that she do that she lacks the power to do. God is omniscient if and only if, for any true proposition P, unless it is logically impossible that P be known or that God know that P, then God does know that P. God knows whatever it is logically possible that God knows. Again, this contrasts sharply with the case of an ordinary human being; no matter how knowledgeable a person may be, there are an indefinitely large number of things that it is logically possible or non-contradictory that he know that he does not know.

The notion of moral perfection is less easily sketched in crisp, brief introductory strokes. It has no relevant content unless some moral theory is true. It is highly problematic at best unless there is a way of rationally assessing competing moral theories. In order for the concept to be rendered usefully determinate, it need not be the case that all moral theories but one are eliminated. It would suffice that various uneliminated theories converge sufficiently so as to agree on a significant range of moral rationales and moral resolutions. Given such convergence, God is morally perfect if and only if the divine being fits the moral ideal that can be constructed from the area of moral convergence.

Alternatively, and more typically, a religious or theological tradition can construct a notion of moral goodness from its scriptural texts. Nor, of course, is this approach necessarily incompatible with the one just described. Notions of moral perfection obviously vary over ethical theories or moral traditions; this fact neither entails that one such notion cannot be discovered to be more adequate than another or that a particular notion of moral goodness cannot be both determinate and highly relevant to a religious tradition. This is not the place to expound some relevant notion of moral perfection, but both traditional and contemporary efforts have produced some determinate and defensible notions of moral perfection. There is appropriate suspicion, then, that Philo's perspective is mistaken.

Two themes are crucial to that perspective. One, shared with Cleanthes, is that one's concept of God, in whatever aspect, must be developed in the context of offering a successful version of the argument from design. To use the language of the philosophy of science, theory construction and theory justification are not independent tasks; in fact, for Philo and Cleanthes, in theology they are a single endeavor. The other is a theory of meaning on which, once one's discourse strays from the concerns of everyday life, its meaning becomes strained, and if it wanders really far from the marketplace and the hearth it becomes incurably vague.

The former constraint is one that few philosophical theologians are likely to accept; it is hard to see why they should reject the alternative view that theory construction should be given free play and only theory justification carried out as rigorously as possible. Indeed, few theologians of any sort are likely to accept Cleanthes' constraint, and while it is perfectly legitimate to see how things turn out when one operates within it, it is also perfectly legitimate to see how things turn out when one operates outside it. Scripture, experience, and reflection (other than merely on the design argument) may and do play significant roles in the development of a concept or doctrine of Deity without thereby altering the appropriate modalities of rational assessment of religious belief, or making it impossible to rationally assess them.

The theory of meaning crucial to Philo's perspective is one that had considerable attraction for Hume, though in the end he abandoned (or at least revised) it. That theory is the subject of a later chapter; it is worth dealing with on its own. If it turns out to be mistaken, Philo's program will be mistaken as well.

Most of the remainder of *Dialogue* Twelve is devoted to a discussion of the relation of religion to morality. Cleanthes briefly affirms the importance of religion—in particular, of a future life with rewards and punishments—for morality. Philo expansively argues that all religion, "except the philosophical and rational kind," has an unfortunate effect on morality. Philo asserts that "all history abounds" with instances of religion's "pernicious consequences on human affairs." No effort is made to distinguish one religion from another, or religion from superstition; indeed "religion" and "superstition" are used interchangeably in this discussion. Philo insists that natural inclination has greater motivational power than fear of hell, even in those who believe in hell. He notes that the inference "Threat of punishment in this life is efficacious in this life, therefore threat of worse punishment in the next life is even more efficacious in this life" is invalid. He contends that appeal to other motives weaken the effect of "the natural motives of justice and humanity" (*D*, 198). He worries about the powers of priests. In all of this discussion, it is Philo who takes positions that Hume elsewhere, in his own name, embraces. There is much in religion, as in any cultural territory occupied by us, that is open to disdain, and Philo is talented at exposing it. Hume's views on religion and morality, as they relate to monotheistic religion, are considered elsewhere in this volume.

Philo's Confession of Faith

In a confession that, in terms of concrete content, comes somewhat short of the Apostles' Creed, Philo says:

If the whole of natural theology, as some people seem to maintain, resolves itself into one simple, though somewhat ambiguous, at least undefined proposition, *that the cause or causes of order in the universe probably bear some remote analogy to human intelli-*

gence: If this proposition be not capable of extension, variation, or more particular explication: If it afford no inference that affects human life, or can be the source of any action or forbearance: And if the analogy, imperfect as it is, can be carried no farther than to the human intelligence; and cannot be transferred, with any appearance of probability, to the other qualities of the mind: If this really be the case, what can the most inquisitive, contemplative, and religious man do more than give a plain, philosophical assent to the proposition, as often as it occurs; and believe that the arguments, on which it is established, exceed the objections which lie against it? [*D*, 203–204]

Obviously, there is nothing, morally or religiously, to *do* with the proposition *The cause or causes of order in the universe probably bears some remote analogy to human intelligence;* it is utterly irrelevant to life and thought. For Philo, that is its beauty. Believing it leaves everything else the same as it was before one believed it. But it does little or no harm to believe it, even from a secondary propensity. After all, as Protagoras said, everything is like everything else in some way or other. Regarding religion, the danger, in Philo's opinion (and in Hume's opinion in the *Natural History*) lies in believing anything more.

Philo closes by saying that "the most natural sentiment which a well-disposed mind will feel on this occasion is a longing desire and expectation that heaven would be pleased to dissipate, at least alleviate this profound ignorance, by affording some particular revelation to mankind, and making discoveries of the nature, attributes, and operations of the divine object of our faith. A person, seasoned with a just sense of the imperfections of a natural reason, will fly to revealed truth with the greatest avidity" (*D*, 204). I take Hume here to be ironic, an agnostic politely saying grace so as not to offend his pious host. Hume did not fly to biblical revelation. So far as we know, he did not seek revelation in the texts of other religious traditions than the Jewish and the Christian. Nor does his philosophy of religion as a whole provide any support for the view that Hume is *not* ironic here; quite the contrary.

Might, though, Hume not wistfully have hoped for something that he would recognize as a revelation? He might have; who knows? But nothing of the sort entered into his philosophy of religion.

CHAPTER 2

The Treatise *Repetition of the* Natural History *Pattern of Explanation*

The Skeptical Prologue

THE PATTERN OF explanation that Hume uses to explicate theistic and polytheistic belief in the *Natural History* is not unique in Hume's writings. Part Four: *Of the sceptical and other systems of philosophy* in Book One of *A Treatise of Human Nature* contains explanations that manifest the same pattern.[1]

In Part Four, Section One: *Of scepticism with regard to reason*, Hume sets the stage for these explanations. He considers a remarkable argument.

> Having thus found in every probability, beside the original uncertainty inherent in the subject [that is, the subject matter], a new uncertainty deriv'd from the weakness of that faculty, which judges, and having adjusted these two together, we are oblig'd by our reason to add a new doubt deriv'd from the possibility of error in the estimation we make of the truth and fidelity of our faculties. This is a doubt, which immediately occurs to us, and of which, if we wou'd closely pursue our reason, we cannot avoid giving a decision. But this decision, tho' it shou'd be favourable to our preceding judgment, being founded only on probability, must weaken still further our first evidence, and must itself be weaken'd by a fourth doubt of the same kind, and so on *in infinitum;* till at last there remain nothing of the original probability, however great we may suppose it to have been, and however small the diminution by every new uncertainty. No finite object can subsist under a decrease repeated *in infinitum;* and even the

vastest quantity, which can enter into human imagination, must in this manner be reduc'd to nothing. Let our first belief be never so strong, it must infallibly perish by passing thro' so many new examinations, of which each diminishes somewhat of its force and vigor. When I reflect on the natural fallibility of my judgment, I have less confidence in my opinions, than when I only consider the objects concerning which I reason and when I proceed still farther, to turn the scrutiny against every successive estimation I make of my faculties, all the rules of logic require a continual diminution, and at last a total extinction of belief and evidence. [*T*, 182–183]

One initial problem with this argument is that so long as one reduces finite probabilities in certain increments (for example, one-half at a time) one can do so infinitely without reducing a finite probability to absolutely zero, though one will approach zero as a limit. Another is that presumably all that Hume needs is to reduce the probability of a claim to .5 or below, not all the way to zero. In any case, to assign probabilities to beliefs to get Humean results, in one way, is easy; there are various strategies that will meet this exegetical constraint and two such will be suggested. How one is to assign probabilities to beliefs *in a rationally justified way* so as to yield Humean results is another matter, and since Hume's conclusion is both false and self-defeating it would seem that no such sufficiently justified assignment is available.

It is not clear how this argument should be stated. Assuming "subject" does mean "subject matter" rather than "believing subject" (compare *T*, 182, which confirms this), we have a proposition *P* in which there is some "original uncertainty inherent." We have another proposition—let us represent it by *H(P)*—to the effect that Hume judges that *P*. We are then to "adjust these two together." Ordinarily, *P* and *H(P)* will be logically independent, neither entailing the other. Hume's concern is with probability. Suppose Hume somehow knows that, while his epistemic autobiography is not flawless, he has nine times out of ten believed truly. Then I suppose the idea is that any proposition of the form *H(−)* is .9, and so this is the probability of *H(P)*. Suppose *P*'s probability is also .9. How do we 'adjust these probabilities together'? Whatever 'adjustment' we make "must weaken still further our first evidence . . . and so on *in infinitum*, till at last there remain nothing of the original probability." *Adding* probabilities will yield *1.8*, a sort of super-certainty. *Subtracting* probabilities will yield zero right away, not gradually (and continuing to do so would yield negative numbers, a sort of super-uncertainty). *Dividing* probabilities will yield a probability of *1.0*. *Multiplying* probabilities will do the trick; it will reduce probabilities slowly towards zero. Suppose this is the appropriate adjustment. The probability result will be .81; apparently this will attach to *P and H(P)*.

Then our Hume is supposed to make a "scrutiny against" the last "estimation"—perhaps this is to assign a probability value to *H[H(P)]*. Being of the form *H(−)*, the probability assignment that *H[H(P)]* rates will be *.9*. Perhaps one is to then multiply *.81* by *.9*, and get a value of *.729* for *P and H(P) and H[H(P)]*. This is one possible strategy that yields Hume's desired results.

Or perhaps we must *tense* each *H(P)*, recording when the judgment is made, so that we have *P* and *H(P)t1* and *H[H(P)]t2* and assign *.729* to *P and H(P)t1 and H[H(P)]t2*.

This sort of assignment of probability with or without tensings is one way to achieve Hume's desired result. A different strategy is possible. The general idea is that it is always a conjunctive proposition that receives the probability assignment. Any relevant conjunctive statement will obviously include propositions expressing assessments of Hume's being right in judging that *P*, as well as an assessment of *P*. Call this sort of proposition an epistemic nesting. Require that a conjunct of propositions of the form *P, H(P), H[H(P)]*, etc. have a probability no higher than that of its least probable conjunct and that the probability of a proposition expressing an assessment of another proposition be lower than that of the proposition it assesses. One might call this the *epistemic nesting principle*. Finally, require that each lowering of probability be of at least the magnitude of (say) *.1*. Then again we will get the result Hume desires.

One could get this result in still other ways. One could require that for any propositions *Q* and *H(Q)*, the probability of *H(Q)* is less than that of *Q*, and for any pair of propositions *H(Q)tn* and *H(Q)tn+1*, the probability assigned to the latter must be lower than that assigned to the former. Then one might specify that the relevant 'adjustment' would be to begin by subtracting *H(Q)t1*'s probability from *Q's*, and assign the resulting probability to the epistemic nesting *Q and H(Q)t1*. The next step would be to subtract *H(Q)t2*'s probability from that of *H(Q)t1* and assign that to *Q and H(Q)t1 and H(A)t2*. The epistemic nesting principle will yield the result that Q's probability declines as the adjustments progress. Require that the probabilities be so assigned that subtraction always lowers the probability of its result at least (say) .1 below what it was subtracted from. Again, Hume's results will follow. I will not criticize these strategies. It would be time for that were they to possess some initial plausibility. Hume does not work out any such strategy, and I have done so only to indicate the sort of conclusion that 'total sceptics's' argument comes to.

Whether this is the, or a, proper way to read the argument, I am unsure. Its general idea is that the possibility of our being wrong (or the fact that we have been mistaken) is to eat away at the evidence for our beliefs until the evidence vanishes, and the only rational alternative is suspense of judgment. (The possibility of our being right, or the fact that we have been right, plays no positive epistemic role.)

Of course Hume, in one sense, makes no pretense of embracing the consequences of this argument. What he offers, however, is neither a counter-argument nor a critique. His reply is simply that:

> Nature, by an absolute and uncontrolable necessity has determ'd us to judge as well as to breathe and feel; nor can we any more forbear viewing certain objects in a stronger and fuller light, upon account of their customary connexion with a present impression, than we can hinder ourselves from thinking as long as we are awake, or seeing the surrounding bodies, when we turn our eyes towards them in broad sunshine. [*T*, 183]

What ultimately determines belief is, not evidence, but human nature.

Hume's intention "in displaying so carefully the arguments of that fantastic sect," the total skeptics,

> is only to make the reader sensible of the truth of my hypothesis, that all our reasonings concerning causes and effects are deriv'd from nothing but custom; and that belief is more properly an act of the sensitive, than of the cogitative part of our natures. [*T*, 183]

Abstractly, apparently Hume takes the *argument* of the total skeptics to be decisive. He writes:

> I have here prov'd, that the very same principles, which make us form a decision upon any subject, and correct that decision by the consideration of our genius and capacity, and of the situation of our mind, when we examin'd that subject; I say, I have prov'd that these same principles, when carry'd farther, and apply'd to every new reflex judgment, must, by continually diminishing the original evidence, at last reduce it to nothing, and utterly subvert all belief and opinion. If belief, therefore, were a simple act of the

> thought . . . it must infallibly destroy itself, and in every case terminate in a total suspense of judgment. [*T*, 184]

Hume supposes that those who try "can find no error in the foregoing arguments" of the total skeptic. So far as their argument goes, they are correct. But they assume that once one discovers one's lack of reasons for a belief, one's belief itself will disappear. They hold, if not an ethic or belief in which one ought to 'proportion belief to evidence,' then a theory of belief (and, indeed, of human nature) according to which recognized total lack of grounds for a belief will remove that belief from one's epistemic storehouse. They thus assume that (known) lack of any grounds for any beliefs whatever will leave one's epistemic cupboard bare. In this, Hume holds, they are mistaken. Rather, "as experience will sufficiently convince any one . . . reasoning and belief is some sensation or peculiar manner of conception, which 'tis impossible for mere ideas and reflections to destroy," (*T*, 182). What the total skeptic's argument would produce in a purely rational agent is suspense of judgment. In Hume's view, such a state is not an option for our species. Thus Hume, so far as I can see, accepts the view that it would be appropriate, as a method of evidence-weighing, to follow some such procedure as that described above.

His interest, it seems plain, lies more in the total skeptics' being wrong about suspense of judgment than in any careful or detailed consideration of their basic argument and its actual strategic details. He even repeats their argument, with apparent approval.

> In every judgment, which we can form concerning probability, as well as concerning knowledge, we ought always to correct the first judgment, deriv'd from the nature of the object, by another judgment, deriv'd from the nature of the understanding. 'Tis certain a man of solid sense and long experience ought to have, and usually has, a greater assurance in his opinions, than one that is foolish and ignorant, and that our sentiments have different degrees of authority, even with ourselves, in proportion to the degrees of our reason and experience. In the man of the best sense and longest experience, his authority is never entire, since even such-a-one must be conscious of many errors in the past, and must still dread the like for the future. Here then arises a new species of probability to correct and regulate the first, and fix its just standard and proportion. As demonstration is subject to the control of probability, so is probability liable to a new correction by a reflex act of the mind, wherein the nature of our under-

standing, and our reasoning from the first probability become
our objects. [*T*, 182]

But again he contends that the psychological *effect* of this evidence-
weighing is not suspense of judgment because, after the "first and
second decision" or act of checking, "the action of mind becomes
forced and unnatural and the ideas faint and obscure" (*T*, 185).

> Where the mind reaches not its objects with easiness and facility,
> the same principles have not the same effect as in a more natural
> conception of the ideas; nor does the imagination feel a sen-
> sation, which holds any proportion with that which arises from
> its common judgments and opinions. The attention is on the
> stretch; the posture of the mind is uneasy; and the spirits being
> diverted from their natural course, are not govern'd in their
> movements by the same laws, at least not to the same degree, as
> when they flow in their usual channel. [*T*, 185]

The checking processes, or the 'reflex act' of considering one's belief
states, or perhaps the continuing multiplication of alleged probabilities, involves an

> effort of thought (that) disturbs the operation of our sentiments,
> on which the belief depends. . . . The straining of the imagina-
> tion always hinders the regular flowing of the passions and senti-
> ments. . . . As the emotions of the soul prevent any subtle rea-
> soning and reflection, so these latter actions of the mind are
> equally prejudicial to the former. The mind . . . seems to be en-
> dow'd with a certain precise degree of force and activity, which it
> never employs in one action, but at the expense of the rest. . . .
> No wonder, then, the conviction, which arises from a subtle rea-
> soning, diminishes in proportion to the efforts, which the imagi-
> nation makes to enter into the reasoning, and to conceive it in all
> its parts. Belief, being a lively conception, can never be entire,
> where it is not founded on something natural and easy. [*T*, 186]

In sum, "nature breaks the force of all sceptical arguments in time,
and keeps them from having any considerable influence on the understanding" (*T*, 187). What epistemology would require, psychology
forbids.

This stage-setting for the explanation of our belief in an external
world contains, then, certain Humean theses relevant to the concerns
of this Chapter. Belief is determined, not by evidence or reasoning,

but by (human) nature; belief is "more properly an act of the sensitive, than of the cogitative part of our nature" (*T*, 183). Belief formation depends "on the operation of our sentiments" (*T*, 185) and is not prevented or undone even by total absence of evidence for the beliefs thereby formed. Put in these various ways, then, Hume offers an essentially acognitive or non-cognitive account of the sources of belief.

If "reason," then, is the name of a propensity, it is the name of a non-dominant propensity. Even if reason is not a propensity, it is something that shares with secondary propensities certain of the latters' defining properties. It does not produce the same beliefs in everyone. Due to its own frailty, and to external factors that it does not control, its operation not merely may be, but (as we do not suspend belief in the absence of relevant evidence) often is, prevented. "Rational animal" is not a plausible candidate for expressing Hume's analysis of our nature. These Humean theses from Section One of Part Four are substantial. If Section One of Part Four sets the stage for what is to come, it also contains important claims of its own.

Belief in an External World: Humean Constancy

In Section Two, *Of Scepticism with regard to the senses*, Hume turns to explaining our belief in an 'external world' in a way that does not require that we have evidence in its favor. Our "assurance of the continu'd and distinct existence of body," Hume says, "must be entirely due [not, for reasons he has given and takes to be sufficient, to reason or the senses, but] to the imagination" (*T*, 193). When we ascribe continued existence to objects, we do so upon having experienced items that manifest *constancy*. At a given time T1, Ann perceives redness, roundness, and (visual) smoothness, all against a white background; she sees a red ball on a white floor. At T2, Ann again perceives redness, roundness, and (visual) smoothness, and again at T3. Ann's perceptual experiences from T1 through T3 manifest *constancy*. At each moment, Ann perceives a new token of each of the types *redness, roundness, visual smoothness,* and *(background) whiteness.* This way of describing Ann's experience, of course, is loaded with assumptions. On it, Ann sees three red tokens, not one red ball; three round tokens, not one red ball; and so on. The *same* token at any given time is a token of each of the different types *redness, roundness,* and *smoothness.* Some philosophers suppose such descriptions to be parsimonious and incorrigible—modest in ontological commitment and secure from human error. Other philosophers suppose such descriptions to be unparsimonious and corrigible—lost in dubious ontological commitment and no more secure from error than experience of ordinary objects. The phenomenologist expresses doubts about objects, the realist about sense data.

Setting such disputes aside here, the qualitative identity or strong similarity between content over time that Ann's perceptual experience manifests is Humean constancy. In such circumstances, according to Hume, Ann will mistakenly suppose that the red token at T1, the red token at T2, and the red token at T3 really are only *one* numerically identical token. She will have no grounds for doing this, and her doing it is to be explained by reference to experiences and propensities, not evidence. Hume's "strict" or "proper" identity is numerical identity. If I am an enduring mental substance or self and remember that I once shook hands with the great Boston Celtic guard, Sam Jones, I am numerically identical to the person whom I remember shaking hands with Sam Jones. Identical twins are not numerically identical; at most, they approach qualitative identity. Perhaps two newly minted coins from the same mint are qualitatively identical. Still, each one of them is the coin it is, and not the other. But if coins are enduring objects, one of the coins at one moment during its history is numerically the same item as that coin at any other moment of its history. In Hume's view, Ann's experience is not of a red ball that endures over time and at one moment is numerically identical with itself at an earlier moment.

At a given time T1, Ann looks out her narrow window and sees a crocodile's head. At T2, her view is of a crocodile's body. At T3, she sees a crocodile's tail. The restless crocodile circles round the cabin, and at T11 Ann again sees a crocodile's head, at T12, a crocodile's body, and at T13, a crocodile's tail. The *T1-through-T3* and *T11-through-T13* sequences exhibit identical *patterns;* they thereby exhibit Humean *coherence.* A particular experiential sequence that yields belief in an enduring object need not contain multiple tokens of a single type. It is requisite only that the *order* of occurring tokens of some types be two or more times the same. (If Ann sees a red dot against a white background at times T1, T2, T3 and T11, T12, T13, constancy reigns *within* each sequence and coherence reigns *between* them.) Upon appearance of a second pattern, Ann mistakenly will tend to assume that she sees again numerically the same item she saw the previous time—to think that she re-identifies, not simply a pattern, but an object or set of objects. One could endeavor to re-describe what Ann sees in non-object terms, limiting ourselves to descriptions that apply to Humean impressions rather than to physical objects. Whether this should, or even can, be done is not our concern here.

Ann may see a token of *redness, roundness,* and *visual smoothness* at times T1 and T3 but not at T2; she mistakenly will take her T3-experience to be a matter of her becoming reacquainted with her T1-friend. Then she will suppose that this token existed unexperienced at T2. Similarly, when experiences manifesting constancy lead Ann to suppose that she re-identifies an object earlier encountered, she will suppose it to have existed between the times at which her experiences exhibited coherence.

Hume contends that

> the imagination, when set into any train of thinking, is apt to continue, even when its object fails it, and like a galley put in motion by the oars, carries out its course without any new impulse. *T,* 198]

> Objects have a certain coherence even as they appear to our senses but this coherence is much greater and more uniform, if we suppose the objects to have a continu'd existence; and as the mind is once in the train of observing an uniformity among objects, it naturally continues, till it renders the uniformity as complete as possible. [*T,* 198]

This, Hume says, "gives rise to the opinion of the continu'd existence of body, which is prior to that of its distinct existence, and produces that latter principle" (*T,* 199). Thus, while one might think the positing of unperceived sets and sequences was enough to yield also the positing of distinct or mind-independent items, Hume denies this; he adds that when we posit mind-independent objects, "'tis only by a fiction of the imagination, by which the unchangeable object is suppos'd to participate of the changes of the co-existent objects and in particular of that of our perceptions" (*T,* 200–201). Hume suggests that, in positing distinct or mind-independent objects, we finesse our data. Given the time difference between one perceptual experience and another of which we are aware, Hume takes it to follow that the tokens comprising one experience are not numerically identical to those comprising another (both sets of tokens allegedly are impressions, and so are fleeing or transient; and the ultimate Humean criterion for change of time is change in impressions or perceptions).

> One single object conveys the idea of unity, not that of identity. [*T,* 200]

> Thus the principle of individuation (among objects) is nothing but the *invariableness* and *uninterruptedness* of any object, thro' a suppos'd variation of time, by which the mind can trace it in the different periods of its existence, without any break of the view, and without being oblig'd to form the idea of multiplicity or number. [*T*, 201]

Thus Hume offers us three propensities: one to fill in gaps in a constancy series, another to fill in gaps in a coherence series, and a third, whether there are gaps to be filled in or not, to mistake qualitatively similar items at two or more times for a numerically identical item. Call these the *constancy, coherence,* and *identity* propensities. In describing the propensities, Hume has also described their eliciting experiences, which operate in a context that involves remembered past sequences of perceptions and which require possession of a common, but nonetheless sophisticated, battery of concepts. For example:

> This fiction of imagination almost universally takes place; and 'tis by means of it, that a single object, plac'd before us, and survey'd for any time without our discovering in it any interruption or variation, is able to give us a notion of identity. For when we consider any two points of this time, we may place them in different lights: We may either survey them at the very same instant; in which case they give us the idea of number, both by themselves and by the object; which must be multiply'd, in order to be conceiv'd at once, as existent in these two different points of time: Or on the other hand, we may trace the succession of time by a like succession of ideas, and conceiving first one moment, along with the object then existent, imagine afterwards a change in the time without any *variation* or *interruption* in the object; in which case it gives us the idea of unity. Here then is an idea, which is a medium betwixt unity and number; or more properly speaking, is either of them, according to the view, in which we take it: And this idea we call that of identity. We cannot, in any propriety of speech, say, the object existent at one time is the same with itself existent at another. By this means we make a difference, betwixt the idea meant by the word, object, and that meant by itself, without going the length of number, and at the same time without restraining ourselves to a strict and absolute unity. [*T*, 201]

Making this mistake is possible only for one whose conceptual framework has considerable sophistication.

The role of background conditions, provided by memory, plus the operations of propensities, is recounted clearly in this extended discussion. Our memory presents us with a vast number of instances of perceptions perfectly resembling each other, that return at different distances of time, and after considerable interruptions.

> This resemblance gives us a propension to consider these interrupted perceptions as the same; and also a propension to connect them by a continu'd existence, in order to justify this identity, and avoid the contradiction, in which the interrupted appearance of these perceptions seems necessarily to involve us. Here then we have a propensity to feign the continu'd existence of all sensible objects; and as this propensity arises from some lively impressions of the memory, it bestows a vivacity on that fiction; or in other words, makes us believe the continu'd existence of body. If sometimes we ascribe a continu'd existence to objects, which are perfectly new to us, and of whose constancy and coherence we have no experience, 'tis because the manner, in which they present themselves to our senses, resembles that of constant and coherent objects; and this resemblance is a source of reasoning and analogy, and leads us to attribute the same qualities to the similar objects.
>
> I believe an intelligent reader will find less difficulty to assent to this system, than to comprehend it fully and distinctly, and will allow, after a little reflection, that every part carries its own proof along with it. 'Tis indeed evident, that as the vulgar *suppose* their perceptions to be their only objects, and at the same time *believe* the continu'd existence of matter, we must account for the origin of the belief upon that supposition. Now upon that supposition, 'tis a false opinion that any of our objects, or perceptions, are identically the same after an interruption; and consequently the opinion of their identity can never arise from reason, but must arise from the imagination. The imagination is seduc'd into such an opinion only by means of the resemblance of certain perceptions; since we find they are only our resembling perceptions, which we have a propension to suppose the same. This propension to bestow an identity on our resembling perceptions, produces the fiction of a continu'd existence; since that fiction, as well as the identity, is really false, as is acknowledg'd by all philosophers, and has no other effect than to remedy the interruption of our perceptions, which is the only circumstance that is

> contrary to their identity. In the last place this propension causes belief by means of the present impressions of the memory; since without the remembrance of former sensations, 'tis plain we never shou'd have any belief of the continu'd existence of body. Thus in examining all these parts, we find that each of them is supported by the strongest proofs; and that all of them together form a consistent system, which is perfectly convincing. [*T*, 208–10]

It is hard to see that *proof* has been offered of anything. It seems that each element Hume introduces into the theory by means of which he explains belief in enduring and mind-independent objects does play a role in that theory; further, the theory does seem self-consistent. *If* we have neither perceptual nor conceptual evidence or reason or ground for belief in public objects, we shall need some such theory to explain that belief. This much, it seems, we may grant to Hume. It is not clear that we should grant him more.

It should be noted that Hume suggests that we have a propensity to posit entities under circumstances in which the absence of such entities would leave us believing contradictory propositions. He does not obviously view this an especially rational propensity, or propensity of our reason, given that the beliefs rendered consistent by its operations are not beliefs we embraced from evidence in the first place, and given that its operations involve 'feigning' objects and finessing data. Still, perhaps the propensity to produce consistent belief-sets falls under the propensity, noted earlier, to adopt a satisfactory system. In any case, the operation of what we may call the *consistency propensity* plays an important role in producing belief in an external world.

> When we gradually follow an object in its successive changes, the smooth progress of the thought makes us ascribe an identity to the succession; because 'tis by a similar act of the mind we consider an unchangeable object. When we compare its situation after a considerable change the progress of the thought is broke; and consequently we are presented with the idea of diversity: In order to reconcile which contradictions the imagination is apt to feign something unknown and invisible, which it supposes to continue the same under all these variations; and this unintelligible something it calls a *substance, or original and first matter.* [*T*, 220]

In a passage that summarizes much of his position, Hume writes:

> Suppose an object perfectly simple and indivisible to be pre-sented, along with another object, whose *co-existent* parts are connected together by a strong relation, 'tis evident the actions of the mind, in considering these two objects, are not very different. The imagination conceives the simple object at once, with facility, by a single effort of thought, without change or variation. The connexion of parts in the compound object has almost the same effect, and so unites the object within itself, that the fancy feels not the transition in passing from one part to another. Hence the colour, taste, figure, solidity, and other qualities, combin'd in a peach or melon, are conceiv'd to form *one thing;* and that on account of their close relation, which makes them affect the thought in the same manner, as if perfectly uncompounded. But the mind rests not here. Whenever it views the object in another light, it finds that all these qualities are different, and distinguish-able, and separable from each other; which view of things being destructive of its primary and more natural notions, obliges the imagination to feign an unknown something, or *original* sub-stance and matter, as a principle of union or cohesion among these qualities, and as what may give the compound object a title to be call'd one thing, notwithstanding its diversity and composi-tion. [*T*, 221]

Hume here offers two propensities as relevant to the production of belief in objects. Suppose that Ann experiences *tokens* or *instances* of redness and roundness—often, and together. Then she tends not to distinguish between such instances. If Ann experiences redness and roundness at time T1, and redness and roundness at T2, and so on, after while Ann has what we may call an *indistinguishability among dis-cernibles* propensity not to distinguish the T1-instance of redness or roundness from the T2-instance of redness or roundness or from in-stances of redness and roundness at other times. But of course these instances are noticeably distinct if we reflectively consider them, and Ann also has what we might call a *distinguishing among discernibles* propensity to distinguish them. In order to reconcile the results of these propensities—that we tend to identify and also to distinguish between the instances—we tend to ascribe the instances to some one thing of which all the instances are seen as properties. While other matters are included in Hume's *Treatise* account of our belief in an ex-ternal world, perhaps we have followed it sufficiently to make clear that its structure is strikingly similar to the explanation of religious belief in the *Natural History*. In particular, the *Treatise* explanation contains essential references to propensities and background conditions and eliciting or triggering experiences.

Belief in an Enduring Self

Notoriously, Hume denies that anyone has a Cartesian *cogito*-experience of oneself as a mental substance and denies that there is any enduring self. Nonetheless, he asks, "What . . . gives us so great a propension to ascribe an identity to these successive perceptions, and to ourselves possest of an invariable and uninterrupted existence thro' the whole course of our lives?" (*T*, 253). Remarking that his concern is with "personal identity, as it regards our thought or imagination," not "as it regards our passions or the concern we take in ourselves," he answers as follows. We have the concept of *identity:* "a distinct idea of an object, that remains invariable and uninterrupted thro' a suppos'd variation of time." We have the notion of *diversity:* "a distinct idea of several different objects existing in succession, and connected together by a close relation." But "that action of the imagination" by which we consider an item under identity and that by which we consider an item under diversity are very similar. And this similarity

> facilitates the transition of the mind from one object to another, and renders its passage as smooth as if it contemplated one continu'd object. . . . However at one instant we may consider the related succession as variable or interrupted, we are sure the next to ascribe to it a perfect identity. . . . Our propensity to this mistake is so great . . . that we fall into it before we are aware . . . we cannot long sustain our philosophy, or take off this bias from the imagination. Our last resource is to yield to it. . . . Thus we feign the continu'd existence of the perceptions of our senses, to remove the interruption; and run into the notion of a soul, and self, and substance, to disguise the variation. But we may further observe, that where we do not give rise to such a fiction, our propension to confound identity with relation is so great, that we are apt to imagine something unknown and mysterious, connecting the parts, beside their relation. [*T*, 254]

Since impressions of reflection resemble one another, our propensity to mistake resembling items for a single item comes into play and produces the idea of a continuing mind; the identity propensity is activated.

Suppose that Ann has a set of impressions or perceptions at time T1—say, *redness, roundness, smoothness, softness*—and that her perceptions at T2 are qualitatively identical save that *hardness* replaces *softness*. Then, at T3, Ann's perceptual experience is comprised by instances of *blueness, roundness, smoothness, hardness*. In such circumstances, we have small changes in the qualitative composition of Ann's perceptual experience which facilitates the operation of the identity propensity, "our propension to confound identity with relation" (*T*, 254). Nor does this propensity operate only if one has sequences of resembling impressions. If one's impressions are, whether resembling or not, the members of a set of impressions so related that they are or seem to be related to some common end, the operation of the identity propensity is facilitated. The same applies if the impressions, successively or simultaneously, are or seem to be related to one another by what Hume calls "sympathy," namely "a mutual dependence on, and connexion with, one another" (*T*, 257). Similar remarks are made regarding the operation of the identity propensity in the case of belief in an external world (compare *T*, 204). The similarity of the structure of this account to the *Treatise* account of belief in an external world, and to the account of religious belief in the *Natural History*, is evident. In both cases, a variety of propensities are said to operate, triggered by various experiences, against various experiential backgrounds.

Principles of Association as Propensities, Causality Included

Upon a little reflection, it is evident that Hume's principles of association are themselves expressible, not as principles of attraction among mental atoms, but as propensities of a mind to think along certain lines. Hume himself is ambiguous between these ways of putting the matter when he introduces the principles of association: "The qualities, from which this association arises, and by which the mind is . . . convey'd from one idea to another, are three, *viz., resemblance, contiguity* in time or place, and *cause* and *effect*" (*T*, 11). He continues:

> Our imagination runs easily from one idea to any other that *resembles* it . . . as the senses, in changing their objects, are necessitated to . . . take them as they lie *contiguous* to each other, the

> imagination must by long custom acquire the same method of thinking. . . . As to the connexion, that is made by the relation of *cause and effect*, we shall have occasion afterwards to examine it to the bottom . . . there is no relation, which produces a stronger connexion in the fancy, and makes one idea more readily recall another, than the relation of cause and effect betwixt their objects. [*T*, 11]

Stated as propensities of the mind, two of the principles of association—resemblance and continuity—go something as follows: if ideas *A* and *B* resemble one another, if a person has had ideas similar to both in the past, and if she has *A* at time *T*, then she will tend also to have *B* at *T* (if the resembling ideas have occurred simultaneously) or at *T* + *1* (if the resembling ideas have occurred successively). Thus even when Hume, as the Newton of the intellectual world, introduces laws of associative psychology intended to be analogous in form and function to the laws of motion, he also states them in the pattern to become familiar in the *Treatise* explanations of belief in objects and selves: biographical background of impressions or ideas, propensity, and triggering experience.

The same holds for the third law of association concerning cause and effect. When Hume comes to "examine [causality] . . . to the bottom," he offers these definitions:

> There may two definitions be given of this relation, which are only different, by their presenting a different view of the same object, and making us consider it either as a *philosophical* or as a *natural* relation; either as a comparison of two ideas, or as an association betwixt them. We may define a CAUSE to be 'An object precedent and contiguous to another, and where all the objects resembling the former are plac'd in like relations of precedency and contiguity to those objects, that resemble the latter.' If this definition he esteem'd defective, because drawn from objects foreign to the cause, we may substitute this other definition in its place, *viz.* 'A CAUSE is an object precedent and contiguous to another, and so united with it, that the idea of the one determines the mind to form a more lively idea of the other.' Shou'd this definition also be rejected for the same reason, I know no other remedy, than that the persons, who express this delicacy, should substitute a juster definition in its place. But for my part I must own my incapacity for such an undertaking. When I examine with the utmost accuracy those objects, which are commonly de-

nominated causes and effects, I find, in considering a single instance, that the one object is precedent and contiguous to the other; and in enlarging my view to consider several instances, I find only, that like objects are constantly plac'd in like relations of succession and contiguity. Again, when I consider the influence of this constant conjunction, perceive, that such a relation can never be an object of reasoning, and can never operate upon the mind, but by means of custom, which determines the imagination to make a transition from the idea of one object to that of its usual attendant, and from the impression of one to a more lively idea of the other. However extraordinary these sentiments may appear, I think it fruitless to trouble myself with any farther enquiry or reasoning upon the subject, but shall repose myself on them as on establish'd maxims. [*T*, 170]

Notoriously, the second definition can be put along some such lines as these: Suppose that at time T a person has ideas A and B, and that idea A (or what A represents) is of kind $K1$, and idea B (or what B represents) is of type $K2$. Suppose, too, that one's experience is such that whenever (something representing) a member of $K1$ has occurred in one's experience, then (something representing) a member of $K2$ has occurred in one's experience with any temporal priority there may be belonging to the (something representing) a member of $K1$. Then upon thinking of (something representing) a member of $K1$, one will also think of (something representing) a member of $K2$, and upon experiencing (something representing) a member of $K1$, one will expect to experience (something representing) a member of $K2$. Briefly, then, this is the well-known background to Hume's remark that "all our reasonings concerning causes and effects are deriv'd from nothing but custom" (*T*, 183). Here, too, we find the remembered backdrop of experience providing background conditions, plus eliciting experiences and relevant propensities. The patterns of explanation present in the *Natural History*, then, are richly exhibited in the *Treatise*.

The *Treatise* Explanations and the *Natural History* Explanation

There is one important difference between the pattern of the *Natural History* explanations and those of the *Treatise*. The *Treatise* explanations fundamentally have to do with primary or original propensities, whereas the *Natural History* explanations fundamentally have to do with secondary propensities. As we saw, secondary propensities, even with relevant background conditions, operate only upon being triggered by both appropriate present experiences and passion. But, Hume says, "A strong propensity or inclination alone, without any present impression, will sometimes cause a belief or opinion" (*T*, 210). Sufficiently strong (presumably primary) propensities, perhaps only with relevant background conditions, perhaps with some supporting passion and perhaps not, but without appropriate present experience, may nonetheless produce belief; they, presumably in contrast to secondary propensities, are sometimes self-starting. But the most important difference, as we saw, is that primary propensities always operate, and always yield the same beliefs, whereas secondary propensities may be thwarted, and when not thwarted yield diverse beliefs. Such belief, in Hume's view, is helped rather than hindered insofar as we accept the 'vulgar' perspective and do not distinguish between 'perceptions' and 'objects' (*T*, 202); Hume's treating impressions as non-representational and ideas as representational, and regarding perception as not a matter of having, but as constituted by impressions (not ideas), involves him in treating sensory experience as non-intentional. (How this relates to the alleged perception/object distinction is too complex to discuss here.)

Conflict Concerning the External World

There is another similarity between the perspectives on explanation in the *Natural History* and the *Treatise*. It will take a while to develop it. As a beginning, consider this passage:

> There is a direct and total opposition betwixt our reason and our senses; or more properly speaking, betwixt those conclusions we form from cause and effect, and those that persuade us of the continu'd and independent existence of body. When we reason from cause and effect, we conclude, that neither colour, sound, taste, nor smell have a continu'd and independent existence. When we exclude these sensible qualities, there remains nothing in the universe which has such an existence. [*T*, 231]

The non-epistemic story relative to our belief in an external world—the non-epistemic "conclusions that persuade us" to accept the existence of physical objects that are distinct from and independent of our perceptual experience—was briefly rehearsed above, and I will not repeat it here. The "conclusions we form from cause and effect," with the accompanying reasoning, go as follows.

In *Of the Modern Philosophy* (Part Four, section Four), Hume, in effect, on the basis of a version of the variation arguments, accepts "the fundamental principle" of the modern philosophy that "colours, sounds, tastes, smells, heat and cold . . . (are) nothing but impressions in the mind" (*T*, 226). (A variation argument infers from premises concerning perceptual variation—the same object appearing one way to one sense or person or in one circumstance but another way to another sense or person or in another circumstance—to a conclusion asserting that the object has no, or no discernable, property that corresponds to the appearance.) At least he says that he finds "only one of the reasons commonly produc'd for this opinion to be satisfactory, viz., That deriv'd from the variation of those impressions, even while the external object, to all appearance continues the same" (*T*, 226). Secondary qualities are accessible to one sense only; primary qualities are multiply sensorially accessible. Thus color is a secondary, and shape a primary, quality. As is well known, the system to which this principle is fundamental holds that secondary qualities do not, but primary qualities do, reside in objects, so that only representations of primary qualities resemble objects. From the "many objections [which] might be made to this system," Hume confines himself to one that he finds "very decisive": "If colours, sounds, tastes, and smells be merely perceptions, nothing we can conceive is possest of a real, continu'd, and independent existence; not even motion, extension and solidity; which are the primary qualities chiefly insisted on" (*T*, 228).

The core of Hume's argument goes as follows:

> The idea of motion necessarily supposes that of a body moving. Now what is our idea of the moving body. . . . It must resolve itself into the idea of extension or of solidity . . . 'tis impossible to conceive extension, but as composed of parts, endow'd with colour or solidity . . . it must at last resolve itself into such as are perfectly simple and indivisible. These simple and indivisible parts, not being ideas of extension must be non-entities, unless conceiv'd as colour'd or solid. Colour is excluded from any real existence. The reality, therefore, of our idea of extension depends upon the reality of the idea of solidity. . . . The idea of solidity is that of two objects, which being impell'd by the utmost force, cannot penetrate each other. . . . Solidity, therefore, is perfectly incomprehensive alone, and without the conception of some bodies, which are solid, and maintain this separate and distinct

existence. Now what idea have we of these bodies? The ideas of . . . secondary qualities are excluded. The idea of motion depends on that of extension, and the idea of extension that of solidity. 'Tis impossible, therefore, that the idea of solidity can depend on either of them. . . . Our modern philosophy, therefore, leaves us no just or satisfactory idea of solidity; nor consequently of matter. [*T*, 228–229]

But if we have no proper idea of matter, the hypothesis that matter exists is no proper hypothesis. One can argue:

(a) body = that which is colored or solid and mind-independent; but

(b) what is colored is mind-dependent; so

(c) body = that which is solid

(d) that which is solid = that which is tangible; but

(e) that which is tangible is mind-dependent; so

(f) body = that which is mind-dependent.

But then a body is both mind-independent and mind-dependent, which of course is logically impossible. One might try to define "body" without reference to any perceptual qualities. But nothing can be *merely* mind-independent, and when we come to ascribe the other properties allegedly relevant to *being a body*, we get the inelegant results noted above. That reasoning requires that we agree that to be colored is to be visually accessible, episodically and not merely dispositionally, and analogously for being tangible, and an astute realist about objects will not grant these analyses of *being colored* and *being tangible*. But the relevant exegetical point is that Hume claims that the "conclusions we form from cause and effect" when we consider the mind-dependency of secondary qualities and the alleged inseparability of primary qualities from secondary qualities lead us to reject physical realism, whereas our nature renders acceptance of physical realism a foregone conclusion. There is, then, this conflict between "our reason and our senses," and it is not a conflict that Hume resolves, or, perhaps, thinks resolvable. For all that, we believe that there is an external world.

Conflict Concerning Enduring Numerically Identical Selves

Hume's highly relevant doctrines concerning the nature of persons or minds will occupy our full attention in Chapter 4; as they are centrally relevant to our present story they must be briefly canvassed here. In a famous passage in the *Appendix*, Hume claims to find another "direct and total opposition," this time concerning personal identity.

> I HAD entertain'd some hopes, that however deficient our theory of the intellectual world might be, it wou'd be free from those contradictions, and absurdities, which seem to attend every explication, that human reason can give of the material world. But upon a more strict review of the section concerning *personal identity*, I find myself involv'd in such a labyrinth, that, I must confess, I neither know how to correct my former opinions, nor how to render them consistent. If this be not a good *general* reason for scepticism, 'tis at least a sufficient one (if I were not already abundantly supplied) for me to entertain a diffidence and modesty in all my decisions. I shall propose the arguments on both sides, beginning with those that induc'd me to deny the strict and proper identity and simplicity of a self or thinking being. [*T*, 633]

Commentators have been puzzled about what problem or problems so disturb Hume. His discussion makes plain that he holds these propositions to be, so far as he can see, true and unchallengeable:

> (1) We have no idea, because no impression, of a simple, individual self or substance.
> (2) Each perception (being distinct, distinguishable, and so separable in thought from every other) can exist alone.
> (3) What (2) asserts to be true of single perceptions is also true of any group of perceptions.
> (4) A physical object, or a self, is but a group of perceptions; and we have no notion of either save as such.

(In (1) through (4), it would seem that "perception" and "impression"—and perhaps "quality" (*T*, 635)—could be used interchangeably without affecting their accuracy as expressions of what Hume says.) At this point, Hume reports: "So far I seem to be attended with sufficient evidence." Then the lights go out.

> But having thus loosen'd all our particular perceptions, when [see *T*, 260] I proceed to explain the principle of connexion, which binds them together, and makes us attribute to them a real simplicity and identity; I am sensible, that my account is very defective, and that nothing but the seeming evidence of the precedent reasonings cou'd have induc'd me to receive it. [*T*, 635]

The core of Hume's problem, then, in his view anyway, seems to concern explaining (i) the principle that connects particular perceptions, and (ii) the (same, or different) principle that makes us attribute simplicity and (numerical) identity to (distinct) particular perceptions. He continues:

> If perceptions are distinct existences, they form a whole only by being connected together. But no connexions among distinct existences are ever discoverable by human understanding. We only *feel* a connexion or a determination of the thought, to pass from one object to another. It follows, therefore, that the thought alone finds personal identity, when reflecting on the train of past perceptions, that compose a mind, the ideas of them are felt to be connected together, and naturally introduce each other. However extraordinary this conclusion may seem, it need not surprize us. Most philosophers seem inclin'd to think, that personal identity *arises* from consciousness; and consciousness is nothing but a reflected thought or perception. [*T*, 635]

The central claims here seem to be: (iii) no connections among distinct perceptions are ever *discovered* or *discoverable*, and (iv) we *feel* a tendency to connect perceptions, and so (v) any connections we posit are *created*. Even here, Hume thinks, his philosophy has "a promising aspect," but his hopes vanish when he tries

> to explain the principles, that unite our successive perceptions in our thought or consciousness. I cannot discover any theory, which gives me satisfaction on his head.
>
> In short there are two principles, which I cannot render consistent; nor is it in my power to renounce either of them, viz. *that all our distinct perceptions are distinct existences*, and *that the mind never perceives any real connexion among distinct existences*. Did our perceptions either inhere in something simple and individual, or did the mind perceive some real connexion among them, there wou'd be no difficulty in the case. For my part, I must plead the privilege of a sceptic, and confess, that this difficulty is too hard for my understanding. I pretend not, however, to pronounce it absolutely insuperable. Others, perhaps, or myself, upon more mature reflection, may discover some hypothesis, that will reconcile those contradictions. [*T*, 636]

The core of Hume's problem here is this. In order for Hume to proffer an explanation of our belief in the external world or causal connections there must be something in the world that has properties relevant to creating or discovering connections. That it *creates* connections between perceptions, thereby creating 'objects,' or *creates* other connections, thereby creating 'causal connections,' whatever other problems it involves, does not raise one problem that arises in explaining our belief in personal identity. Nor would it arise in explaining our belief in other minds, were Hume to tackle that enterprise. The problem is this: in explaining belief in objects or (necessary) causal connections by referring to a propensity-possessor that has a memory which provides a relevant backdrop of experience and that has its propensities brought into operation by passions and present perceptions, one is not—not flagrantly, anyway—presupposing that there are objects or (necessary) casual connections. But in explaining belief in personal identity in this fashion it does appear that one requires the existence of one instance of the very sort of thing whose existence allegedly is being explained. Further, the explanation proffered is such that the item in which we believe exists only insofar as we have created it, so that the Humean explanation of belief in one's own identity has the appearance, if not the very reality, of supposing that the crucial item referred to in the *explicans* is viewed, in the *explicandum*, as having just then been, not discovered, but created. One way of putting the purport of this is that the crucial item referred to in the *explicans* is a *feigned* or *fictional* entity; but then what force can the explanation have? Another way of putting it is to say that Hume's explanation appears to require the existence of a real, enduring substantial self in order to account for the positing of an allegedly unreal self. And the gist of Hume's problem is then that he recognizes this, but sees nothing wrong with premises that led him into this unsatisfactory situation in which the existence of any such self is denied.

Interpreters have noted that these two principles are not logically incompatible:

(1) All our distinct perceptions are distinct existences.
(2) The mind never perceives any real connection among distinct existences.

Why, then, should it trouble Hume that he holds, or even for theoretical reasons must hold, both of them? One way of seeing why involves a simple rephrasing of (2):

(2') There is a mind, and it never perceives any real connection among distinct existences.

How can there be a mind comprised only of distinct perceptions among which there are no 'real connections'? Another way involves the rephrasing of the claim that Hume makes via (1):

> (1′) The mind discovers (or: we know) that all our distinct perceptions are distinct existences.

Which is identical to:

> (1″) There is a mind, and it discovers that all our perceptions are distinct existences.

How could we discover that (1) was true, if it were true? How, that is, could a mind allegedly composed only of distinct existences bearing no 'real connections' with one another ever discover anything? If one doubts that this is the problem Hume sees, or thinks he sees, with his own position, one should remember what he says would remove the problem: "Did our perceptions either inhere in something simple and individual, or did the mind perceive some real connexion among them, there would be no difficulty in the case" (*T*, 636).

We noted earlier that Hume claimed to find "a kind of contradiction between the different principles of human nature, which enter into religion" (*N*, 86). We have seen that he also claims to find a kind of contradiction between the different principles of human nature which enter into our belief in personal identity and an external world. This provides a larger context within which to see Hume's concern that conflicts between secondary or non-original propensities and primary or original propensities do damage to human nature. Even within the relations between primary and original propensities, and within the conditions under which those propensities individually operate, one finds conflict and contradiction. The house that secondary principles threaten is already divided against itself before they present the potential for further strife. The original elements are already boiling in the pot before the secondary elements are introduced.

CHAPTER 3

Religious Belief as a Danger to Human Nature

A Further Similarity

THE *Treatise* perspective resembles that of the *Natural History* and *Dialogues* in yet another way.[1] Hume's explanation of our belief that there is an external world is supposed to make clear how we come to have the concept of a physical object as well as how we come to think that it has application (*T*, 208). (In fact, the explanation comes in terms of a propensity which more presupposes than explains our possession of the concept of an object.) Strictly, given Hume's theory of meaning, we ought not to have this concept. The explanation of our belief in personal identity is preceded by an argument to the effect that we can have no concept of an enduring conscious being (*T*, 251–53). The explanation of our belief in causal connections (*T*, 169–72) is preceded by arguments intended to prove that we have no concept of force or of necessary and non-psychological connections among phenomena (*T*, 155–69). Disputes, then, concerning whether there are enduring objects or enduring persons or one thing brought about by another ought not to occur (the requisite concepts should be unavailable), which is different from saying that they are irresolvable (there is no evidence for either side). All this reminds one of the theme in the *Dialogues* that the theist/atheist dispute is merely verbal, for the discussion of that dispute is plagued by a similar ambivalence between its being taken to be cognitively vacuous and its being taken to be cognitively irresolvable. But since the *Natural History* discussion does not make this central, I but note it here; that the similarity did not escape Hume is indicated by the following footnote in the *Appendix:*

> The same imperfection (hoping in vain to attain an idea) attends our ideas of the Deity; but this can have no effect either on religion or morals. The order of the universe proves an omnipotent mind; that is, a mind whose will is *constantly attended* with the obedience of every creature and being. Nothing more is requisite to give a foundation to all the articles of religion, nor is it necessary we shou'd form a distinct idea of the force and energy of the supreme Being. [*T*, 633]

Hume's deep commitment to the tenets from which this ambivalence arises would make it difficult to remove it from Hume's system without producing a different one. But its presence in Hume's system renders vague the content, and so insecure the intelligibility, that Hume can allow to even those beliefs produced by, not only the secondary, but also the original and primary, propensities. I suggested above that Hume sometimes worried that, assuming his account of human nature to be correct, its conflicting propensities might destroy the capacity for belief, and so for action, altogether. This seemed to be suggested by at least one passage in the *Natural History* (*N*, 86). In the *Treatise*, Hume remarks that "the imagination, according to my own confession, . . . [is] the ultimate judge of all systems of philosophy." He adds:

> I must distinguish in the imagination betwixt the principles which are permanent, irresistible, and universal; such as the customary transition from causes to effects, and from effects to causes: And the principles which are changeable, weak, and irregular; such as those I have just now taken notice of [for example, the propensity to anthropomorphize]. The former are the foundation of all our thoughts and actions, so that upon their removal human nature must immediately perish and go to ruin. The latter are neither unavoidable to mankind, nor necessary, or so much as useful in the conduct of life; but on the contrary are observ'd only to take place in weak minds, and being opposite to the other principles of custom and reasoning, may easily be subverted by a due contrast and opposition. For this reason the former are received by philosophy, and the latter rejected. [*T*, 225]

Perhaps one should add that, given the widespread operation of secondary propensities, most if not all persons, in Hume's view, at least sometimes have 'weak minds.'

Natural Beliefs

Hume distinguishes between beliefs that are natural in the sense of arising from custom and those that (though natural in another sense) are unnatural by contrast to these. He writes:

> One who concludes somebody to be near him when he hears an articulate voice in the dark, reasons justly and naturally: tho' that conclusion be deriv'd from nothing but custom, which infixes and inlivens the idea of a human creature, on account of his usual conjunction with the present impression. But one, who is tormented he knows not why, with the apprehension of spectres in the dark, may, perhaps, be said to reason, and to reason naturally too: But then it must be in the same sense, that a malady is said to be natural; as arising from natural causes, tho' it be contrary to health, the most agreeable and most natural situation of man.
>
> The opinions of the ancient philosophers, their fictions of substances and accident, and their reasonings concerning substantial forms and occult qualities, are like the spectres in the dark, and are deriv'd from principles, which, however common, are neither universal nor unavoidable in human nature. [*T*, 225–26]

Health and maladies both arise from natural causes; yet one is natural and one is not. All beliefs, Hume holds, have natural causes in that they arise from propensities of human nature as they operate in the context of background conditions (usually) upon their being triggered by appropriate experiences and passions; but not every believing-state is equally natural with every other.

This raises the question of what Hume means by "natural," and, of course, he uses the term in several senses. It will be useful to have some of the relevant passages before us. Concerning the principles of vice and virtue, Hume asks:

> Whether we ought to search for these principles in *nature*, or whether we must look for them in some other origin? I wou'd reply, that our answer to this question depends upon the definition of the word, Nature, than which there is none more ambigu-

ous and equivocal. If *nature* be oppos'd to miracles, not only the distinction betwixt vice and virtue is natural, but also every event, which has ever happen'd in the world, *excepting those miracles, on which our religion is founded.* In saying, then, that the sentiments of vice and virtue are natural in this sense, we make no very extraordinary discovery.

But *nature* may also be opposed to rare and unusual; and in this sense of the word, which is the common one, there may often arise disputes concerning what is natural or unnatural; and one may in general affirm, that we are not posses'd of any very precise standard, by which these disputes can be decided. Frequent and rare depend upon the number of examples we have observ'd; and as this number may gradually encrease or diminish, 'twill be impossible to fix any exact boundaries betwixt them. We may only affirm on this head, that if ever there was any thing, which cou'd be call'd natural in this sense, the sentiments of morality certainly may; since there never was any nation of the world, nor any single person in any nation, who was utterly depriv'd of them, and who never, in any instance, shew'd the least approbation or dislike of manners. These sentiments are so rooted in our constitution and temper, that without entirely confounding the human mind by disease or madness, 'tis impossible to extirpate and destroy them.

But *nature* may also be opposed to artifice, as well as to what is rare and unusual; and in this sense it may be disputed, whether the notions of virtue be natural or not. We readily forget, that the designs, and projects, and views of men are principles as necessary in their operation as heat and cold, moist and dry: But taking them to be free and entirely our own, 'tis usual for us to set them in opposition to the other principles of nature. Shou'd it, therefore, be demanded, whether the sense of virtue be natural or artificial, I am of the opinion, that 'tis impossible for me at present to give any precise answer to this question. Perhaps it will appear afterwards, that our sense of some virtues is artificial, and that of other natural. The discussion of this question will be more proper, when we enter upon an exact detail of each particular vice and virtue. [*T*, 473–75]

So we have several senses of "nature." Using their opposites to mark them we have these three: (i) *not supernatural* (not miraculous or caused by God); (ii) *not rare or unusual;* (iii) *not artificial* (not invented by human artifice; not produced by a culture). Hume also remarks:

> To avoid giving offence, I must here observe, that when I deny justice to be a natural virtue, I make use of the word, *natural,* only as opos'd to *artificial.* In another sense of the word; as no principle of the human mind is more natural than a sense of virtue; so no virtue is more natural than justice. Mankind is an inventive species; and where an invention is obvious and absolutely necessary, it may as properly be said to be natural as any thing that proceeds immediately from original principles, without the intervention of thought or reflexion. Tho' the rules of justice be *artificial,* they are not *arbitrary.* Nor is the expression improper to call them *Laws of Nature;* if by natural we understand what is common to any species, or even if we confine it to mean what is inseparable from the species. [*T,* 484]

This gives us: (iv) *is an invention,* but one that is "obvious and absolutely necessary"; (v) *is common to a species;* (vi) *is "inseparable from"* (essential to?) *a species.*

Senses (v) and (vi) suggest yet another sense. In the next to last extracted passage, Hume said that an absolute and obviously necessary invention "may as properly be said to be natural as any thing that proceeds immediately from original principles, without the intervention of thought or reflexion." "Principles," here, are plainly "principles of human nature" (compare *T,* 473), and this gives us: (vii) *proceeds immediately from* (one or more) *original principles* without thought or reflection. An interesting consequence of this sense is that insofar as a belief—say, acceptance of the thin theism discussed in the *Natural History*—involves argument or reasoning, and hence the intervention of thought or reflection, it is to that degree unnatural.

While a belief may be natural in various of Hume's senses, the sense of "natural" most relevant to our present concerns seems clearly to be the last: "proceeds immediately from original principles, without the intervention of thought or reflexion." Beliefs which so 'proceed' will be 'natural beliefs'; beliefs that do not will be unnatural, though they may be natural in, say, senses (i) through (iii). I suspect that beliefs that are natural in sense (vii) are supposed to be, and beliefs not natural in sense (vii) are not supposed to be, natural in senses (iv) through (vi).

Another Humean passage complicates things, however. Concerning pride and humility, Hume writes:

> 'Tis evident in the first place, that these passions are determin'd to have self for their *object*, not only by a natural but also by an original property. No one can doubt but this property is *natural* from the constancy and steadiness of its operations. 'Tis always self, which is the object of pride and humility; and whenever the passions look beyond, 'tis still with a view to ourselves, nor can any person or object otherwise have an influence upon us.
>
> That this proceeds from an *original* quality or primary impulse, will likewise appear evident, if we consider that 'tis the distinguishing characteristic of these passions. Unless nature had given some original qualities to the mind, it cou'd never have any secondary ones; because in that case it wou'd have no foundation for action, nor cou'd ever begin to exert itself. Now these qualities, which we must consider as original, are such as are most inseparable from the soul, and can be resolv'd into no other: And such is the quality, which determines the object of pride and humility. [*T*, 280]

Here a distinction seems to be made between a 'property' (or propensity, or principle) being *natural* and its being *original*. Relevant to a property being *natural* is "the constancy and steadiness of its operations." Relevant to a property being *original* is its being necessary to *other* properties without there being others that are necessary to it (it "can be resolved into no other") and its being (at least closest to being) essential to human nature ("such as are most inseparable from the soul").

Casting our nets of definition over propensities rather than properties, this gives us:

(a) A propensity is original if and only if it is irreducible (basic) and (at least closest to being) species-essential.

(b) A propensity is natural if and only if it operates in everyone producing the same products.

At *T*, 484 we saw that Hume in effect defined natural via:

(c) A propensity is natural if it is species-essential.

This is roughly half of the definition of "original" provided in (a).

Further, consider this passage.

We may, perhaps, make it a greater question, whether the *causes*, that produce the passion, be as *natural* as the object, to which it is directed, and whether all that vast variety proceeds from caprice or from the constitution of the mind. This doubt we shall soon remove, if we cast our eye upon human nature, and consider that in all nations and ages, the same objects still give rise to pride and humility; and that upon the view even of a stranger, we can know pretty nearly, what will either encrease or diminish his passions of this kind. If there be any variation in this particular, it proceeds from nothing but a difference in the tempers and complexions of men; and is besides very inconsiderable. Can we imagine it possible, that while human nature remains the same, men will ever become entirely indifferent to their power, riches, beauty or personal merit, and that their pride and vanity will not be affected by these advantages?

But tho' the causes of pride and humility be plainly natural, we shall find upon examination, that they are not original, and that 'tis utterly impossible they shou'd each of them be adapted to these passions by a particular provision, and primary constitution of nature. Beside their prodigious number, many of them are the effects of art, and arise partly from the industry, partly from the caprice, and partly from the good fortune of men. Industry produces houses, furniture, cloaths. Caprice determines their particular kinds and qualities. And good fortune frequently contributes to all this, by discovering the effects that result from the different mixtures and combinations of bodies. 'Tis absurd, therefore, to imagine, that each of these was foreseen and provided for by nature, and that every new production of art, which causes pride or humility; instead of adapting itself to the passion by partaking of some general quality, that naturally operates on the mind; is itself the object of an original principle, which till then lay conceal'd in the soul, and is only by accident at last brought to light. [*T*, 280–81]

Hume seems here to argue that because "in all nations and ages the same objects [power, riches, beauty, or personal merit] still give rise to pride and humility," these passions are natural; but since the varieties of things that satisfy such a passion (power, riches, beauty, or personal merit) are measureless, pride and humility are not original. The relevant definitions here are (a) and (b), and one would have thought, given the data just noted plus those definitions, pride and humility would be, not natural and unoriginal, but original and unnatural. In any case, it will be useful to construct a definition of "natural" from our Humean materials. My way of proceeding assumes 'property' at *T*, 280 does duty for 'propensity'; Hume speaks also of 'principle' and—at *T*, 473—denies that "every particular instance" of pleasure and pain "are produc'd by an *original* quality and *primary* constitution"; but so far as I can see, while it is important for our purposes to keep *natural*, *original* and *primary*, *secondary* straight, we need not mark off carefully from one another *propensity*, *property*, *principle*, *quality*, and *constitution* when these have to do with *human nature*. Consider, then, these conditions: (1) being irreducible to others (or basic) and (2) being uniform (producing always the same product). It seems logically possible that a propensity satisfy one while failing to satisfy the other. There being, apparently, no single Humean sense of "natural" in its basic sense relevant to our concerns, let us say that a propensity that satisfies at least one condition is *weakly natural*, and one that satisfies both is *strongly natural*.

I think it is fairly clear that Hume's intent is that the propensity to seek a satisfactory system, the constancy propensity, the coherence propensity, and the identity propensity, be strongly natural, and that the design, adulation, visible object, and anthropomorphic propensities are at most weakly so. Obviously, human nature will be defined in terms of strongly natural propensities.

It is not clear whether it is *explanatory* or *definitional* basicality that is in question here. *A* is definitionally basic to *B* if and only if one can define *B* by reference only to *A*'s content but cannot define *A* by reference only to *B*'s content. *A* is explanatorily basic to *B* if and only if one can explain that *B* operates by reference to the operation of *A* but cannot explain the operation of *A* by reference to the operation of *B*. In both the definitional and explanatory cases, something else—rules for definitions, background conditions, and triggering experiences, for example—may be referred to.

Sense (vii) of "natural," noted above, was "proceeds immediately from original principles, without the intervention of thought or reflexion." This, we noted, would fit, not so much propensities as beliefs. Adapting criterion (1)—being irreducible to others—and criterion (2)—being uniform—to apply to beliefs, a natural belief will be (a) irreducible to others (or basic), (b) shared by every human being, and (c) understood in the same way by every human being. On a maximally architectonic model, strongly natural beliefs would be explicable in terms of the operations of strongly natural propensities.

In Hume's view, belief in mind-independent causal connections, mind-independent objects, an enduring self (and presumably, had he thought of the matter, other minds) will be, or will be among, our strongly natural beliefs. Theism and polytheism will not. Without pretending that I have not introduced a bit more system than Hume's actual system contains, I suggest that this anyway is not very far from what his view comes to.

Basic Propensities

Setting aside whatever problems reside in the notion of a propensity, what is a *basic* propensity? Hume's remarks about original as opposed to secondary qualities (*T*, 280) suggest something along these lines. A propensity A is basic relative to propensity B if one's having A does not presuppose that one has B, but that one has B does presuppose that one has A. If *Ann has B entails Ann has A*, but not conversely, then A is basic relative to B. A propensity A is *basic to a person* (say, Ann) if and only if, Ann has A, and for any propensity B that Ann has that is distinct from A it is false that *Ann has A* presupposes *Ann has B*. If every person resembles Ann in this regard, then propensity A is *basic*, period. This allows, but does not require, that two or more propensities be equally basic. The criterion for basicality, I assume, has its primary application to first-order propensities, else all such propensities will be less than strongly natural, contrary to Hume's intention. I take it, that is, that (say) the identity propensity is strongly natural, even if it is true that it not only instantiates, but presupposes, the system propensity which is second order. Second-order propensities will not be basic, but they may be original, and when they are, they are components of human nature. Either the definitional or the explanatory account of basicality can be accommodated by the *entailment* way of putting things here.

Similar definitions, I suppose, can be offered of basic propositions; this would not result in basicality for propositions entailing that such propositions be incorrigible. That is, *this* talk of basic propositions will not make one who embraces it a foundationalist in epistemology (though, on other grounds, I take Hume to be a foundationalist).

No doubt a considerable amount of fine-tuning could be done on the sort of system I, with a little systematizing license, have ascribed to Hume, but I will not engage in it further here. Rather, it is time to turn to a suggestion made earlier.

Religion and Human Nature Again

I suggested that Hume's concern about religious belief lies not only in his oft-repeated (and debatable) contention that religious belief perverts morality. One might, after all, claim that people use bad religion to sanction bad morals that they would cling to even were they unsanctioned or sanctioned differently. It lies, and in a way more deeply lies, in an epistemic concern. Having already quoted some passages in which this concern seems present, let me add another:

> The assistance is mutual betwixt the judgment and fancy, as well as betwixt the judgment and passion; and that belief not only gives vigour to the imagination, but that a vigorous and strong imagination is of all talents the most proper to procure belief and authority. 'Tis difficult for us to withhold our assent from what is painted out to us in all the colours of eloquence; and the vivacity produc'd by the fancy is in many cases greater than that which arises from custom and experience. We are hurried away by the lively imagination of our author or companion; and even he himself is often a victim to his own fire and genius.
>
> Nor will it be amiss to remark, that as a lively imagination very often degenerates into madness or folly, and bears it a great resemblance in its operations; so they influence the judgment after the same manner, and produce belief from the very same principles. When the imagination, from any extraordinary ferment of the blood and spirits, acquires such a vivacity as disorders all its powers and faculties, there is no means of distinguishing betwixt truth and falsehood; but every loose fiction or idea, having the same influence as the impressions of the memory, or the conclusions of the judgment, is receiv'd on the same footing, and operates with equal force on the passions. A present impression and a customary transition are now no longer necessary to inliven our ideas. Every chimera of the brain is as vivid and intense as any of those inferences, which we formerly dignify'd with the name of conclusions concerning matters of fact, and sometimes as the present impressions of the senses. [*T*, 122–23]

In Hume's view, then, "madness or folly," or something greatly resembling these, results when the imagination is disordered in "all its powers and faculties" (perhaps madness simply *is* the imagination being so disordered). In such a state, it cannot distinguish truth from falsehood; 'fictions' influence us as much as memory. Any belief, whatever its source, has as much strength as any other; any proposition is as likely to be entertained, and believed, as any other. Original propensities do not give rise to natural beliefs, and what arises from the imagination is not constrained by past experiences and present triggering perceptions, by constancy and coherence, or by any of the Humean apparatus of intra-cognitive order. Then anarchy reigns in the intellectual world. Why does Hume say madness results from, or even is a matter of, not disordered reason, but a disordered imagination? Given our previous discussion, the answer is not difficult. The imagination, in its fundamental Humean sense, is comprised by certain strongly natural propensities. These propensities produce belief in an external world, causal connections, and personal identity. (Belief that there are other minds seems also a natural, albeit absent, candidate.) Apparently, the *continued* operation of these propensities is required by a *continued* presence of these beliefs. Insofar as Hume's analysis of belief makes beliefs purely or mainly episodic, the presence in Jones at time T (say) of belief in an external world will require the operation of the constancy, coherence, and identity propensities at or around T. Insofar as Hume's analysis of belief allows belief to also be dispositional, things do not radically change so far as our current topic is concerned. For dispositions, or tendencies to believe, can become weak or inoperative or even vanish. If our primary, original propensities should vanish, so, on Hume's view, would our very nature; should they be temporarily inoperative, we would be temporarily without a nature. We might then believe that all there is, is our private sensations: that any event (actually, not only possibly) might be followed by any other or any object accompanied by any other; that we began to exist a moment ago; or anything. In such circumstances, what passed as thought would be reasonably called "madness" and action might well be impossible. This, or something much like it, seems central to Hume's worries.

These concerns surface in somewhat surprising contexts. Hume remarks that there are "*general rules*, which we rashly form to ourselves, and which are the source of what we properly call PREJUDICE". Thus we come to think that "an *Irishman* cannot have wit, and a *Frenchman* cannot have solidity" (T, 146). Hume holds that "human nature is very subject to errors of this kind." Such general rules, Hume thinks, are not overturned by our meeting witty Irishmen and reliable Frenchmen, and he wonders why.

His answer goes as follows. Suppose that Ann experiences several apples, each of which is red. Then when Ann knows she is about to experience a new apple, Ann will suppose it also to be red, without having to experience its redness. Even if Ann experiences a green apple, the result will be that her tendency to expect apples to be red is diminished, but not destroyed.

> From this principle I have accounted for that species of probability, deriv'd from analogy, where we transfer our experience in past instances to objects which are resembling, but are not exactly the same with those concerning which we have had experience. In proportion as the resemblance decays, the probability diminishes; but still has some force as long as there remain any traces of the resemblance. [T, 147]

Further, Hume suggests that though "custom be the foundation of all our judgments, yet sometimes it has an effect on the imagination in opposition to the judgment, and produces a contrariety in our sentiments concerning the same object" (T, 147–148). In so doing, it even operates against the consistency propensity, albeit no doubt also eliciting that propensity.

Hume's view of the fragility of human nature, but also its recuperative powers, comes out nicely in these remarks:

> Thus our general rules are in a manner set in opposition to each other. When an object appears, that resembles any cause in very considerable circumstances, the imagination naturally carries us to a lively conception of the usual effect, tho' the object be different in the most material and most efficacious circumstances from that cause. Here is the first influence of general rules. But when we take a review of this act of the mind, and compare it with the more general and authentic operations of the understanding, we find it to be of an irregular nature, and destructive of all the most establish'd principles of reasonings; which is the cause of our rejecting it. This is a second influence of general rules, and implies the condemnation of the former. Sometimes the one, sometimes the other prevails, according to the disposition and character of the person. The vulgar are commonly guided by the first, and wise men by the second. Meanwhile the sceptics may here have the pleasure of observing a new and signal contradiction in our reason, and of seeing all philosophy ready to be subverted by a principle of human nature, and again sav'd by a new direction of the very same principle. The following of general rules is a very unphilosophical species of probability; and yet 'tis only by follow-

ing them that we can correct this, and all other unphilosophical probabilities. [*T*, 149, 150]

The sort of circumstances Hume has in mind can be represented as follows. Suppose that Ann has experienced tokens of key-turning, pedal-pressing, and car-starting, always followed by car-moving. Thus Ann may come to embrace these two rules of expectation: (*R1*) If *key-turning, pedal-pressing*, and *car-starting* occur at time T, then *car-moving* occurs at T + 1; and (*R2*) If *key-turning* and *pedal-pressing* occur at time T, then *car-moving* occurs at T + 1. Now suppose that at time T + 20, Ann experiences *key-turning and pedal-pressing*, but no *car-starting*. If Ann follows rule (*R2*) then Ann will expect to experience *car-moving* at T + 21. If she follows (*R1*), she will not. Suppose no token of *car-moving* appears at T + 21, and that this is nonidiosyncratic. Then Ann will want to embrace (*R1*) rather than (*R2*); to do the reverse would lead to mistaken expectations and beliefs, and to do the reverse systematically would lead to massively mistaken expectations and beliefs. But some expectations and beliefs are needed for coherent thought and action, and these will be formed *in accord with*, though not therefore *from*, rules like (*R1*) and (*R2*). So for Hume the elimination of rules like (*R2*) is important, not because *reasoning* in accord with (*R2*) will lead to falsehood so much as because expectations and beliefs produced by transitions of the imagination that conform to (*R2*) will be mistaken. A falsehood is to be avoided—but falsehood in the results of elicited propensities rather than in the conclusions of conscious inferences. Yet the elimination of (*R2*) somewhat weakens our tendency to accept general rules, and so even our tendency to accept (*R1*), and this too has its dangers.

Human Nature

What, then, is the result of all this? The result is a Humean view of human nature in which it fundamentally is comprised by certain strong original or natural propensities.[2] Among these are the constancy, coherence, and identity propensities. It presumably also includes certain second-order propensities, of which the just-mentioned first-order propensities perhaps are instantiations—in particular, the system and consistency propensities. (The identity-conditions for propensities are not made clear, so I am unsure whether the consistency propensity is in fact distinct from the system propensity.) The religion-relevant propensities are not natural. They are thus more accompaniments than constituents of human nature; for Hume, they are inessential, though frequent, instantiations of the system propensity.

Natural propensities yield natural beliefs. Possession of these beliefs prevents (perhaps comprises absence of) madness and presupposes the perpetual operation of strong natural propensities. The religion-relevant propensities at times compete in certain ways with the natural propensities. When they do so, they oppose, if they do not endanger, human nature itself, for they threaten to weaken those propensities and hence make intellectual anarchy more of a live option than it otherwise would be.

One way in which they conflict with human nature is by sanctioning what is not universally approved of, or by failing to sanction what is. What is good, for Hume, is what one will approve, if one takes a view Hume describes as follows in *An Enquiry into the Principles of Morals*.

> The notion of morals implies some sentiment common to all mankind, which recommends the same object of general approbation. . . . When a man denominates another his *enemy*, his *rival*, his *antagonist*, his *adversary*, he is understood to speak the language of self-love, and to express sentiments, peculiar to himself, and arising from his particular circumstance and situation. But when he bestows on any man the epithetics of *vicious* or *odious* or *depraved*, he then speaks another language, and expresses sentiments, in which he expects all his audience are to concur with him. He must here . . . depart from his private and particular situation, and must choose a point of view, common to himself with others. [*E*, 272]

Roughly, then, it is Hume's view that what is good is what is approved, and what is evil is what is disapproved, by one who takes the common, human point of view. But adopting one or another religious belief is not part of taking that point of view, and yet often influences what one takes to be good or evil. At best, this introduces irrelevancies into moral judgments. At worst, it produces moral judgments that conflict with those arrived at by the approved procedure. Thus one has two (or more) competing moral judgments, and, incipiently at least, two (or more) competing moralities. This weakens our tendency to have those attitudes and beliefs that arise from moral approval or disapproval (from the common, human point of view), which on a Humean view are the attitudes and beliefs that arise from our moral natures, or our human natures insofar as they are moral.

("Moral" here contrasts, not to "immoral" or even to "amoral," but to "epistemic" or "religious" or "aesthetic.")

More basically Hume is concerned about the degree to which being pulled back and forth from one religious pole (acceptance of a sort of diaphanous theism) to another (acceptance of polytheism) may weaken our capacity for belief. The conflict Hume believed he had found relevant to religious belief, we have seen, is paralleled by not dissimilar conflicts concerning belief in an external world and personal identity and causality, and even concerning our acceptance of general rules. In Hume's view, apparently, our nature is plagued with belief-relevant conflicts. But, with respect to natural beliefs at least, paralysis of belief is presence of (at least something resembling) madness. We have seen that the religion-relevant propensities, the theistic propensity included, are secondary. They are not basic to human nature; indeed, if we have been right to include only original propensities in human nature *per se*, they do not belong to human nature. At the least, they are not at human nature's core. Insofar as they oppose the original propensities by tending to elicit beliefs contrary to those elicited by the original propensities, it is likely that they will lose, for they are less strong. But by means of such opposition, they may weaken the force of the original propensities, and so weaken the grip of one's nature on one's beliefs. We have also seen that Hume describes reason, in effect, as a variety—and not the strongest variety—of sensation. It is thus overturnable; the beliefs to which it would lead are not natural, and so not universally present and always the same. But its overthrow is not, on the Humean account, the overthrow of human nature. Imagination, not reason, has pride of place.

The design argument requires some causal claim or other (for example, order in nature must have a cause analogous to that of order in artifact, because *like effects require like causes*) and ranges over alleged mind-independent natural objects. Notoriously, for Hume we have no rational grounds for belief either in causal claims or in natural objects. Given Hume's overall perspective, then, the sometimes apparently bold talk of argument, already muted in even the design-relevant passages of the *Natural History*, seems to find its place in the context of an overall theory of human nature, of which the *Natural History* itself is an important part. In the end, acceptance of the argument's conclusion rests only a secondary propensity, a backdrop of experience of ordered objects and artifacts and artificers, and a triggering conflation of passion and present experience of order.

Is Hume consistent in holding that some of our beliefs, while natural in some senses of the word "natural," are nonetheless *not* natural in a 'deep' sense—namely, that they are in some way 'against human nature'? I have tried to spell out what sense of "natural" this involves, and see no inconsistency in Hume's holding that, in that sense, some of our beliefs are unnatural—that is, we act unnaturally, or against our interests, in having these beliefs. Of course, consistency is only one of the conditions of truth. For Hume, then, there is a sort of pragmatic protest against theistic belief. It is not an argument that such belief is false, or is held against evidence. It protests that all theistic (perhaps all religious) belief, save perhaps the very thin theism of Philo, endangers epistemic stability.

Hume and Calvin on Human Nature

It is fairly obvious how a timid but clever theist who did not wish to embrace natural theology, or even wish to contend that theism is *more* rational to accept than at least one nontheistic competitor, might alter Hume's theory to construct one more to his or her liking. A more robust theist might begin similarly and continue by criticizing nontheistic alternatives. Calvin's *Institutes of the Christian Religion*, Chapter 3, "The Knowledge of God Naturally Implanted in the Human Mind," begins with these remarks:

> That there exists in the human mind, and indeed by natural instinct, some sense of Deity, we hold to be beyond dispute, since God himself, to prevent any man from pretending ignorance, has endued all men with some idea of his Godhead, the memory of which he constantly renews and occasionally enlarges, that all to a man, being aware that there is a God, and that he is their Maker, may be condemned by their own conscience when they neither worship him nor consecrate their lives to his service. Certainly, if there is any quarter where it may be supposed that God is unknown, the most likely for such an instance to exist is among the dullest tribes farthest removed from civilisation. But, as a heathen tells us, there is no nation so barbarous, no race so brutish, as not to be imbued with the conviction that there is a God. Even those who in other respects seem to differ least from the lower animals, constantly retain some sense of religion; so thoroughly has this common conviction possessed the mind, so firmly is it stamped on the breasts of all men. Since, then, there never has been, from the very first, any quarter of the globe, any

city, any household even, without religion, this amounts to a
tacit confession, that a sense of Deity is inscribed on every heart.
Nay, even idolatry is ample evidence of this fact. For we know
how reluctant man is to lower himself, in order to set other creatures above him. Therefore, when he chooses to worship wood
and stone rather than be thought to have no God, it is evident
how very strong this impression of a Deity must be; since it is
more difficult to obliterate it from the mind of man, than to break
down the feelings of his nature,—these certainly being broken
down, when, in opposition to his natural haughtiness, he spon-
taneously humbles himself before the meanest object as an act of
reverence to God. [10–11]

Calvin, then, holds that a propensity to theism is basic and universal.
It does not, however, always produce the same belief because people
not infrequently fight it and rechannel it to idolatrous belief. But if
recognition of divine existence, being a rebuke to human pride or
haughtiness, finds a resistance that (say) belief in objects does not,
the *strength* of the propensity to theism is revealed in idolatry; idolatry
is the unwilling compliment human pride pays to an original propensity to theism. Refusing to acknowledge God, the idolater in her pride
bows before a stick or a stone, and in worshiping an unworthy object
simultaneously perverts and obeys a basic propensity. (Some would
argue that at least many cases of alleged idolatry are merely cases of
using objects as symbols of a transcendent Deity; in cases in which
this is so, the propensity to theism is not thwarted after all.)

It is clear that Hume too readily assumes that the data of polytheism suffices to prove that the theistic propensity is unoriginal.
There may be—Calvin thinks there are—strong factors this propensity must overcome that other original propensities need not overcome, and it may be that polytheism, in the way indicated, is itself
evidence of the status of the theistic propensity as original in, and so
as part of, human nature. Calvin continues his argument by criticizing the popular claim that religion was created by priests so that they
could lord it over their gullible flocks or by society to make the masses
manageable, and refers to the fear of God as further evidence of the
strength of the propensity to theism.

It is most absurd, therefore, to maintain, as some do, that religion was devised by the cunning and craft of a few individuals,
as a means of keeping the body of the people in due subjection,
while there was nothing which those very individuals, while

teaching others to worship God, less believed than the existence of a God. I readily acknowledge, that designing men have introduced a vast number of fictions into religion, with the view of inspiring the populace with reverence or striking them with terror, and thereby rendering them more obsequious; but they never could have succeeded in this, had the minds of men not been previously imbued with the uniform belief in God, for which, as from its seed, the religious propensity springs. And it is altogether incredible that those who, in the matter of religion, cunningly imposed on their ruder neighbours, were altogether devoid of a knowledge of God. For though in old times there were some, and in the present day not a few are found who deny the being of a God, yet, whether they will or not, they occasionally feel the truth which they are desirous not to know. We do not read of any man who broke out into more unbridled and audacious contempt of the Deity than C. Caligula, and yet none showed greater dread when any indication of divine wrath was manifested. Thus, however unwilling, he shook with terror before the God whom he professedly studied to disdain. You may every day see the same thing happening to his modern imitators. The most audacious despiser of God is most easily disturbed, trembling at the sound of a falling leaf. How so, unless in vindication of the divine majesty, which smites their consciences the more strongly the more they endeavour to flee from it. They all, indeed, look out for hiding-places, where they may conceal themselves from the presence of the Lord, and again efface it from their mind; but after all their efforts they remain caught within the net. Though the conviction may occasionally seem to vanish for a moment, it immediately returns, and rushes in with new impetuosity, so that any interval of relief from the gnawings of conscience is not unlike the slumber of the intoxicated or the insane, who have no quiet rest in sleep, but are continually haunted with dire horrific dreams. Even the wicked themselves, therefore, are an example of the fact that some idea of God always exists in every human mind. All men of sound judgment will therefore hold, that a sense of Deity is indelibly engraven on the human heart. And that this belief is naturally engendered in all, and thoroughly fixed as it were in our very bones, is strikingly attested by the contumacy of the wicked, who, though they struggle furiously, are unable to extricate themselves from the fear of God. [11–12]

In contrast to Hume, Calvin speaks of a "uniform belief in God, [from] which . . . the religious propensity springs." What Hume sees as a set of secondary propensities that includes various propensities that lead to polytheistic beliefs, Calvin reads as perversions of a single strong propensity to theism that possesses positive moral relevance. It seems clear that Calvin, were he to use our rephrasing of Hume's terminology, would call this propensity original and natural. It is clear that Calvin reads the history of religion, in various ways, differently from Hume; for example, what Hume sees as the operation of secondary, polytheism-relevant propensities, Calvin sees as perversions of an original, primary propensity. Both perspectives, to be complete, would have to include reference to varieties of religion with which neither had much, if any, acquaintance. It is not clear that Calvin is wrong; he presents an interesting alternative to Hume regarding the criteria for the originality of a propensity and the naturalness of a belief. He thus presents an alternative notion of what belongs to human nature. On his view, Hume's pragmatic protest against monotheism could not be made.

The Rights of Reason and the Rights of Religion

In a remarkable passage in the *Treatise* Hume writes as follows:

> 'Tis certainly a kind of indignity to philosophy, whose sovereign authority ought everywhere to be acknowledged, to oblige her on every occasion to make apologies for her conclusions, and justify herself to every particular art and science which may be offended at her. This puts one in mind of a king arraigned for high-treason against his subjects. There is only one occasion, when philosophy will think it necessary and even honorable to justify herself, and that is, when religion may seem to be in the least offended; whose rights are as dear to her as her own, and are indeed the same. If anyone, therefore, should imagine that the fore-going arguments are anyway dangerous to religion, I hope the following apology will remove his apprehensions. [*T*, 250]

It is sufficiently obvious how to interpret these remarks if Hume is protecting himself against prejudice and persecution. But can they be read as things he said and meant without irony?

The "following apology" is expressed in these terms:

> There is no foundation for any conclusion *a priori*, either concerning the operations or duration of any object of which 'tis possible

for the human mind to form a conception. Any object may be imagined to become entirely inactive, or to be annihilated in a moment; and 'tis an evident principle *that whatever we can imagine is possible*. Now this is no more true of matter than of spirit; of an extended compounded substance than of a simple and unextended. In both cases the metaphysical arguments for the immortality of the soul are equally inconclusive; and in both cases the moral arguments and those derived from the analogy of nature are equally strong and convincing. If my philosophy, therefore, makes no addition to the arguments from religion, I have at least the satisfaction to think it takes nothing from them, but that everything remains precisely as before. [T, 250–251]

In one sense, this is straightforwardly true; whatever arguments were sound and valid before Hume wrote are so afterwards, and similarly for those arguments that are unsound or invalid. So far forth what he says is *necessarily* true. But presumably Hume's interest is also in how what he has written impacts on our understanding of these matters.

There is a way of reading at least some of these remarks "at the foot of the letter." Hume does not regard religion as having a high investment in the bank of evidence and argument. He does not suppose that any version of the principle of sufficient reason is known to be true nor does he suppose that anything can have logically necessary existence. So no set of what Hume will accept as *a priori* premises will yield any metaphysical or theological conclusions, pro or con. In *a priori* contexts, if Hume is right, materialism and theism are equally poorly off. This is quite compatible with Hume's overall philosophical position.

But in what way, from a Humean perspective, do philosophy and religion have "the same interests"? (That would explain religion's interests being "as dear to philosophy as her own.") Well, what are *philosophy's* interests?

Hume contrasts superstition and philosophy in these terms:

'Tis certain that superstition is much more bold in its systems and hypotheses than philosophy; and while the latter concerns itself with assigning new causes and principles to the phenomena which appear in the visible world, the former opens a world of its own, and presents us with scenes, and beings, and objects which are altogether new. Since therefore 'tis almost impossible for the mind of man to rest, like those of beasts, in that narrow circle of objects which are the subject of daily conversation and action, we ought only to deliberate concerning the choice of our guide, and ought to prefer that which is safest and most agreeable. And in this respect I make bold to recommend philosophy, and shall not scruple to give it the preference to superstition of every kind or denomination. For as superstition arises naturally and easily from the popular opinions of mankind, it seizes more strongly on the mind, and is often able to disturb us in the conduct of our lives and actions. Philosophy on the contrary, if just, can present us only with mild and moderate sentiments; and if false and extravagant, its opinions are merely the objects of a cold and general speculation, and seldom go so far as to interrupt the course of our natural propensities. [*T*, 271–272]

Embracing superstitious beliefs interrupts the effects of natural propensities—such beliefs are about different objects that those caused by natural propensities and relates them by different causal connections. Philosophical beliefs usually do not, though the Cynics are exceptions to this generalization. (The Cynics sponsored asceticism, seeking to render physical wants scant in order to have an independence of mind like the gods. They rejected traditional inhibitions, customary duties, and temporal goods in order to want, and—they assumed—hence lack, nothing.) When Hume adds that "Generally speaking, the errors in religion are dangerous; those in philosophy only ridiculous" (*T*, 222) he uses "religion" and "superstition" interchangeably. Obviously, this contrasts to his use of religion in which it refers to the very thin theism that he favors insofar as he favors any religion at all—the sense of "religion" in which philosophy's interests coincide with those of religion. Philosophy's interest, in contrast to superstition's, is that "the course of our natural propensities" not be interrupted. The same emphasis is found if we switch our attention from the interests of philosophy to the character of a "true philosopher":

Nothing is more requisite for a true philosopher, than to restrain the intemperate desire of searching into causes, and having established any doctrine upon a sufficient number of experiments, rest contented with that when he sees a further examination would lead him into obscure and uncertain speculations. In that case his enquiry would be much better employed in examining the effects than the causes of his principle. [*T*, 13]

CHAPTER **4**

Hume's Account of Persons as Propensity Bearers

Two Models of Human Nature

AS WE HAVE SEEN, Hume's *Natural History* carries on in the *Treatise* tradition for which mathematics, natural philosophy, logic, morals, politics, and natural religion "have a relation, greater or less, to human nature" (*T*, xix). His *Treatise* conception of human nature, on which his explanation of belief rests, seems equally important in the *Natural History*. It is appropriate, then, to consider more fully his theory of persons as the bearers of propensities to believe.

As Hume's later countryman, the great Scottish preacher Alexander White, noted, the Book of Genesis begins "in the beginning God created" and ends "and Moses lay in a coffin in Egypt." Presumably, in between, something inelegant happened. That is a story for another occasion.

Hume begins *A Treatise of Human Nature* with high optimism. With great confidence, he launches his program to become the Newton of the intellectual world (*T*, xxi). In the *Appendix* to the *Treatise* (*T*, 633 and following), Hume laments the failure of his Newtonian theorizing. Presumably, in between launch and lament, something inelegant has happened. That is the story for this occasion. What follows is my attempt, without concern for originality, to tell it.[1]

The strict Newtonian Model of the intellectual world finds impressions and ideas (of sensation and reflection) serving as mental atoms and the laws of association (resemblance, contiguity, and cause and effect) serving as laws of mental motion, repulsion, and attraction. This is how the Humean account goes in introducing the furnishings and laws of the intellectual world that allegedly is open to everyone's introspection in those deceptively naive opening pages of the *Treatise*.

When it comes to explaining our beliefs that there are mind-independent physical objects, enduring selves, and necessary causal connections, we saw, Hume's practice is to speak of backlogs of remembered experiences and propensities to come to have certain beliefs upon having certain new experiences. An apparently enduring mind, equipped with a memory of past experiences and a set of propensities, upon proper stimulation, produces predictable and uniform beliefs. One might accuse Hume of having the Newtonian Model as his orthodoxy, but using a Propensity Model when he comes to do his hardest philosophical work. On a Propensity Model, perceptions are not so much associated as they are bound together.

Insofar as Hume was aware of any difference between the models he uses, I take it plainly to be his intention that the Propensity Model is a handy way of speaking that can be replaced without loss by the Newtonian Model when precision requires—Newtonian explanations are to be understood as ready and waiting to replace propensity explanations once we turn to the task of deciding what there is. Until then, we may speak common parlance without the guilt of bloating the universe beyond necessity.

A feature of the Newtonian Model is that the laws of association do not define the atoms of the mind; they but describe the contingent patterns into which these atoms fall. Laws are not descriptive of the essences of the items over which they range. Other laws might hold and these very same items exhibit them. And, as Hume says, the laws state no real relations among Humean perceptions; they but say what patterns can be observed by one who watches one's perceptions with care, and are of course purely descriptive and contingent and neither prescriptive nor necessary. On a Newtonian Model, perceptions are not so much bound together as they are associated.

The Appendix Summary

Hume follows his lament with a summary. He writes: "I shall propose the arguments on both sides, beginning with those that induced me to deny the strict and proper identity and simplicity of a self or thinking being" (*T*, 633). The summary is long on expounding the denial of the identity of any simple self and short on explaining the problems of his reasoning concerning personal identity. Hume is unwilling to go back on any of the claims that cause the problem. The claims concern his theory of meaning, and what he supposes follows from it, and his claims concerning the non-subtantival but rather bundle-of-perceptions nature of the human person. Interpretation of these *Appendix* remarks invovles relatively smooth sailing.

The next few sentences have provided turbulent waters. "But having thus loosened all our particular perceptions, when I proceed to explain the principle of connection which binds them together, and makes us attribute to them a real simplicity and identity; I am sensible that my account is very defective, and that nothing but the seeming evidence of the preceeding reasonings could have induced me to receive it" (*T*, 635).

It is natural to ask, "Where is the contradiction in Hume's theory of the intellectual world?" Examining the propositions to which Hume refers us is initially discouraging. Plainly *all perceptions are distinct* entails *there is no real connection among perceptions* and *there is no connection among perceptions* entails *the mind perceives no real connections among perceptions*. The first of the propositions Hume specifies entails the second. This is not encouraging for there being a contradiction in maintaining both of them.

What troubles Hume, I suggest, can be seen in two stages. The first is this: if what Hume says true—if perceptions are distinct and held together by no real connections—then neither this, nor anything else, could be known. The second is this: something is known. From these claims, it obviously follows that what Hume says is not true—perceptions are not distinct and are held together by some real connections.

Two brief comments are in order. One concerns knowledge and skepticism. That something is known is not incompatible with Humean skepticism. A skeptic presumably knows the distinction between skepticism and its denial; that much anyway a consistent skeptic can know. But that is enough to make it true that something is known.

The other concerns the contradiction Hume says that he sees but does not specify. If my "two stages" remarks are correct, the contradiction can be stated as follows. Let the claim *perceptions are distinct and there is no real connection among them* be *P*, and let *Hume knows that perceptions are distinct and there is no real connection among them* be *Q*. My suggestion is that Hume came to see that the following proposition is true: *P entails that not-Q* or *Q only if not-P* or *Q presupposes not-P* or *If P is true then Q is false*, whichever you prefer. Perhaps *P entails not-Q* is best. Then Hume's position is contradictory, for it includes both *P* and

Q as essential elements, and it cannot be the case both that *P* is true and that *Q* is true.

This casts the contradiction in epistemological terms. Metaphysical ways of putting it are readily available: Any world in which *P* is true is one in which *Q* is false. Any world in which all perceptions are distinct is a world in which there is no knowledge. No world has both of these properties: *containing only distinct perceptions* and *containing knowledge.* My strategy in defending this interpretation will be to derive it from Humean premises—to show that what Hume holds entails both *P: Perceptions are distinct and there is no real connection among them* and *Q: Hume knows that perceptions are distinct and there is no real connection among them,* as well as *If perceptions are distinct and there is no real connection among them then no one knows anything,* which together with *P* will entail *not-Q.* This requires that Hume accept some such claim as *R: Knowledge exists only if there is a real connection between perceptions.* In sum, I must show that Hume holds *P* and *Q* and *R,* either directly or by holding views that entail them.

The Soul or Person

Hume tells us that the soul is "a system or train of different perceptions . . . all united together, but without any perfect simplicity or identity."[2] A person, then, at a time is a bundle of perceptions. Over time, a person is a series of such bundles. But what, exactly, is a perception? What ties perceptions-at-a-time into bundles? What ties bundles-over-time into a series? What is "perfect simplicity or identity"? Our understanding of Hume's theory will languish without an understanding of his answers to these queries.

It is easy to give examples of Hume's claim that there are no real connections among perceptions. Here is one familiar consideration that Hume offers in its favor. Hume contends that since all perceptions are "different and distinguishable, and separable from each other, and may be separately considered, and may exist separately" it follows that they "have no need of anything to support their existence" (*T,* 252). Indeed, if we meant by "substance" only *"something that can exist by itself,* 'tis evident every perception is a substance, and every distinct part of a perception a distinct substance" (*T,* 244). If minds are bundles, a single perception cannot be a mind; but a single perception can exist. Such a perception would be a perception without a perceiver—a piece of consciousness that was no one's. Every perception is a possible world, as it were.

However implausible this may seem, it follows from part of Hume's account of what perceptions are and what relations perceptions can stand in. Seeing this consequence, he accepts it. So much for proof-texting in favor of the claim that Hume holds that perceptions are independent, not only of a mind, but of one another. What lines of philosophical reasoning provide the context for this claim?

There are at least two. One concerns Hume's theory of meaning. The other concerns his denial of substance. Both are specified in the *Appendix* passage discussed earlier.

Meaning

Hume's theory of meaning is relevant to various issues in his philosophy of religion; my concern here is strictly limited. Its relevance to our present topic is that Hume takes us to have no concept of a substance. His argument is that the word "substance" is meaningful only if we have an idea of a substance. We have the idea of a substance only if we have impressions that are (or are like) a substance. A substance is something that exists independently, endures over time, has properties, and is not itself a property or a mere collection of properties. None of our impressions satisfies this description. So the word "substance" is meaningless.

It is fairly standard in Hume interpretation to say that for Hume (or ourselves) to understand the premise in his argument that tells us what a substance is, or the premise that tells us that no impression has the properties it would have to have to be or resemble a substance, he (or we) must have the concept of a substance. To understand the argument we must have the very concept its conclusion denies to us. At least so it has seemed to many commentators, and I think (as is so often the case) that things seem this way because they are the way they seem.

Do Simple Perceptions Endure?

In one sense of the term "complex perception"—the standard one for Hume, I take it—a complex perception consists of simple perceptions that coexist. It endures only if its components do. Unless simple perceptions can endure, a complex perception that endures is "complex" in a second sense of that term—it is a series of perceptions-at-a-time or of bundles-at-a-time. Either way, the question will arise as to whether simple or noncomposite perceptions can endure.

Speaking of a hypothetical Cartesian introspector, Hume writes that "He may, perhaps, perceive something simple and continued which he calls *himself*, though I am certain that there is no such principle in me" (*T*, 252). Concerning the thesis "that the idea of duration is applicable in a proper sense to objects, which are perfectly unchangeable," Hume says that to be convinced of its falsehood we need but to reflect that "the idea of duration is always to be derived from a succession of changeable objects, and can never be conveyed to the mind by anything stedfast and unchangeable" (*T*, 37). Thus Hume argues: an idea fits or is accurate only to what it was derived from. The idea of duration was derived from, and only from, various sequences of distinct items. So it applies, and only applies, to sequences of distinct items. Without sanctioning the argument, one can note its role in Hume's defense of the claim that perceptions do not endure. On this point, both of the Humean lines of reasoning we are exploring agree.

Substances

Hume tells us that:

"We have no perfect idea of anything but a perception. A substance is entirely different from a perception. We have, therefore, no idea of a substance. Inhesion in something is supposed to be requisite to support the existence of our perceptions. Nothing appears requisite to support the existence of a perception. We have, therefore, no idea of inhesion. What possibility then of answering that question, 'Whether perceptions inhere in a material or immaterial substance?,' when we do not so much as understand the meaning of the question? [*T*, 234]

Not all of this argument rests on his claim that there is no idea of a substance. Part of it rests on a doctrine of introspection on which mental substances are not possible objects of introspection (matched by a doctrine of sensory perception on which physical substances are not possible objects of perception).

As we have noted, Hume often and emphatically insists that each perception is ontologically distinct from and exists independent of every other; thus if it were sufficient for something to be a substance that it be an item that exists distinct from and independent of every other, every perception would be a substance. A substance would not be "entirely different" from a perception.

A substance, though, is supposed to be an item in which other items inhere; for X to inhere in Y is at least for X's existence to depend on Y's (and presumably not conversely). So presumably one can take Hume to be arguing: a substance is some item in which perceptions inhere; perceptions do not inhere in anything; so there are no substances.

Further, Hume writes "I may venture to affirm of the rest of mankind, that they are nothing but a bundle or collection of different perceptions, which succeed one another with an inconceivable rapidity, and are in a perpetual flux and movement" (T, 252–253).

So presumably we can take Hume also to be arguing that a substance is something that is simple or non-composite and enduring; no perception is simple and enduring—simple perceptions do not endure and the phrase "perceptions that endure" will refer only to a *series of successive perceptions;* perceptions are all that we experience; so we do not experience substances.

This is part of the 'no real connections among perceptions' line; it is not all. Part of that story also relates to Hume's views concerning identity.

Identity

Hume's central passage regarding identity occurs at T, 200–201. The suggestion there seems to be this: we have the concept of *something that retains numerical and qualitative identity over time* or *something that changes and yet endures.* There is no problem with this concept, so long as it is not thought that the thing in question is simple or non-composite. A given perception cannot endure over time and a bundle-at-a-time cannot endure over time. But a given perception can be part of a *series of perceptions over time* and a bundle-at-a-time can be part of a *bundle-over-time.* The notion of *a constant and unchangeable object* is the notion of an item that exists over time without changing. If we have a series of perceptions that are qualitatively identical, each but the first preceded by a twin so that the series exists from one moment to the next but each frame of the series looks the same, we have a *series over time* that has both numerical and qualitative identity. It endures and changes not; time passes and it remains the same. Such a concept is that of unity (one series) or that of number (many perceptions, many times), according to the view in which we take it. Of course, we still do not know what ties perceptions into a single series, but I take it that this was not intended to be part of the story just told. Of course the story just told does presuppose that there are such ties.

According to Hume, what we cannot do is to form a coherent concept of something that is simple or non-composite and endures over time. One reason, at least, why he thinks that we cannot do this, has to do with his view of time and the making of time discriminations.

Time

The notion of a temporal instant is closely related to that of a perception: "time cannot make its appearnce to the mind, either alone, or attended with a steady unchangeable object, but is always discovered by some *perceivable* succession of changeable objects" (*T*, 35).

The line of reasoning engaged in here seems to be something like the following: Time changes only if its doing so is perceptible; that the time has changed is perceptible only if one can notice that there is a change in one's perceptual field; so time change occurs only if there is change in one's perceptual field. Perceptual fields change only by virtue of perceptions changing. If a perception can endure, the time must change during its existence; if time changes, then perceptions must change by changing their properties or by coming to be or else ceasing to be; so if a perception can endure, it must not change while other perceptions do change—and since time-change is relative to perceptual fields and (non-derivatively) measured only within such fields, it must be able not to change while another perception in the same perceptual field does change. But a perceptual field is just a bundle of perceptions at a time. If any part of the bundle changes, the bundle as a whole changes. If the bundle as a whole changes, each of its members has changed. So one perception cannot fail to change while its temporal brothers and sisters change. Hence no perception can endure.

Something like this seems to be Hume's view. But, one wishes to ask, *why* can't a single perception decline change while its cohorts embrace it?

I think that two short sequences of claims give the Humean answer to this question. One claim-sequence is that, upon a full analysis, bundles-at-a-moment are comprised by *simple* perceptions—perceptions that are temporally minimal as well as spatially minimal. Necessarily, temporally minimal perceptions, being temporal *minima* or indissoluble atoms, cannot endure. Each temporally minimal perception is coexistent only with temporally minimal perceptions that occupy—strictly, for Hume, constitute—the same moment. Any change in such temporal minima will constitute a change of time. Two temporal minima cannot overlap only partially. Suppose we have temporal minima A and B such that B immediately succeeds A. Then consider temporal minimum AB that overlaps with the last half of A and the first half of B. Then A and B were not temporal minima after all; they have temporally divisible halves, which in turn may or may not be temporal minima. So the proposed overlap cannot occur if A and B really are temporal minima. (There are problems concerning the relation of one 'private' bundle of temporal minima to another, and concerning whether Hume's view does not illegitimately presuppose perception-independent time-slots, but we cannot deal with that here.) So when a perception seems to enjoy isolated endurance while its temporal colleagues suffer corruption, what really occurs is that one series enjoys qualitative identity and others do not.

The other claim-sequence is this. Strictly, a perception cannot change. It can come to be and cease to be, but it cannot gain or lose qualities or relations. A perception 'pops' into existence and 'poofs' out of existence, and thereby *marks* because it *constitutes* the march of time. The notions *change* and *alteration* no more attach to single, simple, perceptions than do the concepts *hungry* and *unhappy* attach to the number four. If you want things that can change or alter, you must go on to a series-over-time or a bundle-over-time.

In sum, that is why a changeless and a changing perception cannot dwell together in peace.

The idea of duration, Hume says (*T*, 37), is derived from successions; what a word is derived from is what it applies to; so the idea applies to successions and never to non-successions. My point here is not that this Humean theory of the application of terms is correct. It is that his claims concerning duration accord nicely with the line that a change of time is a movement from one moment to the next, and a movement from one moment to the next is a replacement of one perception (or bundle of coexisting perceptions) by another. Time alteration is exchange, not change. Perceptions come to be and pass away, but do not change in the meantime; indeed, there is no meantime.

Humean perceptions, then, do not, and cannot, endure. But they can be related, associated into bundles-at-a-time, and in a series of bundles-at-times. On the 'no real connections between perceptions' line, what ties them into bundles, and what ties a sequence of bundles-at-a-time into a series? The resources for an answer are limited to contiguity, resemblance, and a mild cause and effect involving no more than constant conjunction.

Contiguity at a Time

Some perceptions can be spatially contiguous; some, being non-spatial, cannot. Hence spatial contiguity cannot be the whole story regarding personal identity, since bundles contain perceptions that on Hume's account are not spatially contiguous to anything. But on reflection it turns out that it cannot serve as any *underived* part of that story at all.

A perception Q1 and another perception Q2 are spatially contiguous only if they are members of the same bundle at the same time. So unless one has a notion of what "same bundle at a time" comes to, one will not be able to say what "spatially contiguous at the same time" comes to. Allocation of bundle identity is presupposed by allocation of spatial contiguity. Bundle-identity rests on perception-identity and bundle-identification rests on perception-identification.

Turning from spatial to temporal contiguity, *all* perceptions at a time will belong to the same mind if having temporal contiguity is sufficient for belonging to the same bundle. And of course existing at the same time is necessary for perceptions to belong to a bundle at the same specific time. If one objects that this commentary requires that one take a non-Humean 'container' view of time, I note that Hume himself seems to suppose that temporal simultaneity is intersubjective (which is all my remarks require)—see *T*, 31, for example—and that if we cannot make some such assumption then temporal placing will be a matter of being located in a bundle-at-a-time. Then bundle-at-a-time-identity will be basic to perception-identity; bundles-at-a-time will be our Humean primitives and perceptions will be derivatives or constructions or something else non-simple. But that is clearly the reverse of a natively Humean perspective.

In sum: it is necessary for perceptions A and B to be temporally contiguous at a time in order for them to be in the same bundle at that time, but not sufficient; it is sufficient for two perceptions at a time to belong to a bundle at that time that they be spatially contiguous, because only perceptions from a common bundle are spatially located relative to one another at a time, but it is *belonging to the same bundle* that is presupposed by *are spatially contiguous perceptions* and not conversely.

Resemblance at a Time

It seems plain that perceptions A and B resembling one another more than either resembles perceptions C and D is nothing like sufficient to place A and B in one bundle and C and D in another. Consider Rupert and Ruth who tend to have only one image in their minds at a time. Each may have an image of a glass of milk so similar as to be qualitatively identical; each bundle, to put things Humeanly, may consist of one set of perceptions, each set a twin of the other. Yet they are distinct persons. Personal identity cannot be tracked through impressions by following the path of resemblance at a time.

Cause and Effect at a Time

Hume's treatment of causality has merited more discussion than most topics; my comments here cannot contribute to the discussion or defend one line rather than another. Suffice it to say that Humean causal connections hold between perceptions insofar as they are classifiable via observed resemblances into nominalistic classes whose experienced members are in one-to-one correlation with the member of one class always temporally precedent. Extensions of this account can be made to deal with the cases in which we ascribe causal connections upon experiencing a single pairing of perceptions, Hume's famous remark concerning a counterfactual element in causal statements (*T*, 12, 584), and the like. Necessity enters into Humean causality only insofar as one refers to the felt expectation that past regularities will be matched by future ones in particular cases—where, having experienced A-type and B-type perceptions only in *A,B* and never in *B,A* sequences, upon experiencing another A, one expects a new B.

This introduces the element of constantly conjoined perceptions. There are causal connections only if there are nominalistic classes of perceptions related as described. If there are such, then there are statements—one for each pairing of classes—that express what do duty as causal laws. Call the pairings that these laws describe "causal pairings." Causal pairings occur *over* time, not *at* a time. So they cannot fully or partially constitute the identity conditions of a bundle-at-a-time.

I have considered the allowed relations one by one. One could consider them together (a task I leave as an exercise for the reader). Either way, I can see no satisfactory answer to the question: what ties perceptions into a bundle-at-a-time. I turn to the question as to what might tie bundles, if we had them, together in a series over time.

Contiguity Over Time

If we take Hume's own line on time, so that time is a relation of successive perceptions as space is of simultaneous (leaving aside what to do with "successive" and "simultaneous," which seem to be un-analyzed temporal terms on this account), we can make temporal dis-tinctions only after we have made a distinction between perceptions. Time is viewed as relation, not as container. But on this view of time, as well as on a container view, two things are true. That bundle-at-a-time A and bundle-at-a-time B are temporally contiguous is not a suf-ficient condition of A and B belonging to the same series (for then every bundle-at-time-T1 and bundle-at-time-T2 would be members of the same series). That bundle-at-a-time A and bundle-at-a-time B are temporally contiguous is not a necessary condition of A and B being members of the same person-series, since Hume allows for time-gaps in persons.

So far as I can see, *are spatially contiguous* can be a relation that holds only between perceptions in a common bundle-at-a-time. Only they straightforwardly occupy the same perceptual field, which seems to be the condition for two perceptions being spatially contiguous. But if there can be spatial contiguity between bundles-at-different-times, it seems that this can occur only if they belong to the same se-ries; *belonging to the same series* is a necessary condition of *being spa-tially contiguous* insofar as we are considering a bundle-at-one-time and a bundle-at-another-time.

So neither spatial nor temporal contiguity-over-time seem to help us, either regarding tying perceptions-at-a-time into a bundle or tying bundles-at-a-time into a series.

Resemblance Over Time

The perception-sequence W,X may belong to one bundle-over-time, and the perception-sequence Y,Z belong to another, even though W is very much more like Y than either is like X or Z, and even though X and Z are very much more like one another than either is like W or Y. Two people seeing the same television show at the same time, weeping over the events it portrays, do not slice into one double-watcher and one double-weeper.

Cause and Effect Over Time

Suppose that Terry and Ralph both suffer from a rare malady that afflicts only those who have spent years in the Indian jungles. An eerie gasp accompanies a deep queasiness in the stomach that is followed by a vision of a man-eating tiger in flight in turn followed by a sensation of teeth sinking into one's neck. They know that most tigers are not man-eaters and that the few who are usually have been wounded so that quicker prey is unavailable to them, but this knowledge does not cure their malady. Further, Terry and Ralph are both highly suggestible. One evening as they sit at dinner in their club, at time T1 Terry feels queasy and groans that distinctive groan causing Ralph to feel queasy at T2; at T2 and T3, Terry continues to gasp and at T3 Ralph has the tiger vision. At T4 Terry unfortunately dies and Ralph has the teeth-sinking-into-the-throat sensation that lasts the remainder of the evening. The causal chain goes from Terry at T1 to Ralph at T2 through T4; but Ralph at T5 is not thereby made the reincarnation of Terry who died at T4. Personal identity over time cannot follow *all* causal paths; so there being a causal path from one bundle to another is not sufficient for the bundles belonging to a single Humean series or train.

While no doubt the point could be discussed far more fully, I do not see any way of reshuffling the allowed relations that will provide the Hume of the 'no real connections between perceptions' line with a way of satisfactorily dealing with personal identity at-a-time or over-time. As I noted, he seems to have agreed.

A Brief Look Backward

At this point it seems appropriate to ask, Just where are we? Here is the answer. Humean perceptions do not endure. They are connected by no real connections. On a Newtonian Model, they do not need to be connected by real connections. One perception may bear the relation of resemblance, contiguity, or cause and effect (construed in a constant conjunction fashion—construed, as we shall say *mildly*) to another without either being dependent on the other for existence or qualities. The laws of association describe these ever-so-gentle relations that obtain among independent relatees. A person at a time is a bundle of perceptions so construed; a person over time is a series of bundles-at-a-time. The perceptions in a bundle are tied together by resemblance, contiguity, and/or cause and effect; the bundles in a series are connected serially by resemblance, contiguity, and/or cause and effect. The ties between the atoms of the mind relate without binding, and every knot is a bow, gently tied and easily loosed. So far as I can see, no metaphysics of personal identity is constructible from these materials.

An Example of the 'Real Connections Among Perceptions' View

In discussing causation and personal identity, Hume writes that perceptions are related in strong ways: they "mutually produce, destroy, influence, and modify one another" (*T*, 261). In the body of the *Treatise*, then, there are suggestions of the view that perceptions bear real connections to one another. The commonwealth analogy (*T*, 261) suggests a rather different view of the mind than does his theater analogy (*T*, 253) where he takes great care to deny any such connotations as those with which his commonwealth analogy bristles. The *T*, 261 passage seems to say that perceptions are related in 'real' ways. The appearance of these contrasting analogies some eight pages apart provides strong motivation to think that Hume supposed them not to be incompatible or in conflict. No doubt he did. My suggestion is that by the time he wrote the *Appendix* the 'tension' (to use the polite word) between them had become manifest.

Self-Awareness

Hume is insistent that self-awareness is a pervasive and important feature of our experience. The *Treatise* is replete with passages that ring curiously in the ears of one who has read Hume's rejection of a substantival view of the self and expects that with the absence of a doctrine of a substantival self there also must be an absence of claim to self-awareness. With a flagrant disregard for redundancy, he repeats such claims as this: "'tis evident that the idea, or rather the impression of our ourselves is always intimately present with us" (*T*, 317; compare 320, 339, 340, 341). He writes, for example, that:

> What is casual and inconstant gives but little joy and less pride. We are not much satisfied with the thing itself; and are still less apt to feel any new degrees of self-satisfaction upon its account. We foresee and anticipate its change by the imagination; which makes us little satisfied with the thing: We compare it to ourselves, whose existence is more durable; by which means its in-

constancy appears still greater. It seems ridiculous to infer an ex-
cellency in ourselves from an object which is of so much shorter
duration, and attends us during so small a part of our existence.
'Twill be easy to comprehend the reason why this cause operates
not with the same force in joy as in pride; since the idea of self is
not so essential to the former passion as to the latter. [*T*, 293]

Relative at least to what is inconstant and of short duration, Humean
persons are constant and more durable.

Two relevant claims are reiterated in these passages: that there is
an enduring self, and that it is an object of (at least relatively and perhaps strictly) constant self-awareness. The analysis of these claims, I
take it, is the following: the enduring self is a series of bundles-at-a-
time; for a bundle-at-a-time to be self-aware is for it to contain a perception that is second-order relative to its first-order members. For a
bundle-at-a-time to be aware of a series of bundles-at-times (minimally) is for it to contain a perception A that is second order relative to
perception B' that represents another (actual or merely possible) perception B as past and as the cause of B.' Being second-order relative to
a first-order perception is a real relation. So perceptions are held together by at least one real relation.

Observability and Transparency

Some philosophers, Hume included, have held that our own perceptual (including introspective) experiences are in some manner objects of knowledge concerning which error is impossible, so that
among the range of descriptions of these experiences are some guaranteed true by the fact that we know their sense and believe them
true of their referent. No matter how attentive we are to our perceptions, not every description of them is one that we cannot go wrong
about. If we describe an impression or an idea as *the fourteenth of its
kind today* or *darker than the average perception* or *had only by the very dis-
cerning*, we can be wrong. One naturally wonders how to discern
those descriptions that we cannot go wrong about as opposed to
those that we can. It is tempting to say that what we cannot go wrong
about, so long as we are attentive to our perceptions, is the properties
we *observe* them to have. If we limit ourselves to describing perceptions in terms of their observable properties, the properties that we
are directly aware of them as having, we cannot go wrong. Hume
seems to turn this temptation into a doctrine when he says that all

sensations of the mind (actions, too, though I leave that aside here) "must necessarily appear in every particular what they are, and be what they appear" (*T*, 190).

Foundationalism

Hume, like Descartes, is a foundationalist: "the only existences of which we are certain are perceptions, which being immediately present to us by consciousness command our strongest assent, and are the first foundation of all our conclusions." Our strongest assent, it seems, is tantamount to justified certainty: "the perceptions of the mind are perfectly known" (*T*, 366). "Since all actions and sensations of the mind are known to consciousness, they must necessarily appear in every particular what they are, and be what they appear. Everything that enters the mind, being in reality a perception, 'tis impossible anything should to *feeling* appear different. This were to suppose that where we are most intimately conscious, we might be mistaken" (*T*, 190). So perceptions as items of immediate consciousness or non-inferential awareness provide the foundations of our epistemic structures.

Certainty and Personal Identity

What has all of this to do with the question of what Hume's analysis of personal identity amounts to? A part of the answer is this. If one is engaged in giving an analysis of something—call them Z's—that everyone agrees exist, in terms of something else—call them W's—that not everyone agrees exist, it is convenient if one can be confident that there really are W's and sure that skepticism about W's is unjustified. For if there are no W's, then the fact that one's analysis proffers W's as the only genuine constituents of Z's is a substantial defect in one's analysis. Whatever his success, Hume mightily wanted his analysis of minds to escape this defect. He wanted no doubt that there are perceptions, and so no problem about the mental atoms of his mind being there to come together into bundles. That the opening pages of the *Treatise*, in which the tone is that of a philosophical Jack Webb sticking to just the facts, constitute one of the most theory-laden sets of opening pages of any document ever written I take to be obvious. Nonetheless, Hume's strategy was to stick to direct awareness, which he thought the least likely of anything to mislead.

Transparency and Real Connections

Another part of the answer is that transparency wreaks havoc with the 'no real connections' view. If X is transparent to S, then for any property P, X has P if and only if S is aware of X's having P. (The problem will not change if we say instead that X has P if and only if S is aware *that* X has P.) Suppose that X is perfectly transparent to S at T. Then if S had not existed at T, neither would X have existed at T; X is dependent for all of its properties on S's being aware of X's having them. But according to Hume every perception is perfectly transparent to the mind that has it. So no perception is independent of the mind that it partially comprises, and no perception can exist independent of comprising some mind.

Presumably the *every perception is transparent* doctrine holds only for first-order perceptions, lest the mind have to have an unending series of higher-and-higher-order perceptions. One could hold that *for every perception A of order N, it is possible that there be another perception A* of order N + 1 such that A is transparent to A*.* It could be left as a sort of empirical question how high actual orders went. Further, just as a fully transparent first-order perception is dependent for its existence on the second-order perception to which it is transparent, so a second-order perception is dependent for its existence on those perceptions that are first-order relative to it. So a first-order perception A that is transparent to a perception B that is second-order relative to it and B itself are so related that neither can exist without the other existing. Then there is only a distinction of reason existing between them. Then they are not 'really distinct' after all. If a bundle-at-a-time is tied together by there being a second-order perception that is second-order relative to each first order perception in the bundle, and each first-order perception is not 'really distinct' from the second-order perception, then none of the first-order perceptions are 'really distinct' from one another. None can exist without the others. A bundle-of-perceptions-at-a-time is a second-order perception that has one or more first-order perceptions as objects where every perception in the bundle is non-distinct from every other. All 'real relations' among independently existing items will be among one bundle-at-a-time and another bundle-at-another-time by virtue of which they form a series. Insofar as 'real connections' hold only between 'really distinct' items, all such relations will hold among distinct bundles, not 'within' bundles.

This line of reasoning, of course, will not establish that no differences can hold between the perceptions that constitute one bundle-at-one-time and those that constitute another bundle-at-another-time. The bundles-at-various-times that allegedly enter into a single person-constituting-series are really distinct bundles, whatever may be true of their constituents in turn. This line of reasoning "saves" Hume's view that at least same-time perceptions cannot really be related by arguing that the apparently distinct perceptions that enter into a bundle-at-a-time by virtue of being first-order relative to a second-order perception that ties them together are actually all one perception—that what we have called bundles-at-a-time are single perceptions, albeit with a considerable range of possible internal complexity. This is not how Hume conceives of bundles-at-a-time—not at least in his 'no real connections' passages. If you like, the defense, if it is a defense, is not descriptive but revisionary.

Even partial transparency—where X is partially transparent to S at T if and only if there is some set A of properties that does not contain all of A's properties such that X does have A and X has A if and only if S is aware of X's having A—would introduce more interdependency among perceptions that Hume in his 'no real connections' reasoning was prepared to allow, namely none at all. But this does give us a Humean way of bonding perceptions-at-a-time into bundles.

Why We Believe in Personal Identity

Hume explains, of course, why we believe there to be an enduring and substantival self. As we saw, the explanation follows the pattern of Hume's *Treatise* explanations of our belief that there are mind-independent causal connections, our belief that there are mind-independent physical objects, and his *Natural History* explanation of our belief that the cause of order in nature bears some remote analogy to human intelligence. In each case, a backlog of experiences of certain sorts are stored in the memory, a new experience occurs, and a one-or-more-membered set of propensities is elicited. Against a backdrop of relevant past experiences, and upon the stimulus of a current experience, one or more specifiable propensities of the mind produce a belief that requires us to accept a fiction. Central to the cases of belief that there are mind-independent physical objects and belief that there is an enduring self is a propensity to mistake a plurality of similar sucessive perceptions for a single perception. Memories of past experiences and propensities that belong to bundles of perceptions that operate so as to produce other perceptions are part of the explanatory content of this account.

Memory and Personal Identity

As is well known, Hume relates memory and personal identity in some intimate way. In one respect, Hume's doctrine of memory is simple. If the metaphysical distinction between memory and imagination is found in the constraint that memories must copy the past, the epistemological difference, Hume characteristically insists, must lie in something immediately evident to the attentive mind—something we can be conscious of. But this concerns only what we might call *event*-memory. Having memory also involves our ability to know who we are, how to find our way home, who our friends are, what we do for a living, and where we have lived and who our parents are. The capacity to use language involves memory, as does our exercise of various motor capacities and our powers of inference, our capacity to assess theories, our capacity to read and write, and on and on. Hume knows this, and just as he also uses the term "imagination" as his preferred term for the phrase "human nature" so he also speaks of "memory" in the deeper and richer sense that includes but goes beyond event-memory.

For example, "Had we no memory, we should never have any notion of causation, nor consequently of that chain of causes and effects, which constitute our self or person" (*T*, 262). "The memory not only discovers [personal] identity, but also contributes to its production" (*T*, 262). If there are persons, and if to be a person is to be a series of bundles-at-times, then there are cases in which one bundle-at-a-time-T causally impacts another bundle-at-a-time-T1, and causes in the T1 bundle some second-order perception that represents some portion of the bundle-at-T as being cause to the representing portion of the bundle-at-T1 as effect. The representing perception in the bundle-at-T1 is a Humean memory. Series in which such memories occur are Humean persons. There being memory-perceptions in bundles-at-times that occur in series of bundles-over-times constitutes at least a necessary condition of there being Humean persons, and these memory-perceptions occurring are necessary conditions of our coming to know that there are series of the very sort in which they themselves occur. This, or something much like it, seems to be Hume's doctrine: we come to believe that we are enduring substances (according to the *Treatise* account in "Of Personal Identity") because we have memories of past conjunctions of similar perceptions, and given that memory plus the propensity to run similar perceptions together into putative perceptions of single things over time, we concoct the fiction of enduring single or simple items. So memory is crucial to both the allegedly mistaken belief that there are enduring simple selves and the allegedly not mistaken view that there are enduring complex selves.

Memory, then, is crucial in the Humean story concerning the tying of various bundles-at-various-times into a series. A perception A is a memory of perception B only if A is a second-order perception relative to first-order perception B' where B' is caused by B, and represents B (where *A represents B* entails *A resembles B*; *T*, 233). Such memory perceptions occur in one or another bundle-at-a-time; only if a series of such bundles contains at least some of these memory-perception-containing-bundles-at-a-time can it constitute a Humean person. No doubt a memory-perception also must include a 'sense of pastness' that is phenomenologically familiar and hard to illuminatingly describe; this will constitute an observable property of such a perception that is perhaps more encouraging as an identifying feature than sheer force and vivacity; or maybe it is a modality of this feature.

As a metaphysical analysis of a person as a bundle-series, some of the memories in such a series must be veridical; what they represent must have occurred, and occurred earlier in the series in which the memory-perception itself occurs. The perceptions in the bundle-at-T1 must be more than mildly causally related to the perceptions of a prior bundle-at-T or there is no series to which both belong short, perhaps, of one great series containing all perceptions in what for Hume would be a sort of Spinozistic nightmare. Without some veridical memories within a bundle-series, a person is only an apparent bundle-series, and this is not Hume's view.

It is more plausible to suggest that epistemologically, insofar as reference to memory-experience is essential to explaining how we come to have the notion of a bundle-series, the memory-experiences need not be veridical; their sense of pastness need not correspond to an actual past.

It is not clear that Hume's account of memory will do. Suppose that Jane, sensitive to beauty, sees a glorious sunset at T1. At T2, she calls her best friend Hope and describes it, and falls into dreamless sleep at T3. Due to Jane's gift of description and Hope's imaginative powers, Hope at T3 has an experience that is caused by Jane's, resembles Jane's, and represents the sunset Jane saw. Hope's experience then meets the Humean conditions for being a memory of the sunset. But Hope did not see it. Nor will it do to add the requirement that the memory must be in the same series as what is remembered, for a series being the same (in part at least) is a matter of its being bound together by memories. But this relates to the correctness of Hume's views, not their interpretation.

Agency and Morality

Far from assenting to the so-called Hume's Law that 'one cannot derive an "ought" from an "is,"' Hume holds that "when you pronounce any action or character to be vicious you mean nothing but that from the constitution of your nature you have a feeling or sentiment of blame from the contemplation of it" (*T*, 591). Here, rather complex content becomes first-order relative to a second-order perception.

In a striking passage Hume writes:

> If any *action* be either virtuous or vicious, 'tis only as a sign of some quality or character. It must depend upon some durable principles of the human mind which extend over the whole conduct and enter into the personal character. Actions themselves, not proceeding from any constant principle, have no influence on love or hatred, pride or humility; and consequently are never considered in morality . . . only the quality of character from which the action proceeded. These alone are *durable* enough to affect our sentiments concerning the person. Actions are, indeed, better indications of a character than words, or even wishes and sentiments; but 'tis only so far as they are such indications that they are attended with love or hatred, praise or blame. [*T*, 575]

Here, *durable* qualities are ascribed to a person.

I assume, too, that Hume has no quarrel with the principle that a person is justly rewarded or punished for a deed only if she is the person who performed it—a principle that requires that the culprit or hero still be around if just punishment or prize for a past deed is meted out in the present.

If there is a series of bundles-at-a-time related to other bundles-at-other-times in such a manner as to constitute a person, then there must be veridical memories. If there are agents, capable of virtue or vice and even in a compatibilist sense responsible for their deeds, there must be persons. For Hume, what endures is a later bundle-at-a-time that occurs after earlier bundles in the same series, related together in a more-than-mild causal manner.

Summary of the 'Real Connection' Line of Reasoning

Hume holds that "tho' we commonly be able to distinguish pretty exactly between numerical and specific [that is, qualitative] identity, yet it sometimes happens that we confound them, and in our thinking employ the one for the other" (*T*, 257). It is his controversial view that mental substantivalists do exactly this when they conclude that there is an enduring and non-complex mind or mental substance, just as materialist substantivalists do exactly this when they conclude that there is an enduring and non-complex physical substance.

For all that, there is for Hume an enduring person, complex rather than simple, comprised of a series or train of bundles-at-a-time. On the 'no real connections' line of *Treatise* reasoning, perceptions are tied into bundles-at-a-moment, and bundles-at-a-moment are tied into a single series, by nothing stronger than associations that fall under the rubrics *resemblance, contiguity,* and *(mild or constant conjunction) cause and effect.* Even in the *Appendix* to the *Treatise,* this perspective is not recanted.

Also in the *Treatise,* alongside the 'no real connections between perceptions' line, there runs another line that asserts 'real connections' between perceptions. That one perception may be second-order to another is required by considerations of transparency, and indeed is required by our being able to make even the reports concerning perceptions that are required by, and result in, the 'no real connections' view. Thus perceptions are bonded into bundles-at-a-time by means of being first-order relative to a second-order and uniting perception to which they are said to be transparent. Hume's contention that "memory not only discovers the [personal] identity but also contributes to its production by producing the relation of resemblance among the impressions" (*T*, 261) makes memory, and hence more-than-mild causality, central to his account of the relations of bundles-at-a-time to bundles-over-time. The association of ideas, and the transition from one resembling perception to another, that for Hume produces the confounding of numerical and qualitative identity are *acts* of the mind (in contrast to the status of perceptions as *inert*) (*T*, 255). While the association of inert perceptions goes with the Newtonian Model, the binding together of perceptions into bundles-at-a-time by order-

ing relationships and the binding together of bundles-at-a-time into
bundles-over-time by memory and acts of mind, belong to the Propensity Model. Whether or not the Propensity Model's answers to the
questions "What ties perceptions together at a time?" and "What ties
perceptions together over time?" are adequate, they are both *different
from* and *more adequate than* the corresponding answers to those questions provided by the Newtonian Model. The Propensity Model is not
reducible to the Newtonian. The Propensity Model, and its stronger
bonds between perceptions, is more adequate to Hume's epistemology and his moral philosophy—his discussions of transparency, introspection, virtue and vice, and liberty and necessity—
than is the Newtonian Model. It even seems required by them.

Conclusion

Hume's account of personal identity has more resources than at
first appears. Its richness is also an embarrassment. The only even
plausible Humean answer to "What ties perceptions-at-a-time into
one bundle?" is that various simultaneous perceptions are tied together by all being first-order relative to a single second-order perception that is aware of them. The price of this answer, viewed from
Hume's perspective, is that the items so tied are no longer independent but are 'really connected.' To return to our earlier characterization, he holds *P: Perceptions are distinct and there is no real connection
between them* (our discussion of the 'no real connections' line of reasoning establishes this). That same discussion also establishes that he
holds *Q: Hume knows that perceptions are distinct and there is no real connection between them.* But he also holds *R: Knowledge exists only if there is
a real connection between perceptions* (our discussion of the 'real connections' line of reasoning establishes this). But of course *P, Q,* and *R* are
a contradictory set; not surprisingly, there is the sort of contradiction
Hume said there is.

There is more than one way to cash the contradiction in. One could
put it: the Newtonian Model is adequate for Hume's epistemology
and ethics, the Propensity Model is not compatible with or reducible
to the Newtonian Model, and the Propensity Model is required by
Hume's epistemology and ethics. Or one could express it in these
terms: that there are persons requires no relation among perceptions
stronger than mere association; ordering-connections and more-than-
mild causal connections are stronger than mere associations; that
there are persons entails that there are ordering-connections and

more-than-mild causal connections among perceptions. The expression is different, but the theme is the same.

The Humean contradiction is caused by the Humean labyrinth. The Humean labyrinth is comprised by two incompatible lines of reasoning—the 'no real connections' line and the 'there are real connections' line. The two lines are associated with two incompatible models—the Newtonian and the Propensity, respectively. In his "more strict review" of the *Treatise* Hume saw this, and it is this that explains his confession.

A subtantivalist will see one thing in Hume's confession. Hume makes appeal to propensities, acts of the mind, ordering-connections among perceptions, more-than-mild causal connections, enduring bundles-over-time that constitute a person as a numerically identical series that can remember past events, be vicious or virtuous, and properly be held responsible. The substantivalist will see these as concessions in the direction of there being a substantival self, mental or material. A non-substantivalist will see in Hume's enrichment of his position hope for a successful non-substantivalist account of the nature of persons, though it seems clear that Hume is right that the *Treatise* account of that matter will not do. Arguably, at least, persons as propensity bearers must have more by way of identity and durability than Humean bundles can provide.

CHAPTER 5

Hume's Explanation of Religious Belief

A Brief Review

WE HAVE NOW described Hume's explanation of religious belief. What can be said in assessment of it? A brief review is in order. As we have seen in *The Natural History of Religion*, David Hume offers a not unsophisticated account of the fact that persons hold religious beliefs. In so doing, he produces an explanatory system analogous to that which occurs concerning causal belief, belief in 'external objects,' and belief in an enduring self in the *Treatise*. The explanation of the occurrence of religious belief is more detailed than the explanation provided in the other cases just mentioned. In the *Natural History*, Hume devotes a short volume to explaining religious belief, while in the *Treatise* the causal, external object, and enduring self beliefs merit but long sections.[1] More important, however, than length of treatment is the fact that the pattern of explanation is identical in each instance. The *Natural History* could be embedded without categorical clash into the *Treatise*, perhaps as Book Four with fifteen sections, and each formerly separate volume would shed light on the program and tactics of the other.[2] My interest here is in the epistemic features of the explanatory system Hume developed in the *Natural History*.

The Elements of Hume's Explanation

Hume forthrightly proclaims that *The Natural History of Religion* in fact is an attempt to explain the occurrence of religious belief. He

writes, "What those principles are, which give rise to the original belief, and what those accidents and causes are which direct its operation, is the subject of our present inquiry" (*N*, 21). "Original belief"
here does duty for "original *religious* belief," and as he takes religious
belief to be nearly but not altogether universal in scope and astonish-
ingly diverse in object, he supposes the principle, or cause, of such
belief to be secondary in the sense that its operation is (so to say) de-
feasible and its product diversified. Hume's powerful critique of the
argument from design in Sections Two through Eight of the *Dialogues*
is not the only reason for doubting that his occasional kind remarks
concerning it should be taken as indicating that he supposed it sound
and valid. The very fact that Hume wrote a book intended to explain
the occurrence of religious belief by identifying as its cause a built-in
principle and its eliciting stimuli should give us pause about Hume's
apparent acceptance of something like the argument from design. For
while in the *Natural History* he says that "the whole frame of nature
bespeaks an intelligent author; and no rational enquirer can, after serious reflection, suspend his belief a moment with regard to the primary principles of genuine Theism and Religion" (*N*, 21), he speaks,
not of a conclusion having been proved true, but of a belief having
been rendered unsuspendable. Further, neither we nor Hume will ordinarily offer a detailed causal account of the fact that a person has a
belief unless there is doubt that the person has sufficient reason for
holding it. He does not, for example, offer any such explanation of
our acceptance of sincere present-tense, first-person psychological reports concerning the truth (indeed, the incorrigibility)[3] of which he in
the *Treatise* confidently affirms:

> For since all actions and sensations of the mind are known to us
> by consciousness, they must necessarily appear in every particu-
> lar what they are, and be what they appear. Every thing that en-
> ters the mind, being in *reality* as the perception, 'tis impossible
> any thing should to *feeling* appear different. This were to suppose
> that even where we are most intimately conscious, we might be
> mistaken. [*T*, 190]

Or, even more modestly, and without assuming a causal-account
and a sufficient-reason-account of a belief to be competing (or even
necessarily *different*) explanations, we may note that Hume proposes
to explain the occurrence of religious belief by reference to propensity
and eliciting stimuli without making reference to reasons or argu-

ments as items possessing epistemic function or evidential force, but only as items capable of triggering a built-in response.

Hume endeavors to explain religious belief without supposing it (in any of its forms) to be true as well as without supposing it to be false. His tactic is to expose the propensities relevant to the production of religious belief, together with their eliciting stimuli, and the following catalogue roughly covers the resources of Hume's explanatory system. He affirms that persons have certain propensities (or instincts or principles) which, upon being activated or triggered, produce religious beliefs. Among these are:

> (1) The propensity to believe in an "invisible, intelligent power" which is the source of order in nature. [N, 197]

> (2) The propensity to focus attention on, and ascribe the power one believes in to, visible objects. [N, 51]

> (3) The propensity to conceive intelligence or power as always possessed by a human or else a superhuman being. [N, 40]

> (4) The propensity to seek and adopt a system that gives rational satisfaction [N, 40]
> (5) The propensity to ascribe infinite perfection to the intelligent power belief in which is caused by a propensity already noted. [N, 86]

Thus Hume suggests that there are what we respectively may call the deistic, empiricist, anthropomorphic, rationalist, and adulationist propensities, each of which often plays its role in the production of religious belief. Further, these propensities operate upon being triggered by such stimuli as recognition of the (at least apparent) order of nature, ignorance of what causes affect human destiny combined with hope and fear as to what may lie ahead, and fear of pain, disease, and death. The propensities just listed, then, are triggered by various human cognitions and emotions, and as emotions vary in their force and vivacity and in their combinations, and persons vary in their circumstances, the propensities vary in their degree of efficacy, and therefore the belief produced differs from instance to instance. Hume thinks that:

> Any of the human affections may lead us into the notion of invisible, intelligent power; hope as well as fear, gratitude as well as affliction: But if we examine our own hearts, or observe what passes around us, we shall find that men are much oftener thrown

on their knees by the melancholy than by the agreeable passions. [*N*, 43]

Even without further elucidation, the general pattern of Hume's system for the explanation of religious belief has now emerged. In any case, its details were reviewed in previous chapters.

Hume's system is open-ended in that the addition of further propensities of the same sort (or of further triggering stimuli), provided they possess explanatory power, will fortify rather than falsify the system in question—a system for which Hume makes at least no explicit claim of completeness. Further, the system is non-epistemic and causal in that while it traffics with such occurrences as the hopes and fears and reasons and recognitions of individuals, all these factors are treated similarly as items in a causal mix rather than as emotions appropriate (or not) to their objects or as cognitions evidentially supportive (or not) of their intended conclusions. Again, the system is psychological and individualistic; any role social or economic or sociopsychological or anthropological factors might have, singly or in combination, in the origin or the shape of religious beliefs is ignored. Each person is treated by Hume as an autonomous set of belief-producing propensities, whether it is religious belief or causal belief or external object belief or enduring self belief that is being accounted for. Still further, the 'secondary principle' of Hume's Introduction to the *Natural History* has obviously become a whole set of propensities. Finally for present purposes, no explicit commitment is made to the truth, or to the falsity, of any religious belief, and indeed even religious experience itself, whether numinous or nirvanic or otherwise, is assigned no role in the production of religious belief. Such experience is not so much treated as epiphenomenal as it is simply ignored.

This last seems clearly a mistake on Hume's part, though not necessarily a serious one. It is not serious if religious experience itself, in each of its varieties, is explicable along the same sort of lines as Hume attempts for religious belief. If the order in nature is, say, propensity-plus-triggering-stimulus produces religious experience which produces religious belief, then Hume has but explained a sequence of the form A-yields-B-yields-C in terms of A's yielding C, as we might explain the light going on by referring to the flicking of the switch without bothering to mention the intervening flow of current. Or if the propensity-plus-triggering-stimulus produces both belief and experience, Hume has but explained a sequence of the form A-yields-both-B-and-C by referring only to A's yielding B, that being what interested him.

A Critique of Hume's Strategy

The Humean strategy outlined above seems admirably modest in its epistemic pretensions. Is it successful? There are certain problems with it. One such problem is endemic to any attempt at explaining religious belief. It is impossible to have any legitimate confidence that a particular psychological or sociological or anthropological or economic account, singly or together with others, is a sufficient explanation of a person's (or a group's) religious beliefs. One reason for this is the sheer complexity of the phenomena and the high likelihood in such cases that one will have left out crucial causal factors. The sheer and obvious fact of multiple, plausible-sounding competitive explanations reflects this complexity and likelihood.

Further, without some *direct* assessment of religious belief, we have no notion of whether there are religious causes to be taken into account. This aspect of this problem is philosophically more interesting. If God exists, presumably sometimes divine activity is part of the cause of the occurrence of numinous experience. If so, then to claim to have a sufficient explanation of all numinous experiences without referring to the existence of God is to claim to know, or to have sufficient reason for believing, that God does not exist. Hence the claim that one has elicited the sufficient conditions of a religious experience will raise the question as to whether the truth conditions of any religious belief is among those sufficient conditions or not. If so, one's explanation requires the truth of some religious doctrine; if not, it requires the falsity of some religious doctrine. Either way, religious neutrality—lack of commitment to the truth or the falsity of any religious claim—is not sustained. The same result follows if one replaces "religious experience" in this argument by "religious belief." So it is clear that Hume has failed to offer a religiously neutral explanation. Of course, no other attempt to offer a religiously neutral explanation could succeed.

The Critique Assessed

There is something to be said for, and something to be said against, this critique of Hume. First, the something against: Hume's strategy in the *Natural History* is (roughly) to produce an explanation of the occurrence of religious belief that itself contains no religious claim and that is at least equiplausible with any religious claim that, by itself or as a member of a set of claims, also might explain the occurrence of that religious belief. Thus, if Hume's hopes are realized, his explanation explains the occurrence of religious belief *at least* as well as does any religious (or other) explanation and it provides as good an explanation of the occurrence of religious belief as we have. It does not entail any religious belief, or its contradictory. The intent is that, given the success of Hume's explanation, the fact that religious belief or experience occurs is no evidence that some religious belief is true. Further still, exactly the same claims hold for any antireligious claim as hold for any religious claim. So the occurrence of religious belief can be explained without supposing that any religious claim is true and without claim that any religious belief is false.

Now of course Hume's focus in the *Natural History* is simply on the belief that God exists. By contrast, the compleat *Natural History of All Religion* would have to cover other religious beliefs, including nontheistic ones. Further, religious experience of various sorts would require explicit attention analogous to that given religious belief. The sort of treatment required can be seen by replacing "religious belief" by "religious experience" in the opening sentences of the preceding paragraph. These matters, however difficult and important they may be, would be extension of an old pattern, not creation of a new one. Given the treacherous difficulties of both natural theology and natural atheology, Hume's program makes excellent sense.

This, or something much like it, is what can be said for Hume and against the critique. What can be said for the critique and against Hume is the following. The judgment that an explanation (that is, a set of explanatory claims) is equiplausible with regard to a religious claim involves *some* direct epistemic assessment of the religious claim.[4] As Hume's various writings on issues in the philosophy of religion bear eloquent witness, such direct assessment can be desperately complex. Hume's strategy requires that the pro-assessment and the con-assessment be, or nearly be, tied; this provides, so to say, the epistemic backdrop to the requisite suspense of judgment in such cases and opens the way for explanations of the sort Hume proposes. The assumption that assessment is only or mainly a matter of discovering presence or absence of valid arguments whose soundness is guaranteed by the premises all being either self-evident or evident to the senses greatly facilitates the conclusion that the *pro* and the *con* contentions tie, for it is the absence of such arguments that seems obvious to most observers. Yet Hume himself, whatever his view of his own enterprise, often interestingly argues his own case for his own views (of human nature, of morality, of the philosophic enterprise, and so on) without providing such arguments. So the assumption that renders the postulation of a tie between pro-considerations and con-considerations plausible, to say the least, is dubious. Further, the assessment of one religious claim will normally involve assessment of its web of belief. Since such assessment is often a subtle matter, claims of equiplausibility will themselves be debatable.

Hume's procedure also requires that the set of propositions constitutive of his own explanation of religious belief be not worse than equiplausible with the belief being explained. Thus his program requires that there be various ties between a variety of propositions and is in trouble if any of these fail to obtain. Perhaps it often is; perhaps it never is. Trying to decide *that* issue is beyond the scope of this chapter. For the present, it is enough that the pattern is ingenious, and in any given case worth trying; the epistemic results of failure will be as interesting as the epistemic results of success.[5]

It is an open question whether there is any case in which one can claim that an explanation (of the Humean sort) of the occurrence of a religious belief is at least equiplausible with any religious claim that by itself, or as a member of a set that is not less plausible than the religious claim alone, explains the occurrence of the same belief, *where this claim of equiplausibility is neutral with respect to the religious belief's truth value.* So it is an open question as to whether Hume's pattern or ideal is ever in fact fulfilled (including, of course, whether the *Natural History* itself fulfills it).

Religious Experience and Hume's Explanation

Hume's treatment of religion, we noted, does not explicitly deal with the epistemology of religious experience. Nonetheless, his explanation of religious belief is easily adapted to religious experience. Consider these descriptions of religious experience:

> In the year that King Uzziah died, I saw also the Lord, sitting upon a throne, high and lifted up, and his train filled the temple.[6]

(This passage describes a vision of the prophet Isaiah.)

> When I see thy vast form, reaching the sky, burning with many colors, with wide open mouths, with vast flaming eyes, my heart shakes in terror: my power is gone and gone is my peace, O Vishnu.[7]

(The passage describes a vision of the devotee Krishna.) The passage from *Isaiah* continues as follows:

> Above him stood the seraphim . . . and one called to another and said "Holy, holy, holy is the Lord of hosts; the whole earth is full of his glory." . . . And I [Isaiah] said "Woe is me, for I am lost; for I am a man of unclean lips; for my eyes have seen the King, the Lord of hosts."[8]

The vision concludes with Isaiah's repentance eliciting divine forgiveness and a prophetic task. The passage from the *Bhagavad Gita* also describes a part of a vision that culminates with the Deity saying:

> Hear again my word supreme, the deepest secret of silence. Because I love thee well, I will speak to thee words of salvation. Give thy mind to me, and give me thy heart, and thy adoration. This is my promise to thee: thou shalt in truth come to me, for thou art dear to me.[9]

These experiences seem to their subjects to be experiences of, or encounters with, entirely real and independently existing beings. Such experiences occur at many times and in many cultures. The Humean pattern, applied to such experiences, will posit one or more propensities and an eliciting non-religious experience that occurs in the content of the additional stimulus of some emotion. No element of the explanation will require that the experience be, or not be, veridical; the explanation will be neutral in that regard. A variety of social science explanations can fit the pattern, and a reference to a combination of needs and circumstances can substitute for or supplement reference to experience as triggering phenomenon.

Social science explanations themselves tend to carry a heavy theoretical load. This load manifests itself most plainly in the appearance in the social science theory of propositions neither descriptions of empirical data nor generalizations over such descriptions. Such propositions express the content of the theory in question—they articulate its content and structure. Consider these examples of 'structural' propositions:

> [1] In order to understand human society, and the cultural framework of the human condition, one must distinguish between the universal and the particular, the moral and the appetitive, the categorical and the empirical, and the sacred and the profane.[10]

[2] Culture resolves itself into two orders of reality: a phenomenal order having to do with *observable* regularities in behavior, and an ideational order having to do with *discoverable* regularities in thought.[11]

[3] A myth is an artful expression of a person's most fundamental cognitive processes: one's capacity to identify antithetical elements in one's experience, to represent them symbolically, and thereby to resolve inherent paradoxes through the creation of cultural mediators.[12]

These propositions neither report perceptual or introspective experiences nor generalize over such reports. They explain and interpret observations; they articulate theory.

Suppose that one or more of the social science explanations relevant to religious belief is correct; indeed, insofar as they are not incompatible, suppose they all are. What effect, exactly, will this have on the question of whether the religious experiences so explained are, or are not, veridical?

The commonly accepted assumption is that the effect will be that the experiences are not veridical, or at least are not reasonably taken to be veridical. This assumption rests on a claim regarding sufficient explanations. Simply put, if one of the social science explanations is sufficient, or if all together are, then reference to God as the cause, or part of the cause, of such experiences is entirely unnecessary. All the explaining needed is done before one gets to God.

One might respond that theism is no worse off here than materialism: if a materialist wants there to be reasonable belief, then he must embrace the view that beliefs that have sufficient non-epistemic explanations also have positive epistemic explanations and if the theist wants there to be religious experiences reasonably taken to be veridical she must embrace the view that experiences that have sufficient social science explanations also have positive epistemic explanations. The materialist may insist that we do have reason to suppose that some among our beliefs are reasonably held, and the theist may insist that we do have reason to suppose that some of our religious experiences are veridical. But what reasons will the theist offer?

Belief that God exists is a structural belief. It is also a belief that is *existential* (it is true if and only if a being of a certain sort exists) and *singular* (it is true if and only if one particular being exists). As existential and singular, it may be supported by experiential grounds even if, as a structural belief, it can be reasonably held in the absence of such grounds. What grounds, or experiential epistemic support, might there be for theism? Giving an answer requires a short detour.

Elements of an Argument from Religious Experience

"Seems" has at least three senses. One tentatively expresses an opinion (I seem to remember that his first name was Octavius). One contrasts appearance with reality (She seems gentle, but don't get her angry). The important one for us reports without commitment (The drapes seem beige to me, but for all I know they are really chartreuse). Consider Timothy, who is easily confused. Timothy either successfully proposed to Agatha last night, or dreamed he did, but really cannot remember which. His report is that "I seem to remember her saying 'yes.'"

Sensory or religious experience is evidence only under some description or other. Watching a sea gull land is evidence that there is a gull only because such sentences as "I see a gull" and "I am watching a sea gull land" fit the structure and content of my sensory awareness. But I do not *infer* from that structure and content to a report about, or to the existence of, a sea gull. The recognition of the accessibility of the experience to some such report is part of, not something in addition to, having the experience at all. That I often do not consciously formulate any of the sentences that I could truly report is irrelevant. This is no more evidence that the structure and content of the experience is not apt to such reports, or that I do not recognize that aptness—that the descriptions do not fit it nicely or that I do not know that they do—than the fact that one has never formulated the proposition "I am not now inside an alligator" entails that one does not know whether or not one has been or is.

This accessibility to description, it should be emphasized, does not somehow set an epistemological distance between oneself and one's experience. Many seem to view language as a veil between mind and world and sometimes the accessibility of experience to description is viewed as a kind of convenience for interpersonal communication but external and accidental to (and even as necessarily distortive of) the experience itself. An experience equally accessible to all possible descriptions, per impossible, would have to possess logically incompatible properties; an experience accessible to no possible description, per impossible, would have to lack properties altogether.

Accessibility to description is necessarily inherent in experiences. That is, experience is inherently potential evidence. This, of course, holds for numinous experience as well as for sensory.

Within Judaism, Christianity, Islam, and Bhakti Hinduism one finds descriptions of what Ruldolph Otto called numinous experiences. Using "seems" in that sense, noted above, in which to say "I seem to experience an O" neither contrasts appearance to reality nor expresses an insecure opinion, but reports how things appear, so to say, 'from within' the experience reported—using "seems" phenomenologically—the subject of a numinous experience seems to experience a being that is awesome, majestic, unique, righteous, overpowering, holy, intensely alive, and the like. Alternatively, the subject seems to experience a being to whom reverence, awe, recognition of one's guilt, humility, gratitude, and worship are appropriate responses. The varieties of numinous experience, even if we limit our attention to instances central to the monotheistic traditions rather than considering as many sorts as does Otto, are of course richer than this brief characterization suggests. But numinous experience is as flagrantly subject-consciousness-object in structure as is sensory experience.

I will not assume that there is any experiential modality peculiar to having numinous experiences. It may be that such experiences in some manner supervene on visual, auditory, etc. experiences, and/or on moral or aesthetic experiences. The phenomenology of such experiences no doubt deserves detailed analysis. But for present purposes I shall only note that, as seems patent from the reports their subjects offer, they are subject-consciousness-object in structure and seem to be of a mind-independent object.

A Principle of Experiential Evidence

The core premise of an argument based on numinous experience can be cast in these terms:

> (N) For any subject and numinous experience, if her having that experience is a matter of its (phenomenologically) seeming to her that she experiences a numinous being, then if she non-culpably has no reason to think that (i) she would seem to experience a numinous being whether or not there is a numinous being that she experiences, or (ii) if the experience is non-veridical she could not discover that it was, or (iii) if the experience is of a type such that every member of the type is non-veridical, she could

not discover this fact, then the numinous experience provides her with evidence that there is a numinous being.

Are there, then, ways of testing numinous experience? In particular, would there seem that there is a numinous being to the subject of a numinous experience whether there was one or not, and are there analogues to the publicity and multiple modalities that perceptual experience provides?

It is true that one at least is more likely to have had a numinous experience (or its counterfeit) if one has ingested certain substances and is in a religious setting (seated in a high-ceilinged chapel, say, before stained-glass windows, with Handel's *Messiah* being played on a good pipe organ). Depending on what credence is to be given to various psychological theories, one may be somewhat more likely to have numinous experiences if one has had certain past experiences (say, loss of father when one was young) or if one suffers from certain maladies (for example, reference is often made to the alleged epilepsy of the Apostle Paul when his experience on the road to Damascus is being discussed). Then that one has never ingested such substances, has a healthy father, and shows no traces of epilepsy will bar the attempt to 'explain away' one's numinous experience by appeal to these explanations, and it will also be the case that (a) were one in any of these conditions, one could know it, and (b) if one knew that one were in one of these conditions, and knew that there was a reliable theory that said that if one was in one of these conditions then one would (probably) have a numinous experience, one would know that it would probably seem to one that one experienced a numinous being whether one did experience one or not. Suppose that there is a strong theory that entails that if one is in a certain state, then it will seem to one that there is a numinous being. The stronger the theory is known to be, the better the position of one who knows that theory and also knows she has not been in the state that the theory specifies, and that she could tell whether she was in that state or not. She will know that were she in a condition where she would seem to experience a numinous being whether she actually did so or not, she could discover that she was in that epistemic condition. Knowing she is not in that state, she knows that the theory in question does not serve to call her experience into question.

So far as I am aware, there are no especially plausible or persuasive psychological theories that link up being in a certain psychological or physiological state as cause to numinous experience as effect, save perhaps for those that link drug intake with the having of such experiences. So I am inclined to think that if one knows that one has ingested (say) nothing stronger than aspirin within (perhaps) the last seventy-two hours, and one has a numinous experience, one can non-culpably assume that (so far as condition (i) goes) one's seeming to experience a numinous being is evidence that there is one. But if there exist such theories, then one can learn them and (if the theories are worth much) find out whether one is in the conditions they specify, and if one is not and one has a numinous experience (or knows of someone else who has one and is not in the conditions they specify) then one—so far forth—has evidence that a numinous being exists. (Obviously one can also refer to such matters as food deprivation, sleep deprivation, and so on, in these contexts.) It is perhaps worth noting that sensory experiences of various sorts can also be drug induced. The fact that alcohol consumption can produce insect hallucinations does not serve to call entomology into question.

One can, of course, compare the description of one numinous experience with the description offered of another, and one can compare descriptions offered at one time and place with those offered at another time and place, compare descriptions offered within one culture with those offered within another, and compare descriptions offered within one religious tradition with those offered within another. (Similar comparisons are often available for sensory descriptions and are highly useful, as when an astronomical theory is tested by its retrodictions concerning past events through records kept by past astronomers over centuries in various cultures).

There seems in fact (and perhaps surprisingly) to be considerable agreement in such descriptions of numinous experiences, once one allows that different metaphors, similes, symbols, and even literal ascriptions may vary greatly from one culture to another even while predicating roughly the same sort of characteristics. So there are cross-cultural and cross-traditional as well cross-spatiotemporal comparisons to be made in the case of numinous experience, and if the important epistemological point behind the publicity and multiple modality of sensory experience is that it provides experiential testability for claims based on sensory experience, there seems to be considerable experiential testability for claims based on numinous experience, even though it lacks publicity and multiple modalities. Hence there is significant similarity regarding testability.

Of course there are differences. Similarly placed perceivers looking in the same direction with their perceptual systems intact will both see the Great Dane standing on the lawn; if one does not, explanation is required that may call into question the reliability of the apparent sighting of the dog. Two similarly placed worshippers sitting in the same pew may one have a numinous experience and the other not. While no doubt this too has an explanation, the mere experiential disparity does not call into question the veridicality of the numinous experience. One thing that lies behind this difference is that spatial and temporal predicates play a role in identifying the putative object of a sensory experience that they do not play in identifying the putative object of a numinous experience. Another is that physical objects lack, and God has, the property *being experienced only if wishing to be experienced*.

The second condition on (N)—our principle of experiential evidence concerning numinous experience—requires that one be able to discover that one's experience is non-veridical, if it is. Notoriously, there is widespread skepticism—or perhaps failure of nerve—about whether any religious belief can be in any fashion an object of any rational assessment (unless perhaps it is negative). The tendency is strong to put religious belief 'beyond the pale of reason.' For all that, arguments concerning whether there is any successful version of the problem of evil, or of one of the theistic arguments, continue relatively unabated. Should some devastating anti-theistic argument ever succeed, then, I suppose, (ii) would be satisfied. Alternatively, one could discover that a particular numinous experience was non-veridical, or was at least reasonably believed so, by discovering that the numinous experience in question conflicted in its putative information content with the information content of most others in a context in which there was no good reason to overturn majority testimony.

Suppose that there are propositions known or reasonably believed to be true that have the form *Necessarily, if there is a numinous being then it has property A* and that an experience occurs that in other ways seems to be of a numinous being but nonetheless represents its putative numinous object as lacking *A* by virtue of possessing some property *B*, where *being B* is incompatible with *being A*. Then that numinous experience must be non-veridical in at least that respect, and if all numinous experiences represent their putative object as being *B* they are all at least in part non-veridical. (This will assume that the evidential credentials of *If there is a numinous being, then it has A* do not include essential reference to numinous experience.) In these ways, then, condition (ii) in (N) seems discernibly satisfiable.

It is perhaps easiest to consider other ways one might meet condition (ii) as applied to numinous experience by considering also condition (iii)—that if numinous experience as a type of experience is non-veridical, this should be discoverable. Suppose that one of the attempts to disprove theism by appeal to evil has at least apparent success. One would then have reason to be highly suspicious of numinous experience in the presence of strong reason to think monotheism false. Or suppose that one discovered a contradiction in the concept of a numinous being, or at least had good reason to think one had. Then one would have good reason to suppose that there is no numinous being, and so to suppose that numinous experiences are all non-veridical. Or suppose that there was good reason to accept some variety K of religious experience other than numinous as veridical, where if K-type experiences are veridical then monotheism is false. Or suppose (as many believe) that some purely secular explanation of the occurrence of numinous experience is known to be 'sufficient' in some sense that precludes any reason to think that it is caused by anything numinous. What condition (iii) requires is that there be a way, in principle, to discover that numinous experience, as type (or, if one prefers, in all of its tokens) is non-veridical, if it indeed has this inelegance. It seems that, in principle, there are a variety of ways—namely, those just mentioned—in which one could discover this.

It is not required, of course, that one actually discover that numinous experience is non-veridical, or that one find good reason to suppose that it is, or the like. That would absurdly require that numinous experience is evidence only if we know that we have good reason to think that it is not. What is required is that one be able to specify one or more ways in which the global non-veridicality of numinous experience might be discovered, if that is the truth of the matter regarding such experience. We have noted several possibilities in that regard.

Our concern here has been, so to say, with the 'stronger' or 'closer to maximally numinous' of numinous experiences. Roughly, such experiences have this feature: if they are veridical, they are experiences of God. Even such experiences as these underdetermine the theistic claims based on them, which is not surprising since sensory experiences underdetermine the claims typically based on them. Viewed analytically, theological traditions wed numinous content with metaphysical constraints (for example, explanatory adequacy) to yield claims about omnipotence and omniscience. Obviously, this story is very complex, and I will not deal with it here. But there is at least no *a priori* reason to think that there is no non-arbitrary way to 'fill in' the conceptual distance between experience and doctrine.

Social Science Explanations and the
Argument from Religious Experience

There are various social science explanations of religious doctrines, institutions, rites, and experiences. That there are such explanations is not by itself reason to think that numinous experiences—at least ones that occur under conditions that are not ruled out by considerations specified in (N)—are not pro-theistic evidence. Since this is not exactly universally accepted, it is appropriate to argue explicitly for this claim, even if briefly.

Suppose that one accepts a psychological explanation of religious experience that fits the pattern *Whenever psychological factor PF is present in a person, he is likely to have a numinous experience under circumstance C*, and a sociological explanation of the form *Numinous experiences occur with greater frequency in societies in which social factor SF is present than in those in which SF is absent*, and an anthropological explanation of the form *Numinous experiences are frequent in cultures in which anthropological feature AF is present and rare in cultures in which AF is absent*. Suppose that Kim lives in a society in which exhibits *SF*, a culture blessed with *AF*, and that Kim plainly manifests *PF*. Even if Kim is found in circumstance *C*, of course Kim may not have a numinous experience. But suppose that Kim does have a numinous experience.

To whatever degree our psychological, sociological, and anthropological explanations each has plausibility, and is not reducible to the others (or any other), it is also plausible that appeal to just one of the factors that one of the explanations specifies by itself is not sufficient to explain Kim's having a numinous experience. Suppose that these respective social sciences, and that only the factors that they specify, are relevant in proffering a social science explanation of Kim's experience. Then reference only to *PF* is sufficient in psychology for explanation of Kim's experience. The same goes for reference only to *SF* in sociology, and *AF* in anthropology; it is enough to refer to the specified factors as one in these disciplines explains religious experience. Each explanation is sufficient in its own discipline. Suppose that no other social science is relevant to numinous experiences, and combine our three explanations into one grand social science explanation. Then the grand explanation is social science sufficient regarding Kim's experience. But that it is social science sufficient and true does not entail that Kim does not meet all the conditions relevant to (N) regarding Kim's experience and so that experience can be evidence that a numinous being exists even though there is a grand explanation that is both social-science-sufficient and true. Kim's experience satisfying (N) is sufficient for it being evidence that a numinous being exists.

Even a grand explanation seems clearly not to exhaust what needs to be said regarding even the necessary conditions of an experience. There are presumably physiological states of Kim such that, were Kim not in them, Kim would not have a numinous experience. (The same holds for Kim's perceptual experiences.) Combine the physiology/physics explanations, and any other natural science explanation relevant to Kim's having a numinous experience, into a grand explanation that is sufficient in natural science regarding Kim's experience. Regard the grand social science explanation as reducible, or as not reducible, to the grand natural science explanation, as you like. It is not contradictory that the one is natural science, and the other is social science, sufficient regarding Kim's experience, and that Kim meet all the conditions (N) as applied to numinous experience requires that Kim meet in order that the experience be evidence that a numinous being exists. The answer, then, to our question as to whether, if Hume's extrapolated explanation of religious experience is correct, such experience can provide grounds for theism is that it can. Everything depends on whether the experience satisfies the proper principle of experiential evidence. (We have assumed that [N] states such a principle, though if it does not let it be replaced by some more adequate formulation of the principle that tells us what conditions an experience must satisfy in order for it to be evidence.)

PART TWO

Hume's Discussion of Natural Theology

CHAPTER 6

Hume's Evidentialism

Hume and Radical Religious Evidentialism

A RADICAL EVIDENTIALIST regarding religious belief will require that a religious belief is reasonably accepted only by someone who has evidence in its favor—better evidence for than against if the evidence is mixed, evidence that raises the probability of the belief being true over .5 if quantifiable evidence is relevant, but in any case data of some solid sort that supports the belief in question. Evidentialists need to be careful about their evidentialism. Evidence, it seems, stops somewhere; some belief or other must be rationally embraceable without one's having to have still more propositional evidence for it. In this context, evidentialists may refer to 'self-evident' propositions—propositions that wear their truth on their sleeve (for example, *No proposition is both fully true and partly false.*) They may also refer to empirical grounds; *seeing a frog* may be evidence for *There are frogs*, and one then bases one's acceptance of a proposition, not on one's acceptance of another proposition, but on one's having had a confirming experience. Propositions that are rationally believed without one's needing the evidence of other propositions are *basic* propositions. So are propositions whose rational acceptance rests, not on one's acceptance of other propositions, but on experiential grounds. Such basic propositions serve as the foundations or epistemological starting points for evidentialists.

One might be an evidentialist regarding all belief, including religious belief, and think that some religious propositions are basic—either as self-evident or based on experiential grounds or as 'structural' propositions that serve as 'axioms' in a powerful explanatory theory (or the like). But a radical religious evidentialist denies that any religious propositions are basic. Then whatever there is, if anything, by way of reasonable religious belief will be based on non-religious evidence.

Bishop Butler on Probable Evidence

Probable Evidence is essentially distinguished from Demonstrative by this, that it admits of degrees; and of all variety of them, from the highest moral certainty to the very lowest presumption. We cannot, indeed, say a thing is probably true upon one very slight presumption for it; because, as there may be probabilities on both sides of a question, there may be some against it; and though there be not, yet a slight presumption does not beget that degree of conviction which is implied in saying a thing is probably true. But that the slightest possible presumption is of the nature of a probability appears from hence—that such low presumption, often repeated, will amount even to moral certainty.[1]

These remarks suggest one probablistic perspective regarding evidence. If we have non-demonstrative evidence that some proposition is true, it comes in increments. Seeing the tide rise once gives a little evidence that *The tide will rise a year hence.* Seeing it rise tomorrow adds to that evidence. Seeing it rise three hundred and sixty-four days in a row makes it morally certain that the tide will rise on the three hundred and sixty-fifth. Evidence provides moral certainty for a claim if it provides "ground for an expectation, without any doubt of it."[2]

How probability is to be measured, and at what degree of evidence moral certainty is reached, is not discussed. That there is some evidence for a claim does not entail that the claim is true or that it would be reasonable to accept it, since there may be relevant evidence against the claim, or even if there is not the evidence may not be sufficient in quantity to provide moral certainty. Estimates of probable evidence and issues regarding moral certainty arise only for creatures whose information and/or epistemic powers are limited. Whatever lack of precision may characterize these remarks, they are all of a piece, expressing a single overall sketch regarding probability and evidence.

Other comments, also from the Introduction to the *Analogy of Religion,* suggest a further view.

From these things it follows, that in questions of difficulty, or such as are thought so, where more satisfactory evidence cannot be had, or is not seen, if the result of examination be that there appears, upon the whole, even the lowest presumption on one side, and none on the other, or a greater presumption on one side though in lowest degree greater, this determines the question even in matters of speculation; and in matters of practice will lay us under an absolute and formal obligation, in point of prudence and of interest, to act upon that presumption or low probability though it be so low as to leave the mind in very great doubt which is the truth. For surely a man is as reasonably bound in prudence to do what, on the whole, appears according to the best of his judgment to be for his happiness, as what he certainly knows to be so.[3]

It is not very clear that these comments "follow from these things" (the comments that preceded them). But the view they present combines nicely with the view expressed earlier. The further view can be put along these lines. In practical matters, where one must do something, any evidence is welcome. If all the evidence I have favors doing A if I want B, and I badly want B, then it is reasonable to do A— providing it is reasonable to want B, that I want nothing incompatible with B at least as badly as I want B, that I do not reasonably want not to do A at least as badly as I want B, and the like. This is so, even if my evidence is very weak. If a sporting murderer will leave me alone if I can throw either at least one six or a total of six, but kill me otherwise, I am wiser to use two dice rather than one die, since my odds of throwing a six or a total of six with a die are one in six, where with the dice they are four in nine. If I know the odds, it may be unreasonable of me to believe that, either way, I shall throw a six or a total of six; either way, the odds are against it. But it is reasonable to prefer the dice to the die.

Butler also holds, however, that a slight leaning of the evidence "determines the question even in matters of speculation"—matters where it is belief more than action that is in question. One (perhaps revisionary) way to understand this suggestion is to distinguish between belief and acceptance. To believe that A is to suppose A true. To accept A is to use A as an assumption in constructing theories, planning experiments, deriving hypotheses, and the like, without supposing A true. Thus that Ann believes that A does not entail that she accepts A, nor does the converse entailment hold. If there is a little evidence that A is true, and no other relevant evidence, then on this suggestion, A merits acceptance but not belief. Butler writes so as to suggest that it is *degrees* of belief that properly correspond to degrees of evidence; this suggstion treats the lower degrees of belief as amounting to acceptance—as strictly being prolegomena to belief rather than being belief *per se*.

Whether one plausibly interprets Butler along these lines depends on how Butler views belief to be connected with "saying a thing is probably true." If to believe something involves saying, or being prepared to say, that it is probably true, then since "a slight presumption does not beget the degree of conviction which is implied in saying a thing is probably true," an uncontested slight presumption in favor of a proposition will yield acceptance rather than belief. If belief that *A* does not involve saying that *A* is probably true, then perhaps we do not need the accept/believe distinction, or one like it, in order to state Butler's position.

Butler takes things a step further when he says that "in questions of great consequence, a reasonable man will think it concerns him to remark lower probabilities and presumptions than these; such as amount to no more than showing one side of a question to be as supportable and credible as the other; nay, such as but amount to much less than this."[4] Thus if one has almost no chance of keeping afloat in a leaky boat, but no chance whatever of survival otherwise, it is rational to stick to the boat. If bailing the boat is very unlikely to keep it afloat, but it is sure to sink if one does not bail, then it is rational to bail.

Various issues, then, come up in these few comments by Butler concerning probability and evidence. There are at least these: (i) when is it reasonable to believe that a claim is true; (ii) when is it reasonable to accept a proposition without believing it; (iii) when is it reasonable to act as if a claim is true; and (iv) when is it reasonable to act against the odds.

Something like the following answers seem plausible: (i) when the evidence for the claim, on balance, is better than that against it and renders it more probably true than not; (ii) when the evidence there is favors the claim, but not enough to make belief reasonable; (iii) when it is not certain that the claim is false and acting as if it were true increases the chances that it will be true; and (iv) when it is not certain that one cannot succeed, and one is reasonable to care whether one succeeds or not.

One could refine the questions, and the answers. One could defend other answers to the questions and ask other questions. For example, one could ask: (v) when is it reasonable to accept a claim against which we have some evidence, and for which we have none? One answer is: when the gains that accrue to accepting the claim will be great if it is true and the loss involved in accepting it if it is false is negligible, whereas the gains of not accepting the claim, if it is false, are negligible and the loss of not accepting it, if it is true, is great.

What matters most in the *Analogy*, though, is religious belief. Butler's comment here contrasts the case in which the evidence for a claim is "so low as to leave the mind in very great doubt which is the truth" but where one believes it anyway with the religious case: "This course is reasonable, but more is required in religion. Its evidence must be sufficient not only to show how its duties may be performed, and to indicate the prudence of obedience, but strong enough to cause full belief in a reasonable mind. Belief is a condition of salvation, and is involved in full submission to God."[5]

Butler knows that it is Christian doctrine that one "who would come to God must believe that He exists and rewards those who seek Him." Such faith includes assent to the proposition *God exists* and submission to God. Such assent or belief, Butler suggests, comes to a rational person only if the available evidence regarding God's existence renders it more likely than not that He does exist, and the person knows this.

There is neither need nor pretense that one can *quantify* the evidence that Butler is concerned with, nor that we can quantify the probability with which such evidence allegedly invests its target claim. *It is more probable than not that Billy ate all ten cookies, since they were his favorite kind, he is sick now though he was well earlier, and his hands and face are freshly washed long before dinner* can be understandably true without there being any way, even in principle, to quantify either the data or the degree of credibility the data give to the claim.

In contemporary terms, then, Butler is an *evidentialist*. He thinks that it is reasonable for one to believe that God exists only if one has evidence for this. Indeed, as we saw, his standards seem to be that religion itself—Christianity anyway, and perhaps any monotheism—requires a belief that is available to a rational person only if her evidence renders *God exists* more probably true than not.

Chains of evidence stop somewhere. The evidence that Charles took the diamond may end with its discovery in his pocket; this may be the evidence that is decisive and, for all practical purposes, unchallengeable. Evidence is evidence only under some description. "Having a hard object hidden in a trouser appendage" is not a description under which Charles is convictable. Evidence is propositional—expressible in propositions, though not always expressed. Experiential grounds are expressible in terms of the (or a) proposition they are grounds for accepting. *P* is evidence for *Q*, for a probabilist like Butler, means something like *Q is more likely true if P is true than if P is false.*

One can classify evidence into types in various ways. One way is conceptual versus experiential. Our evidence that *All A are B, All B are C, so All A are C* is a valid argument form, or that *There is a prime number higher than seventeen,* is conceptual. Our evidence that some swans are black is experiential. Another way is in terms of evidence provided by reflection, introspection, and sensation. Reflection tells us that no contradiction can be true, introspection tells us whether or not we feel dizziness or fatigue or hunger, sensation tells us what color our socks are. Dealing with our knowledge, say, of morals or aesthetics will require a more sophisticated analysis of the sources of evidence. However the classification is done, however, some propositions will be evidence for others without there being other propositions that are evidence for them. Some propositions, we saw, will be evidentially basic. No other propositions will be both better evidenced than they are and provide evidence for them. Butler's view is that *God exists* is not evidentially basic. He here agrees with Hume.

A proposition might be evidentially basic relative to one type of evidence and not evidentially basic relative to another. Suppose, for example, that *God exists* is confirmed by certain religious experiences and also provable by one or more of the traditional theistic arguments. Suppose, for example, Ann were both to experience God—to have an experience in which it seemed to her that God spoke to her, and He did—and to discover a sound and valid version of the ontological argument. Then *God spoke to me* (which, of course, entails *God exists*) might be experientially basic for Ann; there might well be no experientially based proposition that was both better evidenced to Ann than *God spoke to Ann* and such as to evidentially support *God spoke to Ann.* But if Ann could also prove the claim *God exists*, it would not be conceptually basic in its role as conclusion of an argument; whatever served as the premises of Ann's version of the ontological argument would be evidence for its conclusion. Butler's view seems to be that there is no type of evidence with respect to which, or within which, *God exists* is evidentially basic. Hume agrees with Butler on this point.

Butler, of course, thinks that *God exists* is strongly evidenced—that there are propositions we can know to be true that amply support this claim. Hume, on the view presented here, does not. He is an evidentialist in that he thinks that *God exists* in no way is evidentially basic and that a person can be reasonable in accepting it only if one believes it on the basis of sufficient evidence. He differs from Butler by way of thinking that there is no such evidence. So his explanation of people's believing that God exists significantly differs from Butler's. Butler's explanation refers to evidence and argument, Hume's to the operation of secondary propensities.

Butler expresses a modest epistemic confidence in these terms:

> I shall not take it upon me to say how far the extent, compass, and force of analogical reasoning can be reduced to general heads and rules, and the whole be formed into a system. But though so little in this way has been attempted by those who have treated of our intellectual powers, and the exercise of them, this does not hinder but that we may be, as we unquestionably are, assured that analogy is of weight, in various degrees, toward determining our judgment and our practice. Nor does it in any wise cease to be of weight in those cases, because persons given to dispute or who require things to be stated with greater exactness than our faculties appear to admit of in practical matters, may find other cases, in which it is not easy to say whether it be, or be not, of any weight; or instances of seeming analogies, which are really of none. It is enough to the present purpose to observe that this general way of arguing is evidently natural, just, and conclusive. For there is no man can make a question but that the sun will rise tomorrow, and be seen, where it is seen at all, in the figure of a circle, and not in that of a square.[6]

For Butler, if it is natural to accept evidence, then it is also just and conclusive. "Natural" no doubt means "from human nature." "Just" means something like "epistemologically appropriate" and "conclusive" means something like "evidentially conclusive." It is matters of *evidence*, not psychological acceptance, that is in view. From Hume's pen, these words would have a subtly different sense. "Natural" can bear the same meaning, but "just" would mean much the same as "natural" and "conclusive" would become a psychological rather than an evidential matter. In Hume's philosophy of religion, the Butlerian calculus of evidence is exchanged for a Humean calculus of belief; theory of objective evidence becomes theory of intersubjective acceptance.

One need not be an evidentialist about religious belief. More than one non-evidential perspective is available. In 1742, Henry Dodwell, Jr. published *Christianity Not Founded on Argument; and the True Principle of Gospel-Evidence Assigned*. He wrote: "I am fully persuaded that the judging at all is not the proper province of reason, or indeed an affair where she has any concern."[7] His intention was to prove:

> First, that reason, or the intellectual faculty, could not possibly, both from its own nature and that of religion, be the principle intended by God to lead us into a true faith. Secondly, that neither is it so in fact from the plain account given us of it in Holy Scripture. And, thirdly, by tracing plainly from the same indisputable authority what it positively is, and by ascertaining the proper and prescribed means to come at the knowledge of divine truths.[8]

This sort of non-evidentialism builds a wall between religious belief and rational assessment. All religious belief, by its nature, is immune from rational assessment. Rational assessment, by its nature, is irrelevant to religious belief. For Dodwell, this is to the discredit of neither. At the heart of Dodwell's non-evidentialism is his view that God has decided to make rational assessment irrelevant to religious belief; it is largely a theologically based non-evidentialism that ends with the biblical quotation "Trust thou in the Lord with all thy heart, and lean not unto thine own understanding." Dodwell, then, is a fideist non-evidentialist.

Alternatively, one can embrace non-evidentialism without building Dodwell's barriers. One can hold that while belief that God exists is evidentially basic, there being no proposition better evidenced than it is that entails or otherwise evidentially supports it, still it is not immune from rational assessment. One way of developing this theme is to suggest that *being evidentially basic* and *being disconfirmable* are no more incompatible that *being evidentially basic* and *being explanatorily powerful*.

Contrast the rule of inference *Modus Ponens*—given *P*, and *If P then Q*, one may validly infer *Q*—with the rule of inference *Modus Tollens*—given *Not-Q*, and *If P then Q*, one may validly infer *Not-P*. The evidentialist may be represented as claiming that there is some (perhaps complex) proposition *P* such that *P* and *If P then God exists* are true, and entail *God exists*. (Or, perhaps, what is true is *If P then Probably, God exists* so that it is *Probably, God exists* that follows.) It is Modus Ponens that is basic to the evidentialist's strategy.

The non-fideist non-evidentialist may maintain that *God exists* is explanatorily powerful. There are many things—that at least much of what exists might not have existed, that natural phenomena are orderly in such a manner as to make science and everyday life possible, that there is an objective difference between right and wrong, that people in various cultures have had numinous experiences, that human beings possess theoretical and practical reason, and the like—that have two features: they are things it is rational to seek an explanation for and the truth of the claim that there exists an omnicompetent creative Providence explains them. This sort of explanatory force gives theism much of its importance. The idea is not that having this explanatory force *confirms* theism, but that it gives interest to the question as to whether theism is true.

If only theism explains these things, or explains them *best*, an evidentialist will claim that as a proof, or at least as evidential support, of theism. A critic will deny that only theism explains them and that theism best explains them. A critic may deny both that some of them *need* explanation and that theism actually does explain those that do need it. The non-fideist non-evidentialist is likely to deny the critic's contention but also to deny the evidentialist claim that only if there is evidence that God exists can we reasonably believe that He does.

A non-fideist non-evidentialist will be alert to possible disconfirmations of theism. Her claim will be that theism is not refuted by anything that we know to be true. She will assert that there is no proposition Q such that it is true both that *God exists entails Q* and *Q is false,* and perhaps also that there is no proposition Q such that it is true both that *God exists entails Probably Q* and that *Probably not-Q* or *Not-(Probably, Q).* But she may allow that there are interesting candidates for propositions that provide such disconfirmation. Indeed, the non-evidentialist, fideistic or not, may expend the same sort of effort and ingenuity on refuting attempted disconfirmations that the evidentialist spends on establishing attempted confirmations. If so, it is arguments of a *Modus Tollens* form—*If God exists, then Q, Not-Q, therefore God does not exist*—that attract her attention, though of course not her support. One variety, at least, of non-fideist non-evidentialism, then, will hold that it is reasonable to believe that God exists provided there is no evidence against it (and, perhaps, provided it has explanatory power), even if there is (otherwise) no evidence for it.

Theistic non-evidentialists hold that some religious claims—perhaps the claim that God exists—in some sense are basic. A proposition is *evidentially basic* if there is no better-evidenced proposition that entails or evidentially supports it. (This is a *weak* criterion; on it, both a proposition and its denial can be basic.) A proposition is *basic to Ann* if Ann believes it and there is no proposition than Ann believes from which Ann infers it. A proposition is *basic to a conceptual system,* and so is *conceptually basic,* if it is essential to that system and serves as an axiom in it. (A proposition is essential to a system if that system serves its point if that proposition is included in it—solves the intended problem, answers the relevant question, provides the desired explanation or the like—but does not do so if that proposition is excluded. An axiom is a proposition that is underived from other propositions in the system to which it is essential but from which other propositions are derived.) The same proposition, of course, can be either evidentially or conceptually basic in one system but not in another. A proposition can be evidentially basic and known so by a person in whose system of belief it is also conceptually basic. But a proposition also can be evidentially basic in the system of belief of a person who knows that it is not conceptually basic in her system. *I see the Great Dane on the lawn* is likely to be evidentially basic, grounded on a familiar sort of experience; but it is unlikely to be conceptually basic. If one believes that God exists because one accepts one or more of the arguments that propose to prove His existence, and goes on to make *God exists* basic to one's worldview, belief that *God exists* is conceptually but not evidentially basic in one's system of belief.

If one believes *I feel tired* without inferring it from any other belief, it is an evidentially basic belief but is not likely to be one of one's conceptually basic beliefs. But that one has evidence for a proposition does not entail that one is irrational to believe that proposition without inferring it from the proposition or propositions that express that evidence, and this circumstance is easily understandable if the proposition also is basic to a conceptual system that one believes.

Both evidentialists and non-evidentialists can agree that some propositions are evidentially basic. The core of the radical evidentialist position regarding religious belief lies in two claims: that no religious claims are evidentially basic and that one is not reasonable in accepting any claim that is not evidentially basic or derivable from claims that are evidentially basic. For a consistent radical religious evidentialist, the fact that various religious claims may be conceptually basic—in particular that *God exists* may be so for many who accept it—will not excuse such beliefs from the evidential requirement. Being basic, a conceptually basic proposition cannot be derived from other propositions. For the radical evidentialist, then, if such a proposition is rationally accepted, it rests on experiential grounds. A religious non-evidentialist will reject at least one of the radical religious evidentialist's claims, for the core of the non-evidentialist position lies in the claim that *God exists* is a proposition that a person rationally can accept as evidentially as well as conceptually basic. A fideist will be a non-evidentialist who denies that rational assessment of religious belief is possible. But a non-evidentialist need not be a fideist.

A non-evidentialist who is not a fideist finds his most plausible examples in religious propositions that are conceptually basic. These, he will claim, rationally can be taken as conceptually basic whether they are evidentially basic or not, but in particular at least some conceptually basic claims can be accepted rationally even in the absence of experiential grounds or self-evidence. If his strategy is to embrace a version of monotheism that has high explanatory power and consider its epistemic fate as it is exposed to rigorous attempts at falsification, he will face no need to restrict the properties ascribed to God to those one can extrapolate by use of the design argument. This will give him an important advantage over an evidentialist of Cleanthes' sort.

Hume is a radical evidentialist concerning religious belief, and indeed belief generally. What complicates his evidentialism is his view that we lack evidence for those of our beliefs that are most widely accepted as conceptually basic: belief in an external world, causal connections, an enduring self, and (perhaps) other minds. Here we believe without evidence. What determines our belief is neither evidence nor reason, but imagination or the original propensities constitutive of human nature. We cannot but have these beliefs, so long as our human nature has not crumbled. It is not unreasonable to have these beliefs. But we have no reason to think them true. This is Hume's mitigated skepticism. It is *skeptical:* we have no reason to think that our conceptually basic beliefs that are produced by our original propensities are true. It is *mitigated:* lack of evidence for these beliefs does not prevent our inevitably having them. But Hume's critique of religious belief is largely based on his assumption that radical evidentialism is true regarding religious belief.

CHAPTER 7

Hume's Theory of Meaning

Incomprehensibility

IN THE *Dialogues*, Philo plays the role of the critic of natural theology or of the attempt to prove religious belief without appeal to religious authority. Cleanthes unwaveringly supports the argument from design but opposes other pieces of natural theology. Since he constrains his notion of Deity to what he thinks the design argument substantiates, his concept of God is considerably less rich than that of orthodox Judaism or Christianity. Demea opposes the design argument, but favors the *a priori* portion of natural theology. While Demea is represented as an orthodox Christian, the representation is dubious. Besides championing *a priori* arguments for God's existence—a position compatible with but not required by Christian orthodoxy—he contends for divine incomprehensibility. The doctrine of divine incomprehensibility has a mild and a severe form. In the mild form, to comprehend something is to understand it fully—to have it altogether within one's comprehension. What, exactly, that involves can be understood in more than one way. If it amounts to knowing everything that is true of something, being aware of every property a thing has, or the like, neither God nor anything else is comprehended by any human being; *everything* is incomprehensible. Since there are an infinite number of truths about anything you like— my golden retriever, for example, is identical to none of the whole numbers—anything you like enjoys an innocuous infinitude that puts it beyond the strict comprehension of every Dick and Jane. If to understand something is to know 'how it works,' then lots of things fail to come under the comprehension of lots of people, and God and the more complex of created things are comprehended by none of us. Perhaps it is essential to any of the standard theisms, and at any rate it is true, that in any of these senses (or ones like them) God is not comprehended by any human being. (The atheist will think this true because He does not exist, and the theist because He is too complicated.) But nothing of particular philosophical interest arises from this. It is severe incomprehensibility, or ineffability, that is highly controversial.

An Introduction to Ineffability

As opposed to senses in which "ineffable" serves to emphasize what follows it ("ineffably sublime" means "supremely sublime," "ineffable pain" is pain that hurts more than most, "ineffable joy" is joyous in the extreme, etc.), there is a *philosophical* sense of ineffable in which (a) ineffability has no degrees—something is either ineffable or it is not, and (b) ineffability is a matter of being literally indescribable. Thus: (1) X is ineffable if and only if for any description D, D is false of X or: (2) X is ineffable if and only if for any concept C, C does not apply to X: express the relevant sense of ineffability. There is an obvious inelegance, however, in (1) and (2). According to (1), to say that God is ineffable is to say that (1G). For any description whatever, that description is false of God. But (1G) itself offers a description of God—not a very 'thick' one, perhaps, but a description nonetheless. There is a similar infelicity in (2). According to (2), to say that God is ineffable is to say that (2G). For any concept whatever, that concept does not apply to God. But of course *the concept of no concept applying to God* is itself a concept, not a very rich one, perhaps, but a concept nonetheless. According to (1) and (2), then, something is ineffable only if it is not. For (1) and (2) supposedly say what it is to be ineffable; but if (1) or (2) are true of something, then just because (1) or (2) is true of it, it is not ineffable after all. Perhaps, then, the right way to approach strict ineffability is like this: God (or anything else) is ineffable if and only if the concept of ineffability applies to Him, but no other concept does, or if the description *God is ineffable* is true of Him, but no other description is true of Him. But this will not do either. *God is ineffable*, for example, entails *God exists*, and if a description D is true of God, whatever descriptions D entails are also true of God. In turn, *God exists* entails *God has some properties other than ineffability* for nothing can exist and have no other properties than just existing and being ineffable (even if *existence* is itself a property). But then whatever those other properties are that God has, the descriptions that say He has them are true, and so if the description *God is ineffable* is true of God then other descriptions are true of Him too. But then God is not ineffable. (The same point can be made about concepts—talk about concepts applying to God, and about descriptions being true of God, are just two ways of saying the same thing. So it is not surprising that (1) and (2) have parallel defects.) It is clear, then, that (1) and (2) will not do, and that revising them so that they say "no descriptions are true of X, except this one" or "no concepts apply to X, save for this one" will not do either. Those characterizations of ineffability necessarily do not properly characterize anything.

One might try, then, not just *ineffability*, but *ineffability relative to a language*. The idea goes like this. Any language presumably will have some logical structure. It will, that is, have resources for expressing (i) *quantifiers*—for example: some, all, none; (ii) *inferences*—for example: so, hence, therefore, implies, entails, if . . . then; (iii) *negation*—not; (iv) *connectives*—for example: and, not, but; (v) *subject terms*—nouns and pronouns; and (vi) *predicate terms*—adjectives and adverbs. Consider two 'languages': *flowerese,* which besides (i–iv) above contains only color terms as predicates and names of flowers as subjects, and *moralese,* which besides (i–iv) above contains only moral terms as predicates and names of persons as subjects. Consider the sentences: (A1) *Roses are red.* (A2) *Violets are blue.* (B1) *John is a rat fink.* (B2) *Mary is a saint.* A1 and A2 are ineffable relative to moralese and B1 and B2 are ineffable relative to flowerese. Then one might try to say *God is ineffable* by asserting (3) *God is ineffable relative to English (and any other language humans speak).* However, (3), too, fails. Either "God" in (3) means something like "The Creator of heaven and earth" or "That being than whom no greater can be conceived" or "Jehovah" or "The Father" or "Allah" or "Brahman with qualities" or the like—in which case (3) is false—or it means nothing and is merely a placeholder, in which case (3) amounts only to: (3') *. . . is ineffable relative to English (and any other language humans speak).* Then (3') leaves us wondering what is supposed to be ineffable; it does not say that God is ineffable, or that anything else is. But once we fill in the blank in (3') in order to have a claim that something or other is ineffable, we face the same problem as we faced with (3). I have used "God" as my example in our discussion of ineffability. The same results will obtain if we use some other example—"Nirvana" or "Moksha" or "the Eiffel tower" or "the largest egg in Wausau, Wisconsin" or whatever you like. It would appear that the claim that religious entities and/or experiences are ineffable (in the strict, literal sense) is false. *Were* that claim (*per impossible*) true, it would follow that no religious experience was evidence for anything, for experiences, if they are evidence for anything, are evidence *under some description or other.*

Ineffability: Another Look

As we have seen, the severe form of incomprehensibility requires that for any property we can mention, God lacks it. He is said to be entirely beyond thought and speech—our thought and speech at any rate—and to be *strictly* ineffable. For something to be strictly ineffable is for it to be such that *no* human concept applies to it. God will not be assigned this status because He is too complicated—too rich and complex a person—but because He is "wholly other."

Ineffability has no degrees; you have it or you do not, and anything that has it, has it to the same unrestricted extent as anything else that has it. Ineffability is like perfection or existence in that respect. But with understandable license we speak of things that come closer than others to meeting a standard of perfection as being more perfect than their weaker kin. So also we speak of pain as inexpressible (and thereby communicate its dire intensity), crimes as unspeakable (when they can be all too clearly described), and joy as unutterable (thereby ranking it first in its class). Such *degreed* uses of ineffability and its surrogates are irrelevant here. If God is ineffable in the sense of being harder to describe than elk, eggs, or elm trees, this is not surprising or philosophically revolutionary. Only ineffability, strictly meant, is problematic. It is strict ineffability that Demea means. What this amounts to merits another look.

Two apparently innocuous claims can be made to yield severe incomprehensibility or ineffability. One is that all descriptive concepts apply only to things that we can perceive or introspect. The other is that we can neither perceive nor introspect God. Then no descriptive concept applies to God. Hume writes: "Our ideas reach no further than our experience; we have no experience of divine attributes and operations; I need not conclude my syllogism: You can draw the inference yourself" (*D*, 142, 143). Given the fact that Humean experience is limited to introspection and perception, it is clear that the simple argument had not escaped his notice.

Descriptive concepts provide the content or semantics of our discourse. Logical terms provide its syntax or structure. Thus *not*, the quantifiers *all* and *some* and *none*, the connectives *and* and *or* and *if-then*, and the inferential terms *so* and *hence*, among others, give discourse shape. If logical concepts can be applied to only those things to which descriptive concepts apply, and every concept is descriptive or logical, then *no* concepts apply to God. This account of concepts of course goes too quickly, but its shallowness serves us well insofar as it allows us to see, in bare bones terms, an influential argument for ineffability.

An argument can be influential without its conclusion being consistent. Let us say that a concept C applies to an item x if and only if it is the case that what x *is* C expresses is *either true or false*. Thus, as *The number 14 is red* is false, the concept *being red* applies to the number 14. By contrast, let us say, item x *satisfies* concept C if and only if what x *is* C expresses is *true*. Thus the number 14 does not satisfy the concept *being red* though that concept applies to it; *being even* applies to the number 14 and it satisfies that concept. (If one wishes to traffic in numerals rather than numbers, let these references to the number 14 be replaced by references to a white numeral fourteen.)

The ineffability thesis claims that although God exists, He satisfies no concept and that no concept applies to God. The thesis is not encouraging. If no concept applies to God, then those concepts requisite to expressing the ineffability thesis do not apply to God (so the thesis is meaningless). Since God satisfies no concept, the thesis cannot be true about God, and indeed is false of God. So the thesis is both meaningless (neither true nor false) and false.

People of a certain cast of mind find such objections trivial. Like careless check writers, they blithely write bad checks on a bankrupt account. A thesis that is meaningless, or false, or (per impossible) both cannot be true nor can it provide the basis for a philosophical theory.

Perhaps a simple revision will help. The problem thus far is that the concept *satisfying no concept* must apply to an ineffable God, but the concept *having at least one concept apply to one* is a concept that an ineffable God must satisfy. These conditions for ineffability cannot be satisfied; anything that meets one condition fails the other. So we need a revised notion of ineffability. A first-order concept is a concept of something not itself a concept; a second-order concept is a concept of a concept. The ineffability thesis, revised, says that no first-order concept applies to God (and so He satisfies none). But second-order concepts apply to God (for example, that of *satisfying no first-order concept*) and He satisfies some of them (at least that of *satisfying no first-*

order concept). Thereby, the suggestion goes, the thesis escapes the problems noted.

Properties are not concepts; the concept of being virtuous can be had by a dictator who lacks the property, and in a moral agent who has the concept, the property of being virtuous is one thing and the concept of being virtuous is another. Nothing can exist without having properties, and to any possible property a (first-order) concept may correspond. In principle, as they say, concepts apply to anything that has properties, and thus to anything that exists. So some concepts apply to God—at least some concepts that there might be would apply to God if they existed—if God exists. The revised ineffability theme says that none of the first-order concepts *that we have* apply to God. Presumably the reason for this is that the sort of concepts that apply to God for some reason are concepts that we cannot have.

This returns us to the Positivistic suggestion that all descriptive concepts apply to items that we perceive or introspect. This suggestion seems plainly false; science is full of counterexamples: quark, black hole, neutrino, and the like. Further, "descriptive" here does not contrast to "normative," so moral terms such as "good" are (for present purposes) descriptive. So are "wise," "powerful," and "knowledgeable." After all, these words are not expressive of any of the logical concepts, and a concept is either logical or descriptive, either syntactical or semantic. But of course *being morally good, being wise, being powerful,* and *being knowledgeable* are not perceivable or introspectable properties. So we have descriptive concepts beyond those the Positivistic suggestion would allow us.

One reply to this objection goes as follows. If one takes a narrow view of perception, what is perceived is color, taste, sound, odor, or tactility, and perhaps objects possessing properties falling within these modalities. On a similarly narrow account of introspection, one can internally sense dizziness, fatigue, pain, pleasure, mental imagery, and the like, and perhaps a self whose states these are. But on a wider and more adequate view, one can perceive someone else lift a weight that one could not budge and thereby observe that she is powerful, or master a task that had one baffled and observe that he is knowledgeable. Events as well as objects, and capacities as well as qualities, can be observed. Moral qualities supervene on perceptual qualities; to perceive that John has integrity is to observe John's response to severe moral testing and see that he does what is right. This involves our seeing John, and what John does, and hearing what he says, and the like, though it involves more than this. So an adequately wide notion of perception and introspection allows the theory of concepts under review to escape various counterexamples that are successful against a theory that unnecessarily truncates our perpetual and introspective capacities.

This much (while vague) is correct. But it does not deal with theoretical concepts in science. One way to handle such notions is to take them not to correspond, or even to be intended to correspond, to actual entities or states of affairs, but to hold that the terms that seem to them in actuality to be sheer counters to be used in correlating statements about what we can perceive. But that is not what science seems to be about and that line faces familiar and powerful objections. In particular, the explanatory force of science seems to require that the terms in question do refer to what they seem intended to refer to.

There remains the problem that *being an event, being meaningful, being a concept,* and the like are not observable properties of anything. Given that Josephine has the concept of an event, she can recognize such events as an apple being sliced or the sun rising. But the concept she uses to understand what she sees is not the sort of concept the traditional empiricist took the concept of being red to be. *Being red,* the traditional empiricist held, is a property isolable from all others to which we can apply, or with which we can associate, the term "red," which itself is then an isolable building block of language.

However isolable the property *being red* is, the concept of being red is the concept of a color and of a property, and can serve to express the subject (*Being red* is a property) or the predicate (Your typical apple is red) of a proposition. It bears interesting connections to other concepts and to have it is to be aware of at least many of those connections. No concept is an island. To isolate the concept of being red from other concepts one has is to contrast it with those other concepts in ways that themselves require a knowledge of a system of concepts to which it belongs. However the fact may upset theories it is natural to find plausible or even self-evident, there necessarily is no such thing as beginning to have concepts by learning a single concept and then adding a second and a third, whether or not such concepts correspond to items we perceive or introspect. (It does not follow from this that one cannot *add* a single concept to a system one has already mastered.) Further, any system of concepts that yields empirical beliefs will contain concepts of causes and effects, properties, objects, events, and the like, that bear no necessary tie to perceivable or introspectable phenomena.

One way of putting these points in perspective is to notice what happens when we enrich the notion of observation in the way suggested. What can be observed is not limited to the sorts of things traditional empiricism officially envisioned; to observable properties and collections of observable properties are added objects, events, and causal connections, as well as vices and virtues and habits and capacities. Hume's empiricism countenanced the expansion of traditional empiricism only to the degree that he held that we apply concepts beyond the range of what we are justified in doing so. We "feign" when we cannot properly infer. But if we accept the expanded sense of "observation" in order to escape the problems encountered by the more restricted doctrine, then we can no longer offer the simple argument for ineffability. In describing what we observe, whatever the origin of the concepts we use—whatever the truth about how we acquire them—these concepts are usable by theory-builders as well as by travelers, by theologians as well as by truckers, each for his or her own purposes.

In the *Enquiry Concerning Human Understanding,* Hume writes:

> When we analyse our thoughts or ideas, however compounded or sublime, we always find that they resolve themselves into such simple ideas as were copied from a precedent feeling or sentiment. Even those ideas which, at first view, seem the most wide of this origin are found, upon a nearer scrutiny, to be derived from it. The idea of God, as meaning an infinitely intelligent, wise, and good Being, arises from reflecting on the operations of our own mind, and augmenting without limit those qualities of goodness and wisdom. [*E,* 19]

I doubt that, strictly, we can do what Hume says. We are supposed to be without, say, the notion, of omniscience, but possessed of the notion, say, of knowing that snow is white. Then we "augment without limit" to reach the notion of an omnipotent being; presumably this means adding to the notion of one who knows that snow is white the notion of one who also knows that spinach is green, and so on until one reaches the notion of someone who possesses omniscience. As concepts come in clusters, propositions come in phalanxes; perhaps we need to begin with known *sets* of propositions, but this affects where one starts, not how one proceeds. It seems plain that if there are an infinite number of propositions to be known, then one can never complete the process. One will never get close in a lifetime. Descartes's suggestion is that all this is unnecessary; if one knows that one is *not* omniscient, one must have the concept of omniscience in order to tell. We already know that an omniscient being is one who knows everything that it is logically possible to know, and that we do not know anything like this. No 'augmenting' is necessary.

Whether or not Hume's explanation of our having the concept of God is right, his *Enquiry* remarks make two things clear: Hume grants that we have the concept of omniscience, and sees that our recognition of our own limitations, upon analysis if not upon augmentation, provides the basis of a justification of this claim. A broadened account of observation that allows us to observe our own cognitive limits, restricted power, and our moral imperfection, whether explained or analyzed along Humean or Cartesian (or other) lines, once again requires our possession of the concepts of properties that we do not discern in the things we perceive or introspect. Nor is omnipotence, or omniscience, or moral perfection, a *negative* concept—one that expresses a mere lack of impotence, or ignorance, or immorality; they are as positive as concepts get.

Descartes asks, if one has no concepts applicable to God, how one can say

> that God is infinite and incomprehensible, and that He cannot be represented by our imagination? How could he affirm that these attributes belonged to Him, and countless others which express His greatness to us, unless he had the idea of Him? It must be agreed, then, that we have the idea of God, and that we cannot fail to know what this idea is, nor what is meant by it; because without this we could not know anything at all about God. It would be no good saying that we believe that God exists, and that some attribute or perfection belongs to Him; this would say nothing because it would have no meaning to our mind. Nothing could be more impious or impertinent.[1]

There is no resource for the ineffability thesis here.

Neither the original nor the revised version of the ineffability thesis receives adequate support from an empiricist theory of concepts, and the unrevised version is incoherent. Is the revised version at least coherent?

Nothing can exist to which no possible first-order concepts apply. Consider, however, the thesis that something exists to which no first-order concepts *that we can have* apply. Is this suggestion coherent? It is not. The concept of existence is itself a first-order concept, and (like those that follow) is a concept that we have. Further, if anything exists, the first-order concepts *being something that has properties* and *being self-identical* and *having only consistent properties* apply to it; necessarily, such concepts apply to whatever exists. Let a first-order concept that necessarily applies to anything that exists (including the concept of existence itself) be an *existence-entailed* concept. To claim that something exists is to claim that the first-order, existence-entailed concepts that we have apply to it. So another revision is required: something exists to which no non-existence-entailed, first-order concept that we can have applies. Is *this* a non-self-defeating version of the ineffability thesis?

It is not enough for a version of the ineffability thesis that something (in particular, God) be such that no concept that we now have applies to it, for that is compatible with our tomorrow having a concept (and, given the way concepts go together, therefore more than one concept) that does apply to God. Interesting ineffability is not merely accidental. It must deal in concepts that we do not have because we cannot have them.

What, though, are we to make of the notion of a concept that no human being can have? Perhaps this: suppose that no human being can have a functional IQ of more than (say) 212—the human brain simply breaks down upon any activity that would, if brought to fruition, involve functioning at an IQ level of 213 or above. Suppose, too, that there is a set of difficult concepts that are such that no being of a functional IQ of less than 213 can have them; call these *esoteric concepts.* On this account, no human being could have any esoteric concepts.

This alone will not give us any variety of an ineffability thesis. For that, we need something further along these lines. Suppose that there is one set of beings to which non-existence-entailed concepts apply only if they are esoteric concepts; call these *esoteric beings.* The claim that there are esoteric beings, given our previous two claims, will be the claim that there are ineffable beings.

The motivating story behind this suggestion looks highly suspicious. It is sometimes maintained (I read it somewhere the other day) that those who later do really creative work in the sciences tend to be "B-plus" students who get by on as little work as possible until they discover that they can contribute to some science rather than just reading about it. Their IQ scores are not off the high end of the scale. If this is so, the postulated connection between IQ and possession of esoteric concepts is implausible. But waive this and other possible objections, and suppose the story true. Do we have a version of the ineffability thesis?

It is at least not clear that we do. Suppose that the esoteric beings are very intelligent—way off our IQ scales. Then they are at least as intelligent as the average physics teacher, because they are vastly more so. But no being of which it can be said with truth that it is at least as intelligent as the average physics teacher is ineffable. Similar considerations apply if we suppose esoteric beings to be powerful to an astonishing degree, and so on. Esoteric beings, if ineffable, must lack intelligence and power and everything else we have any concept of; otherwise, they are not ineffable. (What religious interest they might have thus becomes somewhat puzzling.)

Those defenders of ineffability who face this point tend to exhibit the sort of schizophrenic reaction of a miserly book addict in an excellent used-book store: the desire to spend and the desire to hoard wrack his soul. The defender of ineffability wants both to retain the interest, indeed fascination, of the Ineffable without sacrificing the Ineffable's ineffability. So one is provided with a classic case of simultaneous approach and avoidance, a giving and taking back. God, we are told, is indeed powerful—but not with power *at all* like any we know; He is omnicompetent, but it is not true of Him that He can part the Red Sea (for if He can part the Red Sea then some non-existence-entailed, first-order concepts that we *can* have, since we *do* have them, apply to God). Similarly, He is omniscient, but (for the same reason) He does not know that two plus two is four. As it is often put, to say that God has knowledge or power is but to say that God lacks ignorance or impotence but to leave unsaid what God *has*. Or to say that *God parted the Red Sea* is to say something like *The Red Sea parted and God caused this* without the latter entailing or presupposing, for any property we might think relevant to parting the Red Sea, that God has that property.

The temptation is to object to this view on the grounds that *God caused the Red Sea to part and for any property necessary for doing this, God lacks that property* is a contradiction. So it is; but this is not quite what the defender of ineffability intends. She offers rather *God caused the Red Sea to part and for any property of which we have any concept such that having that property seems to us necessary for doing it, God lacks that property*. This is a dubious improvement. *God causes the Red Sea to part* (and similar claims where "produces," "brings it about that," or "efficaciously wills" replaces "causes," with any changes this otherwise may require in the phrasing of the claim) entails *God has the power to part the Red Sea*. To understand a proposition is to know what it entails. If we have no concept of power of which it is true that *God causes the Red Sea to part* entails *God has the power to part the Red Sea*, then we have no concept of cause that allows us to understand *God causes the Red Sea to part* (and similarly for various substitutes for "causes"). This evacuates all content from *God causes the Red Sea to part;* we are left with only *God —— the Red Sea to part.* Since any other term we use relative to an allegedly ineffable God will be in the same boat as "causes," the term "God" loses its sense, and we are left with —— *the Red Sea to part*, which is nonsense. We can substitute *The Red Sea parts* and try to make do with that. But theology and monotheistic religion have vanished.

Hume, who admittedly has less to lose here than monotheists who lust after divine ineffability, sees more clearly than they. He recognizes that, whatever its philosophical fate (which seems highly inelegant), the theological and religious impact of the ineffability thesis is devastating. God can be no more to us than *something to which no fist-order non-existence-entailed concepts apply*. No room is left here to render any ritual or institution more appropriate than another, or indeed to render it appropriate (or not) that there be any religious rituals or institutions. No morality can rest on this conception. You cannot make stew from dust, and only dust is left. So not only have we no defensible notion, as yet at least, of ineffability; it remains puzzling why any monotheist would *want* it.

Still another defense of ineffability is possible. One can argue as follows: the concept of a being greater than any that we can conceive of is a second-order concept, so its applying to a being (and that being satisfying it) is not incompatible with that being possessing ineffability. A being greater than any that we can conceive of is worthy of worship, and from this one can go on to generate relevant ritual, institution, and morality. The claim as to what one can go on to do is worth investigating only if what precedes it is correct. The defender of ineffability has cheated at least once. A being *other* than any that we can conceive of need not be *greater* than any that we can conceive of. The assumption of the defender is that an ineffable being is somehow nobler or better or more elegant than an effable one. This need not be so. As has been noted, the defender of ineffability is not entitled to begin, say, with power, knowledge, and goodness and then to go on beyond our experience in the direction begun if this involves God being more powerful, knowledgeable, or good than we are. This would leave God knowing what we know, and more; being able to do what we can do, and more; and so being effable. Nor can one consistently say that God has something *more like power* than anything else (but still not power), for then the first-order concept of having a property more like power than any other property would then apply to God, and that of course is a concept that we have. (Of course one could ask the defender of ineffability how she *knew* this, and how she knew that the property is not the property of being *omnipotent*, and what makes the property in question more like the property *having power* than any other; but we need not press this here.) The idea of carrying on in the direction of some sort of greatness, and inconceivably surpassing it, is essential to the idea that the ineffable is *greater* rather than merely *other*, or is "other" in a sense that includes "greater," or that a being that is ineffable is rich and complex rather than thin and ailing. This idea is perfectly illegitimate and groundless.

Demea reiterates the theme that obviously God exists (in some sense or other of the word "God"). He writes of "that fundamental principle of all religion . . . No man; no man, at least, of common sense, I am persuaded, ever entertained a serious doubt with regard to a truth so certain and self-evident. The question is not concerning the *being* but the *nature* of God" (D, 141). *That* God is, is certain; *what* God is, is "altogether incomprehensible and unknown to us." Demea's qualification "no man, at least, of common sense" is echoed in Philo's supposed "reversal" in Part Twelve, and for now I simply note the occurrence of this reference to the "man of common sense."

Divine Incomprehensibility and Negative Theology

Demea's position concerning God's nature is Malebranche's, or at least Hume's interpretation of Malebranche. As Demea asserts that "next to the impiety of denying his existence, is the temerity of prying into his nature and essence, decrees and attributes," so he quotes Malebranche to this effect:

> One ought not so much to call God a spirit, in order to express positively what he is, as in order to signify that he is not matter . . . we ought not to imagine that he is cloathed with a human body . . . neither ought we to imagine, that the Spirit of God has human ideas, or bears *any* resemblance to our spirit . . . his true name is, *He that is*, or in other words, Being without restriction, All Being, The Being infinite and universal. [D, 142][2]

Now Demea's (and presumably Malebranche's) motives are religious ones; presumably piety, neither priestcraft nor a desire to subvert religion from within, motivates the firm rejection of any possible knowledge of God's nature. Of course this piety is not pure in the sense of being free from philosophical taint. It is quite open to doubt that the divine answer ("I am that I am") to Moses' query ("Who are you?") is to be read as if it said "I have no properties, or at any rate none you can understand." For all the effusive plethora of Malebranche's "Being without restriction, All Being, Being infinite and universal," it is far from clear that all this about Being is really only putting "He that is" into other words.

It takes no great amount of reflection to see how one might wonder, supposing he knew that "All Being, infinite and universal, exists" was true, what to do about this curious datum. For "infinite" here just means "not finite"; and so "omnipotent" will mean "not impotent" but will *not* mean, or include or entail, say, "is more powerful than Paul Bunyan." Analogously, "omniscient" will mean "not ignorant" but will *not* mean or include or entail "knowing more than Einstein." The religious dullard will suppose that God can *do* things, for example, change water to wine, and that God knows things, for example, what is in one's heart, and so on. Demea and Hume's Malebranche know better. Being religiously wise, they are aware that however strong the tendency of the insipid intellect to think otherwise, no sentence of the form "God has property A" entails that God actually *has* the property "A" connotes or denotes, or any property like it, or indeed any property at all. The net result, Cleanthes rightly insists, is that this pious denial of all properties to God is indistinguishable from atheism. For the difference between "God exists—but for any property you can mention, He does not have it" and "God does not exist" is, to put it charitably, not easy to make out. The path from a certain sort of piety to a religious agnosticism indistinguishable from atheism is short, steep, and slippery and the illusion of wisdom to which its travelers often succumb only serves to make the slide more pleasant without alleviating its perils or altering its course. With friends like Demea, orthodoxy needs no enemies.[3]

Meaning, Verification, and the Designer Hypothesis

If we mean by "God" just "the being who caused the universe," then in this minimal, almost trite, sense, Hume's view is that all or most persons of common sense agree that God exists. But where does this leave us? Religously, we remain ill-informed. For Philo notes that if we follow Demea's pietism (which looks for all the world like skepticism with religious motives and in clerical dress) we must grant that as all perfection is entirely relative, we ought never to imagine, that we comprehend the attributes of this divine Being, or to suppose, that his perfections have any analogy or likeness to the perfections of a human creature. Wisdom, thought, design, knowledge; these we justly ascribe to him; because these words are honourable among men, and we have no other language or other conceptions, by which we can express our adoration of him. But let us beware, lest we think, that our ideas any wise correspond to his perfections, or that his attributes have any resemblance to these qualities among men. He is infinitely superior to our limited view and comprehension; and is more the object of worship in the temple, than of disputation in the schools. [D, 142]

Nor is "affected skepticism" (I do not know whether "affected skepticism" means "the sort of skepticism no one can really embrace" or "the sort of skepticism that Demea embraces from pietistic motives") the only basis for this ignorance of the divine nature. We can instead argue purely philosophically in this manner:

Our ideas reach no farther than our experience: We have no experience of divine attributes and operations: I need not conclude my syllogism: You can draw the inference yourself. And it is a pleasure to me (and I hope to you too) that just reasoning and sound piety here concur in the same conclusion, and both of them establish the adorably mysterious and incomprehensible nature of the supreme Being. [D, 143]

Cleanthes has no commitment to Demea's skeptical pietism, nor need he be impressed by quotations from Malebranche. Philo's argument is another matter. Cleanthes claims he can prove that God—the God of the argument from design—exists. If Philo's conclusionless syllogism is cogent, Cleanthes cannot make good his claim. So Philo must be answered—not his "pious declamations," but his argument.

We should underline the bipolarity of Philo's argument (and the consequent bipolarity of Cleanthes' rebuttal), and note a certain parochiality about Hume's conduct of the discussion.

Philo's argument permits the following phrasing. Where "S" is any person whatever:

(1) If S has not experienced a referent of the word "x," then "x" has no meaning to S.

(2) No S has experienced a referent of "divine attributes and operations."

So:

> (3) For all S, "divine attributes and operations" has no meaning to S.

It would be interesting to know exactly how Philo knows that (2) is true, but I leave that question aside. Assuming (1) and (2), Philo purports to have shown that all "claims" concerning divine attributes and operations are meaningless. One can ring the changes on senses of the word "meaning" in the way recently fashionable, and allow that such "claims" have "emotive meaning" (people tend to have certain emotions upon hearing the meaningless sounds or seeing the meaningless marks which "express" these "claims") or "conative meaning" (upon hearing the meaningless sounds or seeing the meaningless marks which "express" these "claims," people tend to make, or be confirmed in, certain choices). But all this is putting Band-Aids on the Titanic, and if it passes as subtlety perhaps the thing to do is remember a certain famous remark of P. T. Barnum.

Another parsing of Philo's syllogism is less natural but equally relevant to the argument. Where "S" is any person and "P" any contingent proposition, it runs:

> (1') For all S and P, if S cannot verify proposition P by experience, S cannot verify P at all.
> (2') For any person S and for any proposition P whose subject or predicate term is "divine attributes and operations," S cannot verify P by experience.

So:

> (3') For all S and P, S cannot verify a proposition P at all if P's subject or predicate term is "divine attributes and operations."

Now plainly the first version of Philo's argument is vague and its premises implausible. It, and arguments like it, were considered earlier in this chapter. The second is also rather vague. I do not propose to be concerned about that matter just now. For the present, it suffices to note that version one challenges the intelligibility, version two the verification, of Cleanthes' claims. The success of the former version would yield the result that Cleanthes has no religious claims to make, whereas the success of the latter would make Cleanthes the proponent of an unverified religion. Both themes are woven in and out of the dialogic pattern.

Nevertheless, neither theme is well founded. Consider the claim

that if one (in principle) cannot verify a proposition by appeal to experience (perception or introspection) then one cannot verify it at all.
What perceptual or introspective evidence or experience could verify
that claim? The answer is simple and devastating: *no* experience veri-
fies it. So if it is true, it cannot be verified. If one ought not to accept
unverifiable claims, then one ought not to accept it.

Consider the claim that if one has not experienced a referent of a
word, then the word has no meaning to one. Consider the sentence
form "I know that I have never experienced a ———." Many people can
use sentences of this form to say things that they know to be true;
many people, for example, know that they have never perceived or
introspected a black hole, a dodo, or a dinosaur. But were it the case
that if one had never experienced a black hole, a dodo, or a dinosaur,
the words "black hole," "dodo," and "dinosaur" were meaningless to
one, one could not use sentences of the indicated sort to say things
that one knew to be true. If it is objected that the examples are *complex*
things, the reply is that things are no better for the position in question if our examples are "a purple pinprick of color," "a microsecond
of deafening sound," or "a miniscule taste more bitter than lemon,"
and that "black hole" at least is not in any case a concept we can have
by constructing it from concepts of perceptual and introspective
simples. Of course one can reformulate Philo's sort of position, and
reformulate the criticism to match, for quite some time. But there is no
reason to think that any defensible position will yield Philo the conclusions he wishes.[4]

Divine Incomprehensibility Again

The discussion concerning "the mysterious, incomprehensible nature of the Deity" continues into Part Four. But the dispute concerning the meaningfulness of such predicates as "is intelligent" is
not reopened. The exchange continues to involve only Cleanthes and
Demea. The former pointedly asks:

> The Deity, I can readily allow, possesses many powers and at-
> tributes, of which we can have no comprehension: But if our
> ideas, so far as they go, be not just and adequate, and correspon-
> dent to his real nature, I know not what there is in this subject
> worth insisting on. Is the name, without any meaning, of such
> mighty importance? [*D*, 158]

And he asks whether "mystics who maintain the absolute incomprehensibility of the Deity differ from sceptics or atheists" (*D*, 158). The queries, we have noted, have a point. If for every predicate *A*, "God is *A*" is meaningless, theists and atheists make in common the mistake of supposing that "God exists" is meaningful. If no property and no relation can be meaningfully ascribed to God, the word "God" has no meaning. Why worry about a sound or mark that means nothing? The sort of piety that makes God, in this sense, incomprehensible does not indeed reduce to atheism. It reduces to nonsense.

Demea offers no response to this argument. Instead, he attacks Cleanthes' views.

> In reality, Cleanthes, consider what it is you assert, when you represent the Deity as similar to a human mind and understanding. What is the soul of man? A composition of various faculties, passions, sentiments, ideas; united, indeed, into one self or person, but still distinct from each other. [*D*, 159]

Humans think their thoughts in sequence. They change their minds, learn, and forget. They love, hate, hope, and fear, and their thoughts and moods vary in the

> most rapid succession imaginable. How is this compatible with that perfect immutability and simplicity, which all true theists ascribe to the Deity? By the same act, say they, he sees past, present and future: His love and his hatred, his mercy and his justice are one individual operation. . . . No succession, no change, no acquisition, no diminution. . . . He stands fixed in one simple, perfect state. [*D*, 155]

Demea here appeals to a hoary doctrine whose history is more imposing than its rational credentials. Briefly, the view is that God, as First (that is, uncaused) Cause must exist with necessity. A being that exists with necessity is at least one that cannot be put out of existence by another, nor can it simply fade away. Contingent beings—those that lack necessity—are composite, and their demise comes by way of the parts going each its own way. Nothing, then, could be both composite (in constant danger of coming unglued) and necessary. But everything that is, is necessarily either composite or simple. So a necessary being will be non-composite or simple.

Consider, then, the claim that God is both merciful and just. If *being just* is one property of God and *being merciful* another, then it is possible that He have one property but not the other. Having a composite of distinct properties is as dangerous as being a composite of distinct parts. While *we* distinguish between divine justice and divine mercy, this view claims, the properties as they are in God are really one single property. Plainly, by following the same line of reasoning, such as it is, all properties God has become *one* property, looked at as it were from various angles. The analogy of light breaking into various colors as it passes through a prism was pressed into service to express this view: God's nature, seen through the mind of such creatures as we are, breaks into various properties but is single-propertied in itself.

Indeed, even this is not quite enough to guarantee complete simplicity. For it allows God to be a being who has a property. Is, then, the property one thing, and God another? Then God is in danger of being a bare particular. So on this view not only are all God's properties one property, but God and his one property are also identical. Our concepts can't begin to capture all this, but so much the worse for them. Demea points out to Cleanthes that some theists have held firmly to divine simplicity, and that he (Cleanthes) can't.

Cleanthes cheerfully consents: "A mind . . . that is wholly simple, and totally immutable . . . is a mind which has no thought, no reason, no will, no sentiments, no love, no hatred; or in a word, is no mind at all. It is an abuse of terms to give it that appellation" (*D*, 159).

The philosophical issue is whether one can give to "divine mind" a meaning which neither makes of the Deity a "simple being" in the sense characterized above nor one exactly like a human mind (or so close that the difference doesn't matter). Demea thinks there is no way to accomplish this, and insists on God being a simple being. Cleanthes apparently agrees that no third sense of "mind" or sort of mind is available and is content to make the divine mind very like that of a human being. The crucial issue is that on which Demea and Cleanthes (and Hume) agree, and the defense of their view on this crucial issue is Hume's theory of meaning—which, we have argued, is a mistaken theory. Philo, who does not quarrel with Cleanthes' rendering of "divine mind," denies that Cleanthes offers good reason to think there is a Deity.

CHAPTER 8

Design, Causality, and Purpose

The Causal Principle and the Causal Maxim (*Dialogues*, Part Two)

D EMEA REITERATES the theme that obviously God exists (in some sense or other of the word "God"). He writes of "that fundamental principle of all religion. . . . No man; no man, at least, of common sense, I am persuaded, ever entertained a serious doubt with regard to a truth so certain and self-evident. The question is not concerning the *being* but the *nature* of God" (*D*, 141). *That* God is, is certain; *what* God is, is "altogether incomprehensible and unknown to us." Demea's qualification "no man, at least, of common sense" is echoed in Philo's supposed "reversal" in Part Twelve, already discussed and I simply note the occurrence of this reference to the "man of common sense."

While Hume's point that one version of piety (discussed in our previous chapter) leads to a position which differs from atheism only as an elderly spinster differs from an old maid is important, true, and oft-ignored, it is not his main thrust. That status is reserved for his argument that a philosophical theism based on the argument from design fares no better than its pious cousin.

Thus Philo, in agreeing with Demea, quotes no authorities. Instead, he sketches two arguments. The first begins with what Hume, for the sake of the argument, does not challenge in the *Dialogues*.

> Where reasonable men treat these subjects, the question can never be concerning the *being*, but only the *nature* of the Deity. The former truth, as you well observe, is unquestionable and

self-evident. Nothing exists without a cause; and the original cause of this universe (whatever it be) we call GOD; and piously ascribe to him every species of perfection. Whoever scruples this fundamental truth deserves every punishment, which can be inflicted among philosophers, to wit, the greatest ridicule, contempt and disapprobation. [*D*, 142]

That it is self-evident that a cause of the universe exists is dubious, and perhaps no one knew this better than Hume, whose *Treatise* critique classically called into question the necessity of "Every event has a cause." Both his own critique, charitably construed, and his rebuttal of Locke, Hobbes, and Clarke, who defended the necessity of the causal principle, are powerful and, so far as I can see, quite successful. Further, even if every event and thing must be caused, perhaps the universe itself—construed as a collection of events and/or things—need have no cause save as its constituents have causes. A universe composed of a frog on a log, given the necessity of the causal principle, will require a past containing the cause of the frog and the cause of the log. Perhaps its past need not include some further cause of the complex the-frog-and-the-log. Obviously, the considerations raised by "Is the causal principle necessary?" and "Must the universe have a cause?" are more complex than these brief remarks suggest. The interesting thing is that Hume does not concern himself here with such matters. He simply supposes that both questions have an obvious answer, and that the answer is affirmative.

His reasons for proceeding in this manner are complex. The argument from design, at least in Cleanthes' formulation, requires some such premise as "like effects have like causes" in order to generate the conclusion that natural objects have a designer from the premises that natural objects resemble artifacts and artifacts have designers. Whether or not the argument is successful with that premise, it clearly will fail without it. Obviously, then, a critique of the claim that like effects have like causes also will be a critique of the argument from design. Again, if one doubts of two resembling events or things that both (or either) *has* a cause, she will doubt that both (or either) is an effect at all, so that even if like effects do have like causes this will be nothing to the point when we come to consider the events in question, for they are not known to be effects. Why, then, does Hume—who after all has said something important on these topics—mainly ignore them in the *Dialogues?*

I suggest several reasons. For an obvious first, he has already had his say on these other matters and the effect on the argument from design as well as the argument from contingency is obvious enough. Further, if one can grant one debatable premise to an opponent and show that even then he cannot make his case, this makes for a more potent critique than basing one's case on the rejection of that debatable premise. This remark supposes of course that Hume *rejects* the argument from design as a proof that it is more probable than not that God exists, and the discussion to follow will endeavor to justify this assumption.

But there is a more fundamental reason. Hume does hold that the argument from design—more carefully, the data to which that argument directs our attention—in some circumstances and for some persons elicits belief in God. While the argument fails as a piece of natural theology, it plays an effective role in natural religion. Inadequate as a proof, it may be effective in producing assent, for, as every advertising agency knows, rational inadequacy is not incompatible with persuasive efficacy.

While the causal principle lacks a self-contradictory denial and so is not certifiable as true by appeal to logic alone, we cannot help but believe it anyway. Analogously, showing how the critique of the causal principle undermines the rational credentials of the argument from design will not affect the argument's persuasive effectiveness. As Hume might well have put it, the question is not whether there be a God, but why (most) people believe there is. (Compare: "We may well ask, *What causes induce us to believe in the existence of body?* but 'tis in vain to ask, *whether there be body or not?* That is a point, which we must take for granted in all our reasonings.")[1]

Of course Hume also deals with the question, "Is it reasonable to believe (discernibly more probable than not) that there is a God?" just as he deals with the analogous question concerning material objects. Hume has the critic Philo affirm his assent to the causal principle (*D*, 142) and the causal maxim (*D*, 147). In effect, he grants these principles for the sake of the argument. Thus he can concentrate on the question "Given the causal principle and the causal maxim, does the argument from design show that it is more probable that God exists than that He does not?" In the *Natural History*, Hume followed the same procedure concerning the question "Why do people believe in the God of the argument from design?" Since belief—in God as in objects—is not affected by the fact that the causal principle and maxim are *not* self-evident, and since in any case there are other problems with the argument from design, Hume can afford to grant the causal .

principle (and the causal maxim, "Like effects, like causes"), for the sake of the argument, to the proponent of the argument from design. So he has Philo grant—indeed embrace—these principles.

We should note in passing that it is surprising to see Philo heartily approve Demea's argument from authority. For while Demea is content to quote his sources and follow their lead, this is hardly the path for "the careless scepticism of Philo" (*D*, 128). But note what Philo says: "After so great an authority, Demea . . . as that which you have produced, and a thousand more, which you might have produced, it would appear ridiculous to add my sentiment . . . surely, where reasonable men treat these subjects, the question can never concern the *being*, but only the *nature* of the Deity" (*D*, 142). He need not add his sentiment to *what*? Obviously, the *sentiments* of others. And if you want to know people's sentiments, quotation is not an illegitimate way of proceeding. Further, Philo joins in those sentiments as one of those "reasonable men [who] treat these subjects"—where I take it that "reasonable people" are "people of common sense."

Theism and the *Dialogues*

Conspicuous by her absence in all this is the theist who neither relies on the argument from design—either to provide meaning or proof for her doctrines—nor is so skeptically pious that she ascribes no properties to God. Denying the verificationist theories of meaning suggested by version one of Philo's argument and the restricted scope of criteria for truth implied by version two, she ascribes to God such properties as omnipotence, omnibenevolence, and omniscience and such actions as creating the world, calling Abraham from Ur of the Chaldees, and becoming incarnate in Christ. She does not understand these as negative properties, or privative ones either. Nor does she follow Cleanthes in ascribing to God a large but limited amount of power and knowledge.

It is obvious that no figure in the *Dialogues* holds this position, and of course there are other varieties of rather orthodox theism that one might mention. But one ought not to simply infer from the fact that no participant in the discussion holds a particular view that nothing said in the discussion is directly relevant to that view. None of the participants is very representative of classical theism. But we will nonetheless want to ask what effect, if any, the arguments that appear in the *Dialogues* have on this position.

The Design Argument: Initial Formulation

Returning to Cleanthes' use of the argument from design, we can now see what Cleanthes will hope to accomplish by this use. He will wish to point to features of our experience that both give meaning to the use of terms like "intelligent" and "powerful" as applied to God and justify the ascription to God of the properties or capacities these words designate. He will hope thereby to show that skepticism about the divine nature, whether motivated by pietistic feeling or supported by philosophical argument (or both), and whether universal in scope or concerned only with matters beyond the ordinary affairs of life, is simply mistaken.

Cleanthes begins his task with this tentative statement of the argument from design:

> I shall briefly explain how I conceive this matter. Look round the world: Contemplate the whole and every part of it: You will find it nothing but one great machine, subdivided into an infinite number of lesser machines, which again admit of subdivisions. . . . All these various machines, and even their most minute parts, are adjusted to each other with an accuracy which ravishes into admiration all men who have ever contemplated them. The curious adapting of means to ends, throughout all nature, resembles exactly, though it much exceeds, the productions of human contrivance; of human design, thought, wisdom, and intelligence. Since therefore the effects resemble each other we are led to infer, by all the rules of analogy, that the causes resemble one another; and that the Author of nature is somewhat similar to the mind of man; though possessed of much larger faculties, proportioned to the grandeur of the work, which he has executed. By this argument *a posteriori*, and by this argument alone, we do prove at once the existence of a Deity, and his similarity to human mind and intelligence. [*D*, 143]

The argument on which Cleanthes fastens his hopes can be laid out formally along these lines: Let us say that something possesses *designedness* if it is composed of parts that uniformly behave in a specifiable manner to produce a predictable product. Ford assembly lines and bubble gum machines possess designedness; so do rabbits and carrots. *X possesses designedness* does not by itself entail *x was designed*. Not even Paley thought it logically impossible that a watch appear full-made at the end of a designerless process, though he rightly thought that this never occurred. What impresses Cleanthes is that artifacts and natural objects both possess designedness. Quill pens and wigs look for all the world as if they were designed; and they were. What makes pens and wigs look so patently planned? Cleanthes' answer refers us to "the curious adapting of means to ends"—in sum, designedness. Quill feathers and earwigs possess designedness too. So they too, at least upon careful scrutiny, look for all the world as if they were planned. We can thus argue:

(1) Natural objects and artifacts possess designedness.
(2) Artifacts are designed.

So:

(3) Probably, natural objects are designed.

And the move from (1) and (2) to (3) is eased by appeal to what we may call Axiom (A2):

If two effects E1 and E2 resemble one another, then their respective causes C1 and C2 resemble one another.

In appealing to (A2), Cleanthes plainly supposes that natural objects and artifacts are effects, that is, have causes. It is difficult to see how this supposition could be sustained without appeal to some axiom about causality. In any case, in the context of the *Dialogues*, this supposition obviously is based on Axiom (A1):

Every event (and object) has some cause.

And since Hume is granting (A1) and (A2) for the sake of the argument, Philo—who has already affirmed (A2)—appeals to (A1) in his response to Cleanthes, as we shall see. For now, Demea presents a subsidiary point for consideration.

On Proportioning Degrees of Belief and Evidence

Demea objects to Cleanthes' procedures because they do not yield certainty. The conclusion of an *a priori* argument—which presumably is an argument all of whose premises are *a priori*—will also be *a priori*. If the premises are true and the argument valid, the conclusion will be true—an *a priori* truth if the argument is an *a priori* argument. While "*a priori*," and its sometime contemporary twin "conceptually necessary," are less than lucid in connotation or denotation, at least part of the preference of Demea for *a priori* proofs is that an *a priori* claim, if true at all, is (in some sense) *necessarily* true and so can be accepted without reservation. The idea is perhaps that if *P* is necessarily true then upon recognizing *P*'s necessity one can embrace *P* unreservedly. But were *P* only highly probably true, then one must keep a corner of one's heart from *P*'s attraction, for one must proportion the degree of one's belief to the degree of probability of the truth of what is up for belief. One hundred percent belief (subjective certainty) must be granted only to claims with 100 percent likelihood of truth (objective certainty). But religion requires 100 percent belief. Hence if a proof of a religious proposition *P* yields only, say, 80 percent likelihood that *P* is true, then one cannot rightly grant *P* the degree of belief that religion requires. Much has been written concerning the "religious requirement" of certainty versus the less imposing degree of belief (psychological acceptance) justified by the relevant evidence.

There is rather plainly a large dose of artificiality about this notion of proportioning belief to evidence. It is not logically possible that my pen both be in my left hand but not be there. It is not logically impossible that I have no pen. So (on the 'obligation to proportion' line) I ought to believe that "My pen is not both in my left hand and not in my left hand" is true with greater firmness than I believe that "I have a pen" is true. And down the line toward the slot on the belief continuum titled "rightly disbelieved," though not *very* close to it, are the claims expressed by "My family loves me," "I have tenure," and "Hume was a greater philosopher than Mill." All of this bristles with problems. How does one *measure* degrees of belief? What degree of control do I have over my beliefs, and over their intensity?

One criterion that sounds plausible is: Al believes *P* to the degree that he is willing to act on belief that *P*. Accordingly, perhaps Al believes that *P* more firmly than does Bob if Al is willing to act on belief that *P* on more occasions than Bob is willing to act on that belief. But this seems inadequate. Suppose that there are occasions on which Bob is willing to act on the belief that *P* that involve more risk—may cost Bob more if *P* is false—than Al will risk on the occasions on which he is willing to act from belief that *P*. But this will be relevant only if Al and Bob *know* the risks involved—so perhaps we could measure degree of belief more relevantly along the lines of the risks Al and Bob *believe* they would take in various circumstances. But of course Al might just be a more conservative person than was Bob, and that would have, I suppose, to be somehow taken into account. So would the questions of how one measures the risks taken, do both Al and Bob agree on how much risk each acting-on-belief-that-*P* will involve, and how one measures willingness to take more risks versus willingness to take fewer but greater risks. Or one might say, instead, or in addition, that Al believes that P more firmly than does Bob if Al's P-acceptance colors his conceptual scheme more, or is more basic to his life-style, than does Bob's acceptance of P. Probably measurements of emotional intensity (including physiological ones) will be of little aid, since belief is better analyzed so that disposition to act is central and pro-feelings peripheral rather than conversely. And so the issue of measuring degrees of belief provides a host of problems that are not easily solved, and while we have put most of these problems in terms of comparative firmness of belief between Al and Bob, a closely corresponding issue plainly arises if only Al's firmness of belief (never mind how he compares to others) is involved.

Do we have the sort of control of our belief-states suggested by the supposed (moral?) principle that one ought to proportion degree of belief to degree of evidence? Probably not insofar as belief states are viewed as involving adopting a feeling, a pro-attitude, to a claim. Perhaps so insofar as belief states are (more plausibly) viewed as also involving willingness to act. Future dispositions and episodes that enter into the composition of our beliefs may be more open to our influence than are our present episodes and dispositions.

Is there some criterion for degrees of evidence? Surely there are some at least rough criteria: we know it is more likely that a regent criticize the university president than that the legislature will double faculty salaries, and it would not be too hard to specify at least roughly the measuring stick that allows such comparisons. Can one then *compare* slots on the degree-of-belief continuum with slots on the degree-of-evidence continuum and thereby compare firmness of belief with fecundity of evidence? Perhaps, though I suspect this will be even more imprecise than placing a belief on its continuum or a claim on its. Can everybody, or anybody, be expected to perform the continuum placing and comparisons relevant to following the supposed principle "Proportion degree of belief to degree of evidence?" At best, only *very* intuitively and roughly.

I suspect that the supposed principle has been grossly overrated. The principle is neither very clear nor very central in actual human reasoning, and I cannot see either that it is likely to become very clear or that it should be made central. The same goes for its alternative formulation (for to believe P is to disbelieve *not-P*): proportion degree of disbelief to degree of evidence. No doubt atheists can charge theists with violating the maxim in its former formulation and theists return the favor by accusing atheists with violating it in its latter statement. Then agnostics can join the game by noting that the two formulations are but one side of the same coin, and only those who have no belief on important but hard-to-resolve matters obey the principle. It is very hard to see that anything really substantial relevant to the assessment of religious belief is at issue here. Further, Hume is not himself committed to the principle, as his remark "Nature by an absolute and uncontrollable necessity, has determined us to judge as well as to believe and feel" (*T*, 183) indicates and as our earlier discussion has made clear.

The remark about proportioning belief to evidence is not utterly pointless. People do take risks that they are unwise to take; sometimes they do so *knowing* that it is unwise. It is unwise to drive while drunk, or leave guns and ammunition where children can get at them; yet people do such things. They do not proportion action-disposing belief to evidence. Probably we all do things that we really know better than to do. Sometimes the price we pay is high. To act as if something is a sure thing, or a safe risk, when we really know it is not, is to fail to proportion action to evidence. It is in cases in which belief soon leads to conduct whose impact affects life and limb in determinable ways that it seems most natural to talk of proportioning belief to evidence. It was from such cases that the philosopher W. K. Clifford extrapolated in the principle's favor (his favorite example concerned ship owners whose concern for profit overcame their scruples about the risks they encouraged their employees to take). Clifford extrapolated to the claim that "it is wrong always, everywhere, and for anyone, to believe anything upon insufficient evidence."[2] Whether an average Zande tribesman, medieval peasant, English queen, or contemporary politician has sufficient evidence for embracing the fundamental features of their various world views, and if not whether they deserve moral censure for lacking it, I leave aside. It seems plain, however, that while Clifford's ship owners may have balmed their consciences by trying to believe dubiously safe ships were seaworthy, their chief sins were not epistemic. Whatever they managed to come to believe, they had information relevant to their employees' safety that they held back, and permitted others to take risks they were unaware of in order to line ship owners' pockets. Their sins were sins of conduct and of omission more than of private assent. Talk of "proportioning belief to evidence," recast in terms relevant to actual wrongs done, will purchase plausibility for the principle at the low price of revealing its irrelevance to the present dispute.[3]

I do not suggest that there is no ethics of belief. But what there is seems to me not much related to talk of proportioning degree of belief to strength of evidence.

Arguments from Experience

Philo is not shocked by Cleanthes' appeal to *a posteriori* arguments, though he professes to lament that among arguments from experience the argument from design appears "not to be even the most certain and irrefragable of that inferior kind." Strong arguments from experience, his examples suggest, have at least these features:

(1) An event E (the effect) is experienced which is a member of a class k1.

(2) There is another class k2 (a class of causes) such that the experienced members of k2 are in one-to-one causal correlation with the experienced members of k1, E being the lone exception.

Under such circumstances, we can infer that there was another member of k2 (say, C) such that C caused E, though we did not experience C. Or, if we have experienced C, we can, by the same reasoning *mutatis mutandis*, infer to an effect E of C, even though we did not happen to experience E.

Both events of the cause-class and events of the effect-class often have been experienced, and always together. No relevant dissimilarities appear between various instances of the cause-class and none appear between various instances of the effect-class. Weak arguments from experience, those "confessedly liable to error and uncertainty," involve a class of causes whose members are relevantly dissimilar and/or a class of effects whose members are relevantly dissimilar. That stones fall and fire burns (Philo's examples) can be shown by strong arguments from experience. So far as falling goes, when you've seen one stone, you've seen them all. But a house (or any other artifact) and the universe scarcely bear causal comparison.

Philo, in effect, adds a new axiom to the "everything is caused" principle and the "like effects, like causes" principle, namely:

(A3) The more properties effects E1 and E2 share, the more reasonable it is to suppose that their causes C1 and C2 share many properties.

Conversely, where "E1 and E2 do not share property X" means "Exactly one member of the set *E1, E2* has X" rather than "Either exactly one member of the set *E1, E2* has X or neither does:"

(A4) The more properties not shared by E1 and E2, the less reasonable it is to suppose that their causes C1 and C2 share many properties.

In Philo's words,

> Exact similarity of . . . cases gives us a perfect assurance of a similar event; and a stronger evidence is never desired or sought after. But wherever you depart, in the least, from the similarity of the cases, you diminish proportionately the evidence; and may at last bring it to a very weak *analogy,* which is confessedly liable to error and uncertainty. [*D,* 144]

One question about (A3) and (A4) is what denotation to allow to the word "property" (or in Philo's phrase, what range to allow the "exact similarity"). *Being round, being red,* and *weighing two pounds* are properties in anyone's book. *Being read, heaving spent an hour in Eric's pocket,* or *being thought about by all living physicists* are more debatable candidates. The endeavor to alleviate the problem by noting that the members of the former group of properties are monadic or non-relational whereas the members of the latter group are, if properties at all, relational or two-or-more-place properties (pedantically, properties whose symbolic expression requires two-or-more-place predicates), patently will not do. *Being an effect* and *being a cause* are themselves relational properties, as are spatial and temporal properties. Surely "property" covers such cases. In any case, probably the safe route is to allow as properties such widely divergent candidates as *being brown, being made only of lead, being seven inches long, having once been touched by Spinoza but owned only by Leibniz,* and *having been thought of once by Richard Nixon.*

However this question be resolved, it is not the central issue. Cleanthes points up the crucial matter in these remarks:

> Is the whole adjustment of means to ends in a house and in the universe so slight a resemblance? The economy of final causes? The order, proportion, and arrangement of every part? . . . this inference, I allow, is not altogether . . . certain, because of the dissimilarity which you remark; but does it, therefore, deserve the name only of presumption or conjecture? [*D,* 145]

"This inference" is that "legs are also contrived for walking and mounting," but of course it is the inference to a designer that is Cleanthes' major concern, so no license is taken when I apply his remarks to the argument from design.

Cleanthes, then, grants that there are many dissimilarities between the universe and that representative artifact, a house. But not every dissimilarity weakens an argument by analogy. Rocks may be dissimilar in color, weight, location, size, shape, value, and whether they have ever been pocketed by a little boy. They fall when dropped nonetheless. The universe and a house are unlike in size, but they are alike (according to Cleanthes) in possessing designedness. So if designedness-bearing is evidence of having being designed, all goes well with the argument from design.

To Philo's axioms, then, Cleanthes offers this appropriate emendation:

> (A5a) The more properties relevant to their causes C1 and C2 each being A that E1 and E2 are known to share, the more reasonable it is to suppose that C1 and C2 each is A.
>
> (A5b) The less properties relevant to their causes C1 and C2 each being A that E1 and E2 are known to share, the less reasonable it is to suppose that C1 and C2 each is A.

And where "being A" does duty for "being a designer," Cleanthes affirms, the relevant properties are "adjustment of means and ends," "economy of final causes," "order, proportion and arrangement of every part"—in sum, designedness. A house possesses this feature. So does the universe. So while your average house is composed of wood, cement, and nails but contains neither zebras nor galaxies, whereas the universe contains galaxies and zebras as well as wood, cement, and nails among its constituents, this is beside the point altogether. Diverse as they are, a house and the universe possess designedness, and that is all that is needed for, or relevant to, the argument from design. To take, say, size and diversity of components into account in the house-universe case, given that both a house and the universe possess designedness, is as unreasonable as taking into account that one rock is prized by Willie Jones but despised by Suzy Smith, whereas another is loved or hated by no one, when we ask: Will both drop when released?

Inductive Arguments and Lawlike Connections

Philo, apparently, is prepared to shift from (A3) and (A4) to (A5a) and (A5b). This seems quite right; given the proposition that the universe is a very complex thing comparable *qua* thing with artifacts, Cleanthes is right to press (A5a) and (A5b) into service.

Philo, of course, tries again by affirming that "all inferences . . . concerning fact are founded on experience" (*D*, 147). By fact, Philo presumably means "matter of fact," where a sentence expresses a matter of fact if and only if it expresses neither a necessary truth nor a contradiction and it is in principle testable by reference to sensory and/or introspective experience. (The roughness of the definition is patent but nonetheless faithful to Hume's view.) "Experience" includes only introspective and sensory experience. Moral, aesthetic, religious, or other varieties of experience are not included; more carefully, they are for Hume reducible in some sense to sensory and/or introspective experience. Thus that two plus two equals four is not, in this context, a fact, nor is "seeing that" two plus two is four in this context to be accounted an experience, being neither sensory nor introspective.

Philo takes a while to get to the idea behind his remarks about inference and experience, in the meantime raising sundry objections that we will consider shortly. But he comes to his point when he says:

> When two *species* of objects have always been observed to be conjoined together, I can *infer*, by custom, the existence of one wherever I *see* the existence of the other: And this I call an argument from experience. But how this argument can have place, where the objects, as in the present case, are single, individual, without parallel, or specific resemblance, may be difficult to explain. [*D*, 149]

Normally, arguments from an effect to its cause will have a certain pattern. Philo *defines* "argument from experience" by reference to this pattern. The element of such an argument will be: (a) an event or object E which is an effect and a member of kind K1; (b) other, past members of K1; (c) past members of kind K2 whose experienced members have been in one-to-one spatio-temporal correlation with past, experienced members of K1. The pattern of inference, roughly stated, starts with "All past, experienced members of K1 were in one-to-one spatio-temporal correspondence with past, experienced members of K2," and "Here is a newly experienced member of K2," and moves to "There was a member of K1 in spatio-temporal contiguity with this member of K2." Inference from effects to causes requires that the causes as well as the effects be members of species. Further, past experience must have included encounters with various members of both effect-species and cause-species.

Cleanthes' argument has a more complex pattern than the one just noted, for two effect-species and two cause-species are in question. By itself, this raises no insuperable difficulties. Its elements will be effects of E1 (of kind K1) and E2 (of kind K2), and causes C1 (of kind K3) and C2 (of kind K4). So we will infer from resemblance (in one respect) between E1 and E2 to resemblance (in another respect) between C1 and C2. The pattern will be:

(1) E1 belongs to K1, and whenever a member of K1 has been experienced it has been preceded by a member of K3, which is its cause.

(2) E1 is very like E2.

So:

(3) Probably, E2 has a cause that belongs to K4, whose members are very like the members of K3.

Filling in the variables:

(1′) Every house has been experienced to be preceded by a designer.

(2′) A house and the universe resemble one another regarding designedness.

So:

(3′) Probably, the universe has a cause that resembles a designer.

But, Philo argues with Peirce, universes are not as plentiful as blackberries. The universe is not a member of a species. Hence no argument from experience is possible concerning the cause, or any other property or relation, of the universe. As God is no more a species-member than is the universe, one could ring the changes on Philo's critique and note that no argument from experience *to a cause* is possible unless the cause inhabits a species, just as no argument from experience *from an effect* is possible unless the effect dwells inside some species' boundaries.

Philo contends, then, for Axiom (A6):

If the existence of a cause can be established with probability by an argument from experience, the *effect* must be a member of a species some of whose members we have experienced.

In stressing the uniqueness of the universe Philo is denying that it is such an effect. And while he does not here stress the matter, a natural supplement to (A6) is:

(A7) If the existence of a cause can be established with probability by an argument from experience, the *cause* must be a member of a species some of whose members we have experienced.

What Philo is driving at is probably best put in other terms than talk about species. What concerns him is this: if a connection is to be established by experience between a member of kind K1 and a member of kind K2 by an argument from experience, past experience must give us some reason to suppose that a lawlike connection holds between members of K1 and members of K2. Thus that the universe be a member of various classes is not sufficient for a conclusion of the form "the universe is" is to be derivable from an argument from experience. The universe must, under some description that classifies it with other things, be related to a member of another class *in a lawlike manner*. This is a relationship the universe cannot have to anything else, whether one takes a "constant spatio-temporal contiguity" view of lawlike connection or requires further and more stringent ties.

Inductive Argument and Argument by Analogy

At this point, those who chide Hume for dealing only with an analogical, but not an inductive, formulation of the argument from design do him (and the argument) a disservice. For *qua* inductive reasoning the argument from design is bankrupt whereas as analogical reasoning it may possess some force. The universe lacks constant spatio-temporal juxtaposition with anything in it you can name (or has it with everything in it, if one prefers). It hence has no lawlike relations with anything. Thus conclusions concerning the universe as a whole cannot be established by an inductive argument. But if the universe-designer relation is analogous in relevant ways to the artifact-artisan relation and the universe-artifact analogy is sufficiently cogent, perhaps the argument from design offers some reason to suppose there is a designer. But unless there is a resemblance between the universe and an artifact, even this version of the design argument fails.

Philo, then, contends for some such axiom as this:

(A8) If it is inductively inferred (from an argument from experience) that the cause C1 of E1 belongs to or resembles the members of a class K1 of causes, it must be the case that: (a) E1 belongs to a class of K2 of effects; (b) The experienced members of K2 have been discovered to be in one-to-one causal correspondence with the experienced members of K1, with the K2 items being effects and the K1 items being causes.

Thus a lawlike connection must exist between E1 and C1. Since the universe enters into no lawlike connections with anything, no inductive version of the design argument is possible. This, or something much like it, seems to be the purport of Philo's remarks about species.

The Design Argument and Postulation of Theoretical Entities

The lack of lawlike connections between the universe and any particular type of phenomenon destroys the analogy between the designer hypothesis and the postulation by scientists of unobserved and perhaps unobservable entities—for example, Newton's "minute anatomy of the rays of light." Astronomers require "other earths" (sun, moon, planets, stars) than our own in order to establish "the Copernican system" and Galileo proved the moon and earth to be made of the same sort of stuff by

> its similarity in every particular to the earth; its convex figure, its natural darkness when not illuminated. . . . After many instances of this kind, with regard to all the planets, men plainly saw, that these bodies became proper objects of experience; and that the similarity of their nature enabled us to extend the same arguments and phenomena from one to the other. In this cautious proceeding of the astronomers, you may read your own condemnation, Cleanthes; or rather may see, that the subject in which you are engaged exceeds all human reason and enquiry. [D, 151]

Philo's attack has two prongs: the astronomers infer that A is like B only if: (1) A and B are members of species (enter into lawlike concourse with other things); and (2) A and B are both "proper objects of experience" (are both directly observable). By appeal to the "minute anatomy of light" (not to mention atoms, elementary particles, neutrons, etc.) Cleanthes can escape (2); scientists do infer to unobserved objects—at least, to objects that are unobserved in any sense that Philo or Hume would accept. But by appeal to (1) Philo can indeed derail Cleanthes' design argument as a supposed train of inductive inference from the experienced to the unexperienced in the manner of the sciences, for scientific and other inductive reasoning requires that (1) be satisfied and the design argument violates (1).

We noted that it took a while for Philo to get to the point. He makes several stops along the way to pursue points of polemic not directly related to the main road of inquiry. Having followed the main road to its end (so far as Part Two is concerned) let us now look at the byways.

Relevant versus Irrelevant Properties

Philo begins with the point that "experience alone can point out . . . the true cause of any phenomenon" (146). Here, he and Cleanthes agree. If Cleanthes did not, he could appeal to other arguments than that from design in order to establish a cause of order in the universe. The design argument is intended as an *a posteriori* argument. Part of the force of this can be put in our previous language, by saying that "X possesses designedness" does not entail "X was designed." If it did, the argument from design would be unnecessary, though perhaps an argument *to* designedness would still be required.

Philo, in effect, grants that when considering whether the universe, like a house, is designed although there are plenty of properties not shared between them, only *relevant* properties need be considered. But can we rightly be as confident as Cleanthes that we *know* which are relevant to being designed? "Unless the objects be quite familiar to us, it is the highest temerity to expect with assurance, after any of these changes (i.e., dissimilarities), an event similar to that which before fell under our observation" (*D*, 147). Cleanthes' reply, presumably is that we do know this; *the* property relevant to having been designed is simply *possessing designedness*.

The Fallacy of Composition

Again, is not Cleanthes guilty of the "fallacy" of composition, inferring from 'The parts of the universe are machine-like' to 'The universe is machine-like' or from 'The parts of the universe possess designedness' to 'The universe possesses designedness?' It is true that such reasoning is not always fallacious; if we know that all the parts of a machine are made only of lead, we are entitled to infer that the machine is made only of lead. In moving from 'The parts of X are A' to 'X is A,' one's success depends on what property "A" turns out to be. It is also true that 'is a machine,' 'has a purpose,' and 'possesses designedness' are properties whose possession by the parts of a whole does not guarantee the whole's possession of them. A collection of machines need not be a machine; a set of items each of which has a purpose need not itself have a purpose, and a class of objects each of which is so arranged that its parts produce a uniform product by a predictable process need not itself yield any further uniform product via predictable process of its own. But it is also the case that the whole *may* have the property its parts distributively possess, and even if Cleanthes may sometimes illegitimately infer from part to whole he also at times argues that the whole (the universe) has design-relevant features (designedness) without the illicit inference. Further, he seems right on this score.

Philo also remarks that in our experience order is associated with other things besides intelligent design. "Intelligence . . . is no more than one of the springs and principles of the universe, as well as heat or cold, attraction or repulsion, and a hundred others, which fall under daily observation" (*D*, 147). The "hundred others" are reduced later to generation, vegetation, necessity, and instinct (178) and Philo will develop and press this important objection then. In Part Two he only adds that in our experience more order comes from non-intelligent causes than from intelligent, an allegation we shall consider later.

Opposing Analogies

Still another point should be noticed. Philo balances Cleanthes' analogy between the universe and an artifact with a different analogy. Cleanthes' analogy provides, in part, one way of looking at natural phenomena—seeing them as productions of a superhuman (but not omniscient or omnipotent) intelligence. Philo, in effect, produces another perspective. This analogy *seems* to support Cleanthes: as stones do not put themselves together into a cathedral, so molecules do not put themselves together into a stone. What strikes Philo is the implausibility of the analogy:

> Admirable conclusion! Stone, wood, brick, iron, brass have not, at this time, in this minute globe of earth, an order of arrangement without human art and contrivance: therefore the universe could not originally attain its order and arrangement, without something similar to human art. But is a part of nature a rule for another part very wide of the former? Is it a rule for the whole? Is a very small part a rule for the universe? Is nature in one situation, a certain rule for nature in another situation, vastly different from the former? [*D*, 149]

Philo is again more impressed by the disanalogy than the analogy.

Another matter deserves brief mention. The "beyond our weak

capacities and ordinary experience" theme appears again as Philo re-
signedly answers that "I never should expect any success from its
[reason's] feeble conjectures—in a subject, so sublime, and so remote
from the sphere of our observation" (*D*, 149). At least part of the point
of this remark is to keep a promise to Demea that "with your assis-
tance . . . I shall endeavor to defend what you justly call the adorable
mysteriousness of the divine nature, and shall refute this reasoning of
Cleanthes" (*D*, 146). Thus does Hume keep this theme before our
eyes without here making it preeminent.

Is the Universe a Thing?

Two other matters relevant to Part Two deserve brief mention.
One is that, as he has thus far conducted the argument from design,
Cleanthes is committed to the assumption that the universe is some
sort of thing. If this meant that the universe must be treated as having
spatial boundaries when it is perhaps infinite, or as having temporal
boundaries when perhaps its duration is without start or finish, or as
weighing so many pounds, or the like, it would be objectionable for
fairly obvious reasons. But so far as I can see all that Cleanthes requires is that the universe be a thing in the sense of actually possessing some property or properties, and in *that* sense of "thing" the universe is one. For surely the universe, whether finite or infinite in
extension, is larger than my left thumb, and whether of beginningless
or endless duration or not, it is older than my shoelaces. Necessarily,
there is only one universe; it has what we might dub "necessary
uniqueness" in the sense that it can have no actual twin. Nonetheless,
its existence is logically contingent ("Nothing exists" being neither
senseless nor contradictory) though not therefore causally contingent, for its causal contingency is a further question.

While I have deliberately ascribed some properties to the universe
that not all philosophers would agree belong to it, others on my list
look innocuous enough. So the universe has some properties, and is
in that sense (the sense Cleanthes' argument requires) a thing.

Perhaps one reason why the universe is sometimes disallowed
from even this thin sort of thinghood is that the universe is supposedly only a *class* of items, not itself an item in a class. Thus my
body is a class of what Saint Paul (in the King James version) called
the "bodily members," but is also itself a thing or a member of the
class of bodies. But the universe, while containing many members, is
not a member of the class of universes, there being no such class.

It seems to me that this line of reasoning bristles with problems. From one point of view, for which Leibniz is famous, there *are* various possible universes though only one can exist. So the truth of the matter is that our universe is a member of a class—the class of all possible universes—only one member of which can be actual. One might retort that necessarily, if anything is a member of a class then it can be joined by other members of the same class. But what justifies this dictum?

If being a member of a class is simply being something sorted out from other things by the fact of possessing a (one-or-more-membered) set of properties the universe belongs to lots of classes and there are plenty of necessarily one-membered classes. Thus the universe is a member of the class of things containing more than a billion members and the class of things larger than my left thumb, and the class of first reader of Hume's *Treatise* and the class of most recently deceased authors are necessarily singly populated if populated at all. In this sense, the universe is a member of many classes as well as being a class of many members, and it is a member of the class of classes that are instantiated at most once.

Or perhaps the detractors of the universe's thinghood are impressed by the body's being an organism but take the universe to be a mere collection. A tally of the body's parts yields a taxonomy but a tally of the universe's parts provides an unwieldy grocery list. But this seems false, as the current stress on ecology suggests and such principles as the conservation of energy require. Physicists consider the physical universe as a closed system in which no total energy loss or gain occurs, each plus shift being perfectly balanced by a minus shift.

In sum, scientists and philosophers tend to view the universe as a *system*, not a collection. Some philosophers have taken the universe to be at least analogous to an organism and for Leibniz there is, as it were, a conceptual ecology among the monads. There is some point to the organism analogy, and in any case the universe is plausibly viewed as possessing a taxonomy all its own.

One reservation more deserves mention.

The number five has properties too; is it a thing? If we take "the number five" to refer to an entity, a quasi-Platonic denizen of an abstract universe, it is not a class and is an individual. Like Plato's Forms it will have instances but not members, participants but not parts. While this formation is clearer in what it denies than in what it affirms (what *is* it to have *instances* or *participants* in *this* sense?), five as an entity is no class. Or if "the number five" just connotes all the five-member-sets there are (or might be? were? will be?) then perhaps it is a class but not also a thing, though things will comprise its parts. Just, then, as "the number five" can be construed as applying to *one* thing which has neither members nor parts, or as a class of five-membered classes, but not both in the same sense of the term, so the universe may be construed as applying to one thing or as applying to very many classes of things but not both in the same sense of the term.

But this argument seems wrong. "The class of all-five membered sets" has a mere collection as what it denotes. "The universe" does not. If "the universe" denotes a class—the class of everything there is, or everything that is except God—it also (like "body") denotes a system governed by laws and wedded together by the concourse of its constituents. Not so for the class of all five-membered combinations.

Being Designed and Having a Purpose

A more serious issue arises at this point. Suppose we grant that, in the sense the design argument requires, the universe is a thing. Does it possess designedness? More carefully, if it does, do we know that it does? If not, the argument from design, at least in its present version, is at an end.

Cleanthes emphasizes "the economy of final causes" in the universe, but he is surprisingly reticent concerning the purpose the universe itself serves. Unlike such things as houses, legs, and eyes (but quite like such things as rocks and earwigs) it is not easy to assign an end that the universe serves or ought to serve. Perhaps we are to understand that Cleanthes does not know what the purpose of the universe is. Can he then plausibly claim that it has a purpose though he does not know what that purpose might be?

Suppose that Herbert Jacobsen, crossing the Sahara alone, discovers a five-foot cube whose corners and edges are sharply defined but whose material is old. Obviously, someone has *made* the cube. Left to itself, the material would erode and the sharp edges and corners be worn down. Herb may not ever discover what possessed its artificer to produce this artifact. But he can nonetheless rightly claim to know it *is* an artifact.

It may then be suggested that no corresponding property can be mentioned which is such that, if the universe is known to possess it, then it is known to have a purpose, whether or not its purpose is known.

A distinction is required here. Herb knows the cube is an artifact (has an artificer); he does not know why the artificer artificed. Nor does he strictly know whether the cube has or had a purpose. An artisan presumably can carve aimlessly, so producing a cube; or carve a cube as he intended without intending to do anything with the cube (including creating an art object). "X is an artifact" entails "X was produced by an intelligent being." It does not entail "X has a purpose" or "The intelligent being had a purpose in producing X." Knowing that the universe was artificed neither entails nor presupposes knowing *that* it has a purpose nor that its artificer had a purpose in producing it. Hence knowing that the universe was artificed neither entails nor presupposes knowing *what* its purpose is.

If this in one way lessens Cleanthes' burden, it also decreases the significance of his conclusion. Suppose he proves that more probably than not the universe had an intelligent artificer. *By itself*, what possible difference could that make? Would it show that "mind is more ultimate in this world" than, say, Bertrand Russell thought? Yes, slightly. But the artificer might himself have arisen from purely non-intelligent causes, so only slightly. Should we rejoice? Yes, if the artificer wishes our weal and can aid us. But on neither point does the argument provide any information. Should we fear? Yes, if the artificer wishes our woe and can bring it to pass. But again we are uninformed. Not every possible purposive world is a good, or even a pleasant, one. So far as simply being purposive goes, a world designed so that all people suffer injustice equally, eternally, and incessantly is admirably qualified. The moral, religious, and practical impact of the discovery simply of an artificer, no further information forthcoming, seems to be nil. There is no reason why anyone should care. That *God* exists is another matter altogether.

Could one know that the universe has a *good* purpose without knowing what that purpose is? Yes, surely, if he knew that an all-good and all-powerful God created the world for a purpose. But Cleanthes cannot utilize this move, for it is the existence and intelligence of God that the argument from design is intended to establish. Hence Cleanthes must know that whether or not the world has a purpose, it at least possesses designedness, without having to know that God so much as exists.

Does the world possess designedness? Perhaps the strongest reason for saying so is the *de facto* existence of scientific inquiries which find the universe to be a system shot through with regularities. Various scientists have been impressed with the "as-if-designed" appearance of natural phenomena, and an Omnicompetent Mathematician has been postulated as the source of this massive orderliness. No doubt for any possible state of affairs there is some way or other in which it is ordered—in which an intrepid mathematician could discover some pattern and describe it by some formula. But the universe has seemed to many of its students to possess a magnitude of orderliness far above the minimal whether or not they postulated a designer. It seems plausible that, given the success of the sciences (and that the order they recount has been discovered, not imposed) the universe indeed possesses designedness.

By now, however, it should be clear that even if designedness were undeniable proof of a designer, it does not show the existence of a purpose of the universe. For, as we have seen, an artificer can display intelligence by aimlessly artificing (that is by unintentionally producing what only an intelligent being can unintentionally produce) or by intentionally producing something which has no purpose at all. Rube Goldberg machines have a purpose of sorts—to turn themselves off? A cube carved by a careless whittler need not be even Rube Goldbergish. Even if "the universe has designedness, so it has a designer" is good reasoning, the designer may be good and providential, or a cosmic Rube Goldberg, or a careless whittler grown larger than life. Hume, in his own way, raises similar issues as we shall see. Since considerations of multiple purposes, whether all part of the overall purpose or not, raises no new issues, we can ignore it here without loss.

CHAPTER 9

Inductive Arguments and Analogical Arguments

Cleanthes' Attempt to Avoid Philo's Critique (*Dialogues*, Part Three)

PHILO'S CRITIQUE is plainly powerful. Cleanthes does perhaps the one thing left to do besides quit the field. The plausibility of an axiom of inductive inference is reduced or removed if a plainly successful inductive argument violates it. In part, the art of constructing axioms of inductive inference rests on intuitions about which inductive arguments initially (that is, prior to rules) are cogent and which initially are not.

Then one can ask what renders the unacceptable inductive endeavors subject to cognitive disapproval. If one is so fortunate as to discover an axiom that many unreliable arguments and no acceptable ones violate, perhaps one has found a perfectly general axiom of inductive inference. Conversely, one can query an axiom by discovering an apparently bad argument that it sanctions.

What a clever Cleanthes will try, then, is to discover a patently acceptable inductive argument that violates Philo's axioms. If he can discover such a valuable property, he can reject those axioms with impunity, or at least raise an important doubt about them, thereby reviving his design argument.

Inductions from Single Cases

Cleanthes, then, offers two inferences that he takes to be patently allowable. The premises (as Cleanthes of course is aware) in each case are false, and it is the *pattern of inference* that is crucial. The first inference (slightly festooned) is from (1) to (2):

(1) There is an articulate voice heard at the same time all over the globe, by each nation in its own language and dialect, that speaks a message both profound and beneficial to all people, providing information which would have been inaccessible without the voice having announced it.

So, probably:

(2) This voice has an intelligent cause.

The second inference pattern goes from (3) to (4):

(3) There is a single language shared by all people which is also the language of "natural volumes" (books "which perpetuate themselves in the same manner with animals and vegetables, by descent and propagation") that contain profound and beautiful reasonings.

So, probably:

(4) The language and natural volumes have an intelligent cause (one which bears "the strongest analogy to mind and intelligence").

Cleanthes supposes that the second inference concerns a state of affairs closer to reality than the first, and we will see why he makes this less than obvious suggestion shortly. Our main interest is in the inference from (1) to (2) and in the inference from (3) to (4). They are similar inferences; let us for the moment concentrate on the inference from (1) to (2).

Cleanthes stresses several things about it: (i) the voice is unlike other, human voices in regard to loudness, being broken into diverse dialects, possessing great profundity of thought and expression, and so on; it is an effect dissimilar in various ways from other verbal effects; (ii) it is not logically impossible that the voice "proceeded . . . from some accidental whistling of the wind" (*D*, 153); (iii) the voice occurs but once; (iv) it has no lawlike connection with anything in our experience; (v) nonetheless, it would be wrong to deny that the inference from (1) to (2) is altogether more plausible than any other inference from (1), and more reasonable than no inference at all.

Cleanthes' strategy seems altogether appropriate—he picks at least *a* correct way of challenging Philo's axioms. Further, the voice example is a plausible one. If such a voice were heard, it does seem that the most reasonable view of it would be that its cause was an intelligent being—if we found that no known device that might produce such an effect existed, and no known natural phenomenon could produce such an effect. This will be so even though Cleanthes' argument can neither appeal to nor establish a lawlike connection between the voice and its cause. Hence the availability of lawlike connections between those things over which its premises range is not after all a necessary condition of the success of the design argument.

At this point, perhaps a deep parting of the ways occurs. A follower of Philo can insist that it remains a condition of good inductive arguments from experience that relations between things *like* the items (for example, voices and intelligent beings in ordinary cases) over which the premises range be capturable in lawlike statements. At least, a Philonian may hold, there must be analogous classes of causes and effects, with members of both classes falling within our experience as causally connected. A follower of Cleanthes may deny this, holding that no law-like connection need hold between the natural volumes and their cosmic author, or between the articulate voice and its source in order for the argument to be a good one. Then either causality does not hold only between items that are related in a lawlike manner, or the author/volume and source/voice connections are not to be understood causally. (Then, of course, an account is needed of how they are to be understood.)

Suppose that Cleanthes endeavors to construct the design argument along the Philonian line that requires that things like source and voice be causally connected within our experience. Cleanthes, then, in effect is affirming that the design argument is a two-stage argument. One stage will concern the artificer-artifact relationship, viewed as experienced and causal (and perhaps lawlike). The other state will involve an inference by analogy to a cosmic designer of the universe. Only stage one is an inductive argument from experience. The first stage is an inductive argument which can perhaps be put in this fashion. It will be useful here to make use of a somewhat artificial notion that we shall dismiss later. Let us coin the term "shartifact" for anything that (a) is not known to have no human designer, (b) has parts in an order never knowingly observed to have been produced by unaided natural processes, (c) possesses designedness, and (d) raises the suspicions of at least some of its reflective and rational examiners that it had a designer. Obviously, I suppose, all (or very many) artifacts are shartifacts, and necessarily, all artifacts have designers. But are all shartifacts artifacts? Well, there are various relevant sub-classes of shartifacts, one being *those known by observation to be artifacts,* and another *those not known by observation to be artifacts.* Were we to read "known by observation" strictly, only cars *observed* to come off the assembly line and only hand-carved wood figurines made by *attentive* artisans would fit into the former class. Were a productive machine to be left unattended, or a whittler to carve a figurine without noticing what he was doing, the product would not be *known by observation* to be an artifact. But we can use "known by observation" more generously, so that if the machine stamps "made in Hong Kong" on its products or the whittler notices that he has unwittingly produced a figurine while attending to the antics of his favorite football team, their products too fit our first class. Suppose, however, that we find an item with no known artificers, no stamp or signature, in a place hitherto (so far as we know) unoccupied and unvisited by human beings. Let the item be possessed of (a) through (d) above so that it is clearly a shartifact. We can then argue:

(1) Many shartifacts are artifacts.

(2) This item shares many properties with known artifacts (in particular, designedness).

So:

(3) Probably, this item is an artifact.

The item is not complex or large enough to elicit reference to a non-human designer, but does deserve full artifactual status, including being ascribed to a designer. The argument, our Cleanthean will maintain, is an ordinary inductive argument of the form: previous members of the class K2 (things having designedness) are known to belong to the class K1 (things having designers). Here is a new member of K2. So probably it belongs also to class K1. The Cleanthean hope now will be that the axiom

(A8) If it is inductively inferred that the cause C1 of E1 resembles the members of a class K1 of causes, it must be the case that (a) E1 belongs to a class K2 of effects (b) a large sub-set of the experienced members of K1 have been discovered to be in one-to-one causal correspondence with a large sub-set of the experienced members of K2, with the K2-items being effects and the K1-items being causes.

is not violated if we conceive of shartifacts as divided into the two indicated sub-classes. The class of shartifacts contains another pair of sub-classes. It contains *things known by observation to be artifacts* and *things known by inductive inference to be artifacts*. A 1966 Valiant belongs to the former; Paley's watch to the latter. If Philo is right, the universe belongs to neither of these sub-classes since it bears no law-like relations to a set of species co-members. Nonetheless (if Cleanthes is right) it is like a shartifact, sharing properties (let us grant) (b) through (d) with such items. It plainly possesses designedness and many suspect it has an intelligent cause. Arguably, it possesses designedness, looks designed, has parts in an order never knowingly observed to have been produced by unaided natural processes; suppose, then, that the universe is like a shartifact. If we consider these sub-classes of shartifacts, then to claim of a shartifact that it is also an artifact we will need some proof of this fact beyond any yielded by an inductive argument. For if we try to construct an argument for "The universe is an artifact" analogous to that for "Paley's watch is an artifact" we shall run afoul of (A8). For the universe, lacking (a), is not a member the appropriate class K2 of effects. A follower of Philo, then, will claim that (A8) is violated after all.

What is crucial, then, is not merely that the universe lacks membership in some such class as those described above. What is crucial is that the universe—the orderly heap of all causes and effects, save God—is not *itself* related by any lawlike proposition to any of its members. It is not related as cause to its components, nor as effect. So while we can describe various classes of which the universe is a member, we cannot describe a class of which the universe is a member, all of whose members—the universe included—is related as cause or as effect to the members of some other class. No law is such that it has the form "—— is the cause of . . ." or "—— is the effect of . . ." where (i) "the universe" fills in one of the blanks, and (ii) the other blank is so filled in that the result is a pair of classes whose members are in one-to-one causal correlation.

Review and Prospect

Things have become a little complicated. We have the Philonian possibility that law-like connection must hold between members of classes over which inductive arguments range. Then, as the artificer's relationship to her artifact is not law-like, the design argument cannot get off the ground. The Cleanthean rebuttal is that the author/volume and source/voice inferences are perfectly rational. While they can be so stated as to be deductively valid, so can any inductive argument. Both of the following arguments are deductively valid.

Argument A

(1) This item has designedness.

(2) Every experienced object discovered to have designedness about which we have learned whether or not it was designed has turned out to have been designed.

(3) If (1) and (2) are true, then it is probable that this item was designed.

So:

(4) Probably, this item was designed.

Argument B

(1) This item is an artifact.

(2) Necessarily, if this item is an artifact, then it had an artificer.

So:

(3) This item had an artificer.

But *A* is a probability argument and *B* is not. The interesting issues about the rational credentials of *A* lie mainly in questions about premise (3) of that argument; these are the same questions as would arise if (3) were removed from *A* and we simply inferred from premises (1) and (2) to the conclusion (4).

Next, consider:

Argument C

(1) An articulate voice was heard over all the earth, speaking wise things intelligible to persons of every dialect and tongue.

(2) If (1), then probably the voice has an intelligent cause.

So:

(3) Probably, the voice had an intelligent cause.

Argument *C* is another probability argument. It is deductively valid, but its rational credentials, insofar as propriety of inference is concerned, depend on the epistemic status of premise (2). The issues about that premise are the same issues as arise if we drop premise (2) and infer directly from premise (1) to the conclusion (3).

The Cleanthean contention is that arguments A and C are good arguments. They contain no inferential impropriety. Premise (3) of argument A, and premise (2) of argument C, are true. This is so even though the items over which those arguments range are not related in a law-like way. Both arguments are probability arguments—inductive arguments, if you please. So an inductive argument can be in good inferential form even though it does not range over items that stand to one another in law-like relationships.

Cleanthes, then, can claim that causality can relate items that are not related in a law-like manner. Philo could grant this and endeavor to recoup his losses by insisting that nevertheless the items over which an inductive argument from experience ranges must, *under the relevant descriptions*, be at least possible objects of experience, where the relevant descriptions are simply those under which the objects make their appearance in an inductive argument from experience. Since "being the cause of design in the universe" and "having design-edness that is caused by a cosmic artificer" are not descriptions under which anything could be observed, they are not descriptions under which anything may appear in an inductive argument from experience. Since these are the descriptions that are crucial to the design argument, that argument, Philo can contend, cannot be an inductive argument from experience.

So Cleanthes has a new response to construct, if he can. This response can be developed along the lines of a two-stage argument, the first stage of which is an inductive argument from experience and the second stage of which is an argument by analogy that rests for its cognitive force on the propriety of Cleanthes' reasoning in the voice and volume cases—on the inferential propriety of argument C and its analogue concerning natural volumes.

The Philonian argument necessitates an addition to axiom (A8), and all later reference to this axiom will be to this refined version:

> (A8) If it is inductively inferred that the cause C1 of effect E1 resembles the members of a class K1 of causes, it must be the case that (a) E1 belongs to a class K2 of effects, (b) a large sub-set of the experienced members of K1 have been discovered to be in one-to-one causal correspondence with the experienced members of a large sub-set of K2, with the K2 items being effects and the K1 items being causes, and (c) the members of K1 and K2 must be experienceable under the descriptions of them contained in the premises and the conclusion of the argument.

Under condition (b), even if we sometimes do not experience an effect belonging to K2 when we experience a cause belonging to K1, we may still infer that there was such an effect if (b) is satisfied—especially if we can explain our failure to observe the new effect other than by its not being there to be observed. *Mutatis mutandis*, the same thing holds for the case where we observe a member of K2 but observed no member of K1. "Causal correspondence" is so understood here as not to require law-like connection.

We lack an appropriate axiom to cover the second stage of this Cleanthean response. We can, however, in the light of Cleanthes' voice example, formulate the axiom:

(A9) If it is inferred by analogy that the cause X of effect Y resembles the members of a class K1 of causes, it must be the case that (a) there is a successful inductive argument to the effect that E1 is caused by C1, (b) E1 and Y must be analogous, (c) X can only be said to be as analogous to C1 as is Y to E1, (d) there is no Z such that Z is as analogous to C1 as is X.

Of course, (A9) is rather roughshod. For example, how are we to measure "as analogous as?" Still, something like (A9) is what Cleanthes requires—and his voice example perhaps gives (A9) some plausibility. Further, later Philo in effect picks up the question of what to do with "as analogous as." So let us grant Cleanthes (A9) for the sake of the argument, at least to see how the argument fares with this addition.

A Two-Stage Design Argument

On the present account, then, of the design argument, it contains two stages, the first of which is an ordinary inductive argument from experience. The first stage, that is, is an argument sanctioned by (A8). While Cleanthes does not himself offer such a rephrasing, one can be constructed along the lines indicated above. It will look something like the following: Let an item that is observable under a description appropriate to an inductive argument from experience be *inductible*. Then the first stage of our Cleanthean argument runs:

(1) Each inductible member of the class of artifacts is caused to possess designedness by some member or other of the class of designers.
(2) Each inductible member of the class of artifacts possesses instances of the members of the property set (a) through (d).

(3) Each inductible member of the class of shartifacts possesses instances of the members of the property set (a) through (d).

So, probably:

(4) Each inductible member of the class of shartifacts is caused to possess designedness by some member of the class of designers.

Items possessing instances of (a) through (d) that are found in archaeological digs presumably are shartifacts concerning which premise (3) is true. Premises (1) through (3) are to be read as entailing that the classes in question have members; they express logically contingent claims. So, of course, does (4).

An item that is not inductible, of course, is uninductible. Then the second stage of our Cleanthian argument will run:

(1) Each inductible member of the class of shartifacts possesses the property set (a) through (d).
(2) Probably, each inductible member of the class of shartifacts is caused by some member or other of the class of designers.
(3) Each uninductible member of the class of shartifacts possesses the property set (a) through (d).

So, probably:

(4) Each uninductible member of the class of shartifacts is caused by something that resembles the members of the class of designers as much as a shartifact resembles an artifact.
(5) The universe shares properties (b) through (d) with shartifacts.

So, probably:

(6) The cause of the universe resembles the cause of the class of artifacts.

Being uninductible in the sense defined is compatible with being experienced in a variety of ways. One can observe that the universe is complex, large, and has designedness; the universe is observable under many descriptions. But (the Philonic claim is) none of these descriptions appear in good inductive arguments.

There are, of course, certain problems with the first stage of our Cleanthean argument. For one thing, necessarily an artifact has a designer; but inductive arguments presumably ought to range over properties that belong contingently to the members of the classes with which the argument is concerned. This argument is not decisive. One can argue to the probability of getting three pairs of threes on three consecutive fair throws of a fair pair of dice. But the result is a *necessary* truth; the probability is necessarily what it is. The relevant premises, too, are necessary truths; this is not so in the design argument. Perhaps, then, the relevant response to the objection is that all but one of the properties over which the design argument ranges are contingent. Again, it is not in fact clear that the property-set in question in premise 2 is related *in a lawlike manner* with the members of the class of artifacts. Indeed, it seems rather clearly not related to them in a lawlike manner. Further, analogous remarks apply, *mutatis mutandis*, to premise 3. Still, if one abides by the compromise described earlier, all one will demand is that the items be experiencable under the descriptions under which they make their appearance in the argument. This, not law-like relatedness, is what is essential to inductibility. In any case, here I wish to concentrate on the second stage of the argument.

Restated in the most succinct possible terms, and assuming the conclusion of the first stage, it will run as follows:

> (5) The universe shares properties (b) through (d) with shartifacts.

So, probably:

> (6) The cause of the universe resembles the members of the class of the cause of artifacts.

Of course, one who offered this second stage would have to hope that the universe resembling shartifacts with respect to only properties (b) through (d), but not with respect to (a)—namely, not being known not to have a human designer—is enough of a resemblance to support the inference from stage one and (5) to (6). The relation between the universe and the property-set (b) through (d) is plainly not lawlike, and so *if* the inference from stage one and (5) to (6) is legitimate, then (as intended) appeal must be made to (A9) rather than (A8).

In the second stage, it is inferred that the cause (X) of the universe (Y) resembles the members of a class of causes (C1)—namely, designers—of a class E1 of effects (namely, shartifacts). *If* stage one is a satisfactory inductive argument for premise 4, condition (a) of (A9) will have been met. If premise 5 is true, condition (b) of (A9) is met. The phrasing of the conclusion (6), given condition (c) of (A9), becomes:

(6') The cause of the universe resembles the members of C1 (that is, designers) as much as the universe resembles a shartifact. It is obvious that (6') leaves us wondering "how much is that?" and this question, as we noted above, comes up for later discussion in the *Dialogues* so we may leave it for later treatment in the discussion of this part, and also of Part Seven. That premise 6 satisfies condition (d) of (A9)—that there is no Z such that Z is as analogous to shartifacts as shartifacts are to the universe—is problematic. In explaining why this is so, it will be useful to have a modest notion of an *inductible property*. Suppose that an item is inductible under some description D. Then those properties by virtue of which D is true of that item are inductible properties. Properties that are not inductible, then, are *uninductible*.

Argument by Analogy to Properties of the Universe's Designer

The virtue of (A9) is that it will allow us to argue by induction and analogy that the universe has certain properties. But as things stand, (A9) has a precisely corresponding vice. It allows us to ascribe any property at all to the universe. There is one qualification on this contention, but it is not one that will comfort Cleanthes.

What (A9) allows is this: (i) suppose that C1 and E1 are causally connected or related by law or that C1 and E1 both are experienceable and that an appropriate inductive argument, sanctioned by (A8), has been developed; (ii) suppose that E1 and the universe *qua* ordered (which shares no inductible properties with E1) share uninductible relevant property A; then one may infer that C1 and the universe's cause share an uninductible property B. (So far as [A9] as developed thus far goes, A and B may or may not be the same property.)

Consider some effect E1—say the flight of a ball. On one account, the flight of the ball is divisible into space-time slices. So, on this view, is the universe. Whether or not this view is defensible, it has pedagogical value here. Sentences of the form "―― has space-time slices" are entailed by hosts of inductible descriptions, but not conversely. Nothing is related by law to, or shares being experienceable with, anything else simply because both "have" spatio-temporal slices. So there is an uninductible property A shared by E1 and the universe—namely, having space-time slices. Hence there will be, by some analogy sanctioned by (A9), some property B shared by the cause of E1 and the cause of order in the universe.

Let C1 be the striking of the ball. C1 has, let us suppose, these properties: is a consciously performed action (B1), involves physical motion (B2), requires physical apparatus (B3), is performed on a Tuesday (B4), and is approved by Sharon (B5). Then X—the cause of the universe—shares some property B with C1. What property will B be? It can be, so far as (A9) goes, any of B1 through B5, or all of them, or none of them. Indeed, I suspect that given sufficient ingenuity, for any uninductible property B you please such that "The cause of order in the universe has B" has consistent instances, B can be ascribed to the universe's cause of order on the basis of some argument by analogy sanctioned by (A9).

It may be objected that the last clause—clause (d)—of (A9) refutes my contention. Clause (d) read: There is no Z such that Z is as analogous to C1 as X (the cause of order in the universe). So all we have to do is to find some *one* property B such that nothing not possessing B is as like C1 as is something having it. Finding that property is, in one sense, easy. Consider the single property—set S such that a property P is included in S if and only if C1 has P. The property B that we seek is, maximally, S; anything having S will be as like C1 as you can get. Perhaps some of those properties are necessarily possessed by only one item. So consider set S', which is S minus all those properties which are such that, if anything has them, only C1 does—minus such properties as 'being the second son of Herb and Phyllis.' Then the property B will just be S'. But while C1 has S', C1 and X can share only uninductible properties. So we must consider S^*, which is S' minus all its inductible members; and then $B = S^*$.

What is contained in S^*, though, will depend on what particular event C1 is, and that will in turn depend on which particular inductive argument is chosen to comprise stage one of an argument by analogy. We know what argument Cleanthes has in mind. But Philo will offer other arguments, and these will suggest different analogies. Further, I suspect that, for any property B we wish to ascribe to the cause of order in the universe, we can—given only sufficient ingenuity—select an inductive argument sanctioned by (A8) at least as much as is Cleanthes' stage one argument that in turn will suggest an argument by analogy which (A9) will sanction, where the conclusion of the argument by analogy is "The cause of the universe's order has B." So we are back where we started when appeal was made to clause (d). Hence appeal to clause (d) provides no rebuttal to my contention. (See Chapter 10, especially "Various Models for Understanding Universal Order.")

Further, it should be clear now both how to supplement (A9) so as to guarantee a connection between the property A ascribed to Y and the property B ascribed to X, though by itself the supplement will not help much. The requisite supplement is the following:

(e) The property B ascribed to X must be a property such that the possession of B by X explains the possession of A by the universe, supposing the analogy to provide a proper model for explanation of the universe.

In Cleanthes' argument, the model is designer-designed object. So the substitute for or value of "B" must be such that (a) C1 has it and (b) possession of it by the universe's cause X will explain the occurrence of property A in the universe. But the universe's cause being, say, *something prized by Sharon* will not enter into the explanation of its being ordered.

In considering (e), we had best look more closely at the strategy of the design arguer. She finds a resemblance between order in the universe and order in an artifact. She knows how to explain order in the artifact. She wishes to explain order in the universe in the same way, insofar as this is possible. An artificer of cosmic order of course will be more powerful and intelligent than the designer of even the most complex artifact. The human designer will have a body, but if someone designed the universe then that someone is not himself part of the universe—one does not design his own body. So the cosmic designer has no body, since if he did he would be part of his own design, a piece of his own artifact. (At least, he has one only if he wishes, and non-essentially.) Having no body, he does not use his hands to mold or make anything. So there are these, and other, disanalogies between the cause of cosmic order and the cause of order in a watch, a pen, or a dictaphone. If the design argument is to work, there must be more than these dissimilarities.

There must be similarities too—and the similarities will constitute the crux of the analogy. Indeed, they will *comprise* the analogy. But there are similarities—both the cosmic and the terrestrial designers are intelligent and possess power. They can think and act. "X designs Y" entails "X thought and acted," and if the designer has neither ceased to exist nor undergone a serious atrophy of his powers, he can still think and act; unfortunately, the design argument by itself does not guarantee that the designer still lives and flourishes. "X designed Y" does not entail "X has a body" but it also does not entail "X still lives." (What "X is a designer" entails, besides intelligence and power, can no doubt be disputed; my concern here is to expound the design arguer's strategy.) So with respect to (A9) and any particular class of effects, any particular value of Y, and any specific analogy suggested by the resemblance between the members of the class of effects and Y, one will be able to specify what is the requisite value of "B"—the property or properties to be assigned to Y's cause. Hence not just any old property can be ascribed to the universe by an argument by analogy which is sanctioned by (A9), provided we supplement (A9) by (e). So, at least, a Cleanthean will contend.

The Most Plausible Analogy or Model

There is point to this reply. I think it, or something much like it, will reduce the number of candidates for filling out the sentence form "The universe is ———." But there are various classes of effects to which the universe bears some resemblance, and also various analogies suggested by these resemblances—analogies that each propose their distinct explanation of how the universe came to have the property or properties that constitute the resemblance in question (or perhaps *classes* of resemblances, each class suggesting some particular analogy—or even class of analogies). So long as this is so, at least various candidates for being the appropriate value of "B" are available. Perhaps (A9), with (e) included, orders the chaos a bit by setting higher conditions for candidates for being the value of "B" in an argument by analogy sanctioned by (A9) than were present in (A9) without (e). Still, more candidates are available than can fill the vacancy. We shall need some such addition as:

> (f) The analogy which gives content and direction to stage two of the argument must be the most plausible model for explaining the existence of order in the universe.

But of course the addition of (f) to (A9) will vastly restrict (A9)'s applicability—(A9) will now only apply to arguments concerning cosmic order and is in any case polemically vacuous—what (A9) was for was to help us decide which explanation, or explanation-model, is best. If we have to decide that in order to apply (A9), (A9) is not worth much. It is like a key that opens only unlocked doors.

Miscellaneous Topics

By now, matters mentioned but not explained have piled up. Why does Cleanthes think the "natural volume" explanation so natural? In more detail, why must only uninductible properties be the subject of discourse for arguments sanctioned by (A9) but not (A8)? And what is the qualification on conclusions of arguments sanctioned by (A9) which we said would not comfort Cleanthes?

The Qualification on (A9)

In reverse order, the answers are as follows. As we have thus far discussed the two-stage Cleanthean argument, the conclusion of an (A9)-sanctioned argument has been "X has B," where "B" was shared by X (the universe's cause) and the members of K2 (the class of causes whose effects resemble the universe). This is not quite correct. As the premise strictly reads not "Y (the universe) and the members of K1 share A" but "The members of K1 have A, and Y (the universe) resembles the members of K1" and so the conclusion can only read "The members of K2 have B and X resembles the members of K2." Just as both "Y has A" and "Y has A*, where A resembles A*" equally render the premise true, so "X has B" and "X has B*, where B resembles B*" are equally satisfactory truth conditions of the conclusion. Only the *weaker* claim, "X has B*" is justified, or (if one prefers) what the argument justifies is "X has B or X has B*"—if, of course, the argument justifies any conclusion at all. But the qualification—the shift from "Y shares A with the members of K1" to "Y resembles the members of K1 in virtue of having either A or A*," and the analogous specification with respect to X, B, and B*—is of course not one to encourage the design arguer. It weakens the resemblance between designer and Cleanthean deity. Many more things are *like* designers than *are* designers.

Uninductible Properties and (A9)

Why are only non-inductible properties allowed to appear in (A9)-sanctioned arguments? Simply, because if one can justify the claim that "X has B" where "B" is an inductible property, the argument must be sanctioned by (A8), and will not require the analogical stage to which (A9) is relevant. But there is a more interesting answer.

Suppose a Cleanthian insists that there can be an inductible property B such that an argument along the following lines could be constructed:

(a) The members of K1 have B, the members of K2 have A, and K1 and K2 are such that their members are in one-to-one causal correspondence with the members of K2 being effects; so:

(b) A and B are inductible properties,

(c) given some plausible analogy, the universe too has A

(d) so the cause of the universe has B.

Can't analogies, or models for explanation, ascribe inductible properties (in the sense defined above) to their *explicans?*

We have argued that (A9) either does not sanction only successful stage-two Cleanthean arguments—arguments by analogy that ride piggyback on (A8)-sanctioned inductive arguments from experience— or else does so only after such arguments (if any) have already been identified without any need to refer to (A9). In sum, (A9) is false or useless. Chapter 10 follows Philo as he skillfully details this point in his discussion of various models for explaining natural order. For now, we need to finish our discussion of (A8).

In order to give room to Cleanthean strategies, we did two things in our discussion of disputes about (A8). One thing was to require that the properties appropriately ascribed to objects by descriptions that occurred in the premises of arguments sanctioned by (A8) meet a certain condition. The condition was that they be experienceable—if a premise in an (A8)-sanctioned argument contained the expression "x's have A" then property A must be something that one could experience an x as having. *Being red* and *leaning to the left* would do; *being caused to have order by a cosmic designer* would not do. Inductive arguments from experience sanctioned by (A8) then will center on correlations of experienceable properties, or on objects as their experienceable properties are correlated.

This strategy is probably too lax. Either experienced correlation is *some* reason to think that the correlation is not accidental, or it is not. If it is not, then experienceable correlations are irrelevant to inductive arguments. If it is, then one may as well simply deal in terms of non-accidental (that is, law-like) correlations in the first place. If experienced correlation is evidence of law-like connection only under certain constraints, or plus other considerations, or the like, then it is experienced correlation under those constraints or in those conditions that is relevant to an inductive argument from experience, and only descriptions of items under which they are experienceable as correlated under those constraints or in those conditions will be allowable in such arguments. It is (at least presumptive) law-like relations that will ground inductive arguments from experience, and so it is law-like relationships, or their epistemological marks, that should be referred to in inductive arguments from experience. Hence it is such relationships, or their marks, that should be specified in an axiom designed to do the work expected of axiom (A8). Whether or not one could base this Philonian reasoning on Hume's own metaphysic and philosophy of science, there is much to be said for it. Inductive generalizations over, or inferences from, data that does not even presumptively militate against accidental correlations are epistemically wimpish. Probably, then, one should revise (A8) so that the members of the classes over which the premises of arguments that (A8) sanctions are causally connected, where causal connections hold only between items that are related in law-like ways. Only items experienceable as related in such ways properly are referred to in arguments that bear (A8)'s stamp of approval, and even then only under descriptions by which they are recognizable as being so connected. Thus the conditions of inductibility should be raised so as to require law-likeness among its instances. (I will not try to give an account of law-likeness here.)

The other concession made in order to give room for the exploration of Cleanthean strategies involved the use of the notion of a shartifact. Perhaps some will agree that the universe resembles a shartifact slightly more readily than they will assent that it is or closely resembles an artifact. Artifacts, shartifacts, and the universe arguably share some apparently uninductible properties not irrelevant to the question of whether they are designed, whether or not all shartifacts are designed. Some experienceable shartifact properties are not irrelevant to the question of whether shartifacts are designed. A great many shartifacts are artifacts. Some shartifacts not experienced to have had designers are experienceable—that is, could have been experienced—as having them; we could have seen them caused to have designedness. So reference to shartifacts, artificial and not made in the *Dialogues*, served to provide a temporary if shaky bridge between the two stages of a Cleanthean argument. But now we can dismiss the notion.

Causally Relevant Descriptions

We now can put Philo's contentions regarding (A8) a bit more fully and precisely. We have seen that for Hume "C1 causes E1," where C1 and E1 are particular events, entails:

(1) E1 is a member of a class K2.
(2) C1 is a member of a class K1.
(3) The members of K1 and K2 are paired in one-to-one spatio-temporal correlation with the member of K1 being temporally precedent.

It is fairly easy to see what restriction this rather minimal statement of the meaning of "causal connection" sets to properties over which the premises of an inductive argument from experience can range. Let us say that if, for two events C1 and E1 the three conditions just noted are met, C1 and E1 are *related by law*. (Arguably, stronger conditions are required for causality, but we need not pursue that here.) Let C1 be the striking of a ball and E1 be its flight. The lawlike relation between striking and flight is expressible by an obvious specification of the law-schema "—— causes. . . ." Appropriate values for the first opening of the schema will be (among many others) "the striking of the ball," "the imparting of a blow to a round object," and the like (or their more scientific replacements), and appropriate values for the second opening will be (among many others) "the flight of the ball" and "the rapid motion of the round object along an arched trajectory" (or their more scientific replacements). We may call the appropriate descriptions of the cause-event and the effect-event—those whose paired occurrence in the law-schema will yield an instance of a law— *causally relevant descriptions*. So the cause-event and effect-event descriptions just noted will be causally relevant ones. But even if the ball is in fact the object most prized by Eric, the thing most coveted by Karen, and the item David likes best to drive over the hedge, the descriptions "the striking of the object most prized by Eric," "the imparting of a blow to the thing most coveted by Karen," "the striking of the item David likes best to drive over the hedge" will not be causally relevant descriptions of events. *Under these latter descriptions*, the events in question enter into no lawlike connections with anything. Indeed, it is only chance that, for example, the thing most prized by Eric is strikable at all. He might have most prized his mother's smile. So some event-descriptions are causally relevant, and some are not.

We may also note that an easy extension of *causally relevant event description* yields the concept of a causally relevant *object* description. Examples of causally relevant object descriptions are "ball" and "round object." Examples of descriptions that are not causally relevant are, of course, "object most prized by Eric," "object coveted by Karen," and "object David likes best to drive over the hedge." What renders an object-description causally relevant is that an object, *under that description*, is *related by law* to another object (or one event occurring to an object is *related by law* to yet another event which occurs to it). Otherwise put, causally relevant object descriptions can be part of (are appropriately included in) causally relevant event descriptions.

Finally, a *causally relevant property* is any property A such that there is a causally relevant event or object description D such that "D is true of X" entails and entailed by "X has A." Thus an object possessing such a property is a sufficient condition for that object being a partner in a lawlike connection. The only properties of objects or events, then, that may be ascribed to them by the premises of an inductive argument from experience are causally relevant properties. This is yet another way of putting what Philo has in mind in his talk about species, and so another way of putting the thrust of (A8)—only ascription of causally relevant properties can be justified by inductive arguments. A consequence of this restriction, as we have seen, is that while inductive arguments about the location of the planets or the relative size of earth to other solar bodies is possible (since these items, as Philo puts it, belong to species), no inductive argument from experience by itself will justify the claim that *the universe* has (or fails to have) any particular property. (A8), then, should not be weakened. A Cleanthean could then claim that the relations between source/voice, intelligence/volumes, and designer/designedness are causal and lawlike; then she faces the challenge to produce the relevant laws. Or she could argue that teleological explanations are causal but do not posit law-like relations between agent and action, and that designedness is best explained teleologically. This opens a new dispute that raises issues that go well beyond the *Dialogues*. Short of entering that dispute, Philo's critique of Cleanthes stands victorious so far as (A8) considerations go. We will look at one more issue relevant to (A9) after considering the "natural volumes" examples.

The "Natural Volume" Inference

Why does Cleanthes favor the "natural volume" inference to the voice inference? Here, I think, the reasons are historical. Berkeley thought of sensory experience, composed of ideas in Berkeley's extremely technical sense of the word "idea," as a divine language. In Berkeley's view, nature (the collective objects of sensory experience—more carefully, the sum of the private non-intentional sensations that constitute Berkeleyean perception) is natural revelation. It is God's word to every person's sensory capacities, as the Bible is God's word of special revelation concerning the forgiveness of sins through the death and resurrection of Christ. Natural order is a sign of divine benevolence, and the answer to "How do we know the future will be like the past?" was for Berkeley "We don't, save as we rest our confidence in Providence." The order of nature was in fact an order sustained by a gracious Deity who thereby makes both common sense and science—daily life and high-flown theories—possible. So the fact that sensory experience exhibits recurring patterns is a product of divine grace. It is this sort of view—in Berkeley's idealistic mold, as well as in Butler's, and later Paley's, realist version—that Cleanthes voices when he says:

> But if there be any difference, Philo, between this supposed case [the natural volumes] and the real one of the universe, it is all to the advantage of the latter. The anatomy of an animal affords many stronger instances of design than the perusal of [the works of] Livy or Tacitus. . . . Choose, then, your party, Philo, without ambiguity or evasion: Assert either that a rational volume is no proof of a rational cause, or admit of a similar cause to all the works of nature. [*D*, 154]

Nonetheless, the voice inference seems the more forceful. It provides a (hypothetical) instance that is much harder to "explain away" in the effective and damaging way with which Philo deals—especially in his "multiple models" argument in Part Seven—with the usual design argument. But, taken literally, its premise is false. It rationally motivates some such claim as that (A9) is a correct axiom of analogical reasoning. But, as we saw, it establishes no premise for the design argument.

(A9) and Ultimate Explanations

The initial promise of (A9) was deceptive. Even supplemented by (e), it is impotent without (f) as well. With (f), however, we know that an argument satisfies (A9) only provided we know first that its analogy is the best explanatory model. But if we somehow know that before we apply (A9) to our argument, the argument itself is only window dressing. What we should concentrate on is however in the world one tells how to correctly fill in the blank in "Analogy . . . provides the best explanatory model for order in the cosmos."[1]

A rather formal variety of the design argument has been suggested that might provide the answer. Most of the *explicanda* we encounter are instances of temporal order—such sequences as selecting a necktie from among various rejected consequences or the shift of traces in a Wilson cloud chamber. What spatial order we encounter, such as the arrangement of books in a library or petals on a daisy, are generally explicable in terms of temporal sequences. Perhaps the majority of instances of temporal order are explicable non-teleologically—

that is, without reference to the ends, motives, intentions, purposes or the like of an intelligent agent. The physical sciences notoriously have excommunicated such explanations and many social scientists hope for the same measures to securely govern their own disciplines. Nonetheless, in common life and still in various social sciences, teleological explanations continue to be offered. Perhaps they are irreplaceable, not merely practically (for example, people not trained in the sciences have to use them) but theoretically (for example, some phenomena—say, human behavior—are not fully explicable without, or are best explained by, teleological explanations).

In any case, the more formal version of the design argument (or, if one prefers, a possible successor) can be stated as follows: Let us say that an explanation E1 is *ultimate* with respect to another explanation E2 if every event E2 explains is explained at least equally well by E1 but there are events that E1 explains but E2 does not or that E1 explains better than does E2. An explanation that is ultimate with respect to every event whatever is a *total ultimate explanation*.

Assume, for the sake of the argument at least, that teleological explanations and non-teleological explanations are irreducibly different in that sense that if T is teleological and M is not, and if both T and M are offered as explanations of *x*, *T explains x* has one set of truth conditions and *M explains x* has another; further, if *T explains x* is true, it is also (that is, therefore) true that some agent exists whereas if *M explains x* is true this is not entailed. This is so even if T is inappropriate in some contexts in which M is not (and/or conversely), even if the conditions of T's truth and those of M's truth can coexist (so that *T and M explain x* is consistent), and even if both T and M are required in order to fully explain *x*. (Further still, even if we do not need T in order to explain *x*'s occurrence, the facts to which T directs our attention might be both important and non-describable save teleologically. For example, in an epiphenomalistic world—a world that contained purposes, intentions, motives, etc., but only as effects—it might be impossible to fully describe the significant features of that world without use of teleological locutions even though no feature of that world would require teleological explanation.)

Assume, further, that if we can get by with only one type of explanation, that is (in some sense) preferable to having to use two types of explanation. And assume, finally, that if it is possible to have only one type of explanation included in, or constitutive of, the *explicans* of a total ultimate explanation, then that is rationally preferable (in some sense) to having two sorts of explanation included in, or constitutive of, the *explicans* of a total ultimate explanation. These last two assumptions are, so to say, principles of parsimony of explanation-types.

Now suppose it is shown that:

(1) There is a total ultimate explanation which is (a) teleological, (b) superior to every other, teleological explanation, and (c) superior to any non-teleological explanation, unless it is reducible to some such explanation.

Suppose that our characterizations of teleological and non-teleological explanations, and their relationships, has been correct. Then, given our first assumption, it follows that there is no non-teleological explanation to which the alleged superior explanation is reducible. Given our second assumption, it follows that if we can explain a set of phenomena by appeal to this explanation alone, we ought not to refer at all to a non-teleological explanation with respect to those phenomena. But it seems fairly clear that for some purposes and in some contexts we will in fact need to use non-teleological explanations. The natural sciences, and many portions of the social sciences, probably are such contexts. The point to be stressed, then, is that if some version of the teleological argument under consideration is successful then when we come to the basic, or most general, sort of explanation, or when we come to giving a total ultimate explanation, it will be the case that (1) our (supposed) total ultimate teleological explanation explains everything any ultimate non-teleological explanation explains but not conversely; or (2) it explains everything at least as well as any ultimate non-teleological explanation explains it, and explains some things better; or, perhaps, (3) explains more things better, though perhaps some things not quite so well, as the best among the ultimate non-teleological explanations.

Given our third assumption, it (in some sense) will be rationally preferable to adopt this (supposed) total ultimate teleological explanation. And *if* (but only if) the relevant sense of "is rationally preferable" legitimizes the inference from "X is the rationally preferable explanation" to "It is more probable that X is true than that any other explanation is true" (as opposed to merely entailing that it was simpler to calculate using X, or that X is more aesthetically pleasing or elegant, or that it was rational to accept but not rational to believe the explanation, or the like), then our total ultimate teleological explanation presumably would be justified in something like as strong a sense as the design arguer hopes that the designer hypothesis is justified. Further, were we to know this explanation to be justified, we would know that there was an agent to which the world was related in some telic manner or other without thereby knowing (unless the explanation happened to tell us) what purpose he had (or whether he had a purpose) in producing our ordered world.

Now all of this offers a rather abstractly described, and certainly insufficiently precisely characterized, route that a design arguer might follow if he were to develop his contentions along the lines of what might be called explanation-theory. His case would depend on how things now are in the natural and social sciences, and on how he might be able where necessary to improve how things are in the sciences in ways favorable to his own viewpoint. It might help his case, for example, if he could resuscitate vitalism—or at least eliminate reductionism—in biology. It might help him along if he could show that human behavior is not an epiphenomenon of anything that is non-teleologically explicable, and is not itself non-teleologically explicable. It would help even more, I suspect, if he could show this to be so *uberhaupt* and not merely from some useful point of view, or show this to be so from some point of view that was absolutely central to some or all of the social sciences.

It is obvious, of course, that the critic of the design argument could follow a strategy similar to the one open to the design arguer herself, though with different conclusions in mind and different contentions about the role of teleological explanation as supports for those conclusions. The critic likely will ascribe to some non-teleological ultimate explanation the status ascribed above to a teleological ultimate explanation, and try to defend that ascription. So even if it is just conceivable that one might in the long run justify something like the designer hypothesis along the lines very roughly characterized in the above few paragraphs, it is equally just conceivable that one might criticize that hypothesis along the same lines of inquiry. But of course neither line of inquiry is very close to any that appear in the *Dialogues*, and I do not myself have any clear idea of what the outcome of a dispute carried out along these lines might be.[2]

It does seem fairly clear that the design arguer is endeavoring to show that in some sense the design hypothesis is the best explanation of order in the universe; that is, he wants to show that with respect to the designedness of the universe, the activity of a (non-human) Designer is the superior account. It seems clear, then, that in answering the query as to whether the design argument succeeds, one is ultimately forced to ask what an explanation, or perhaps what an explanatory model, amounts to. One is also forced to ask how one appraises the relative merits of competing explanations or models. For the design argument is in fact an argument to the effect that the cosmos itself, *qua* orderly system, requires explanation and that the explanation it requires is teleological. At the very least, it requires that some *parts* of the universe be such that they are orderly, that no non-teleological explanation of their order is sufficient, and that no teleological explanation of their order is sufficient, which refers only to human agents (and/or animal agents). It is to this issue that later parts of the *Dialogues* are addressed. But pursuing these matters very far along the lines abstractly described above would take us far beyond the limits of the *Dialogues*, and (so far as I know) also well beyond anything that might plausibly be called points of agreement among philosophers of science.

CHAPTER 10

Design Arguments and Multiple Models

Ramifications of and Alternatives to the Designer Hypothesis
(*Dialogues* Part Four)

P HILO BEGINS at this point a task that continues through Part Five, namely, acquainting Cleanthes with

> the inconveniences of that anthropomorphism, which you have embraced; and I shall prove that there is no ground to suppose a plan of the world to be formed in the divine mind, consisting of distinct ideas, differently arranged, in the same manner as an architect forms in his head the plan of a house which he intends to execute. [*D*, 160]

Philo begins by querying what advantage one reaps by adopting Cleanthes' position. Suppose we grant that the order of the universe is caused by an intelligent being whom we shall call "Intellectus." Since everything has a cause, Intellectus has one. Even in the knowledge that Intellectus is, one does not reach the end of explanations. But suppose one grants this. Not even Intellectus basks in inexplicable existence. What then? (The cosmological argument contends that a sufficient explanation of there being something rather than nothing, and/or of there being things of a sort that might not have existed, requires reference to a being that in some manner is *necessary;* this issue comes up in Part Nine. One could supplement the design argument by the cosmological, though one then needs to argue that the conclusions of the two arguments are true of the same being.)

Philo notes that in our world order arises from various causes. If we can offer the argument:

(1) The universe and a house possess designedness.
(2) A house has a designer.

So, probably:

(3) The universe has a design.

We can also offer the argument:

(1') The universe and a carrot possess designedness.
(2') A carrot is produced by natural growth.

So, probably:

(3') The universe is produced by natural growth.

If within our experience both intelligent action and vegetative process yield ordered states, and if the argument to a cosmic designer possesses plausibility, Philo contends, so does the argument to a cosmic vegetative process possess plausibility. Since this type of argument is stated more fully in Part Seven we will discuss it in detail when considering that section. But clearly a cosmic vegetation will not serve even Cleanthes' purposes—*that* hypothesis would provide no "sufficient foundation for religion" and would lead to no cosmic designer.

Philo presses still further. Nothing in the design argument prevents Intellectus from having a *material* cause, or a *non-intelligent* cause. (In a deleted passage, Hume understates the difficulty: "that the Deity arose from some external cause . . . will be adopted by very few.") Along the same lines, but not made explicit, is an implication of Philo's remark that we "have also experience of particular systems of thought . . . which have no order," (*D*, 162). As material order collapses into disarray (for example, a log decomposes) so cognitive order sometimes degenerates into madness. So far as the design argument goes, Intellectus is not safe from the latter danger—nor for that matter is his body (if any) secure from the former. (That decay and madness are new varieties of order is a possible reply, but one that offers Cleanthes little comfort.) The explicit point of the *matter corrupts/mind corrupts* discussion is that in the cases of both material and immaterial systems order sometimes arises without known cause, or from a cause intrinsic to the system itself. If, as we are for the purposes of discussion, we insist that there must be a cause of order in the universe, why can't the cause of the present order be tendencies always implicit in the system, on the analogy of acorn-oak or seed-carrot or egg-chicken?

Philo dismisses the Peripatetics' *faculties* or *occult qualities* ("bread nourished by its nutritive faculty, and senna purged by its purgative" [*D*, 162]) in one paragraph and in another Cleanthes reports that he stops asking about causes once he has "found a Deity" (*D*, 163). Philo then concludes the section in these words:

> Naturalists indeed very justly explain particular effects by more general causes; though these general causes themselves should remain in the end totally inexplicable: But they never surely thought it satisfactory to explain a particular effect by a particular cause, which was no more to be accounted for than the effect itself. [*D*, 164]

In so doing, he reiterates three criticisms: (a) inductive arguments from experience require lawlike connections between the items over which the argument's premises range and the universe bears no lawlike connection to anything (and neither does Intellectus); (b) even if order in the universe is explained by Intellectus, another explanation—this time of Intellectus—is required; (c) if one is rationally at ease without inquiring "whence Intellectus," one can with equal propriety be rationally at ease without inquiring "whence natural order." Further, if the one is viewed as "having the cause of order within itself," so may the other be, and hence, having the universe on our hands anyway, we may as well quit there. The first of these objections is especially important; as we have seen, it is central in Philo's contention that no inductive formulation of the argument has any hope of success, and it appears unanswerable.

More Ramifications of the Designer Hypothesis (*Dialogues*, Part Five)

Continuing his Part Four program, Philo proposes to show Cleanthes "still more inconveniences . . . in your anthropomorphism." He reiterates the previous axioms that *like effects prove like causes* and *the liker the effects are, which are seen, and the liker the causes, which are inferred, the stronger the argument.* He adds: "Every departure [that is, dissimilarity] on either side [that is, between causes, between effects] diminishes the probability, and renders the experiment less conclusive" (*D*, 165).

These are our old friends (A2), (A3), and (A4). As we enumerate the suggested inconveniences, we shall ask whether appeal to by Cleanthes (A5a) and (A5b) would prevent them.

First, Philo contends that the degree of intelligence and power that would be required to produce the regularities in planetary and stellar movement discovered by astronomers greatly surpasses that of any human artificer. The disanalogy in degree of intelligence requisite to produce one effect to that necessary to produce the other renders any argument based on comparison of the effects less cogent that it would be were the same degree of intelligence required in each case. Philo says that "according to the true system of theism" these "new discoveries in astronomy, which prove the immense grandeur and magnificence of the works of nature, are so many additional arguments for a Deity," and I suppose the "true system of theism" is the sort of very thin theism that Philo himself confesses in Part Twelve and that Hume favors in the *Natural History*. Must Cleanthes' sort of theism regard these arguments as difficulties?

In one sense, it need not. Cleanthes is right that "these are surely no objections. . . . They only discover new instances of art and contrivance. It is still the image of mind reflected on us from innumerable objects" (*D*, 166).

If the designedness–designer connection is strong enough to license the inference that comprises the design argument, the Philonic objections do not break that connection.

In another respect, though, Philo is right. Cleanthes' first problem was how to start ascribing properties to the cause of cosmic order. His method was argument by analogy and his first properties were intelligence and power. He likes these properties and is content not to scrutinize them too carefully. Philo scrutinizes, wondering if Cleanthes can stop once he has begun. He concludes that Cleanthes cannot stop where Cleanthes wishes to stop, and his argument to that effect is potent. Indeed, the comparative difficulty of what precedes and what follows contrasts sharply with the easy triumph of Philo which follows this exchange:

> These surely are no objections, replied Cleanthes; they only discover new instances of art and contrivance. It is still the image of a mind reflected on us from innumerable objects. Add, a mind *like the human*, said Philo. I know of no other, replied Cleanthes. And the liker the better, insisted Philo. To be sure, said Cleanthes. [*D*, 166]

Philo "with an air of alacrity and triumph" marks some consequences of Cleanthes' use of the design argument as "the sole theological argument." First, if one grants for a moment that the argument proves that *something* intelligent (again, call it "Intellectus") exists, that something cannot be proved to be infinite by this argument. For no greater cause may be postulated than one potent enough to produce the effect. The universe "so far as it falls under our cognisance" could be produced by a being whose power fell considerably short of omnipotence, whose knowledge fell well short of omniscience, and so on. Thus no "omni-property" is shown by the design argument to be legitimately ascribed to Intellectus, who *ex hypothei* caused cosmic order. (One argument for God's existence that, if successful, would prove Him, say, omnipotent would be a version of the "God is a perfect being, perfect beings have all perfections, and necessary existence and omnipotence are perfections" argument. Or if one could show that a necessarily independent being exists, and that a being is necessarily independent only if it is omnipotent, this would do; some versions of the cosmological argument endeavor to do this. Hume includes considerations relevant to the argument in Part Nine.)

Further, still supposing the design argument to prove the existence of Intellectus, Intellectus may have made multitudinous mistakes in his universe construction. Species that faded from the scene may be errors in the blueprint—cosmic Edsels, as it were. If God is omnicompetent then apparent difficulties seem so only "from the narrow capacity of man." Not so if Intellectus is in charge.

It is compatible with the design argument that Intellectus used trial and error methods, is in his infancy (or his senility) as an artificer, is embodied, has a family, and so on. For all that the design argument shows, "Intellectus" may be a pseudonym for a whole array of artificers.

What concerns Philo is that given only the design argument, four things are true. First, no *determinate* degree of intelligence or power is ascribable to Intellectus—"enough to produce the observed order in universe," to be sure, but how much is that? Second, blunders, ignorance, false starts, and so on are as legitimately ascribable to Intellectus as is success in giving the world an order, for the line of reasoning: (1) Defunct species are like scrapped artifacts in that they manifest designedness. (2) Scrapped artifacts testify to the ignorance or ineptitude of a human designer; so probably (3) defunct species testify to the ignorance or ineptitude of a cosmic designer: is a good argument if the design argument is good. Third, no determinate *number* of designers is legitimately specified by the design argument. Fourth, Intellectus, by analogy with human artificers, is most plausibly viewed as himself possessing a body, and by now Intellectus looks more like Zeus than Jehovah. As Philo puts it,

> a man, who follows your hypothesis, is able, perhaps, to assert, or conjecture, that the universe, sometimes, arose from something like design: But beyond that position he cannot ascertain one single circumstance, and is left afterwards to fix every point of his theology, by the utmost license of fancy and hypothesis. [*D*, 169]

Most importantly, even if the design argument is impeccable so far as it goes, it goes only so far as proving *something like* a designer. (More on the "something like" qualification in a moment.) At best we (almost) get an intelligent designer. By itself, this is hardly enough for religious purposes. Even if we were justified in inferring to a designer, this would not be enough for religious purposes. Creation, Providence, Redemption, Judgment—these and their kin are the stuff of monotheistic religion. The existence of a cosmic tinkerer is not worth an "Amen," let alone a "Hallelujah."

But suppose we take our clue as to where to go from here from the design argument itself. Then we face a plethora of properties less to Cleanthes' taste—properties like *being embodied, being male or female, being a maker of false starts,* and the like. Without what William James called "overbeliefs"—in this context, beliefs not justified by the argument from design—the religious relevance of Intellectus is less imposing than that of the Unmoved Mover. With the overbeliefs suggested by filling in (or following out) the artificer analogy, we get a cosmic colleague all too like a magnified Robert Fulton or Walter Chrysler. More carefully, what we get is determined by the "utmost license of fancy" and the philosopher has become the fictionist. With regard to the various possible fictions—the Pandora's box of analogies with which 'Intellectus' may be festooned—Philo bluntly admits: "From the moment the attributes of the Deity are supposed finite, all these have place. And I cannot, for my part, think that so wild and unsettled a system of theology is, in any respect, preferable to none at all" (*D*, 169).

Hume has a fine sense of the wisdom of the orthodox in insisting on ascribing the "omni-" properties to God. Cleanthes' confident-sounding reply, "by the utmost indulgence of your imagination, you never get rid of the hypothesis of design in the universe; but are obliged, at every turn, to have recourse to it. To this concession I adhere steadily; and this I regard as a sufficient foundation for religion" (*D*, 169), looks for all the world like whistling in the dark.

Philo keeps another (by now familiar) topic afloat without making it central to the discussion. "An intelligent Being of such vast power and capacity, as is necessary to produce the universe, or, to speak in the language of ancient philosophy, so prodigious an animal, exceeds all analogy, and even comprehension." And he adds that the design argument at best shows "that the universe, sometime, arose from *something like design*" (*D*, 169, my italics). The qualification is no slip of the pen; Hume replaced "some kind of design" by "something like design." The conclusion of the design argument, then, cannot be "there is a designer." Strictly it at most can specify that "there is something like a designer." And a good many more kinds of things can be "something like" a designer than can *be* designers. The difference in formulation of the conclusion is hence not very subtle. Consider the difference between being sane (or alive, or solvent) and being *something like* sane (or alive, or solvent). Perhaps the only bigger change wrought by this 'little' alteration is that produced by adding or deleting "not."

Alternatives to the Designer Hypothesis Again (*Dialogues*, Part Six)

After Demea complains that Cleanthes' Intelligent cause, of which we must simply hope there is only one, that it still exists, that it is not too imperfect, seems hardly a candidate for veneration or obedience, Philo begins to formulate a new and powerful criticism. It is perhaps best cast initially in the form of an argument to the animality of the universe:

> (1) The universe resembles the body of an animal in that both are ecological systems.

So:

> (2) Probably, the universe is an animal.

The suggestion is that while this conclusion is hardly self-evident, it fares no worse than Cleanthes' own contention.

Cleanthes offers two criticisms of the argument to animality. One is that the analogy is

> effective [*sic*, defective] in many circumstances, the most material [that is, relevant]: No organs of sense, no one precise origin of motion and action. In short, it seems to bear a stronger resemblance to a vegetable than to an animal; and your inference would be so far inconclusive in favor of the soul of the world. [*D*, 172]

The other is that

> your theory seems to imply the eternity of the world; and that is a
> principle which, I think, can be refuted by the strongest reasons
> and probabilities. [*D*, 172]

The first objection raises a familiar problem. The universe bears some
resemblance to an artifact, but also to an organism, and among organ-
isms it bears some resemblance to an animal and some to a plant. Artifacts are artificed, animals born, and plants germinated. So we have
about equal evidence, such as it is, that the universe is designed,
produced by parents, or grown from a seed. All of this is laid out in
detail in Part Seven. The inference to a particular cause of the universe
is shaky in any of these cases, and that for exactly similar reasons.

The second objection gives rise to a peculiar argument. The universe cannot have existed forever in the past because vines have been
growing in France for only two thousand years and cattle have been
raised in America for only three hundred, though vines and cattle
thrive in these environments. Surely were the world without beginning there would long since have been French vines and American
cattle, for someone would in all that time have brought them sooner
to their present environments.

> Is it possible that, during the revolutions of a whole eternity,
> there never arose a Columbus, who might open the communica-
> tion between Europe and . . . [America]? We may as well imag-
> ine, that all men would wear stockings for ten thousand years,
> and never have the sense to think of garters to tie them. [*D*, 173]

Surely nothing is more unimaginable than that!

That argument for the relative infancy of the universe is more secure, Cleanthes suggests, than the argument from "the late origin of
arts and sciences," for that phenomenon might be explained by previous learning having been lost, as indeed "ancient learning and history
seem to have been in great danger of entirely perishing after the inun-
dation of the barbarous nations" (*D*, 172, 173) whereas only natural
convulsions could "destroy all the European animals and vegetables,
which are now to be found in the Western world" (*D*, 174). And of
course Philo responds, "And what argument have you against such
convulsions" (*D*, 174). For some reason, it is not mentioned that the
same argument could be offered had vines been grown in France for
two billion years. There is "as much time" before two billion years ago

as there is before two thousand years ago if the universe has infinite past duration. So the argument can succeed only if the thesis that "the universe has an infinitely long past" is incompatible with there being *any* first occurrence of an event; and this thesis plainly is *not* incompatible with events occurring for the first time.

It seems to me natural to wonder what in the world possessed Hume to discuss this particular argument. It is hardly essential to his overall argument that he consider whether the fact that French vine-yards are relatively recent features of the landscape has some important entailment about the age of the world. I suggest three reasons. One is that Hume is perhaps replying to certain literature of his or an earlier day—literature that has received its deserved oblivion. Another is that he wishes to reintroduce in this context the determinism he favors in the *Natural History*. The third is that he wishes to present another argument that concerns a conclusion about matters far from common life, that also would (if developed) turn into a two-stage argument composed of an inductive argument from experience and an argument from analogy, that also has quite close counterpart arguments that defend with equal success (or failure) their different and incompatible conclusions, and that hence leaves skepticism in the sense of "no verdict" the only rational conclusion.

Philo's remarks suggest the last two reasons:

> Were I obliged to defend any particular system of this nature (which I never willingly should do), I esteem none more plausible than that which ascribes an eternal, inherent principle of order to the world; though attended with great and continual revolutions and alterations. This at once solves all the difficulties; and if the solution, by being so general, is not entirely and completely satisfactory, it is, at least, a theory we must, sooner or later, have recourse to, whatever system we embrace. How could things have been as they are, were there not an original, inherent principle of order somewhere, in thought or in matter? And it is very indifferent to which of these we give preference. Chance has no place, on any hypothesis, sceptical or religious. Everything is surely governed by steady, inviolable laws. And were the inmost essence of things laid open to us, we should discover a science, of which, at present, we can have no idea. Instead of admiring the order of natural beings, we should clearly see, that it was absolutely impossible for them, in the smallest article, ever to admit of any other disposition. [*D*, 175]

Philo proposes the theory that the cause of the order we experience is that the universe itself, conceived either as immaterial or material as you like, is viewed as possessing an order inherent to itself and deterministic in its outworkings and may be viewed as oscillating between ordered and chaotic stages. Several points are made in these remarks. First, the question "How old is the universe?" is not central to the dispute that Cleanthes and Philo are engaged in. If the universe is young, its source of being and order is in something older—a designer is one possibility, a precedent state of an always-ordered universe is another, earlier stages of the universe in which it oscillates between *being ordered* and *being chaotic* is still another, and so on. So even if we knew, say, that the universe (in the sense of "the system of matter described by current physical theory") was (say) exactly twenty thousand years old, this would be nothing to the point. It would neither establish nor refute the design argument. Second, Philo contends that if we agree that there must be a cause of natural order, decide to seek what that cause might be, and agree that we shall keep on seeking a cause of order until we find something whose order is intrinsic to itself, then the simplest (most parsimonious) thing to do is just to say that there is "an eternal, inherent principle of order to the world" (*D*, 174). This is compatible with the present order being a temporary state (on a geologic time scale) such that the universe at regular intervals goes random and then recoups its order. It is also compatible with the theory that the present order is the eternal status quo. Either way, he says, this hypothesis "solves all difficulties." Third, this theory does not appeal to chance as the source of order—it does not deny, that is, that order has a cause, or a sufficient explanation. Fourth, it is neither materialist nor immaterialist; the cause may be an immaterial intelligent being, a material intelligent being, an immaterial non-intelligent being or a material non-intelligent being. But it is, as Philo presents it, a deterministic theory. And Philo here "speaks for Hume" in that Hume himself, in both *Treatise* and *Enquiry*, perhaps quite surprisingly, is persuaded (on grounds rather difficult to discern) that some version of determinism is true.

Philo concludes his argument in these words:

> Were any one inclined to revive the ancient Pagan Theology, which maintained, as we learn from Hesiod, that this globe was governed by 30,000 Deities, who arose from the unknown powers of nature. You would naturally object Cleanthes, that nothing is gained by this hypothesis; and that it is as easy to suppose all

men and animals, being more numerous, but less perfect, to have sprung immediately from a like origin. Push the same inference a step farther; and you will find a numerous society of Deities as explicable as one universal Deity, who possesses, within himself, the powers and perfections of the whole society. All these systems, then, of scepticism, polytheism, and theism, you must allow, on your principles, to be on a like footing, and that no one of them has any advantages over the others. You may thence learn the fallacy of your principles. [*D*, 175]

In the preceding passage, Philo has noted that were he to accept any position on the cause of cosmic order, what that position would be. In the present passage, he backs off from even that position. For given the axioms or principles to which Cleanthes appeals, one cannot justify *any* system, for competing explanations of order are as much, or as little, justified by appeal to experience plus appeal to analogy as their competitors. It is this theme that Philo presses in detail in Part Eight. He adds the important point here that while one use of the principle "Postulate no more entities than required to explain the phenomena" will reduce 30,000 deities to one, one more application will reduce us to simply the universe itself, unaccompanied by any deity at all (or itself regarded as a deity). So while Philo's "committee of deities" hypothesis is unparsimonious, so is Cleanthes' "single designer" view. (Whether this sort of appeal to parsimony has any real evidential force is another matter.)

The Universe, Vegetables, and Animals (*Dialogues*, Part Seven)

Philo picks up again the universe-animal and universe-vegetable comparisons at the outset of Part Seven.

If the universe bears a greater likeness to animal bodies and to vegetables, than to the works of human art, it is more probable that its cause resembles the cause of the former than that of the latter, and its origin ought rather to be ascribed to generation or vegetation than to reason or design. Your conclusion [Cleanthes], even according to your own principles, is therefore lame and defective. [*D*, 176]

Philo's move is the by now characteristic one: "Supposing, Cleanthes, I grant you your last response. Even so, your argument does not succeed for the reason I now bring forth."

So Philo enters fully into the spirit of offering explanations of cosmic order.

> There are other parts of the universe (besides the machines of human invention) which bear still a greater resemblance to the fabric of the world, and which therefore afford a better conjecture concerning the universal origin of this system. These parts are animals and vegetables. The world plainly resembles more an animal or a vegetable, than it does a watch or a knitting-loom. Its cause, therefore, it is more probable, resembles the cause of the former. [*D*, 176]

Appealing in effect to (A9) in these words, Philo next fills out his conjectural arguments as follows:

> The cause of the former [i.e., animals and vegetables] is generation or vegetation. The cause, therefore, of the world, we may infer to be something similar or analogous to generation or vegetation . . . as a tree sheds its seed into the neighboring fields, and produces other trees; so the great vegetable, the world . . . produces within itself certain seeds, which, being scattered into the surrounding chaos, vegetate into new worlds. . . . Of if, for the sake of variety (for I see no other advantage) we should suppose this world to be an animal; a comet (or other orderly sub-system) is the egg (or bodily organ) of the animal [*D*, 176, 177]

We are spared further specifications of these analogies. Philo insists that while "we have no data to establish any system of cosmogony," still

> if we must needs fix on some hypothesis . . . by what rule, pray, ought we to determine our choice? Is there any other rule than the greater similarity of the objects compared? And does not a plant or an animal, which springs from vegetation or generation bear a stronger resemblance to the world, than does any artificial machine, which arises from reason and design? [*D*, 177]

Various Models for Understanding Universal Order Again

Various answers can be given to this question. That is the problem, after all—how to sort out (A9)-sanctioned arguments so that one is justified in retaining only one. It is not Philo's concern to defend any one argument. His purpose lies elsewhere, and he expresses it in clear terms. I bypass Demea's brief objection that "vegetation" and "generation," and Philo's response that "reason" too, "mark only certain powers and energies in nature, whose effects are known, but whose essence (and operation) is incomprehensible" (*D*, 177, 178). Admitting that "one of these principles, more than the other, has no privilege for being made a standard to the whole of nature" (*D*, 178), Philo insists that:

> It may reasonably be expected, that the larger the views are which we take of things, the better will they conduct us in our conclusions concerning such extraordinary and such magnificent subjects. In this little corner of the world alone, there are four principles, *reason, instinct, generation, vegetation*, which are similar to each other [as similar as is the universe to a shartifact, for example], and are the causes of similar effects. What a number of other principles may we naturally suppose in the immense extent and variety of the universe, could we travel from planet to planet and from system to system, in order to examine each part of this mighty fabric? Any one of these four principles above mentioned (and a hundred others which lie open to our conjecture) may afford us a theory, by which to judge of the origin of the world. [*D*, 178]

He adds that "these principles are all known to us from experience" but "their manner of operation . . . [is] totally unknown," but this is not the central point. His concern here is not with any particular factual or structural defect of the design argument. Rather, his point is that the design argument suggests one explanatory model of the cosmos. Other cosmic models are available; we may follow Cleanthes in extrapolating from design of artifacts to design of the world. We may also follow the lead of some of the Ancients in extrapolating from human mind-body relations to a cosmic mind-cosmos view of the world, or of others in extrapolating from the processes of an animal body to the view that the cosmos is an animal. Sticking to Philo's categories, we have these models: (a) *reason*-production of cosmic order by the intelligent power of an agent; (b) *generation*-production of cosmic order by reproduction and growth (compare "cosmic egg" mythologies); (c) *vegetation*-production of cosmic order by its progressive realization of latent capacities; (d) *instinct*-production of cosmic order by the subsystems which comprise the universe interacting so as to produce order. Of course (b) through (d) are directed to the same point. Hen-from-egg, plant-from-seed, migration due to instinct, adult-from-embryo, and so on are each cases of order arising from causes which had no prevision of their effects. There are more instances in our experience of order being produced by causes having no prevision of their well-martialed effects than there are of causes with foresight. Foresight aside, there are more non-intelligent causes of order than there are intelligent causes. To conclude that *Probably, the causes of cosmic order have no prevision of their effect* (an argument Philo suggests but does not emphasize) would go considerably beyond the evidence, but would also be beside the point at hand. That point is that cosmic order can be multiply explained. Models involving no intelligent cause are very well represented among these explanations. Unless we can give rational grounds for preferring at least one among the models that include an intelligent agent, the design argument has no hope. The fact that one *can* explain cosmic order under its rubric, or along the lines of its model, does not entail that one *should* if one *also* can explain cosmic order about equally well (the criteria here are rough) in other, incompatible ways. No good rational grounds for throwing out *any* of the models have been provided by Cleanthes. So the design argument is simply one of many candidates for an office—that of True Explanation of cosmic order—for which the qualifications are not very clear, and how to apply them is not very clear; and at that, the candidates each offer questionable evidence of their fitness for the post. This point is not vitiated by Demea's claim that a vegetative cause would require an intelligent cause, for even if this is so the intelligent cause will itself (by parity of reasoning) require a further (not necessarily, an intellient) cause, and so on.

In keeping with what is to come in Part Twelve, Cleanthes, while he has no answer to Philo's arguments, contends nonetheless "that such whimsies, as you have delivered, may puzzle, but never can convince us" (*D*, 181). They lack the purchase on 'common sense' and on secondary religious propensities that reference to design possesses.

Alternative Models for Explaining Universal Order
(*Dialogues*, Part Eight)

What you ascribe to the fertility of my invention, replied Philo, is entirely owing to the nature of the subject . . . in such questions as the present, a hundred contradictory views may preserve a kind of imperfect analogy; and invention has here full scope to exert itself. [*D*, 182]

Thus Philo begins Part Eight with a contention he amply illustrated in Part Seven and further illustrates in what follows. Philo's argument in effect begins with appeal to the axiom that:

> (A10) If data D is explicable equally well on Hypotheses H1, H2 . . . Hn, D provides no evidence for H1 over H2 . . . over Hn.

Consider then the fact that the universe is orderly. How are we to account for this fact? Here is one possibility. Suppose that there is a finite number of material particles.

> A finite number of particles is only susceptible of finite transpositions, and it must happen, in an eternal duration, that every possible order or position must be tried an infinite number of times. This world, therefore, with all its events, even the most minute, has before been produced and destroyed, and will again be produced and destroyed, without any bounds and limitations. [D, 182]

While Philo spends some time endeavoring to make the revised Epicurean hypothesis more and more plausible, his goal is only to show that it "affords a plausible, if not a true solution of the difficulty" (D, 185) of explaining cosmic order. Though the Epicurean hypothesis "is so far incomplete and imperfect . . . can we ever reasonably expect greater success in any attempts of this nature" (D, 186)?

So far as appeal to Axiom (A10) goes the Epicurean hypothesis and the design hypothesis come off about even. Every hypothesis concocted to explain cosmic order will contain some "circumstance repugnant to our limited and imperfect experience of the analogy of nature," (D, 186). We thus have no more reason to accept the design hypothesis than the Epicurean, or various others.

Philo concludes the final section dedicated to appraisal of the design argument by offering a parting critique and a reaffirmation of his belief that skepticism with regard to all religious systems is both psychologically possible and "our only reasonable resource." First, then, the critique.

Cleanthes' adoption of anthropomorphism is motivated by an endeavor both to make talk about God meaningful and to express propositions about the existence and nature of a designer for which the design argument provides cogent support. In these respects, anthropomorphism is proposed "the better to preserve a conformity to common experience." Philo has already had his say as to whether appeal to anthropomorphism aids in making talk of the divine more intelligible. He directs his final attack on the claim that the argument from design gives proof of an anthropomorphic deity.

His points are these: (1) in our experience, ideas are copied from objects, not the reverse; (2) in our experience, disembodied or unembodied mind has not influenced matter; (3) the designer, not being embodied, can move matter other than his own body directly (by merely taking choice, as it were) and we have no experience of this type of action occurring; (4) the action of a designer does not come under "the equality of action and reaction [which] seems to be an universal law of nature, supported by all the experience relevant to its confirmation or disconfirmation"; (5) in our experience, no mind is eternal. In these and sundry other respects, the design hypothesis "implies a contradiction to . . . experience"—the ordinary human experience from which its support supposedly comes. Of course appeal to (A9) might focus attention only on the analogies, and if the design analogy were shown to provide the best explanatory model, only those features that it requires (only those properties whose ascription to God are necessary in order for the explanation to work) are relevant, and it will be intelligence and power that are crucial, not possession of a body. What Philo is suggesting is an inductive argument of this sort: all intelligence and power in our experience has been exercised by an embodied being; so probably every being who has intelligence and power is embodied. This argument is in the spirit of Cleanthes' own design argument. The hypothetical reply: a teleological total ultimate explanation is the *best kind* of explanation; that a Designer exists entails an intelligent and potent cause of cosmic order, but entails nothing about his being embodied; hence being embodied is not relevant to the design hypothesis: is not in that spirit. It brings into consideration the nature and appraisal of explanations, leaving us in a changed conceptual environment with new questions and tasks. The *Dialogues* do not much operate in this new environment; they only force one wishing to deal with the design argument to dwell there.

Philo draws the long discussion of Parts One through Eight to a close by insisting that, so far as rational appraisal carries us, all religious systems—meaning the design hypothesis and its competitors—are in the same leaky epistemological boat. So insofar as rational reflection determines belief, skepticism concerning such systems is both psychologically possible and what reflection requires. The remaining question, with which Part Twelve deals, is whether what reflection requires is in fact (as Philo here suggests) satisfied in "all mankind." Thus Philo ends the discussion maintaining the position with which he began it, saying:

> All religious systems, it is confessed, are subject to great and insuperable difficulties. Each disputant triumphs in his turn; while he carries on an offensive war, and exposes the absurdities, barbarities, and pernicious tenets of his antagonist. But all of them, on the whole, prepare a complete triumph for the sceptic; who tells them, that no system ought ever to be embraced with regard to such subjects: For this plain reason, that no absurdity ought ever to be assented to with regard to any subject. A total suspense of judgment is here our only resource. And if every attack, as is commonly observed, and no defence, among theologians, is successful; how complete must be *his* victory, who remains always, with all mankind—on the offensive, and has himself no fixed or abiding city, which he is ever, on any occasion, obliged to defend? [*D*, 187]

So Axiom (9) is neither repaired nor replaced; Axiom (10) is relevant to assessing the argument from design, but does not provide a new platform on which its supporters may stand. With the demise of the initial promise provided by Axiom (9), the design argument dies. If it can be resurrected, it will be in a new world in which consideration of inductive arguments that range only over law-embedded predicates and causal properties, and arguments from analogy that satisfy (A9), is replaced by a confirmationist theory that worries about arguments to a best explanation or a disconfirmationist theory that worries about explanatory value and rigorous failed attempts at disconfirmation.

CHAPTER 11

Other Theistic Arguments

Demea's *a Priori* Arguments (*Dialogues*, Part Nine)

THE NINTH SECTION of the *Dialogues* raises a new problem. As Demea asks, "if so many difficulties attend the argument *a posteriori* . . . had we not better adhere to the simple and sublime argument *a priori*, which, by offering to us infallible demonstration, cuts off at once all doubt and difficulty" (*D*, 188)? The "simple and sublime argument" is the ontological. It endeavors to show that "God does not exist" is a contradiction, and hence "God exists" a logically necessary truth. If successful, the argument thus shows that necessarily, not merely probably, God exists. We are not left asking how many designers or gods there are; there is *one*. Since God is a perfect being, necessary existence being among His perfections, He is omnipotent and omniscient (these too being perfections). So He is not senile, or infant, or inept. He has not retired, nor shall He fade away. In sum, what the design argument—even should it succeed—leaves open to doubt, the ontological deals with definitively—if it succeeds.

Characteristically, Demea points up the usefulness of the argument. Cleanthes appropriately responds that "Argument A is useful for certain purposes if it is sound and valid" does not entail either "A is sound" or "A is valid." So Demea turns to the task of presenting the argument.

There is nothing new or especially insightful about his presentation. It runs:

(1) Necessarily, whatever exists has a cause or reason of its existence.

(2) Either there is an infinite series of causes, or something exists that is necessarily existent.

(3) If there is an infinite series of causes, the series itself must have a necessarily existent cause; an infinite series of causes requires explanation as much as does a single cause.

Hence:

(4) Whether there is an infinite series of causes or not, there must be something which is necessarily existent.

Demea remarks that explaining that something exists by saying it exists "by chance" is no explanation at all. Indeed, "chance is a word without meaning" (*D,* 189). Hume himself agrees that "chance, when strictly examined, is a mere negative word, and means not any real power which has anywhere a being in nature" (*E,* 95), and that "what the vulgar call chance is nothing but a secret and concealed cause" (*T,* 130). This is all that Demea is claiming. Further, Demea remarks, "*nothing* . . . can never produce anything"—which means either that it is a mistake to reify "nothing" (which is patently true) or that premise (1) is true (which is debatable).

In fact, Demea conflates at least three sorts of argument. They can be separated as follows:

Argument A

1) God is a Perfect Being.

2) A Perfect Being has all perfections.

3) Logically necessary existence, omnipotence, omniscience, and omnibenevolence are perfections.

So: 4) There is a logically necessary, omnipotent, omniscient, omnibenevolent Being.

Argument B

1) Necessarily, whatever exists has a cause.

2) Every existent is either caused by itself or by another.

3) If every being is caused by another, there is an infinite series of causes.

4) An infinite series of causes must be caused by something not itself a member of the series; but the series of causes is *ex hypothesi* all-inclusive; so an infinite series of causes cannot be caused by

something not a member of itself; so there cannot be an infinite series of causes.

So: 5) Some being exists which is caused by itself.

Argument C

1) Whatever exists is such that there is a sufficient explanation of its existence.

2) There is a sufficient explanation of the existence of something only if there exists a logically necessary being that (mediately or immediately) caused that thing.

So: 3) There is a logically necessary being.

Each of these arguments, of course, can be—and has been—multiply refined, rebutted, and restated.[1] I will limit myself to the discussion of them by the participants in the *Dialogues*.

The Notion of Necessary Existence

Hume deals primarily with one concept the arguments share, the concept of a necessary existent. His dismissal of this notion is brief and widely supposed to be definitive.

> [1] Nothing is demonstrable, unless the contrary implies a contradiction. [2] Nothing, that is distinctly conceivable, implies a contradiction. [3] Whatever we conceive as existent, we can also conceive as non-existent. [4] There is no Being, therefore, whose non-existence implies a contradiction. Consequently, [5] there is no being, whose existence is demonstrable. I propose this argument as entirely decisive, and am willing to rest the entire controversy upon it. [*D*, 189]

As (4) and (5) rest on what goes before—(4) following from (2) and (3), and (5) following from (1) and (4)—I will discuss only (1), (2), and (3).

To begin, (1) is certainly apropros with respect to Argument A, which is one version of the ontological argument. The intent of the ontological argument is to show that "God does not exist" is or implies a contradiction, hence showing that "God exists" is demonstrable. It is not so obviously applicable to Argument B, for the relevant concept in B is "a being which is cause of itself." Strictly read, *causa sui* is a contradictory concept—one that could apply to a being only if that being possessed logically incompatible properties. 'X causes y to come to be' entails 'x exists in order to do the causing' and 'y does not exist in order to be brought into existence.' Something, then, could pull off the trick of causing its own existence only by both existing (to cause) and not existing (to be brought about) simultaneously. But of course *causa sui* is not to be read strictly. 'X is self-caused' is to be glossed in part as 'there is nothing distinct from x on which x depends for its existence.' But that is only a partial gloss, for perhaps it is logically possible that something that did not at one time depend on anything else for its existence might later come to be dependent for its existence on something else, or that an originally dependent thing come in the course of time to be independent. So 'x is self-caused' must be read in some such terms as 'It is logically impossible that x depend on anything (else) for its existence.'

The implicit assumption in Part Nine is that *It is logically impossible that x depend on anything else for its existence* entails *X has logically necessary existence*. That assumption is false. A being *x* that necessarily did not depend on anything else for its existence might simply be one of which the following is true: "'x exists' is logically contingent, but *There is a y such that y is not identical to x and x depends for its existence on y* is contradictory."[2]

Thus (a) *It is logically impossible that x depend on anything (else) for its existence*, entails, not (b) *'x exists' is logically necessary*, but rather (c) *'x exists' is logically necessary, or 'x exists' is logically contingent while 'There is a y such that y is not identical to x and x depends for its existence on y' is contradictory*.

To the considerable extent that Cleanthes' critique of Argument B depends on (a) entailing (b) rather than (c), it is defective. And of course to the considerable degree that Demea's argument conflates arguments A and B, it is importantly confused. Similar remarks apply to the notion of 'a being whose existence is its own explanation' (the crucial concept in argument C) as apply to 'a being that is its own cause.'

Hume's mistake, in sum, is in supposing that the only concept of 'necessary being' relevant to arguments B and C is 'logically necessary being,' and it is a mistake in which Hume has plenty of company (including Kant).[3]

Turning to premise (2) of Cleanthes' argument, I think there is no need to say very much. Being 'distinctly conceivable,' I take it, means something like this: proposition P is 'distinctly conceivable' if there are (logically possible) conditions under which P is true. What one offering the ontological argument is affirming is that there are no such conditions for the proposition 'God does not exist.' What one offering argument B or C is affirming *may* be the same, or it may simply be that he is affirming that there are no possible conditions under which 'God depends on something (else) for His existence' is true.

Cleanthes' premise (3) simply denies the conclusion drawn by the ontological arguer. What (3) says is that there are possible conditions under which 'God does not exist' is true. The ontological arguer claims to *prove* that there are no such conditions, and takes it that 'God exists in all possible worlds (and so in our world)' is true; Cleanthes denies this. I do not find anything *more* than sheer denial. So I do not find that this supposedly definitive refutation has in fact furthered the discussion in any way. At most, it provides a suggestion that a would-be ontological-arguer-refuter might follow up successfully. But I am not aware that anyone has. Thus while Hume's discussion has no doubt been historically influential (along with Kant's dictum that existence is not a predicate or property) in foisting upon us the *dicta* that whatever can be conceived to exist can be conceived not to, and that "necessary existence" is a meaningless (or inconsistent) locution, I cannot see the philosophical depth that others pretend to have found here. "God has logically necessary existence" is true if and only if "The proposition *God does not exist* is contradictory" is true, and either that proposition is contradictory or not. So either it is true that God has logically necessary existence, or it is false. Either way, meaninglessness does not come into the matter. Granted, if it is true that God has logically necessary existence, then it is *necessarily* true that He does, and if He lacks necessary existence, then it is *necessarily* true that He lacks it. But necessary falsehoods, being false, are not meaningless. Whichever side one takes in this dispute, arguments are required; simply denying that the other side's conclusion is true gets one nowhere. What Cleanthes needs, then, is an argument for *Whatever we can conceive as existent we can conceive as non-existent*. But he offers none. The standard defenses of Cleanthes' position assert that *Every necessary proposition is hypothetical* and *Every existential statement is contingent*. But propositions like *There is a prime number higher than 17* and *There is a successor to 251* are necessary and existential but neither hypothetical nor contingent. So the ontological argument, whatever its ultimate fate, thus far seems unscathed by Cleanthes' attack on it.

The remainder of the discussion in Part Nine can be dealt with briefly. Cleanthes dismisses the puzzling suggestion by Aquinas that while 'God exists' is indeed necessarily true (existence is included in God's essence), since we do not know that essence we cannot know that it is necessarily true. Clearly this is no defense of the ontological argument as a piece of reasoning any human being could use to prove that God exists to another human being (or to himself), so it seems fair enough to dismiss it as irrelevant to the question as to whether the argument succeeds—whether it proves its conclusion to be true.

The Universe and Necessity

Cleanthes' next move is, in effect, to grant for the sake of the argument that 'x has necessary existence' is both meaningful and true of *something or other*. Why suppose even then, he asks, that it is true of God rather than, say, the material universe? The answer is that the non-existence of the material universe is not inconceivable; that is, 'The material universe does not exist' is not a contradiction. Cleanthes' reply is that

> it seems a great partiality not to perceive, that the same argument extends equally to the Deity, so far as we have any conception of him; and that the mind can at least imagine him to be non-existent. . . . It must be some unknown, inconceivable qualities, which make his non-existence appear impossible. . . . And no reason can be assigned why these qualities may not belong to matter. [*D*, 190]

It seems fair to put Cleanthes' point in this fashion: What connection is there between *other* properties and *being logically necessary?* Are there other properties such that, if a being has them, then it must have logically necessary existence? What connections are there between *being logically necessary* and other properties? Suppose we know that something or other has logically necessary existence. What *further* properties should we ascribe to it? Why ascribe the property set: is omnipotent, omnibenevolent, Creator and Providence? Why not rather ascribe the set: is composed of material entities, is a system in which energy is conserved, and is deterministic?

One way to show that the theistic rather than the materialistic set of properties should be added to our concept of the *ex hypothesi* necessary being would be to show that there was an entailment relation between having that set of properties and having logically necessary existence. Then its having that set of properties would *explain* the *ex hypothesi* logically necessary existence of our necessary being. But while *X is omnipotent and omniscient* entails *Nothing (else) can put X out of existence*, in fact it does not entail that *X has logically necessary exis-*

tence. Further, even if it did, it might be that some other set of proper-ties—even a set inconsistent with the theistic set—was such that if anything possessed the properties in that set, it too was logically nec-essary. Put schematically, let "T" be the set of properties the theist wants to ascribe to the something or other that *ex hypothesi* possesses logically necessary existence. Let "M" be a consistent set of properties such that (a) if x possesses M, then x possesses logically necessary existence and (b) if x has M, x does not have T. Then even if *X has T* entails *X is logically necessary*, this will give us no more reason for as-cribing *T* to x than for ascribing *M* to x—no more reason for being *theists* than for being (as it were) M-ists. Either line would explain pos-session of logically necessary existence as well as the other. It remains true that we seem to have no very plausible candidates for specifying a relevant set of T, or of M, properties.

Suppose, however, that (c) *X is T* entails *X has necessary existence*, and (d) there is no set M of properties such that M is not identical to T and *X is M* entails *X is logically necessary*. Even so, we do not have suf-ficient grounds for ascribing the theistic properties to our postulated necessary being. For there is no reason for accepting the assumption:

> (N) If there is a logically necessary being x, then there is some set S of x's properties such that (1) S does not include the prop-erty necessary existence, and (2) 'x has S' entails 'x is logically necessary.'

Yet without (N), the fact that *X is T* entails *X is logically necessary* would be irrelevant. *Being logically necessary* seems a superb candidate for the status of an ontologically (and so explanatorily) basic or primi-tive property. So far as I can see, then, this sort of endeavor—the attempt to show that possession of the theistic properties of om-nipotence, omniscience, etc. entails possession of logically necessary existence—is completely bankrupt. On the other hand, *X is logically necessary* does not seem to entail either *X has the T-properties* or *X has the M-properties;* there seems no ontological or conceptual linkage in that direction either.

Another attempt to link 'x is T' and 'x is logically necessary'—one which has the prestige of tradition on its side—is the doctrine that some members at least of T (omnipotence, omniscience, and om-nibenevolence for example) are perfections. Suppose we limit T for the remainder of our discussion to the "omni-" properties. The claim is then that each member of T, and also the property *being logically necessary*, have a (second-order) property in common. All of these properties are perfections. But what does this mean? According to Leibniz, some properties are perfections, and some are not. In order to qualify, a property must be *infinite*, *positive*, and *simple*. These terms can be appropriately defined (for Leibniz) as follows:[4]

> A is an *infinite* property if and only if A is a degree of a property Q such that "x has Q to degree A and y has Q to a greater degree than x has Q" is contradictory.

So perfections are the 'logical upper limit' of properties that have a logically maximal degree. Not all properties have degrees—*being prime* does not. Either a number is, or is not, prime, and no prime number is more so than another. Not all degreed properties have logical upper limits; one thing can be hotter than another, but there is no logical upper limit (though there may be a physical or causal limit) on how hot something can get.

> A is a *positive* property if and only if saying "x has A" affirms that x *has* a property, not merely that x lacks a property.

Being red is a positive property; *not being red* is not. While many things are not red, to not be red is not to possess some property, but to lack a particular property. Not being red is a matter of being deprived of redness, not a matter of being apprized of a 'negative property.' *Being ignorant* and *being impotent*, for example, are not positive properties. They are *not* 'negative properties,' if being a negative property is understood as being a property too. As *not existing* is not a way of thinly existing, so *not-being-A* is not a way of thinly *being A* (or any other property), no matter what property we fill in for "A."

> A is a *simple* property if and only if there is no property B such that (i) B is not identical to A, and (ii) B is a part of A.

As I understand it, A's being a simple property allows for there being what used to be called "a distinction of reason" with respect to A. According to an example sometimes used to illustrate the notion of a distinction of reason, a perfect Euclidean Triangle has the properties *being-three-sided* and *being-three-angled*. But that 'in the triangle' that makes it three-sided is the same thing 'in the triangle' that makes it three-angled. To our "distinction of reason" between *being-three-sided* and *being-three-angled* nothing 'real' corresponds.

So far as I know no *clearer* characterization of what it is to be a perfection is available, even though the characterization just rehearsed is something less than lucid.

In the abstract, the definition of "infinite property" seems clear enough. *Being happy* would appear not to be an infinite property, and so not a perfection. *Being wise* (unless this is identical to *being knowledgeable*) may or may not be an infinite property; it is hard to tell. *God is omniscient* often is construed as *For any proposition P, if it is not logically impossible that God know that P, God does know that P.* It seems possible that a being be omniscient in this sense, but foolish or irrational—that God not *act* in such a way as to take advantage of his splendid knowledge. Perhaps one needs here a notion of *omnisapience*—omniscience wisely used. So stated, it is not patent that we are dealing with an *infinite* property. *Being generous* would *seem* not to be an infinite property. And so it goes. Two points, then, seem worth making. One is that a perfection (roughly and intuitively) is supposed to be a property it is better to have than not, and lots of properties it would be better than not to have are not infinite, even if we limit "better" to "morally better." The other is that it would seem to not always be very clear whether a property is in fact infinite or not.

About the notion of "positive property" I shall say only that the notion has its appeal—though I suspect there again will be cases where it is hard to tell whether a candidate is positive or not. (Compare Descartes's doubts about *being hot* and *being cold*.) Its point, roughly, is that while there is verbal parity between "being potent" and "being impotent," "being potent" being definable as "not being impotent" and "being impotent" as "not being potent," only "being potent" actually names (or connotes) a property. It might be construed in part as a protest against negative properties and (by extension) negative facts.

As to "simple property," what one needs is a criterion for identifying simple properties. An obvious one is: property P is part of property Q if and only if 'x is P' entails 'x is Q.' But *X is Euclidean and three-angled* entails, and is entailed by, *X is Euclidean and (closed and) three sided*, yet if they are distinct only by a distinction of reason, they are part of one another only if something can be part of itself. Another attempt would be: P is part of Q if 'x has P' entails 'x has Q,' but not conversely. But of course *X is a machine and x is made by General Motors* entails *X is a machine*, but not conversely, but *being a machine* is a complex property. Intuitively, at least, *being a perfectly determinate primary red* looks like a simple property, a positive property, and an infinite property. But no one wants to say God has this particular perfection. If one adds that a perfection must be better to have than lack, presumably one eliminates *being red*. This serves to make explicit the moral, or at least evaluative, element in the notion of a perfection. In order to make the notion of a perfection clear, one would have to spell out the moral theory, or evaluative theory, that provides content to "is *better* to have than to lack."

It should be clear by now that the notion of a perfection turns out to be rather complex, and it will vary as one changes the moral (or evaluative) theory that is one of its basic elements. None of this is fatal to making the notion of a perfection clear. But I am not aware of any very satisfactory analysis of it. One could try other criteria and analyses. But it is not clear that any others are in fact non-arbitrary, clearer than those already noted, and serviceable for getting the omni-properties and logically necessary existence together by use of the concept of a perfection.

Suppose, however, that one found a clear sense of "perfection" in which logically necessary existence, the omni-properties, and whatever other properties are desirable from a theistic viewpoint to ascribe to God count as perfections. Suppose, further, that nothing else is, in the requisite sense, a perfection. To do the prescribed job one will still need the proposition:

(P) Anything that has one perfection, has them all.

For the idea was to relate the T properties and logically necessary existence in a non-arbitrary, indeed *necessary*, way. Simply *defining* 'x is God' as 'x is a Perfect Being—one who has all perfections'—will not do. For, a Cleanthean will object, it may still be logically possible that something (say, the material universe) have *one* perfection (say, logically necessary existence) but not the other perfections. Whether or not one can think of plausible examples of items actually having some but not other of these properties, the definition may put together otherwise quite logically independent properties. So apparently this possibility must be ruled out. Indeed, one needs, not merely (P), but:

(P') *Necessarily*, if anything has one perfection, it has them all.

Even a clear definition of perfections on which only T-properties (including all the "omni-" properties, perhaps with others) and logically necessary existence are perfections need not *a fortiori* provide a justification for (P'). Hence Cleanthes' query—why ascribe the omni-properties to an *ex hypothesi* proved necessary existent?—remains unanswered.

Consider, in a Cleanthean spirit, a single elementary particle. It seems conceivable that it not exist. Consider also an omnipotent person. It seems conceivable that He not exist. Suppose that I know (a) that both do exist, (b) that at least and at most one of them is (contrary to appearances) logically necessary. Can I decide which? It would seem not. If it is not possible that the particle not exist, not even an omnicompetent person can destroy it. There is no more an entailment between *X is omnipotent* and *X is a logically necessary being* than there is between *X is an elementary particle* and *X is a logically necessary being*. Nor, of course, is there any inductive, or probability, relation in such contexts.

Suppose, instead, that I know (a) both an omnipotent person and an elementary particle exist, and (c) exactly one of these is (in the sense noted above) causally necessary. Can I decide which one is causally necessary? Again, I think not. There is no entailment between *X is omnipotent* and *'X exists' is contingent but 'x depends for its existence on something else' is contradictory*. Presumably an omnipotent being cannot be put out of existence against its will, for *X, who is omnipotent, always exists* seems to describe a possible state of affairs and also one that an omnipotent being can bring about. (*The world exists uncaused by an omnipotent being* describes a possible state of affairs that an omnicompetent being could not bring about.) But it also seems consistent that *X, who is omnipotent, causes his own demise* or that *X, who is omnipotent, puts his existence at something else's mercy*. If so, then no entailment holds between *being omnipotent* and *being causally necessary*; for a being could have the former property but lack the latter.

It might seem, though, that *X is an elementary particle* does entail *X is causally necessary*, for what it is to be an elementary particle is to satisfy the concept 'elementary particle' in current physical theory, and part of what this involves is not depending for existence on anything else. But that, of course, would not be enough; the concept would have to require that whatever satisfied it be such that it is logically, and not merely *de facto*, impossible that it be dependent on anything else. Even if physical theory required that such particles be eternal, since two eternal entities being co-dependent is not logically impossible, such a requirement would not entail that anything be causally necessary. Even if *An elementary particle depends on no other physical item for its existence* is a necessary truth, the question as to whether it depends on God for its existence remains an open question; hence its causal dependence remains an open question. It seems a perfectly consistent state of affairs that an omnipotent being exist, and that this being destroy the particle. But then the particle would, so to say, depend for its existence on the good graces of its potent cosmic colleague. This points up a distinction we have thus far neglected between *x has causal necessity* and what we may call *necessary causal independence* where *x is necessarily causally independent* if and only if *It is logically impossible that anything distinct from x cause x not to exist*. Were an omnipotent being and an elementary particle to have always existed in the past, and both to possess causal necessity, still neither need therefore possess necessary causal independence. While it might be the case that a physical theory, or a theological system, provided connections which linked *having necessary existence, being causally necessary, being causally independent* (and in the theological case, the traditional "omni" properties) to one another conceptually, these conceptual links would of course be sure to reflect corresponding connections among the objects of these concepts (if any) only to the degree that it was sure that the theory of system was itself justified.

Suppose, finally, that a being was omnipotent, omniscient, *and* perfectly good. It may be a necessary truth that *No omnipotent, omniscient, perfectly good being commits suicide by its own actions or by what it permits another being to do*. Perhaps it is also a necessary truth that *No omnipotent, omniscient being can be put out of existence by anything else against its will*. If so, then an omnipotent, omniscient, and perfectly good being, if it has these properties necessarily or as essential properties, will also possess necessary causal independence. It does not follow that it will have logically necessary existence. Perhaps, so to speak, *necessary causal independence* is the strongest property it will follow that a being with the "omni-" properties will possess.

The point of these rather abstract remarks is this. A not unnatural development of Cleanthes' remarks leads one to note that there is no necessary connection between the various "perfections" as usually conceived, and that while one may be able to develop a system which provides a rationale for ascribing them all to one being—and while orthodox Judaism and Christianity may do this—the rationale depends on the plausibility of the system and not on the force of a single *a priori* argument. These points rather plainly strike deeply at the ontological argument in many, perhaps all, of its traditional formulations. While I will not argue the point here, the same seems to be true with regard to contemporary reformulations of the ontological argument.

Explanation and Infinite Series

Cleanthes makes two brief criticisms in concluding his critique. Demea had assumed that if an infinite series of things, each of which was caused to exist by its predecessor, were supposed or shown to exist, then besides the explanation of the existence of the members of the series, an explanation of the series itself would also be requisite. And this may seem quite clearly mistaken. If we explain that Adam exists because God created him, and Eve exists because God made her, we do not need in addition to explain the existence of the set composed of Adam and Eve. That has already been done. As Cleanthes puts it, "Did I show you the particular causes of each individual in a collection of twenty particles of matter, I should think it very unreasonable, should you afterwards ask me, what was the cause of the whole twenty. This is sufficiently explained in explaining the cause of the parts" (190, 191).

Conceivably, one might need an explanation of why the members of a set had one order rather than another. But that is not an explanation of how some object that was not has come to be. It is rather an explanation, so to speak, of how what already was has come to be where it is.

Perhaps we can put something like Demea's point in this manner: Suppose there is an infinitely long causal chain of objects, each brought into existence by its temporally precedent member. Consider some member A of that chain. A was caused by its precedent member in the chain; but that member is as yet unexplained. It will be explained by *its* predecessor; but then the predecessor awaits explanation. And so we can see that if there is an infinitely long causal series that never began and is ordered so that each member of the series is effect of a prior member and cause of a later member, and if we endeavor to explain the existence of the members of that series one at a time, we shall never be done. Further, at any stage, we shall explain one being by bringing onto the stage another being as yet unexplained. Perhaps we can put something like Cleanthes' reply by saying that still another being is always in the wings whose entry will explain the existence of the as yet unexplained being. Further, we can give a *general* explanation of the form: every being is such that its existence is explained by the existence of its predecessor in the causal chain. Nothing is left out of the general explanation—no being is left over in the sense that its existence is not accounted for (unless we have to refer to some being not a member of the series—but the argument was intended to *establish* that necessity and so cannot *assume* it). On this point, surely, Cleanthes is quite right.

Demea's point, however, may be that *there being logically contingent things that are not necessarily causally independent* needs explanation—this is something that it is appropriate to ask the explanation of, and expect an answer. The existence of a chain of logically contingent things that are not necessarily causally independent, however long successively or simultaneously, will not provide *that* explanation. Perhaps Demea's reasoning, then, goes something along these lines: Cleanthes' explanation assumes the existence of contingent entities that lack necessary causal independence; whether there is one such entity or an infinite number of them ranked in a causal series, that such things exist is not self-explanatory. Hence Cleanthes' explanation contains a non-self-explanatory assumption. On this point, Demea is right.

Cleanthes and Demea may differ here as to where explanations may properly stop. Cleanthes continues: "In tracing an eternal succession of objects, it seems absurd to inquire for a general cause or first Author. How can any thing, that exists from eternity, have a cause, since that relation implies a priority in time and a beginning of existence" (*D*, 190)?

Cleanthes' way of putting the point is somewhat defective. If something is eternal, it is *a*temporal; nonetheless, if x and y are both eternal, still x might depend for its existence on y. 'X is eternal' does not entail 'x is dependent on nothing for its existence.' Contrary to Aristotle, *being eternal* and *being contingent* are *compatible* properties. Thus it makes sense to claim that 'x *eternally* causes y.' Thus, contrary to Cleanthes, something can exist eternally and yet be caused.

Nonetheless, Cleanthes' fundamental point is sound. If we suppose that there is a series of beings, each caused by a temporally prior being, such that the series stretches back forever into the past, we do not make a contradictory assumption. Nor does it *follow* from this supposition that there is a temporally first cause of the series (it follows instead that there is *not*) or that there must be some being not a member of the series on which the members of the series *also* depend (as well as depending on their temporal predecessors). There may be such a further being; the supposition does not tell us. If we can tell, appeal to some further claim will be necessary. Various versions of the principle of sufficient reason are typically appealed to in this context. The dispute between Demea and Cleanthes, at this point, will be over whether a strong enough version to serve Demea's purposes can be justified. A follower of Demea will favor a version that entails that anything lacking necessary causal independence has an explanation and that no explanation of such things is sufficient that does not refer to beings whose hold on existence is at least as strong as that provided by necessary causal independence.

Philonian Determinism

Philo concludes Part Nine with two remarks. One is to effect that, if we postulate the existence of a necessary being, we can go further and postulate that every relation anything bears to anything else is necessary. Of course, we cannot *see* that all propositions of the form 'x is related in way R to y' express necessary truths. Indeed, so far as we can tell, a great many such propositions are clearly contingent. But (though it seems very unlikely) perhaps we may be wrong about this. Suppose that we are, so that every relation anything bears to anything is one that it logically could not but have borne to that thing. This perspective attracts Philo.

At first blush, this may elicit an even greater admiration of the order, and so the artificer, of the cosmos. Imagine, not only great adjustment of means and ends, but an adjustment in which all means-ends relations, as well as all other relations, are *necessarily* as they are! But whatever reflection on these matters does to our admiration of cosmic order, it cannot long sustain admiration for its artificer. For if *Necessarily, xRy* is true, an artificer cannot gain *credit* for the fact that *xRy*. That fact obtains *no matter what*. A *creator* could get credit for there being an x and a y. But a *designer* cannot even get credit for that. A designer can get credit only for the arrangements of his given materials. But on the present hypothesis, all arrangements are as they must be and they could be no other way at all. At best, the "designer" necessarily does what cannot but be done. The designer is herself much more like a (non-random) machine than like a genuine designer.

> It is observed by arithmeticians, that the products of 9 compose always either 9 or some lesser product of nine; if you add together all the characters, of which any of the former products is composed. . . . To a superficial observer, so wonderful a regularity may be admired as either the effect of chance or design; but a skillful algebraist immediately concludes it to be the work of necessity. [*D*, 191]

So the question arises, Is the order manifest in the universe contingent or necessary? If the order is contingent—if things could have been disorderly or otherwise ordered—design remains a viable hypothesis. If the order is necessary, then the design hypothesis must go. For while one may congratulate Pythagoras on *seeing* his theorem, we cannot coherently congratulate him on *making* it *true*.

> Is it not probable, I ask, that the whole economy of the universe is conducted by a like necessity, though no human algebra can furnish a key which solves the difficulty? And instead of admiring the order of natural beings, may it not happen, that, could we penetrate into the intimate nature of bodies, we should clearly see why it was absolutely impossible, they could ever admit any other disposition? So dangerous is it to introduce this idea of necessity into the present question! And so naturally does it afford an inference opposite to the religious hypothesis! [*D*, 191]

The answer to Philo's question seems to me negative. In any case, that a necessary being exists does not entail that every proposition of the form *xRy* is either necessarily true or contradictory. At most, it raises the reflection that this might be so. But this reflection is itself an explanation of designedness which is incompatible with the religious (design) hypothesis and is, strictly speaking, compatible with the data (for it grants that many relations *seem* quite contingent).

Finally, says Philo, not many people *accept* the ontological argument or the argument to a First Cause or Sufficient Explainer anyway. "Men did, and ever will, derive their religion from other sources than from this species of reasoning" (*D*, 192). Perhaps this is so.

CHAPTER 12

Evil, Happiness, and Goodness

Religion and Fear (*Dialogues*, Part Ten)

IN PARTS TEN and Eleven of the *Dialogues*, Hume deals with some among the set of issues usually referred to as "the problem of evil." Demea opens by suggesting that "each man feels the truth of religion within his own breast; and from a consciousness of his imbecility and misery, rather than from any reasoning, is led to seek protection from that Being on whom he and all nature is dependent" (*D*, 193). Philo cheerfully assents that "the best and indeed the only method of bringing every one to a due sense of religion is by just representations of the misery and wickedness of men. And for that purpose a talent of eloquence and strong imagery is more requisite than that of reasoning and argument" (*D*, 193). Demea says that "futurity is still the object of all our hopes and fears" (193), and he and Philo ring the changes on "Religion rises from human hopes and fears" in a way reminiscent of the *Natural History*. Supposedly, they for a while join "the poets, who speak from sentiment, and without a system"; but of course the *Natural History* provides a systematic backdrop for their discussion, although it is a system intended to *explain* rather than *justify* religious belief. Since we have already discussed and appraised that system, all that is requisite here is to note the reappearance in the *Dialogues* of the view that religious belief arises in good part from the darker emotions. We should, then, simply note that here too—as well as in other crucial respects—the concluding portions of the *Dialogues* must be seen in the broader context of Hume's writings, and seen particularly as closely related to the themes of the *Natural History*. I turn, then, to the problem of evil.

Perhaps the first thing to note in this regard is the long discussion (it takes up most of Part Ten) documenting the thesis that "neither man nor any other animal . . . [is] happy" (*D*, 198). The legion causes of human misery are rehearsed *ad nauseam:* "necessity, hunger, want . . . fear, anxiety, terror . . . weakness, impatience, distress, . . . agony, horror" (*D*, 194); one kind making prey of another; fear of imaginary and dream objects; "oppression, injustice, contempt, contumely, violence, sedition, war, calumny, treachery, fraud" (*D*, 195); disease (both mental and physical); fear of death—and the list is incomplete at that. Why the tremendous emphasis on the causes of human misery?

Philo's query provides the point:

> And is it possible, Cleanthes . . . that after all these reflections, and infinitely more, which might be still suggested, you can still persevere in your anthropomorphism, and assert the moral attributes of the Deity, his justice, benevolence, mercy, and rectitude to be of the same nature with these virtues in human creatures? [*D*, 198]

But Hume of course knows that a good many believers have both been aware of each and every "cause of misery" that he lists and have nonetheless firmly held that God is good. In what respect, if any, are they inconsistent in so doing? The remainder of Philo's remark is intended to answer this question.

> His power we allow infinite: Whatever he wills is executed: But neither man nor any other animal are happy: Therefore he does not will their happiness. His wisdom is infinite: He is never mistaken in choosing the means to any end: But the course of nature tends not to human or animal felicity: Therefore it is not established for that purpose. Through the whole compass of human knowledge, there are no inferences more certain and infallible than these. In what respect, then, do his benevolence and mercy resemble the benevolence and mercy of men? [*D*, 198]

Hedonism

Two central themes play their roles in this argument, one obvious and one implicit. The obvious theme is that among human beings what is viewed as good is closely related to what is believed to bring happiness and what is viewed as evil is closely related to what is believed to cause misery. Further, happiness is closely connected with (perhaps, is identical to) the varieties of pleasure and misery with the varieties of pain. "Satisfactions" are contrasted with "pains" (*D*, 198, 199)—and the tone of the discussion, more than the explicitly stated doctrine, is hedonic: the good is what is itself pleasurable or causes pleasure, the evil is what is itself painful or causes pain. Further still, good agents endeavor to so act as to produce happiness and evil agents are those who endeavor to so act as to produce unhappiness. These themes at least move in the direction of ethical hedonism—the doctrine that pain alone is inherently evil and pleasure alone is inherently good.

Insofar as Philo's overall argument concerning the problem of evil rests on hedonism being true (being a correct ethical theory), the argument fails. For while this is not the place to recount them in detail, hedonism has been subjected to very powerful and conclusive criticisms. For example, feeling malice is a matter of taking pleasure in the innocent sufferings and misfortunes of others; while pleasurable, it is also inherently wrong. If a type of pleasure is inherently wrong, hedonism is false. Another criticism of hedonism points out that many good things—knowledge, friendship, love, for example—are at least as plausibly viewed as inherently good as is pleasure and are neither identical to pleasure nor valuable only for the pleasure they may bring. If in an attempt to meet this criticism the hedonist so construes "pleasure" that by definition it refers to *any* good thing, "pleasure" is defined in terms of "good" and not the reverse as was intended. In sum: not all pleasure is good, and some good things are not good merely because they are pleasurable. It is not likely that anyone whom Philo is attacking will be a hedonist. Theistic ethics are not hedonistic ethics—if pleasure is seen as an intrinsic good at all in the context of a theistic ethic, it is not seen as the only one. So Philo cannot make his argument simply *ad hominem*. He must first prove hedonism correct, and then make his critique. But no attempt is made at proving hedonism correct and in any case no such attempt could succeed.

But if Philo's argument sounds the more plausible for its hedonic atmosphere, it does not strictly require that hedonism be true. We can best see this by making explicit the implicit theme referred to above.

The Equivocation Argument

If one examines Philo's remarks, as quoted above, with some care, it becomes obvious that Philo is assuming this claim:

> (1) If 'good' means the same thing (or something closely analo-
> gous) in 'God is good' and (say) 'Isaiah is good,' then God and
> humans share the same moral ends.

That is, if God is good then the things that God regards as morally
worth the seeking or having (for example, knowledge, love) will be
the same as a really good human person regards as morally worth the
having. What a human person rightly believes to be morally good that
other persons seek or possess, God too views as morally good. Happiness (not necessarily hedonistically defined here) is just the sort of
thing that morally good human persons take to be good that human
persons possess. But humans are not in general happy. God could
make them happy—being omnipotent He has the power, omniscient
the knowledge, and omnibenevolent the will (if His goodness is like
ours). So either He lacks the knowledge or the power, or His sort
of goodness is quite unlike the sort we sometimes to some degree
actually possess. So beginning with (1), Philo in effect develops this
argument:

> (1) If 'good' means the same thing (or something closely analo-
> gous) in 'God is good' and (say) 'Isaiah is good,' then God and
> human persons share the same moral ends (prize the same in-
> trinsic goods).
> (2) Humans take their possession of happiness as an intrinsic
> good—indeed, the highest goal a human person can attain.
> (3) In general, human persons are not happy.
> (4) God could make all human persons happy, and if He too
> prized human happiness He would do so.
> So: (5) God does not prize human happiness (at least not as the
> highest good a human person can attain). (*D*, 314)
> So: (6) 'Good' does not mean the same thing (or something closely
> analogous) in 'God is good' and (say) 'Isaiah is good.' (1, 2, 5)

Steps (2) and (3) are to be taken as very general empirical reports,
or perhaps as inductions from relevant representative cases. Step (4)
is intended as a consequence of 'God is omnipotent and omniscient.'
Step (5) seems to result from a decision to leave God's other properties besides omnibenevolence intact, so to speak, and then see what
will follow concerning divine omnibenevolence given (1) through (4).
The conclusion (6) should perhaps be viewed as following from steps
(1), (2), and (5) with the understanding that human happiness encom-
passes all or most other goods (as we view things) or as vastly the

most important good (from a human point of view). Does, then, the argument succeed?

The Equivocation Argument Assessed

For various reasons, it does not. One central issue is just what is to be meant by "happiness." Aristotle long ago reminded us that while it is no doubt true that all seek happiness, what they take happiness to be varies quite considerably. If we agree to rule out (for reasons suggested above) the facile "happiness = pleasure with absence of pain" view, what other accounts of happiness are available? Obviously, very many. Philo's argument will fare better with some than with others. But which ones are relevant? Or are they *all* relevant?

It would seem that Philo's strongest case will be made if he can accept, at least for the purposes of his argument, some doctrine of happiness felicitous to the theists. Then he will need no independent defense of that doctrine, the *ad hominem* route being thereby available.

A theistic account of happiness presumably will develop two themes familiar in, and basic to, Judeo-Christian theism—that human persons are made in the image of God and that the core of morality is the imitation of God. To be happy is to realize one's potential, develop one's capacities, as one made in God's image, in imitation of God (insofar as this is possible to a human being) and in obedience to God's commands. Happiness, so understood, is less the psychological sense of well-being and more the moral character of one who acts toward others in intelligent love. These themes are present in the biblical Old and New Testaments and are frequently referred to in the ensuing theological and philosophical traditions. While their elaboration is not our present task, the resultant concept of moral maturity is one in which suffering looms large and a faith that triumphs over adversity is highly prized. So Job says "Even though He slay me, yet will I trust him" and the author of Hebrews says that even the one whom he regards as God Incarnate had, as a man, to "become perfect [mature] through suffering." Through a life in which suffering has its role, along with many other and more easily embraced experiences, one may grow toward the point where one makes the interests of others one's own. Happiness becomes (as in Aristotle) a condition of character, not a psychological tone—a status rather than a feeling state.

Of course these remarks are sketchy and therefore to a degree vague. But their point should be clear—if one's happiness is one's attaining one's potential as one made in God's image, some or all of the "causes of misery" Hume lists so fully (or their moral equivalents) may be essential features of any world in which such attainment is genuinely possible. The same will be true for other, non-theistic conceptions, which nonetheless share much of the "growth through trials" theme.

All of this becomes relevant to the questions '*Could* God make us happy?' and 'Is this world the sort of world in which, even in the long run, human happiness can be attained?' The answer to these questions is not so obvious as it might seem. That God is omnipotent perhaps does *not* entail that He can make us happy if happiness is conceived as gaining the status of moral maturity. For consider the claims that:

> (P1) A person can gain moral maturity (= happiness) only by making free and morally relevant choices rightly.
>
> (P2) If a choice is made freely by an agent, then it is "up to the agent" how it is made—the agent can in fact choose to perform or not to perform the action in question, given the agent's own past history, the history of the cosmos, and all conditions which exist at the time of the agent's choosing.

If (P1) and (P2) are true, then "God makes agent A happy" (in contrast to "God made A, who is happy") does not describe a possible state of affairs. Whether God can simply *make* a person happy or not depends, not merely on whether He is omnipotent, but in what being happy consists. Hedonic happiness is no doubt producible by fiat, but that is irrelevant.

Correspondingly, for what has unfortunately come to be called the "vale of soul making" view of human happiness (or, better, human maturity), not only is it plausible that fiat will not produce it, but also that some conditions or other of temptation and trial are (not merely causally but) logically necessary. Fortitude without pain, courage without fear, honesty without temptation to lie, compassion without suffering—so at least one traditional view maintains—are logically impossible, no more to be had than triangles without angles or handshakes without hands. Hence step (4) in Philo's argument—which says that God could simply make all people happy—is altogether dubious. Perhaps God cannot make people happy. But then (5)—which claims that God does not prize human happiness—is without support.

It may be (I do not know) that most people—say, more than half—would prefer hedonic satisfaction without concern for moral maturity along Aristotelian or Kantian or Judaic or Christian lines. Suppose that they would, so that the report enshrined in Philo's second step may be read along hedonistic lines. Nothing will follow, so far as I can see, that will in any way aid Philo's case. For what is crucial is not what humans *do* prize, but what they *ought* to prize, or what they do prize *insofar as they are good*. If we prize most something that we ought not to prize so highly, then so far forth we are not good, and the ends we value highest cannot be used to determine what ends good persons most value. What, then, is one to make of (2), which contends that (most) persons prize happiness most highly? I suspect that any sense in which (2) is clearly true will be a very general one of something like this:

> (2') People take their possession of happiness (in some sense or other of the word "happiness") as an intrinsic good—indeed, the highest good one can attain.

And given *this* reading of (2), it is hard to see that it plays much of a role in the argument. As part of the buttressing for (6)—the argument's conclusion—"happiness" must appear in (2) with the same meaning as it has in step (5). No doubt there are senses of "happiness" in which no good being, human or divine, prizes it as the peak of all moral goods. The problem with (2) is that it is simply not clear that, in any determinate sense of "happiness," all or most persons do prize it, and so it is not clear that (2) is true. In some senses of "happiness," as noted, even were (2) true it would be irrelevant to the argument.

Suppose, though, that it is true that all persons prize moral maturity—their own and others'—as the highest good; let *that* be what (2) says, and suppose that this is so. Step (3) says that most people are not, in that sense, happy. But it is altogether problematic that God can, in that sense, *make* anyone happy (as [4] requires). So (5), which says that God does not prize human happiness, and hence (6), the argument's conclusion, both are unsupported.

In sum, it is hard (perhaps impossible) to find any very determinate sense of "happiness" in which (2) is both true and relevant. Further, even if this were accomplished, there is nothing like a guarantee that, in that sense, God can *make* anyone happy. Even given (2), (5) remains problematic. Granting (1) and (3), the road to (6) seems impossible.

Two further, brief comments seem relevant. One objection to the preceding argument is that while this discussion makes moral maturity (as a human achievement) central in theistic tradition, it is grace—unmerited forgiveness of sin by God—that is central. There is much to be said for this reservation, but the same sort of argument can be easily put in the hypothetical objector's terms. For central to the tradition in question is the view that grace, freely offered, must be freely received. Love required is no love at all; grace irresistible is but power in disguise, and a kindly disposed despot is still not a Heavenly Father. So consider the claims:

(P3) While one is "saved by grace, not by works," free acceptance of divine grace is a necessary condition of salvation.

(P4) It is logically impossible that grace be both freely accepted and divinely determined.

The weaving of these remarks into a notion of human happiness relevant to an analogue of the preceding argument is left as an exercise for the reader.

Happier Possible Persons?

Another objection is this: surely of all the people God could have made, there is a subset who (if created) would be happier than the actual denizens of earth. But here we meet a problem. If we wish to speculate concerning persons who might have been created but will not be—concerning unactualized 'possible persons'—then our sample set is surely the persons there are. Inductive inferences to (other than purely formal) propositions of the form "Possible persons would have ——" will require as their support propositions of the form "Actual persons do have ——." It seems evident that such an inference, with the sentence blanks filled in by specification of some particular degree of happiness, will require parity of supplementation. For any degree of happiness, we can justifiably claim that unactualized possible persons would have degree D of happiness only if actual persons have achieved degree D of happiness. Put formally, a (contingent) property may not be ascribed with inductive justification to unobserved members of the reference class (all persons, actual or not) which is not known to belong to any member of the sample class (observed actual persons). So either we cannot project degrees of would-be happiness onto possible persons, or the degrees projected will be the twins of the degrees actually obtained by ourselves and others.

Means and Ends

While there are unending intricacies to the problems of evil, so that any treatment will leave some issues untouched, it seems appropriate to restrict the present discussion of the relevant portion of Philo's argument to one further point. While it seems right to say that if persons A and B are good in the same sense or in closely similar senses, they (at least mainly) agree as to what *ends* are worthy of being morally prized, the same does not hold for the *means* each may appropriately use to attain those ends.

Perhaps this point can best be made in terms of what critics at times use as a supposedly paradigm case of unjustified evil; the painful death of an infant or child. No human being who could prevent such a death and does not, and who had no morally sufficient reason for not doing so, is (at least so far as that act is concerned) a good person. Further, one who can commit sins of omission of that magnitude surely reveals what is charitably called a character defect. Further still, it is hard to see what point there could be to such an "act of omission"—unless it be that the infant or child was known to face imminent incurable insanity or coma. But such justification of a sin of omission comes through appeal to prevented worse evils, not to goods. Allowing an infant or child to die a painful death is not a means that we can use for good ends. (Whether there is *some* exotic circumstance in which this could occur is hardly to the point.)

Nonetheless it is a means a good God might use, provided of course (something God could presumably easily arrange, and something maintained by the tradition) that the person in question survived death. "God is the God of the living, not of the dead." From this perspective, death itself, as well as fear or pain or suffering, might be a means God used for an end of which any good person would approve—even though perhaps we (having no experience in such matters) cannot see how death fits into the providential pattern of growth (in the long run) to moral maturity. That two beings both most highly prize the same end but find that pursuit of that end requires use of different means due to a great difference in the power and knowledge these beings possess, is in no way surprising or objectionable. That two beings are good in the same or a similar sense does not, then, entail that they must use the same means to attain those ends. This point also is relevant to a later argument concerning the meaningfulness of "God is good," an argument to be discussed in the context of Part Eleven.

The Argument of Epicurus

Philo follows the argument we have been discussing with a reference to Epicurus: "Epicurus's old questions are yet unanswered. Is he willing to prevent evil, but not able? Then is he impotent. Is he able, but not willing? Then is he malevolent. Is he both able and willing? Whence then is evil" (*D*, 198)? Formally stated, the argument runs:

> (1) If God is willing to prevent evil, but not able, He is impotent.
> (2) If God is able, but not willing, to prevent evil He is malevolent.
> (3) If God is able and willing, there would be no evil.
> (4) There is evil.

So: (5) God is unable or unwilling to prevent evil. (3, 4)

So: (6) God is impotent or malevolent. (1, 2, 5)

What are we to say about this argument?

Premise (1) apparently can be simplified. If God is not able to prevent evil, whether He is willing to or not, He is impotent. It is a necessary truth that *If God is unable to do x, then God is impotent with respect to x*—with perhaps the proviso that 'God does x' is not contradictory. So we can reduce (1) to:

> (1') If God is unable to prevent evil, He is impotent (with respect to preventing evil).

As an instantiation of a necessary truth, (1') is necessarily true; (1) contains irrelevant material and its purified reformulation is (1'). But this line of reasoning concerning (1) and (1') is not quite fair to Epicurus. The reference to being unable to prevent evil in (1) is not simply unnecessary, and the appropriate replacement for (1) is not (1') but rather:

> (1a) If God does not prevent evil but is willing to do so, then He is impotent with respect to preventing evil.

This is so, even though (reading "is willing to" as "will, if He can") (1a) also is a necessary truth.

The same sort of consideration applies to (2). For part of the idea behind (2) is:

> (2a) If God does not prevent evil, but is able to do so, then He must be unwilling to prevent evil.

With regard to human agents, (2a) would not be a necessary truth. If I can do something and do not do so, it does not follow that I am unwilling to it. Doing it may just never have crossed my mind. But this qualification (and whatever analogous matters there are) *ex hypothesi* does not apply to God. So perhaps (2a) is a necessary truth, concerning God but not humans.

But (2a) expresses only part of the sense of (2). Also requisite is:

(2b) If God is unwilling to prevent evil, He is malevolent.

Consider, then, (1a) and (2a) together:

(1a) If God does not prevent evil but is willing to do so, He is impotent with respect to preventing evil.
(2a) If God does not prevent evil but is able to do so, then He must be unwilling to prevent evil.

We can conflate (1a) and (2a) into:

(A) If God does not prevent evil, either He is impotent to do so or unwilling to do so.

At least one problem remains even with (A) for, according to theistic belief God is not willing that any should perish—but some will. For at least one central theistic viewpoint, if human persons freely choose to reject divine grace, they will be damned even though God wills that none perish. For He also wills that only those who come freely come at all. So some assertions about what God wills will be about what He wills that others will (freely) do. (A) concerns only what God wills that He himself should do. So read, (A) is a necessary truth.

We can now restate Epicurus's conundrum:

(A) If God does not prevent evil, either He is impotent to do so or unwilling to do so.
(B) There is evil.

So: (C) God does not prevent evil. (from [B])
So: (D) God is impotent to do so or unwilling to do so.

The Argument of Epicurus Assessed

So far, so good; but the theist need not be in any way unhappy about admitting (D). But the argument continues:

(E) If God is unwilling to prevent evil, He is malevolent. [= (2b)]
So: (F) God is impotent to prevent evil or malevolent. (from [D] and [E])

(F) is not a proposition that the theist can consistently accept. But why should she, or anyone, accept (E)?

It is important to distinguish between (E) and (E'):

> (E') If God is unwilling to prevent evil, *and has no morally suffi-cient reason for doing so*, He is malevolent.

Then it is clear that it is (E') that is true whereas Epicurus needs (E). Of course (E') plus *God has no morally sufficient reason for allowing evil* will yield (E)—but then we should need a justification of *that* additional claim, and none is forthcoming in the *Dialogues*. Nor, so far as I know, is there such a justification anywhere else. So Philo's appeal to Epicurus does not aid his cause.

If *God is omnipotent and omnibenevolent* and *There is evil* were incompatible, then *God exists* and *There is evil* would (in appropriate and easily supplied context) entail *God is impotent or malevolent or amoral*. Perhaps one could successfully argue that a being who allowed evil for no morally sufficient reason is *im*moral, not merely *a*moral. Then one would have (F) or what is tantamount to it, by a different route of argumentation. But that route (we shall see in discussing Part Eleven) is closed. Nor can I see any other that will yield (E), and thence (F).

Omnibenevolence and the Phenomena

Philo next grants to Cleanthes that one may "ascribe . . . a purpose and intention to nature" (*D*, 198), but that the claim that this purpose is benevolent is unsupported by evidence: "How then does the divine benevolence display itself, in the sense of you anthropo-morphites? None but we mystics, as you were pleased to call us, can account for this strange mixture of phenomena, by deriving it from attributes, infinitely perfect, but incomprehensible" (*D*, 199) Philo here returns to safer ground, no longer arguing that he can prove that God is impotent or malevolent, but arguing instead that God's omnibenevolence cannot be inferred from "the phenomena" nor can a benevolent purpose be therein discerned by our simply taking thought. This, as we have already said, seems quite right.

Still another pair of arguments is suggested by some remarks of Philo.

> Allowing you . . . that . . . human happiness, in this life, exceeds its misery . . . you have done nothing. For this is not, by any means, what we expect from infinite power, infinite wisdom, and infinite goodness. Why is there any misery at all in the world?

Not by chance, surely. From some cause then. Is it from the intention of the Deity? But he is perfectly benevolent. Is it contrary to his intention? But he is almighty. Nothing can shake the solidity of this reasoning, so short, so clear, so decisive; except we assert, that these subjects exceed all human capacity, and that our common measures of truth and falsehood are not applicable to them; a topic, which I have all along insisted on. [*D*, 201]

Of course a substantial part of this "so short, so clear, so decisive" reasoning is rewarmed Epicurus, and the description of this reasoning (for reasons just rehearsed) is hence vastly more optimistic than is justified. But there are hints of two other lines of reasoning. The suggestion that "these subjects exceed all human capacity . . . our common measures of truth and falsehood are not applicable" brings to mind the claim that "good" in "God is good" is equivocal with respect to "good" in (say) "Isaiah is good." Further, the references to chance and causality indicate that perhaps Philo is wondering whether the theist can *explain* the existence of evil, even in the most general possible terms. Both matters appear again in Part Eleven, and we will discuss them in that context.

CHAPTER 13

Evil, Prediction, and Probability

The Prediction Argument (*Dialogues*, Part Eleven)

WE HAVE NOTED that Part Eleven contains arguments which question whether the theist can explain the existence of evil even in the most general terms (whether he can consistently say that God is either the "direct" or the "indirect" cause of evil) and whether "God is good" is intelligible. But though these matters loom large in Part Eleven, they do not begin it. Pride of place is given to the *prediction argument:*

> It must, I think, be allowed, that, if a very limited intelligence, whom we shall suppose utterly unacquainted with the universe, were assured, that it were the production of a very good, wise and powerful Being, however finite [the person was], he would, from his conjectures, form beforehand a different notion of it from what we find it to be by experience nor would he ever imagine, merely from those attributes of the cause, of which he is informed, that the effect could be so full of vice and misery and disorder, as it appears in this life. [*D*, 203–204]

It is not easy to see that one should put much weight on this sort of argument. If the "limited intelligence" has all the moral and causal knowledge she needs in order to answer such questions as: (a) are the ends that can be attained in this world of the highest value; and (b) are the means open to agents in seeking these ends of the morally most appropriate kinds. Then we should perhaps pay her careful attention. If not, and if she lacks even the moral and causal knowledge that experience and growth in character yield (and I take it that this is the intent) it really seems inappropriate that such an agent be surprised at anything at all. If Hume's point is that *we* are sometimes surprised, the question is whether that surprise is *evidence* for anything concerning the moral attributes of God. I do not see that it is, nor is any argument given to this effect in the *Dialogues*. Perhaps, charitably read, the prediction argument simply provides another way of putting Philo's sound point that the design argument does not establish that God is omnibenevolent.

Is Evil *a Priori* Unlikely?

The prediction argument receives much of what force it has from the assumption that there being any evil at all in a world created by God is *a priori* unlikely. It is questionable whether *anything* is *a priori* unlikely, and one of the weaknesses of some theories of confirmation is that they require *a priori* assignments of probability to logically contingent claims. No non-arbitrary basis for such assignments seems available. The *ad hominem* points that Hume's views on induction are incompatible with any such assessment having evidential value and Hume's claim regarding causality that *a priori* anything can cause anything prevent a consistent Humean from pressing the prediction argument.

Even brief reflection on other, initially more promising, grounds for the prediction argument shows the initial promise to be deceptive. It has seemed to some obvious both that an omnicompetent God would create the best of all possible worlds and that such a world would contain no evil. This would support the prediction argument. That there is any coherent notion of a best of all possible worlds is hardly indubitable. Its sponsor, Leibniz, offered as criterion for such a world that it maximize complexity (measured by *kinds* represented in a world), maximize simplicity (measured by the number of logically independent explanatory principles required to account for what a world contained), and maximize the cardinality of self-conscious agents (the more creatures of the sort most like God, the better). I am not aware of a Leibnizean ruling as to which element within the criterion has pride of place when, as seems reasonable to expect, applying one element yields a different judgment regarding the perfection-quotient of a world than does applying another. Aquinas suggested that for any world God created, He could create a better; no world, he thought, could be absolutely as good a world as omnicompetence could produce.

There is no need here to try to adjudicate between Leibniz and Aquinas. It is enough that we consider the impact of *the Leibniz line* and *the Aquinas line* on the prediction argument. The Aquinas line supposes that for any world God creates, He can create a better; necessarily, then, the notion of a best possible world—the best even omnicompetence can do—is incoherent. Since Aquinas and Leibniz embrace incompatible modal claims, one must be mistaken. Since false modal claims are necessarily false, one or the other must have accepted a view that is necessarily false or contradictory. If the Aquinas line is correct, a morally perfect being does not face the duty of creating the best possible world if He creates at all. If the Leibniz line is correct, things are more complicated. God does have that duty, and exactly one world must best satisfy the criteria of minimizing principles and maximizing variety and agents.

Certainly for anything that Hume has *shown*, and not just assumed, a world could be created by God and yet contain evil. If achieving moral virtue involves conquering evil or if moral agents need be free and so capable of making wrong choices or if both of these are correct, a world that contains or possesses any moral worth will or may contain evil. A world created by a morally perfect being is not implausibly thought of as containing or possessing moral worth. Hence, on the present account of the conditions of virtue and the proclivities of free agents, a world created by a morally perfect (and otherwise omnicompetent) being is not implausibly thought of as containing evil. The assumption that the best possible world will not contain evil is far from obvious.

The Aquinas Line

God, on the Aquinas line, is not free of all constraints in what He creates; He cannot create just any world and remain morally perfect. Perhaps he can create any world such that it is better that He create it than not, so that in creating He retains moral perfection. Perhaps He can create any world that it is not better that He not create than that He create, but we will conduct our discussion here on the higher standard stated in the preceding sentence. If a world that it is better that God create than not can contain evil—and it is hard to see that this is not a possibility, since containing evil seems not enough to make a world's non-existence morally better than its existence—then given only the information that God created the world, a "very limited intelligence" who takes the Aquinas line will have no grounds for expecting the world to contain no evil.

The Leibniz Line

God, on the Leibniz line, must create the best possible world. Leibniz did not conceive of that world as lacking evil. In part, this is due to his having what we might call an aesthetic criterion of value— if there being evil results in greater variety of certain sorts, then God is justified in allowing it in circumstances in which, on a purely moral criterion (for example, one that made no essential reference to sheer variety of kinds) He would not be justified. Suppose, then, that we move Leibniz's position closer to what its use for the Humean purpose of defending the prediction argument would require; suppose that we remove from the criterion for a best possible world any element that is other than moral. Still, if moral virtue is possessed only by those who conquer evil and/or if moral agents must be free and if free agents (not of necessity, but in fact) sometimes will choose wrongly, a world containing moral agents will contain evil. A world containing no moral agents also contains no moral worth. So the best possible world will contain moral agents and thus contain evil. Our Humean creature of a "very limited intelligence" who is given the information that God created the world and who takes the Leibnizian line also will have no grounds for expecting the world to contain no evil.

Determinism and Responsibility

Various objections can be made to this criticism of the prediction argument. One might claim that moral agents need not be free in any sense incompatible with a determinism that would allow God to cause agents only to choose rightly; the previous argument has presupposed incompatibilism. Incompatibilism holds that in the sense in which *being free with respect to a choice or action* is requisite to *being responsible for a choice or action* the truth of determinism would preclude anyone's being free with respect to any choices or actions.

Determinism, defined relevantly to this dispute, contends that for any event B there is some other event A and some law of nature L

such that *A occurred* and *L is true* entail *B occurred.* "Event" here is so
understood that a complex of events also counts as an event and that
choices and actions (or the making of choices and the performing of
actions) are events. The descriptions of events that make it possible to
link them through the statement of a law is conceived of as "tight."
Suppose that when an event occurs in a person's central nervous system that satisfies some such description as "is a state of physiological
kind *A*" then if materialism is true that state is identical to, and if dualism is true that state is correlated with, *either* a mental state describable as "choosing to steal a purse" or to a mental state describable as
"choosing to refrain from stealing a purse." Or suppose the mental
alternatives are "electing to embezzle money" or "going for coffee."
In either case, the connection between the relevant descriptions is
"loose," not tight. Using other language, the relation between physical descriptions and mental descriptions is not "one-one" but "one-
many." More than one mental description can apply to the same
physical event, where this linguistically reflects (what would be the
fact on this account of things) that the same physiological state can
encode or embody or correlate with either of two quite distinct mental
events. Conversely, on a one-one physical event-mental event connection, or on a many-one physical event-mental event connection,
the relation between the relevant descriptions will be "tight," not
loose. A given physiological state can encode or embody or correlate
with only one sort of mental event. The point of this "tightness" requirement is that determinism is true only if some particular mental
event is caused by preceding conditions, not if preceding conditions
leave open two or more alternatives. Further, those conditions must
render the resulting mental event inevitable, not merely probable.

If Alan decides to embezzle and determinism is true, then Alan's
decision to embezzle has a long history. Each event at any moment is
caused by an event occurring a moment earlier, and that event in turn
by an event a moment earlier. Some event prior to Alan's birth will be
at an earlier point on a causal chain on which Alan's decision occupies
a later position. Between some such earlier event (if determinism is
true, there are plenty of candidates) there will be an unbroken sequence of events in which each causes, and indeed renders inevitable, the next. Since Alan has no control over what occurred before
he was born, and since what happened before he was born rendered
an event inevitable that rendered another event inevitable (and so on
up until the event that rendered Alan's decision to embezzle inevi-

table) Alan has no control over whether he decides to embezzle or not; that is not up to him. But then it is not something that he is morally responsible for.

One might object to this that causation is not transitive—that *A caused B* and *B caused C* does not entail that *A caused C*. We can escape having to decide concerning the merits of this objection, or its analogue regarding the relation *rendering inevitable*. If determinism is true, there is a series of propositions, each true, beginning with one that says that the relevant event prior to Alan's birth actually occurred and ending with one that says that Alan decided to embezzle such that (given an appropriate statement of laws of nature) each proposition, conjoined with an appropriate law, entails the next member of the series down to the proposition concerning Alan's action. But then that proposition is entailed by the series' earliest member; *entailment* is indisputably transitive. If A entails B and B entails C, then A entails C. Thus determinism is incompatible with Alan's being responsible for his decision. Since Alan's decision represents all, determinism is incompatible with anyone being responsible for anything.

Disanalogies between God and Human Agents

Another objection is that theism does not hold that God earned His goodness by conquering evil. If human persons are created in the divine image, why should they have to earn their virtue by conquering evil? This objection can be pushed in either of two directions, the one concerning divine goodness and the other concerning human goodness. One can argue that even if incompatibilism is true, still there being persons who are caused by God always to choose rightly has some moral value, less perhaps than free persons making their choices rightly but more than free persons making important choices wrongly. The response is that (there being) persons who unfreely always choose rightly has no moral value at all. If one human person always determines what another shall do, the second is but the agent or puppet of the first, and is not an independent person at all. Indeed, that one person makes what might have been a person into her agent or puppet seems deeply evil. Nothing in the case changes in any way that mitigates this result if the determiner is divine.

The objection concerning divine goodness maintains that if God is good but not free to be evil this undermines the claim that human agents can be morally good or evil only if they are free whereas if God is freely good He at least is so without having to have overcome evil. The theist here may argue that there are disanalogies between the divine case and the human. She must pick her disanalogies carefully, since the intended result is that *God is morally good* remains true though the conditions of truth are not identical to the conditions requisite to *John is good.* The alternatives multiply quickly here. God can be conceived as eternal or as everlasting. He can be viewed as existing necessarily or as existing logically contingently though with ontological independence. The line of reasoning will vary, depending on which alternatives are chosen. Alternatively, the theist can hold that God too is free. Then either divine goodness must be a contingent property or God must lack logically necessary existence.

On any standard theistic account, *God is morally perfect* is a necessary truth. On one construal, this claim states a necessary condition of monotheistic divinity; no non-perfectly-good being can be God. On another construal, it states a truth about God's essence. The difference between these claims is analogous to that between *If George Washington is President, then he is Commander-in-chief of the army* and *George Washington belongs to Homo sapiens;* the former states a partial definition of the presidency and the latter remarks on a man's biological essence. (In contemporary technical jargon, the former states a *de dicto*, the latter a *de re*, necessity.) On the former account, were God to do wrong, He, in effect, would resign the office of Deity. He would still be Jehovah or Jahweh, but no longer God. On the latter account, were He to do wrong, since being perfect is an essential property of His, He would commit suicide. Either way, of course, the divine case and the human case are disanalogous. When a human being acts wrongly, no cosmic office is resigned and no essence is destroyed.

If one weds the second view—that moral perfection is an essential property of God—with the view that God has logically necessary existence, then it follows that it is logically impossible that God act wrongly, not merely that He cannot do so and retain divine existence. This introduces another disanalogy or dissimilarity: it is logically impossible that God not be good and it is logically possible that Alan not be good, just as it is logically impossible that God not exist and logically possible that Alan not exist. If God is viewed as having logically contingent existence, no new dissimilarities are introduced.

Finally, God is viewed either as eternal or as everlasting. To be eternal is to lack temporal properties altogether; to do or be nothing before or after or at the same time as anything or anyone else. To be everlasting is to have temporal properties without beginning or end.

On neither alternative is God viewed as having *earned* goodness, so this is another dissimilarity.

One question that arises is whether, given these dissimilarities, God and Alan can be good in the same sense of "good." If both share the same *ends*, both can be. For Alan to be good in the same sense as God is good is for Alan to approve, will, and (insofar as he is able) act for the same ends approved of, willed, and acted for by God. They need not, and will not, always share the *means* available for seeking these ends. Insofar as God wills that agents freely choose rightly, He wills ends that He cannot fiat, though He can fiat the conditions that make it possible that such choices be made. On any alternative on which God can have ends, approve some things and disapprove others, and the like, and do so on non-arbitrary moral grounds, God can be *good* in the same sense as a human being who does likewise. Those who conceive of God as eternal suppose Him capable of having ends, as do those who view Him as everlasting.

One might reply that even this "shared ends account" will give us a universal meaning for "good" in *God is good* and *Alan is good* only if both have libertarian freedom. (Alan has libertarian freedom regarding performing action *A* at time *T* if and only if Alan non-hypothetically has the properties *can do A at T* and *can refrain from doing A at T.*) If God is conceived of as *de dicto* good, whether possessing logically contingent or logically necessary existence, He can be viewed as *freely* good. If He is viewed as *de re* good, and as possessing logically contingent existence, then He can be freely good. This alternative is not open if God is viewed as *de re* good and as existing with logical necessity, though those holding this view sometimes change the topic and say that God is "free" in the sense of "none of His actions being externally caused," as if this were a morally relevant *sense* of "free" rather than a *condition* of morally relevant freedom. At least, these consequences follow if God is conceived as everlasting rather than eternal. If God is conceived as eternal, then presumably He cannot also be viewed as possibly *changing*, as that would entail *being temporal*. But those who conceive of God as eternal often also view Him as capable of acting; if this is coherent, and God is viewed in any other way than as both *de re* necessarily good and possessing logically necessary existence, perhaps here too He can act freely. In some of the construals of divine existence, then, both God and Alan can be free.

There remains the disanalogy that God, always having been morally perfect, cannot have *become* morally good or have *earned* moral goodness by passing from moral neutrality to a morally virtuous maturity. But if He is free He can lose His goodness if He wishes, and is praiseworthy for maintaining it, even if being able *not* to be good is a condition for being praiseworthy for being good. Perhaps it is even logically possible that God, knowing what the consequences of His ceasing to be good would be, deliberately reject that alternative— perhaps even logically possible that He be tempted by that alternative, *being tempted* itself involving no evil, and firmly resist. So there are various abstract possibilities to be investigated here.

All of this, of course, but scratches the surface of some complex issues. It is enough for present purposes that there are ways of conceiving of God on which "good" in "God is good" and "Alan is good" can bear the same sense. That this is so is a necessary condition both of the intelligibility of an essential part of traditional theism and of the prediction argument having any force. But none of it shows that the prediction argument succeeds.

Hume's own sympathies lie with the compatibilist. He would not, then, grant that libertarian freedom is a condition of moral agency. But he also could not argue that divine moral agency requires divine libertarian freedom. Thus he would doubt the 'free will defense' but not be in a position to press alleged disanalogies between divine and human freedom if God is conceived as *de re* necessarily morally good and possessed of logically necessary existence. Of course he would reject the notion of logically necessary existence.

Direct and Indirect Causation

I turn now to a consideration of some lines of argument already mentioned. Philo puts his point in this language: "So long as there is any vice at all in the universe, it will very much puzzle you anthropomorphites how to account for it. You must assign a cause for it, without having recourse to the first cause" (*D*, 212). But why must an anthropomorphite, or any other theist, refuse to "have recourse to the first cause?" Presumably because *God causes evil* is *necessarily* false. But why suppose that? Perhaps because (one suggestion goes) *God is omnibenevolent and omnipotent* is necessarily true, or at least because *God is omnibenevolent and omnipotent* entails *God causes no evil*. On this view, whatever evil there is must be only *allowed* by God. If God is omnipotent, nothing can exist that God does not allow to exist; indeed, an omnipotent creator *sustains* in existence whatever does exist. But this means that God causes whatever evils there are "indirectly" as it were; He brings into being something (a human being, or an earth tremor) that in turn causes an evil (a wrong choice, a tidal wave that takes human life). This, Philo implies, is subterfuge. A person who leaves a time bomb in the President's car, knowing it will go off during the chief executive's ride, is the "indirect" cause of the President's demise. She is no less an assassin for that. There is, of course, a distinction between God creating an evil state of affairs and His creating a universe that will produce evil states of affairs. It is, however, not a distinction that is, by itself, relevant to whether in so doing God can also be omnipotent and omnibenevolent.

We can put the point a bit more precisely in this way. If God is omnipotent and omnibenevolent, perhaps He will either create a universe in which there is a balance of good over evil, or He will not create at all. At least He will create a world that it is better to create than not to create. Suppose, then, that He creates a universe in which there are evils but a balance of good over evil. This is the more utilitarian way of putting the point, and perhaps the way more favorable for the critic's position. "A balance of good over evil" means "no matter *how many* good or evils there are, the *total value* of the goods outweighs the *total* (negative) *value* of the evils." Consider the evils that occupy part of this universe. Some of these evils, we will assume, are the products of human choice. In creating the agents who choose wrongly (assuming that God knows what choices will be made), if God is omnipotent and omnibenevolent, He so creates that for every wrong choice C by any agent A, *A's making C*, or at least (and more plausibly) *A's being allowed to make C*, is (on the whole) better than *A's not making C*, or at least (and more plausibly) *A's not being allowed to make C*. One may be right to allow another to make a choice that neither one or another is right to make. Then God is indirect cause of *A's being allowed to make C*, and perhaps of *A's making C*. Given the condition noted concerning what is better (on the whole), that God is *indirect* cause of evil in this sense seems not problematic. He is morally justified in allowing evils if they are allowed under the conditions stated. It is not contradictory or logically impossible that an omnicompetent Deity be morally justified in allowing evil. Strictly, it seems that God rightly can allow others to do wrong things that He could not rightly do Himself, and that these wrong actions are actions He is morally responsible, not for *doing*, but for *allowing*. Then there seems to be no good reason why the theist, in considering the cause of evil, may not "have recourse to" God.

Another way of developing Philo's concern is to doubt that it can be the case both that God sustains Alan in existence and that any of

Alan's actions be other than determined by God and hence traceable to God as their 'real' agent. Suppose that *A* knowingly renders it inevitable that *B* murder *C*. It is true that *B* may be responsible for killing *C*, or at least blameworthy for doing so, for *B*, whether or not *B* knows *A*'s significant part in the murder, may exult in the deed, may have hated *C* and have enjoyed causing *C*'s demise. It even may be that *B* would have murdered *C* had *A* stayed out of the matter. The fact remains that as things actually happened, *B* was *A*'s agent—*A* murdered *C* by using *B*, and so *A* has used both *B* and *C* as means only, not as ends or creatures of inherent worth. The relevant Philonian worry, then, will be this: if God sustains *A* in existence and sustains in *A* the powers that *A* misuses, is not God also constraining *A* to act as *A* does, so that *A* is God's pawn relative to all things just as *B* is *A*'s pawn relative to murdering *C*.

While the worry is understandable, it is hard to see that it is justified. What conceptual difficulty is there exactly in a genuinely omnipotent being so exercising omnipotence that a human person, with her various properties and powers, is sustained in existence for three score years and ten, and throughout that period allowed to exercise morally significant freedom over a wide range of actions? So far as I can see, if an omnipotent god can sustain a person in existence, then an omnipotent God can sustain a person in existence who exercises morally significant freedom. How much determination of actions the sustaining relation involves is up to God.

One assumption that is not essential to Philo's argument (or is it?) but makes it run more smoothly is that good and evil are closely connected, if not identical, to pleasure and pain respectively. Hume has often been chided for coming close at least to defining "X is morally good" as "X is itself pleasurable or is a cause of pleasure" and "X is morally evil" as "X is itself painful or is a cause of pain." He does seem to suppose the sort of world that a worthy Deity would produce would be a haven of enjoyment rather than a vale of soul making, and we have noted some of the difficulties this involves for his position. So we do not need to consider that issue again here.

The Consistency Question

Philo moves abruptly to the next step in his argument. In the opinion of many, the proportion of moral evil to moral good, he opines, is greater than that of natural evil to natural good—or the percentage of goods in the class of *natural goods–natural evils* is higher than the percentage of goods in the class *moral goods—moral evils.* But however that may be, Philo in effect argues, suppose there to be as few evils, natural or moral, as you please. Suppose there is only one evil in the history of the universe. Still, the existence of that evil is incompatible with God existing and being able and willing to prevent it. If God is unwilling, He is not omnibenevolent. If God is unable, He is impotent. So either He is impotent, or not omnibenevolent (or both), or He does not exist at all. *How much* evil there is, is irrelevant. In one sense, this is quite correct. Provided we have sufficient reason to hold *God exists and is all-powerful and all-good* and *There is evil* are in fact logically incompatible, if we know that there is even one evil we know that God as the orthodox conceive Him does not exist. But efforts to show that these propositions are inconsistent have notably failed with a perhaps unexcelled persistence.[1]

The sheer question of logical consistency is (in one sense) decidable with no great difficulty. Two propositions *A* and *C* can be seen to be consistent if it is the case that *A* and *B* and *C* is a consistent set of propositions. The propositions (1) *God exists and is all-powerful and all-good* and (2) *God has a morally sufficient reason for allowing the evils that exist* entail (3) *There is evil.* Consider the set comprised of these three propositions. *That* set seems consistent. If that set is consistent, then any two members of it, taken together, are consistent. So the first proposition is consistent with the third; that is, (1) and (3) are not incompatible.[2]

Of course one could claim that *God has a morally sufficient reason for allowing the evils that exist* is itself contradictory, perhaps on the grounds that *X is omnibenevolent* entails *X always prevents evil if he can* and *X is omnipotent* entails *X can always prevent evil.* Thus *X is omnipotent and omnibenevolent* entails *X always prevents evil if he can, and he always can;* so if there is an omnibenevolent, omnipotent being, necessarily he allows no evil. So there is no evil he allows for a sufficient reason.

But the same tactic again suggests itself. Consider (4) *God is omnipotent and omnibenevolent* and (6) *God allows evil E.* Together, (4) and (5) *E is an evil such that if it does not exist, good G will not exist (good G exists but evil E does not is a contradiction) and good G is a good state of affairs any omnibenevolent being would bring about,* entail (6) *God allows evil E.* And if the critic says that he takes omnibenevolence to rule out allowing preventable evil, the theist can reply that *he* does not use "omnibenevolent" in that way, but rather uses it in such a manner as to allow (4) and (6) to be compatible. The issue is not merely verbal. The disagreement between critic and theist here focuses on whether there is a defensible moral perspective—an ethical theory—on which perfect goodness can be possessed by a being that allows evil. The theist's claim is that there are theories that are consistent with theism and meet these constraints.

By now it should be evident that more than a purely logical dispute—a dispute about whether two propositions are consistent or not—is involved in the dispute over God and evil. So while it is true that if *God exists* and *There is evil* are incompatible, one actual recognized evil has the same evidential force as a billion, the "if" is a very big one. So far as I can see the propositions *God exists* and *There is evil* are quite consistent (for the reasons noted above). Nor am I aware of any argument that proves the contrary, though the attempts to provide this proof are legion. Philo at times apparently grants this, saying that "there may, for ought we know, be good reasons, why providence interposes not in this manner" (*D*, 207) and that he is "sceptic enough to allow that the bad appearances . . . may be compatible with such attributes" as the theist ascribes to God (*D*, 211). But his emphasis is hardly on the compatibility of the relevant propositions.

Philo's Four Causes

Philo says that there are four logical possibilities concerning the moral features of the "first causes of the universe": that they are perfectly good, or perfectly evil, or some one and some the other, or none either. The first two are eliminated by the fact that the phenomena are "mixed" (some good, some evil). The third is ruled out by the fact that phenomena obey general laws, the assumption being that if some causes of order were good and some evil the causes of order would not produce one uniform system. Hence the causes of cosmic order are neither good nor evil. This argument assumes that there is an incompatibility between there being a morally perfect being and there being evil in the world. As we noted, Philo defended this claim, though unsuccessfully.

This argument from Philo is surprising in at least two ways. The "four hypotheses" are not exhaustive, even if we read "first causes" as "first cause or causes." Suppose that there are two causes. Both might be mainly good, or mainly evil, or one mainly good and one mainly evil. These possibilities are simply ignored though supposedly all possibilities had been included. Further, these hypotheses are compatible with "mixed phenomena," and explain them at least as well as the preferred hypothesis. The argument, then, is surprisingly weak—indeed, the reasoning is sloppy in a way unusual for Philo.

Even more surprising is Philo's willingness to draw conclusions of any sort concerning cosmic order. He has been maintaining that all such matters are beyond reason's tether. For a moment Philo finds himself able to draw explicit conclusions about whether the cause or causes of cosmic order have morally relevant properties—that is, being good or evil or neither. The argument that Philo offers bears close examination.

Philo's Four Circumstances

There seem, says Philo,

> to be *four* circumstances, on which depend all, or the greatest parts of the ills, that molest sensible creatures; and it is not impossible but that all these circumstances may be necessary and unavoidable. We know so little beyond common life, or even of common life, that, with regard to the economy of the universe, there is no conjecture, however wild, which may not be just: nor any one, however plausible, which may not be erroneous. [D, 205]

Still, we must draw what conclusions we do draw given what evidence we have (provided we draw any at all). In so doing,

> all that belongs to human understanding, in this deep ignorance and obscurity, is to be sceptical, or at least cautious; and not to admit of any hypothesis whatever; much less of any which is supported by no appearance of probability. Now this I assert to be the case with regard to all the causes of evil, and the circumstances on which it depends. None of them appear to human reason, in the least degree, necessary or unavoidable, nor can we suppose them such, without the utmost license of imagination. [D, 205]

The four circumstances "which introduce evil" are:

> *First* . . . that contrivance or economy of the animal creation by which pains, as well as pleasures, are employed to excite all creatures to action . . . [and] self-preservation (205) . . . *second* . . . the conducting of the world by general laws . . . *third* . . . the great frugality with which all powers and faculties are distributed to every particular being . . . *fourth* . . . the inaccurate work-

manship of all the springs and principles of the great machine of nature. [*D*, 205, 206]

Philo notes unfortunate effects of each circumstance. A consequence of the first is that sentient beings bear considerable pain, of the second that winds aid the fleets of evil sailors as well as good, of the third that creatures struggle against one another to meet their needs, and of the fourth that rains cause floods and lack of rain causes drought. What he specifies with regard to the second circumstance, Philo intends for all: "this seems nowise necessary to a very perfect Being" (*D*, 206).

Further, in each case Philo gives an example of what apparently would be a better way to run the cosmos: inciting to action by reduction of pleasure rather than by pain, producing such slight variations of general laws (for example, "some small touches, given to Caligula's brain in infancy, might have converted him into a Trojan" [*D*, 207]), as would rid the world of tyrants and give longevity to benefactors; providing all sentient creatures with more capacities or less needs (or in the case of human beings, simply with "a greater propensity to industry and labor" [*D*, 208]), and making rains (and other natural phenomena) "so accurately adjusted, as to keep precisely within those bounds in which their utility consists" (*D*, 210).

So we have "these *four* circumstances . . . [on which] all or the greatest part of natural evil depend" (*D*, 210). Each seems eliminable in such a manner as to make room for a morally preferable replacement which would sustain the good effects of its predecessor—the examples are intended to provide illustrations of such replacements. What, exactly, are we entitled, in Philo's opinion, to conclude from all of this?

> What then shall we pronounce on this occasion? Shall we say, that these circumstances are not necessary, and that they might easily have been altered in the contrivance of the universe? This decision seems too presumptuous for creatures so blind and ignorant. Let us be more modest in our conclusions. Let us allow, that, if the goodness of the Deity (I mean a goodness like the human) could be established on any tolerable grounds *a priori*, these phenomena, however untoward, would not be sufficient to subvert that principle; but might easily, in some unknown manner, be reconcilable to it. But let us still assert, that as this goodness is not antecedently established, but must be inferred from the phenomena, there can be no grounds for such an inference, while

there are so many ills in the universe, and while these ills might so easily have been remedied, as far as human understanding can be allowed to judge on such a subject. I am sceptic enough to allow, that the bad appearances, notwithstanding all my reasonings, may be reconcilable with such attributes as you suppose. But surely they can never prove these attributes. Such a conclusion cannot result from scepticism; but must arise from the phenomena, and from our confidence in the reasonings which we deduce from these phenomena. [*D*, 211]

Philo's contentions, then, are: (a) it is logically possible (involves no contradiction) that God is omnibenevolent and omnipotent and allows all the evils there are plus their attendant circumstances; (b) if *God exists and is omnibenevolent and omnipotent* were established by an *a priori* proof (that is, were known to be *necessarily* true) then we could know God to be good in the same or a similar sense to that in which morally upright human beings are, and this knowledge would not be overthrown or rendered less certain by the existence of evil—though we might not be able to discern in all (or even any) cases what purpose Providence had in allowing them; (c) any inference (deductive or inductive) from phenomena—including inferences constituting a version of the design argument—to an omnibenevolent and omnipotent Deity will be illegitimate. That there are evils in the world prevents us from arguing (from the phenomena that comprise the cosmos) that the cause of cosmic order is known (certainly, or with probability) to be perfectly good. Now *these* conclusions are in fact correct. Indeed, we can see that each of them is true without recourse to the "four circumstances" argument at all.

We have already argued for (a) without making any such reference. And (b) seems rather obviously true, and so not in need of any particular defense. Finally, (c) follows from the already familiar point that if one infers a cause C from an effect E, nothing more by way of properties can be ascribed to C than is required by C's being E's cause. This made justification of ascribing the "omni" properties to God something beyond the capacities of even a successful formulation of the argument from design. So all of this is either clear (and clearly true) on its own, or justifiable without any recourse whatever to the four circumstances. What then is Philo up to? Perhaps we can become clearer about this matter by considering what Philo says about the *non-necessity* of these circumstances.

As we have seen, Philo lists four circumstances of evil, none of which—he suggests—"appear to human reason in the least degree necessary or unavoidable" (*D,* 205). Now in one sense, this is clearly true. If "X is necessary" means "*X does not exist* is contradictory," neither the circumstances Hume names, nor perhaps any others whether good or evil, unless *God exists* is a necessary truth, are "in the least degree necessary." In this sense, Philo's claim is true but trivial.

Presumably Philo means something else by not appearing necessary or unavoidable. Save for "X is logically necessary," "X is necessary" leaves us asking "for what?" In the context of Philo's discussion, the answer seems to be "for the effects to which they give rise." Causally, the circumstances *are* necessary; without them (under the present cosmic regime) their effects won't arise. It is just their causal role that constitutes the difficulty. (This is so whether one accepts a "constant conjunction" account of causality, or substitutes a stronger.) Hume's point, then, is that it is conceivable that insofar as they have moral worth, the same ends that these causes or circumstances yield can be gotten by different and morally better means; the same effects could be conjoined with morally preferable causes—at least so far as we can see. In that sense, these circumstances do not "appear to reason in the least degree necessary or unavoidable."

By itself, the fact that the same ends can be reached by other means is irrelevant. As suggested, the other means must be morally preferable—preferable as the morally good is to the morally neutral and the morally neutral to the morally evil. The idea behind Philo's examples is that were *that* the way the world wagged, things on the whole would be better, at least so far as we can see.

The Four Circumstances Argument

So Philo's argument can be put simply.

(1) There are "circumstances of natural evil" (events themselves evil or the causes of evil) that bring about good ends, such that (a) it seems conceivable that the same goods be caused without these circumstances, but rather (b) by other circumstances that would be morally preferable.

(2) If there are circumstances of natural evil of which (a) and (b) are true, it is probable that God does not exist.

So: (3) It is probable that God does not exist.

One can quarrel with Philo's examples. Is it, in fact, possible to have pleasure but no pain? The suggestion has been made that pleasure and pain are necessarily on a continuum so that "pleasure" refers to experiences toward one end of a continuum of sensations and "pain" to those toward the opposite end. If so (the argument continues), then should we replace the present continuum (the range of sensation states people experience) by another, what was painful would become pleasurable (if the continuum was extended painwards, so to speak) or what was pleasurable would become painful (if the continuum was extended pleasurewards). The 'pleasurableness' of one state arises from its *contrast* to other states, and so (with a reverse contrast, so to speak) does the 'painfulness' of others. So if we regard pleasures and pains as psychological states (and this appears to be Hume's intent), their pleasure-tone or pain-tone depends on their place on the experience continuum. Nothing is gained, for essentially nothing is changed, if one continuum is substituted for another.

Again, it may be doubted that operating the world by "particular providences" (giving the Allied planes fair weather and the Nazis foul, for example) would make the world morally better on the whole. The fact that good intentions found nature cooperative and bad intentions found nature restrictive would be soon noted by agents, and people would favor good intentions from the fact that they could not carry out evil ones. But then where is freedom and moral agency? (It is at this point, and at least equally concerning the third circumstance, that Hume's tendencies toward hedonism psychologically facilitate but philosophically hinder his argument.)

Further (as Philo at times insists) it is not easy to judge the degree, if any, to which particular changes in the cosmic processes would render things morally better. For example, agents might be kept from noticing that nature favored good intentions and frustrated evil ones. Would this enhance the worth of moral agency or make the world morally better?

With respect to the third example perhaps it is true that were goods and capacities more plentiously provided, there would be less competition and less carnage. There would also be less need and opportunity for courage and compassion. Where people can be vicious, they can also be virtuous; where vice is impossible, so is virtue. So far as I can see, there is no important difference between the second and fourth circumstances, and—having commented already on the second example—correspondingly no need to comment on the fourth. So (as one would expect) one can argue about Philo's examples. Maybe they are apt; maybe they are not apt.

There is, however, a sense in which it is unimportant whether or not Hume's examples provide illustrations of circumstances of natural evils of which (a) and (b) are true. For there are some evils whose existence is contingent and whose good effects (if any) appear attainable without either them or any corresponding evils. Animal pain is a notoriously difficult example for enthusiastic theodicists (those who would explain what the point of particular evils is) to deal with. So I think we must grant that step (1) of Philo's rephrased argument is true.

The crux, then, of Philo's argument (revised version) is step (2). Is it the case, as (2) says, that:

> If there are circumstances of natural evil of which (a) and (b) are true, it is probable that God does not exist.

or is some other conclusion at least equally compatible with (1)?

Step (1) is a fact about our knowledge, as it were. There are evils, it says, whose point, if any, is unknown to us, and which indeed appear pointless—either by having no good effects or by having good effects that could be purchased at lower moral price. How forceful this fact is as evidence perhaps can be gauged if we compare it with what we conceivably could have, but do not. Consider, then, the following conditions that are among those that one passing, as it were, full and final moral judgment on the course of the cosmos would need to possess:

> (1) A knowledge of each (actual or possible) good and its value relative to other goods and to each (actual and possible) evil. (This would entail, because it would include, the corresponding knowledge concerning every [actual or possible] evil.)
>
> (2) A knowledge of how the goods and evils in this (actual) universe compare with the goods and evils of other possible universes—the value (on the whole, and in the long run) of this universe versus that of all other possible ones.

Someone with this sort of knowledge could tell whether or not the "circumstances of natural evil" are (in the relevant sense) necessary— that is, whether or not any universe as good, on the whole, as this one would contain at least as much evil as ours does. If she also possessed knowledge as to whether the Aquinas line or the Leibniz line is correct, and other relevant philosophical and theological data, she could also (assuming properly functioning cognitive powers, no mistakes of fact or inference, and no errors of memory) pronounce on whether it was good that God create the actual world (or create at all).

All of us may well join Philo in being sceptical that our actual relevant knowledge comes at all close to meeting these conditions.

A more modest sum of knowledge might serve as well. Suppose we knew:

> (a) that a set *S* of conditions under which an agent who can prevent evil is justified or is not culpable for permitting it is exhaustive (all the cases are included) and determinate (each distinct kind of justification is so described as to be logically independent of every other sort).
>
> (b) for every actual evil, we know whether or not God, who allowed it if He exists, is in fact justified in at least one of the ways specified in *S*.

Then we could tell whether or not any actual evil is one God would be unjustified in allowing. Here, no reference to merely *possible* evils, or to *other* universes, would be required so long as it turned out that some actual evil or other was one that God would be unjustified in permitting. (Were all actual evils known to be ones that God would be justified in permitting, this would not tell us whether or not some other universe was on the whole morally better than our own.) But of course none of us have knowledge that comes at all close to meeting these conditions either.

The question remains as to whether we might not still have enough information as to render a probability judgment. There is, after all, a lot of evil. So isn't it reasonable to suppose *some* of it is unjustified (where to say that an evil is unjustified is shorthand for saying that it is an evil that God is unjustified in allowing)—especially where we cannot even imagine what justification there could be? Philo's claim was only that *probably* God does not exist.

Evil and Probability

There are at least two difficulties with this suggestion. Normally, if we are justified in inductively inferring, regarding member *M* of a class *S* that *M* has *A*, we know that members *M1*, *M2* . . . *Mn* of *S* have *A*, and so infer that *M* also has *A*. But of no evil do we know that God is unjustified in allowing it, though there are many evils such that if God is justified in allowing them, we do not know what makes Him so. That would be evidence that He is not justified in doing so only if it is the case that if God is justified in allowing an evil, we would know how and why; and that is false. So we have no relevant class of evils known to have the property *being an evil that God would not be justified in allowing—being an unjustified evil,* for short—with respect to which, by an inductive argument, we can substantiate the claim, concerning some particular evil *E,* that *E* is unjustified. With regard to probability claims, the difference between

(1a) Many X's are A, so probably X is A.

and

(2a) There are many X's, so probably at least one is A.

is crucial. We need some such claim as

(1b) Many evils are unjustified, so probably evil E is.

in order to make Philo's influence. Instead, we have not (1b) but rather

(2b) There are many evils, so probably at least one is unjustified.

But (2b) will not serve. We have no inductive reason to suppose that the inference embedded in (2b) is legitimate, and (2b) is plainly not a necessary truth.

Perhaps we should shift our ground. Let an evil that in fact serves no justifying point be a gratuitous evil. Even if there are gratuitous evils—evils that serve as necessary conditions to no compensating goods—that will not damage the theist's cause unless it is also true that:

(3a) If God exists and is omnicompetent, then no evil is gratuitous.

It is hard to see how (3a) can be established unless it is by reference to the claim that if God is an all-knowing, all-powerful, all-good, Creator, and Providence, then (so to speak) there is no room in a universe He creates for an evil that is gratuitous. This claim is not obviously true, but suppose we grant it to Philo for the sake of the argument. Thus the backing for (3a) is:

(3b) Necessarily, if God exists and is omnicompetent, then no evil is gratuitous.

Given (3b) plus *God exists,* we obviously get:

(4) No evil is gratuitous.

Even granting (3b), the problem with the argument, briefly stated, is that I cannot know that (A) *Probably, some evil is gratuitous* without also knowing (B) *Probably, God does not exist.* A necessary condition of the truth of (A) being true is that (B) is true. But a condition of a proof being one that extends our knowledge is that we be able to know whether or not its premises are true without knowing whether its conclusion is true or not. Hence Philo's argument (revised version) cannot be a proof that extends our knowledge.

We perhaps can put this point more clearly by asking what conditions premises A and B must meet if they are to constitute a proof of conclusion C in the manner desired by Philo. Of course A and B must together entail C (or, together with some appropriate axioms of probability, entail *Probably, C*). Further, A and B must be known to be true. Further, A must be known to be true without our having to know that C is true; for unless I know that A is true without knowing whether or not C is true, my knowledge of A depends on my knowledge of whether C is the case or not. But I want to prove C in a way in which my knowledge is extended, and if I cannot know whether A is true without knowing the truth value of C, appeal to A is of no help in determining whether or not C is true, for I must know whether or not C is true in order to be secure in my knowledge that A is true. And of course exactly similar comments apply to B as to A. In sum, it must be the case that each premise of an argument that extends our knowledge is logically independent (neither entails nor is entailed by) the argument's conclusion. Further, if the proof is to extend my knowledge, as Philo desires his proof to do, each premise must be epistemologically independent of the argument's conclusion in the sense that I can know that the premise is true without having to know whether or not the conclusion is true. (Plainly, this requirement—and the requirement of logical independence—apply to the premises of an argument distributively, not collectively.)

But the requirement of epistemological independence of premise from conclusion is not met by Philo's argument. That argument succeeds only if it is necessary truth that *If God exists then there exists no evil that is gratuitous.* Call this alleged necessary truth N. N plus *God exists* entails *No evil is gratuitous.* And of course N plus *Some evil is gratuitous* entail *God does not exist.* Were N false, Philo's argument would be bankrupt for that reason; for then that there is gratuitous evil will not entail that God does not exist. But if N is true, Philo cannot know *Some evil is gratuitous* to be true without knowing whether or not *God exists* is true. Hence his argument does not meet the condition of epistemological independence; rather, it is epistemically circular.

The obvious reply is that Philo runs his argument in terms of probability. He hence requires not *N* but rather *P: Probably, if there is gratuitous evil then God does not exist* (that is, *If God exists, probably there is no gratuitous evil*). It is hard to see what justification one could offer for *P* without making appeal to the conceptual relations between there being a God and there being an evil. But these relations are stated in *N*. If they justify anything, then they justify *N*, not *P*.

It would appear, then, that one does not find a successful statement of the problem of evil—one that renders *God exists* either *false* or *probably false*—in *Dialogues* Ten and Eleven.

PART THREE

Further Humeana

CHAPTER 14

Superstition, Enthusiasm, Suicide, and Immortality

Of Superstition and Enthusiasm

Hume views superstition and enthusiasm as "corruptions of true religion" (*O*, 146). He suggests that "the corruption of the best of things [true religion] produces the worst [superstition and enthusiasm]" (*O*, 146). His account of superstition and enthusiasm derives them from emotion run riot. The darker emotions that arise from public or private failure, illness, or melancholy can cause a state of mind in which "infinite unknown evils are dreaded from unknown agents" (*O*, 146).

> Where real objects of terror are wanting, the soul, active to its own prejudice, and fostering its predominant inclination, finds imaginary ones, to whose power and malevolence it sets no limits. As these enemies are entirely invisible and unknown, the methods taken to appease them are equally unaccountable. [*O*, 146]

Hence, Hume holds, arise rituals and ceremonies. What arises, religiously speaking, from the darker emotions is superstition: "Weakness, fear, melancholy, together with ignorance, are, therefore, the true sources of Superstition" (*O*, 146).

There are brighter as well as darker emotions. They lead, in Hume's view, not to superstition but to enthusiasm. Public or private success, health, confidence, boldness, and elation are dangerous too.

> In such a state of mind the imagination swells with great, but confused conceptions, to which no sublunary beauties or enjoyments can correspond. Everything mortal and perishable van-

281

ishes as unworthy of attention; and a full range is given to the fancy . . . the soul is at liberty to indulge itself in every imagination, which must best suit its present taste and disposition. [*O*, 146–47]

God is viewed as the cause of these transports, which are thus taken to be subject to neither reason nor morality since "every whimsey is consecrated." Thus: "Hope, pride, presumption, a warm imagination, together with ignorance, are . . . the true sources of enthusiasm" (*O*, 147).

Hume's account here supplements his *Natural History* explanations, spelling out more fully the role of emotion, as Hume sees it, in the production of types of religious experience and belief. It is propensities, filtered as it were through the darker emotions, that for Hume yield almost all of religious belief. There is no reference here to propensities and triggering experiences. This argues no change in Hume's views. The focus of *Of Superstition and Enthusiasm* is on *the social and political consequences* of superstition and enthusiasm. Seventy per cent of the essay concerns these consequences.

Hume's consequences are a debateable lot. They go as follows. Superstition is favorable to priestly power as it causes its adherents to view themselves as highly unworthy to approach God, and hence as needing priests as mediators; "the stronger mixture there is of superstition [in a religion], the higher is the authority of the priesthood" (*O*, 148). Hume's view here is distinctly "modern." The possibility that there is a God, and that one's sins make one guilty before Him, is not one he takes seriously. That at the core of superstition there is this much truth, Hume does not so much deny as ignore. Enthusiasm, Hume suggests, frees its adherents "from the yoke of ecclesiastics" (*O*, 148). Enthusiasts have contempt for forms and ceremonies and think themselves "sufficiently qualified to *approach* the Divinity, without any human mediator" (*O*, 148). Hume's first alleged social consequence is that superstition favors, and enthusiasm disfavors, priesthoods.

A second "reflection with regard to these species of false religion" is that an enthusiastic religion initially is "more furious and violent" and "produces the most cruel disorders in human society" when compared with a superstitious religion, but then settles down to calmer effects, whereas superstitious religions have an initially more calm and later a more violent aspect. Quakers, Anabaptists, Levellers, Covenanters, and Camisars embrace enthusiasm; "the Romish Church" practices superstition.

Third, Hume claims, superstition is an enemy, and enthusiasm a friend, to civil liberty; superstition leads to submission to priests and enthusiasm to suspicion of authority that is not derived from inner raptures. Enthusiasm "being the infirmity of bold and ambitious tempers, is naturally accompanied with a spirit of liberty; as superstition, on the contrary, renders men tame and abject, and fits them for slavery" (*O*, 150). High-church Tories and Roman Catholics thus support royalty, and Deists and Latitudinarians have dominated in Whig leadership and been "friends to toleration" (*O*, 150). Molinists "are great friends to superstitions; rigid observers of external forms and ceremonies, and devoted to the authority of the priests, and to tradition" (*O*, 150). Those "tyrants of the people, and the slaves of the court," the Jesuits, rule the Molinists. The Jansenists, in contrast, "are enthusiasts, and zealous promoters of the passionate devotion, and of the inward life; little influenced by authority; and, in a word, but half Catholics . . . (they) preserve alive the small sparks of the love of liberty which are to be found in the French nation" (*O*, 150).

Hume's politics I leave aside. His discussion includes a now common tactic of the alleged evaluation of religious belief, one that focuses on social and political consequences. It is not lucid what one *tells* about a religious belief from this sort of assessment.

The method of evaluation is this: one attempts to discover what social consequences embracing a religious belief has, and then judges the religious belief on the basis of the discovered effects. The rationale is that this sort of information about religious beliefs is supposed to be more accessible than are clear answers to questions about what the belief logically entails and whether what it entails is true. Direct assessment of religious beliefs that asks such questions as: *What does this belief entail?; What would confirm it?; What would disconfirm it?; Does anything actually confirm it?; Does anything actually disconfirm it?; What does it explain if it is true?;* and the like, is hard. Those who reflect on these matters see that it is hard. Frequently, it is simply assumed that direct assessment for some reason is impossible. Though the limits Hume sometimes argues attach to meaning, and to epistemology, would have this consequence, Hume (as we have seen) commendably spends considerable effort and ingenuity on direct assessment. But here he engages in indirect.

The assumption that one can tell what the effect of embracing a religious belief is has its own problems. Presumably it is generally easiest to do this in the case of an individual. If Mary was a confirmed drunkard before she was converted, and now stays stone sober and credits her conversion with the change, probably that is the reason for the change. It is at the level of society, or culture, or at least a religious tradition within a culture, that Hume conducts his analysis. Here, judgments regarding consequences obviously are more complex. The *form* of such judgments will be this. One will have a consequence, a set of conditions that hold independent of religious belief, and a (simple or complex) religious belief. One will claim that this religious belief, under these conditions, yields this consequence—a consequence that would not have arisen from those conditions without the presence of that belief, and that would not have risen had the contradictory of that belief, or some other belief, been held instead. It often is not noted that this last element is essential to whatever sort of assessment is involved. Suppose that in a given culture that is at war it is assumed that "If God exists, then He is on our side" but also that "without God, anything is permitted." They believe that God exists, and they pursue war in the belief that God is their heavenly Captain. But should they cease to believe in God, they will also abandon their moral beliefs, and continue to pursue the war in what they perceive as their self-interest. Belief that God exists, in the context, will lead to war; so will belief that God does not exist. What sort of assessment will result here, either concerning the truth, or the pragmatic value, of the belief? The counterfactual element is necessary to whatever assessment is supposed to be going on. Since it enormously increases the difficulty of an often already difficult task, it almost always is ignored. Then the alleged assessment becomes worthless.

Suppose that one does discover that if a particular religious belief predominates in a given cultural context, then a certain consequence will follow, that the consequences will not arise without that belief being held, and that the consequence is highly undesirable. Suppose there is also good reason to think the belief true. Then what should be concluded? That no one in the relevant culture should accept the belief, even though it is true? Suppose that we do not know whether the belief is true or false. Then is the result of assessment that no one should accept the belief? That the belief is false? That no one should *act* on the belief?

One can pursue this sort of strategy as a way of deciding about the truth or falsity of religious belief. Along these lines, one might argue as follows: religious belief B entails a moral principle or rule F, we know that F is false, so we can infer that B is false. One who so argues, however, appeals to ethics, not history; it is moral philosophy, not historical studies, that will confirm, if anything will, the claim that we know that *F* is false.

One can pursue this sort of strategy to argue that the possession of a belief by the majority of those in a culture has had bad consequences—consequences so bad that it would be enormously morally better for them not to occur. Then one must also have good reason for supposing that two things are true: that if the majority had not held that belief then the bad consequences would not have occurred, and that there is no other belief that is such that had the majority not held it then the bad consequences would not have occurred. If one does not know that if the majority had not held the belief in question, then the bad consequences would not have occurred, one also does not know that their having the belief is at least part of the cause of those consequences. If one does not know that there is no other belief such that had the majority not held it, then the bad consequences would not have occurred, then one does not know whether there is also some other belief whose abandonment would be as advantageous as that of the belief in question. Further, one must know that if the belief were abandoned, it would not be replaced by another (the contradictory of the proposition previously believed, or some other) whose effect would be the same, or that suspense of judgment regarding the belief (if that would be the result of abandoning it) would not yield the same consequences. Further, it must be known that the majority of people abandoning the belief would not have consequences just as bad as those that occur because of its presence.

Such things are hard to be confident about. Therefore those who appeal to historical consequences seldom if ever raise them. Hume does not. But without their being raised and answered, we have, not argument, but allegation—suspicion cheaply raised without the hard currency of evidence. (Of course, similar issues arise for one who argues in favor of a religion on the basis of alleged historical consequences of a belief being accepted.)

One can see that the non-moral components of a religious tradition serve to support some moral themes and not others—that, say, a particular theology comports well with respect-for-persons ethics and ill with utilitarianism. If we independently know that utilitarianism is false and know no such thing regarding respect for persons ethics, then so far forth this is to that theology's credit. Asking *What elements of moral philosophy are entailed by a theology?* and *How do those elements fare in moral philosophy?* is fair enough. But attempting to assess the truth of a belief, the morality of a tradition, or the moral advisability of accepting a morality, on the supposed basis of the consequences in history of the belief being accepted requires that one know that those who accepted the belief understood it and applied it properly, plus all of the other matters just rehearsed. The historical-consequences argument is enormously hard to be justifiably confident of; we are highly unlikely to know what we would have to know in order to offer it responsibly. And if we do ever know that much, the proper conclusion has to do with the inappropriateness in certain circumstances (those specified by the arguments' premises) of *acting* on a certain religious belief; nothing more. Anything more will have to come from moral philosophy, or from our knowledge of morality independent of the historical-consequences argument.

As usual, attempts to assess religious beliefs indirectly, by appeal to matters other than their consistency and coherence and explanatory power and relationship to relevant evidence, turns out to be harder to carry out responsibly than direct assessment, and to yield far less by way of results.

On Suicide

> One considerable advantage that arises from philosophy consists in the sovereign antidote which it affords to superstition and false religion. All other remedies against that pestilent distemper are vain, or at lest uncertain. Plain good sense, and the practice of the world, which alone serve most purposes of life, are here found ineffectual. [*O*, 151]

With these words, Hume begins his essay "On Suicide." It presumably is the critical powers of philosophy that Hume is praising— its ability to criticize "superstition and false religion" rather than its ability to substantiate a world view that lacks any superstitious element. This, at least, is the reading suggested by Hume's overall philosophy of religion. His confidence that "superstition, being founded on false opinion, must immediately vanish when true philosophy has inspired juster sentiments of superior powers" (*O*, 151) can be read along these lines. Then the "juster sentiments of superior powers" will be views of such powers more in accord with what Humean philosophy would let us know about such matters (a line of information too thin to support religion of any sort, but also too thin to support superstition) rather than a robust orthodoxy that eliminates magic from the world due to a high view of divine rationality and morality.

Hume's objection against superstition is not so much that it is false or that it precludes one from embracing any very substantial religious truth. It is that the superstitious person is dominated by fear, and even if this fear makes her life hardly bearable, it also prevents her from escaping her burden of fear by suicide.

Hume's essay focuses on presenting and criticizing the arguments against suicide that, in his opinion at least, have their sources in superstition—that is, have premises the acceptance of which renders one superstitious.

Hume also seems to reason in favor of the appropriateness, or at least moral innocence, of suicide by one whose life is miserable. He notes that we have the power to commit suicide and so have a "native liberty" to perform it unless we are so constrained by superstition that we cannot exercise the power we would otherwise have. Consider John who, as a boy, was terrified by a large and angry dog. This man, like the rest of us, has all the capacities requisite for scratching a canine behind the ears. But his childhood encounter has left him unable to extend a hand in the direction of a dog's head. Only upon his phobia being cured can he exercise his native liberty to express affection to "man's best friend." On Hume's view, the superstitious person is rendered, by her superstition, incapable of suicide though she possesses the native capacity to commit it.

Prior to examining the course of Hume's critique, certain things seem clear. One is that Hume's argument for the appropriateness of suicide is a fragile reed. Mary has the native ability to drown her cat, drop her baby from the top of the United Nations building, and poison her husband; it does not follow that such actions would be morally innocent. Another is that Hume for once overestimates the power of reason. John may not be cured simply by persuading him that dogs as a whole are marvelous companions without whom our lives would be impoverished; even believing this, he may not be able to overcome his fear. Even if argument plays a role, it may not be sufficient in working a cure. If John says "I know that Spot is friendly, but I cannot bring myself to pet him," he does not utter a contradiction in terms. Similarly, curing false belief may not cure superstitious behavior. Hume, with a view on which the rational capacities are weak sisters in the family of human natural propensities, is in no position to maintain otherwise. Third, it needs defense that superstition is the only

barrier to suicide's being sometimes permissible. Why should the belief that a human life is of too great a value for it to be permissible to
cut it short, whether this belief rests on a theological premise or not,
be thought *inherently* superstitious?

There is this wrinkle to Hume's view: if philosophy cures superstition, and superstition causes fears that make suicide attractive, then
philosophy presumably will remove such fears by removing their
cause and so render unnecessary what it justifies as permissible. But
this will apply only to cases where what makes suicide attractive is
superstitious fear. It would not affect, say, a case where incurable
pain was the motivation toward suicide, and the pain was not (as it
typically would not be) caused by superstition.

The arguments against suicide that Hume considers are moral arguments. "If suicide be criminal, it must be a transgression of our
duty either to God, our neighbor, or ourselves" (*O*, 152). So Hume's
goal will be to show that even if we grant that theism is true, no duty
not to commit suicide obtains. Hume's argument that the existence of
God does not render suicide morally inappropriate goes as follows.

> In order to govern the material world, the almighty Creator has
> established general and immutable laws, by which all bodies . . .
> are maintained in their proper sphere and function. To govern
> the animal world, he has endowed all living creatures with bodily
> and mental powers . . . by which they are impelled or regulated
> in that course of life to which they are destined. These two dis-
> tinct principles of the material and animal world continually en-
> croach upon each other, and mutually retard or forward each
> other's operation. The powers of men and of all other animals are
> restrained and directed by the nature and qualities of the sur-
> rounding bodies, and the modifications and actions of these
> bodies are incessantly altered by the operation of all animals.
> [*O*, 153]

Hume's own perspective is both mind/body dualistic and deterministic and his description of the world is most naturally read along
these lines; doing so aids the force as well as the flow of his argument.

Assuming, then, that there are bodies and minds (animal and human), each with a set of laws that "impel or regulate," brought about
by God, one naturally reflects that:

> The providence of The Deity appears not immediately in any
> operation, but governs everything by those general and immu-

table laws which have been established from the beginning of time. All events, in one sense, must be pronounced the action of the Almighty; they all proceed from those powers with which he has endowed his creatures. [*O*, 153]

There are problematic features in this characterization of the world. On one account, a law is a statement we make in order to record a regularity that we observe; in this sense of "law," laws have awaited the arrival of scientists; no such law is a cause or something that impels or regulates anything. On another view, a law is a proposition, a mind-independent and presumably abstract entity. Abstract entities are not promising candidates for being an impelling entity or regulator; such an entity can neither consciously nor non-consciously act, or (presumably) be cause or effect.

On another account, what corresponds to a law (here taken in our first sense) is the natures and capacities of the entities referred to by the referential terms of the law. Laws describe, in Hume's language, "the powers" of things. Each kind of thing has its nature; the nature of a thing determines, or else at least partially is comprised of, the capacities that things of that kind possess. The nature of a member of any biological species, for example, differs somewhat from that of the member of any other biological species. What here gives rise to a law is the nature and capacities of a body or a mind, and bodies and minds are thought of as enduring entities that retain the same nature over time as they gain some accidental properties and lose others: as substances of a sort forbidden by Humean ontology. It is hard to see how the perspective can be rewritten compatibly with Hume's own metaphysics. The defense presumably is that Hume here speaks the language of others to explore the implications of their views.

Hume is right to draw a controversial conclusion. Suppose that God creates (or designs) objects whose capacities He causes to operate in a particular way at the moment of creation or initial design (or at some other time) so that what occurs then is determined by Him and what happens later is determined by what happened then. Under those conditions, it is true that God has determined that whatever occurs should occur; whatever obtains is something He directly or indirectly causes to obtain. If everything Mary does is something she is caused to do by Martha, then Mary has no agency of her own; at least, if Martha knows this fact about Mary, then Mary's agency is an extension of Martha's—Martha acts through Mary's body as well as her own. On the supposition noted, everyone is related to God as Mary is to Martha.

This is not the standard monotheistic view, for which God sustains in existence whatever exists dependently without determining, at least if what is in question is an agent, every property it has and every event it participates in. That God so acts as to sustain John in existence does not entail that God causes John to choose or act in one way rather than another. Thus John's actions need not be God's actions. Of course God's sustaining John and Martha in existence is a necessary condition of John speaking cruelly to Martha and of Martha speaking graciously to John. But this does not entail that God thereby has Himself spoken to John or to Martha, either cruelly or graciously or otherwise. The connections Hume wishes to forge between divine action and all that occurs not surprisingly requires Hume's determinism. A monotheism that is libertarian rather than deterministic (as monotheism often is) will not yield Humean conclusions concerning suicide—not, at any rate, on Humean grounds.

Given a deterministic monotheism, one can round out Hume's argument this way: since whatever occurs in effect is God's action, and God does not do wrong, whenever suicide occurs it is not wrong. If Mary commits suicide, on this view, her doing so is God's action in Mary. Of course, anyone who thinks that suicide is wrong will reverse the argument: committing suicide is wrong; God never does wrong; so committing suicide cannot be God's action in Mary; so not everything that occurs is a divine action. Nothing significant is altered if we move from "is a divine action" to "is a divine action or is a result determined by divine action to occur" in stating argument and rebuttal.

When Hume says that "The providence of the Deity appears not immediately in any operation, but governs everything by . . . general and immutable laws" he is denying that any event more manifests providence than another, not that any event you pick manifests providence. His comments suggest one other sense of "law"—a law expresses either how God always acts (this is the analogue-in-heaven of the *causal powers/natures and capacities* reading) or how God has caused things to act (this offers an explanation of the phenomena referred to by that reading). If either of these senses of "law" is fed into the argument just considered, nothing significant changes. It still requires an unproved determinism that is not essential to theism. It still can be reversed by one who believes suicide to be wrong.

A somewhat different argument is suggested by these remarks.

> Shall we assert that the Almighty has reserved to himself . . . the disposal of the lives of men, and has not submitted that event, in common with others, to the general laws by which the universe

is governed? This is plainly false: the lives of men depend upon the same laws as the lives of all other animals [O, 154]

Here his argument is: what God permits to be ended without human agency it is permissible that an agent end. Or, perhaps, what God permits cannot be wrong, God permits suicide, so suicide cannot be wrong. But both of these arguments will as such justify murder as suicide. Other similar arguments can be coaxed from Hume's remarks, with similar results.

A different argument is suggested by this comment: "Is a man's disposing of his life criminal because in every case it is criminal to encroach upon these laws [of matter and motion] or disturb their operation? But this seems absurd." (O, 154).

Every human motion, including those that save life, "innovates on the order of some parts of matter" (O, 155). Hume's argument is confusing here. The laws, said to be immutable, here are said to be things that we can "alter or disturb" (O, 155). But what Hume has in mind is easily enough seen. When one moves a rock out of one's path, one changes it from where it was to another place and thus makes both the present and the future, regarding rock and path at least, different from what they otherwise would be. It is not *laws*, but a bit of the course of nature that one has changed. So one cannot argue that it is wrong to alter the course of nature—to change what its path would otherwise be without our interference. On this view, "it would be equally criminal to act for the preservation of human life as for its destruction. If I turn aside a stone which is falling on my head, I alter the course of nature" (O, 155).

Nor can one argue that God has decided what the time of every human death should be and it is wrong to change that time unless one argues that the time of a human death differs in this respect from every other event, either because God has not decided their times of occurrence or because it is acceptable to alter his decisions about events other than demises. If one abandons Hume's perspective and embraces libertarianism, or accepts Hume's compatibilism, one can view Hume as arguing that liberty has many legitimate exercises, so why not also view its exercise in life-and-death matters as legitimate?

Hume's strategy by now has become divided. He began by trying to derive the conclusion that suicide is permissible by starting with monotheistic determinism and reasoning deductively. His attempts here were less than impressive. The other strategy is to critique attempts to base the prohibition of suicide on premises constitutive of monotheistic determinism. Such attempts, if successful, will be relevant to the views of monotheistic determinists (and to all monotheists if Hume's apparent assumption that monotheism entails determinism is correct). This latter strategy is correct insofar as it involves claiming that one cannot plausibly claim that God has set a time for all events at which they should occur—not at any rate if this includes the idea that this time is built into general laws, for such laws refer to no times or individual events, and not if this precludes the future being affected by actions that themselves are determined.

He comes to considerations that are central to monotheism, libertarian as well as determinist, when he notes that for many, perhaps all, who object to suicide it is

> because human life is of such great importance that it is a presumption for human prudence to dispose of it . . . the life of a man is of no greater importance to the universe than that of an oyster; and were it of ever so great importance, the order of human nature has actually submitted it to human prudence. . . . A hair, a fly, an insect, is able to destroy this mighty being whose life is of such importance. Is it an absurdity to suppose that human prudence may lawfully dispose of what depends on such insignificant causes? [O, 155]

This, of course, is rhetoric, not philosophy. A person is easier to destroy than her cast-iron image. Is the image therefore more valuable? What *rationale* is there for accepting any such claim as *the value of anything is a function of its durability* or *if something is easy to kill then it cannot be of significant moral worth*? To say that the universe does not value human life more than that of an oyster is to say that both die, the death of each is natural, neither death is enormously harder to procure than the other, and the universe at large does not much react to either. It is hard to see what *follows* from this so far as the value of human life goes. The galaxies have no vote on such matters. But if anything did follow, then as the value of human life sank, the barrier to suicide also would go down as would the barrier to murder and moral evil generally. Is Hume willing to argue that murder is wrong only if monotheism is true? Hume can get what he wants for suicide only by paying far more than he is willing to spend. He writes:

> It would be no crime in me to divert the Nile or Danube from its course, were I able to effect such purposes. Where then is the crime of shedding a few ounces of blood from their natural channel? [O, 155]

If murder is not wrong, then self-murder is not wrong. But where was the argument for the antecedent?

Hume even claims that if suicide is not wrong then sometimes it is a duty. If one finds ones life unbearable then

> both prudence and courage should engage us to rid ourselves at once of existence when it becomes a burden. It is the only way that we can then be useful to society, by setting an example which, if imitated, would preserve to every one his chance for happiness in life, and would effectually free him from all danger or misery. [*O*, 160]

But this claim rests, as Hume notes, on the unproved assumption that suicide "be no crime" but "if suicide be supposed a crime, it is only cowardice can impel us to it" (*O*, 166).

Nothing in Hume's essay has shown suicide not to be wrong. Nor are the only alternatives that suicide be always be forbidden and suicide be sometimes a duty. Suppose that suicide is wrong unless one knows, upon competent medical testimony confirmed by a second and independent opinion, that one's life is going to be short and what is left of it will be filled with agonizing pain too powerful to be much mitigated by drugs. It might then be that suicide was permissible but not obligatory. Hume's argument regarding suicide as a duty requires that only *being a duty to* and *being a duty not to* are possible moral situations, and *being permissible to* and *being permissible not to* is an impossible moral situation. This needs proof.

Next, Hume considers suicide and duties to others. Here he argues that "all our obligations to do good to society seem to imply something reciprocal." Benefits received require benefits given. But if one retires from society, one does not do wrong; hermits are not wicked by virtue of being hermits. At least if one has repaid society for its benefits (and it could be argued that no lifetime is long enough for one to have done that) one then has no obligations to others that make suicide impermissible. To the argument that one owes obligations to do good even if benefits received have been paid for in kind, Hume responds that such obligations

> certainly have some bounds; I am not obliged to do a small good to society at the expense of a great harm to myself: why then should I prolong a miserable existence, because of some frivolous advantage which the public may perhaps receive from me? [*O*, 158]

As a public servant may resign from office, so may a person resign from life, without thereby failing to have given society its due, the more so if the person will be a burden to society if suicide is shunned.

Duty to others receives discussion here in impersonal terms; it is duty to a faceless society, not to family or friends, that appears in "On Suicide." What difference this makes, if any, of course is not explored. It seems quite right that one's duties to do good are finite. That they, so to say, are finite enough to allow one to commit suicide is asserted, but not argued. Nor are arguments from duties to others or to a deity *not* to commit suicide much considered—for example, that at least often suicide is a tragic mistake that the person involved would recognize to be such were they to have seen their situation other than through temporarily dark glasses. (This, argument, of course, makes an empirical assumption; so do Hume's arguments.) The case, pro or con, is investigated only briefly.

It does seem that Hume's views regarding suicide differ from those of the thinkers most likely to be his opponents. What Hume takes to be relevant is simply the quality of conscious content—whether life as lived by a person is or is not sufficiently unpleasant presently and in prospect to make him or her to wish it prolonged. The value of *persons* who live lives, as a consideration not reducible to the value of *lives* that persons live, does not come into play for Hume; he denies any such distinction, or embraces the view that such a reduction can be made. Kant affirms the distinction and denies the reduction. One who joins Kant in this may or may not hold that suicide is always wrong. But one who joins Kant here will argue the case on different and more complex grounds.

Finally, Hume considers duty to self.

> That suicide may often be consistent with interest and our duty to ourselves, no one can question who allows that age, sickness, or misfortune may render life a burden and make it worse even than annihilation. [*O*, 159]

Our horror of death, Hume argues, guarantees that if our life is worth keeping we will keep it. No motive short of our life being lived under conditions that make it worse than annihilation will bring us to suicide. One obvious objection is that it might *seem* to one that one had reached such an impasse when one had not; and it is *thinking* that annihilation is better than life that is relevant to motivation to suicide. Many a life has been tragically lost by momentary depression making things seem worse than they are. Hume's response is weak:

> Though perhaps the situation of a man's health or fortune did not seem to require this remedy, we may at least be assured that any who without apparent reason has had recourse to it was cursed with such an incurable depravity or gloominess of temper as must poison all enjoyment, and render him equally miserable as if he had been loaded with the most grievous misfortunes. [*O*, 160]

On this view, every teenager who has committed suicide out of a shocked empathy with a friend who has done likewise was of such "incurable depravity or gloominess of temper" as not to have enjoyed life anyway—a view which needs only to be stated clearly to be seen as false. Hume tempers his claim by saying only that "most people who lie under any temptation to abandon existence" would "prolong a miserable existence" by refraining, and this too underestimates the potential suicide's ability to see things as far worse than an objective evaluation would describe them.

Immortality

In "On the Immortality of the Soul," scheduled for publication in 1757 but withdrawn, Hume begins and ends with a reference to the Christian Gospel:

> By the mere light of reason it seems difficult to prove the immortality of the soul; the arguments for it are commonly derived either from metaphysical topics, or moral, or physical. But in reality it is the gospel, and the gospel alone, that has brought *life and immortality to light* . . . Nothing could set in a fuller light the infinite obligations which mankind have to Divine revelation, since we find that no other medium could ascertain this great and important truth. [*O*, 161, 167]

Between these remarks, which would be sincere in Calvin but are ironic in Hume, he considers arguments for and against immortality that he classifies as metaphysical, moral, or physical.

Metaphysical Arguments

Two metaphysical propositions of most apparent help to the defender of the immortality of the soul are *The soul or mind is immaterial* and *Nothing material can think.* The second, along with *The mind can think*, serves as backing for the first, and the first, together with *The immaterial is immortal* yields the desired conclusion. It, of course, is *substances* that are of interest here. Individual thoughts, even if immaterial, are not immortal, and *The immaterial is immortal* must mean *An immaterial substance is an immortal substance.*

Hume follows Locke in viewing substance as a something, we know not what, in which properties inhere. Thus while we may see the cylindrical black pen or be aware of fatigue and a desire for coffee, it is the properties *being cylindrical* and *being black,* or the states *being fatigued* and *desiring coffee,* that we are aware of. The pen as material substance, and the self as immaterial or mental substance, lies forever beyond our experience. So construed, a substance is propertyless or *bare,* and *inferred* rather than experienced. It is a metaphysical absurdity—what could exist and have no properties?—and an epistemological problem—what could justify the inference? The temptation to stick with properties alone, and forswear substances, looks parsimonious and safe.

The Cartesian account of our experience differs. What one is aware of is *a pen's being cylindrical and black* or *a person's being fatigued and desiring coffee.* There is but a distinction of reason between a substance at a time and its manner at that time of possessing its essential property. (Descartes holds that minds have only mental properties—modifications of *being conscious*—and bodies have only material properties—modalities of *being extended;* but we need not pursue this doctrine here.) The point relevant here is that it is logically impossible that a substance walk about naked or a property take an unchaperoned stroll. Properties that are not properties of still other properties are properties of a substance and a substance always has properties. To experience a substance is not to experience a property and infer a substance; it is to experience a substance-*qua*-propertied. Berkeley thought of *substance* in a Lockean manner and so eschews the term "substance" when he comes to make a list of the furniture of heaven and earth, but he thought of minds along essentially Cartesian lines as self-conscious entities that endure through time and undergo change without loss of essential property. For the reasons indicated, a Lockean conception of substance falls easy prey to Hume's critique. A Cartesian conception of substance is allied with sturdier doctrine, though this is not the place to develop it. Not surprisingly, a Cartesian notion of substance is better adapted to a defense of dualism than the Lockean.

On the Lockean account, a substance is set apart from all properties; it has none of its own, so to say. Thus of course any substance might have any property. If such bare particulars could be classified, some as mental and some as material, then a material substance might have the property *thinking about the Boston Celtics* and so be a mind.

Hume makes appeal as well to his doctrine that *a priori* anything might cause anything:

> Experience being the only source of our judgments of this nature, we cannot know from any other principle, whether matter, by its structure or arrangement, may not be the cause of thought. Abstract reasonings cannot decide any question of fact or existence. [*O*, 161]

Hume did not suppose that there are such abstract objects as universals or Forms or numbers. Still, a Humean might know that such propositions as *If there are abstract objects they do not cause spatial phenomena* and *The number two is not the cause of lunch being served at noon*, and know them as *necessary* truths. This would not be a relevant counterexample to Hume's claim regarding causal knowledge though it certainly goes beyond it.

Hume's contention is that any statement of the form *A causes B* is known only from having sensory or introspective confirmation that the sort of thing "A" refers to is related to the sort of thing "B" refers to by way of being members of classes that occur in one-to-one correspondence, where any temporal precedence there may be goes to the member of the "A" class. He denies that *Bodies can think* is a contradiction. Descartes held that this proposition is tantamount to *An extended thing has an unextended property or state*, and that this is a contradiction. Descartes's view requires that *A thought is unextended* be a necessary truth. Hume agrees with this assessment, though a materialist would not. His *Treatise* position embraces a dualism regarding impressions—some are spatial and some are not. The story of how this dispute continues is not told in Hume's discussion of immortality. There one is left with the assertion that as *a priori* anything can cause anything, bodies may cause thought or thought may be caused in bodies.

Suppose that we discover by experience that *being an oak* is an essence and that only things that have it cause acorns. Some contemporary philosophers hold that such propositions as *Water is H_2O* are necessary truths, describing the essences of the stuff they are about, but are discovered by experience to be true. The essence of a thing proscribes its causal powers, and a proposition of the sort *Only oaks can cause acorns* may be viewed with plausibility as a necessary truth.

Were one to take this non-Humean line, then it becomes an option that Descartes's sort of view be experientially confirmed. One would have to descend from Hume's thesis that *a priori* anything can cause anything to the question as to whether we have experiential grounds for embracing the Cartesian or the Humean account of body and thought, or perhaps some other. That there are essences becomes a matter of experience, and perhaps minds have essences.

There is at least this difficulty with Hume's argument. Hume supposed that the class of propositions that are knowable *a priori* or without appeal to sensory or introspective experience and the class of propositions that are necessarily true are extensionally equivalent, perhaps necessarily so: the epistemological category *knowable a priori* and the metaphysical/logical category *necessarily true* cover the same propositional landscape. To the degree that this assumption is challengeable, Hume's argument concerning bodies being capable of sustaining thought is challengeable. There is at least no necessary connection between *being knowable a priori* and *being necessarily true* if the view described in the preceding paragraph is non-contradictory.

Hume next appeals to an analogy. Material substances come and go. Supposing that there are however many immaterial substances you like, reasoning by analogy will yield the conclusion that they too come and go. In part, the argument here, presupposing again the Lockean substance-detachable-from-all-properties view, seems to be that a substance (should any exist) may for one period be associated with a cluster of properties that constitutes the identity of one individual and at another period be associated with a different cluster that constitutes the identity of another individual. On this perspective, individuals can be ephemeral while substances endure. That part of Hume's argument depends on the plausibility of Locke's account of substance, a doctrine that Hume rightly gives low marks to and wrongly assumes to be all there is to talk of substances. Whether the analogy Hume suggests has any force is another matter; perhaps minds are unlike bodies in ways negatively relevant to the analogy. Hume does not immediately pursue the issue in his discussion of metaphysical arguments; he picks up the topic again as he reviews moral arguments, and yet again as he considers physical arguments. And he returns to it at the end of the section on metaphysical arguments.

Hume concludes his perusal of metaphysical arguments with a brief discourse on change and beginning:

> Reasoning from the common course of nature, and without supposing any new interposition of the Supreme Cause, which ought

always to be excluded from philosophy, *what is incorruptible must also be ingenerable*. [*O*, 162]

How Hume knows this—from what Humean epistemological resources it is derivable—is entirely puzzling. Perhaps the idea is that if any metaphysical themes are cogent, *what is incorruptible must be ingenerable* is cogent (though that too could be debated). It is *natural* immortality, immortality inherent to its owner, that is in view here. The question in the section on metaphysical arguments is not whether God will sustain the lives of persons, but whether by their nature persons or minds escape being subject to corruption. Thus, for example, the Christian view of immortality and resurrection is not here officially under discussion. In fact, Hume and much of the Judeo-Christian tradition *agree* that the human mind or soul is not inherently immortal. The theist typically holds that God will sustain persons in existence beyond the death of the body. Persons in *this* life depend on God for their existence, and the *next* life will not be different in that regard. Hume, of course, does not agree. Hume, and much of the theistic tradition, agree on the *frailty* of human nature, but of course not on their longevity. More carefully, some theists have held that God has created human beings with the property *being immortal unless annihilated by God* and others have held that instead humans have the property *being non-existent unless sustained in existence by God*. This, as it were, involves a difference about the degree of human frailty but not a difference regarding the fact of human dependence. The proposition that Hume sponsors entails that *Minds are immortal* is true only if *Minds are incorruptible* is true, and that *Minds are incorruptible* is true only if it is the case that *Minds are ingenerable*.

At this point, Hume returns to his argument from analogy. He claims that it is true both that *(Non-human) animals have minds* and *Animal minds are not ingenerable*; hence it is the case that *Animal minds are not incorruptible*. So it is probable that *Human minds are not incorruptible*. "Animals undoubtedly feel, think, love, hate, will, and even reason, though in a more imperfect manner than men: are their souls also immaterial and immortal" (*O*, 162)? Hume knows that the metaphysical traditions that have argued for human immortality have answered his question with a "No"; he invites them to do so in the case of the human soul as well. This, Hume suggests, is what parity of reasoning requires. A defender of metaphysical arguments for human immortality, of course, could retain parity by regarding non-human animals as immortal, and shown to be so by the same sort of argument she believes cogent in the human case. Or she can argue that there are relevant differences between human and non-human animals that ruin Hume's analogy. That issue is not explored.

Moral Arguments

Hume grants that there are properties or attributes of God such that, if we have good reason to suppose that God exists and has these attributes, then there is good reason to suppose that God will sustain us in existence beyond the death of our bodies, and perhaps forever. Having said that no claim may be made in philosophy that supposes "any new interposition of the Supreme Cause, which ought always to be excluded from philosophy" (O, 162), he nonetheless must argue against the theological or metaphysical views sometimes used as a basis for concluding that the soul is immortal. He mentions the view that God is just and is "interested in the future [that is, postmortem] punishment of the vicious and reward of the virtuous" (O, 162). Divine love, or promises, could also be appealed to. Hume denies, of course, that there is any good reason to suppose such things. There is need to redress injustice in a future life only if justice remains unredressed in this one. But then we cannot infer from what God has caused or permitted in this life to what God will cause or permit in a next, lest we assume that there too injustice will remain unredressed and we find ourselves without an argument from justice for there being a life to come. If we argue by analogy from what is allowed now to what will be allowed then, Hume suggests, this is exactly our situation.

On the question as to whether humans have a natural desire for immortality or its corollary a natural terror of ceasing to exist, Hume says that "There arise indeed in some minds some unaccountable terrors with regard to futurity; but these would quickly vanish were they not artificially fostered by precept and education" (O, 162) and ascribes such education to priests who gain a livelihood from it. Anticlericalism aside, this is part of Hume's answer to the argument that human beings by nature desire immortality, and there is no natural desire that lacks a corresponding possibility of fulfillment (to thirst corresponds water, to hunger food, and so on). The other part comes in the section on physical arguments, when Hume contends that "Were our horrors of annihilation an original passion, not the effect of our general love of happiness, it would rather prove the mortality of the soul: for as nature does nothing in vain she would never give us a horror against an impossible event." Extrapolating slightly, if we accept *Nature does nothing in vain*, then we have two equiplausible claims: *Nature gives us no desires that are unfulfillable* and *Nature gives us no fears of things that are unrealizable*. If we both desire immortality and fear oblivion, then (on the present assumption) both immortality and oblivion must be live options, and we shall (by appeal to nature doing nothing in vain) have nothing to choose between them. Our reasons for thinking that both the desire for immortality and the fear of oblivion are natural desires are quite comparable, and if *Nature does nothing in vain* is so read as to entail *Nature gives us no desires that are not fulfilled* and *Nature gives us no fears of conditions that are not realized*, then plainly nature must do something in vain after all.

Not surprisingly, in discussing moral arguments for immortality, Hume assumes his own moral theory.

> Whence do we learn that there is such a thing as moral distinctions, but from our own sentiments. The chief source of moral ideas is the reflection on the interests of human society. [*O*, 164–165]

> By what rule are punishments and rewards distributed? What is the Divine standard of merit and demerit? Shall we suppose that human sentiments have place in the Deity? How bold that hypothesis! We have no conception of other sentiments. According to human sentiments, sense, courage, good-manners, industry, prudence, genius, etc., are the essential parts of personal merits. [*O*, 163–164]

Virtue is essentially what makes one agreeable in and useful to society, and vice the opposite. Those who contend that the comments with which Hume begins and ends his essay on immortality are sincere rather than ironic must at least face the fact that Hume's ethic is hardly that of the Christian tradition. Faith, hope, and charity are not on his list of "personal merits." Love of and obedience to a holy God play no role in his moral theory.

His argument, in effect, is this. Virtue and vice, right and wrong, reward and punishment, are tied closely to human society. Such matters have little if any relevance to post-mortem persons and conditions unless those conditions are conceived as largely similar to current conditions, and typically they are not. Thus reasoning concerning what morality entails or justice requires will have little or no relevance to postmortem conditions that are very dissimilar from current conditions. Arguments for immortality that are based on moral considerations involve reasoning of precisely this sort; they consider the consequences of morality or justice for post-mortem conditions than are very dissimilar to current conditions. Hence they establish little or nothing.

It is not surprising that a moral theory not merely applicable to but cut to the cloth of current human society should have little by way of postmortem implications or relevance. Just as a moral theory based on theistic premises should be more promising as a basis for projecting to immortality but highly questionable to a Humean, so Hume's theory, with little promise for such projections, will seem highly questionable to a theist who (independent of the immortality issue) will think its list of virtues and vices arbitrarily restricted and its foundations in human sentiment alone to be intolerably weak. Hume, though, does not develop, let alone defend, his moral theory. Of course that is to be expected in a relatively short essay; the consequence is that while it seems clear what consequences Hume's theory has (and what consequences it lacks) regarding immortality, we are given no reason for supposing that the theory that has these particular consequences is true.

Physical Arguments

Hume writes: "The physical arguments from the analogy of nature are strong for the mortality of the soul; and are really the only philosophical arguments which ought to be admitted with regard to this question, or indeed any question of fact" (O, 165). Hume claims that any logically contingent claim regarding the existence or properties of anything that we do not directly perceive or introspect should be decided by appeal only to arguments whose premises refer only to objects of sensation or introspection and reason by analogy from those premises to conclusions concerning the existence and properties of the items in questions. That is a large and vague claim and this is not the place to dispute or refine it.

Hume takes the physical argument to be heavily against the claim that persons are immortal. One such argument Hume puts as follows: "The souls of animals are allowed to be mortal; and these bear so near resemblance to the souls of men that the analogy from one to the other forms a very strong argument. Then bodies are not more resembling, yet no one rejects the argument drawn from comparative anatomy" (O, 166). The argument, slightly modernized, is this: given the success of argument by analogy involved in the use of animals for medical research, the nature of animal bodies and human bodies is very much the same. Animal minds and human minds are alike in many ways, and traditionally monotheists have not held that animals enjoy immortality. Given other similarities, the relations between animal mental states and animal physical states is analogous to that between human mental states and human physical states. Probably, then, human minds are mortal if animal minds are.

Another Humean argument is stated in these terms:

> Nothing in this world is perpetual; everything, however seemingly firm, is in continual flux and change: the world itself gives symptoms of frailty and dissolution. How contrary to analogy, therefore, to imagine that one single form, seeming the frailist of any, and subject to the greatest disorders, is immortal and indissoluble? [*O*, 166]

Being "in the world" here is to be understood, not as "being located in space," but in "being a member of the set of things called 'the world.'" Of course if, as Hume claims "Nothing is perpetual," that settles the issue against the soul's or mind's immortality. (Whether one speaks of animal mind and human soul, or of animal mind and human mind, matters little here.) What Hume claims is that if the human mind is immortal, it is unique in the world; at least most things are not immortal or perpetual. A naturalist or a dualist might wonder about elementary particles; various philosophers will suggest one or another sort of abstract entity. That at least many entities are mortal is nothing to the point. One could argue that complex things are mortal but simple things are not. Since complex things are made up of simple things, there are more of the latter; if simple things are immortal, then there are more immortal things than mortal, abstract objects (if any) aside. Of course, no Humean will grant that simple things are immortal. Humean simples are minimal impressions and ideas, which are transitory and fleeting and thus far from immortal. But one who holds that the soul is immortal is not likely to hold that the mind or soul is comprised of transitory mental states, even as an unbroken series of such states. If a Humean can clinch the argument only by appealing to the claim that whatever is non-complex is transitory, the best that one can say for the argument is that it derives the claim that nothing is immortal from Hume's own metaphysics. But it is not surprising that this result follows from Hume's metaphysics, which of course Hume's opponent is not likely to share.

There remains the argument from analogy. In a few pages of a short essay, the argument does not get the detailed discussion that the argument from design receives in the *Dialogues*. Nonetheless, the same sorts of questions arise. For example, what are the *relevant* similarities? Is what is often called "self-transcendence"—a complex and variously conceived property involving the capacity to choose in ways not determined by heredity and environment—lacked by non-human minds but possessed by human minds? If so, is that a relevant difference? If non-human rationality is complex, human rationality seems vastly more so; not seeing this requires a peculiarly selective vision. Is *that* a relevant difference? Why so, or why not? No one whom Hume has made aware of the importance of such considerations can accept Hume's argument by analogy without their being raised and answered. They are neither raised nor answered in Hume's essay.

Perhaps no *complex* thing is perpetual; one might suggest that the best physical candidates for immortality will be whatever is taken to be primitive by our best current physical theory (of course whether such items are conceived as everlasting or not will depend on the details of that theory). One wonders: if elementary particles, say, are conceived as everlasting, does that increase (or otherwise effect) the plausibility of the view that souls or minds are immortal? Why should it? Of if something complex should turn out to be everlasting, will that affect matters if the soul is complex but not if it is simple? These are matters that Hume leaves unexplored.

He offers yet another argument, this time not an argument by analogy, that goes as follows:

> How to dispose of the infinite number of posthumous existences ought also to embarrass the religious theory. Every planet in the solar system we are at liberty to imagine peopled with intelligent mortal beings, at least we can fix on no other supposition. For these then a new universe must have been created at first so prodigiously wide as to admit of this continual influx of beings. [O, 166]

There seems to be no good reason to think that this argument is well founded. Hume's assumptions are that every mind always must be embodied (presumably in one body), that each person comes newly into existence at birth, and that space is finite but time infinite, so that sooner or later space will run out. If the soul is immortal then 'old' minds, upon the death of their corresponding bodies, get 'new' bodies and keep them; but 'new' minds also get new bodies, and after while the finite supply of new bodies simply will run out. A view on which minds can exist unembodied, or space is infinite, or the supply of bodies is unlimited, would provide ways around this argument. (Strictly, it is not clear whether Hume's assumption is that *space* is finite or that the amount of *matter* is finite—in each case *fixedly* so.)

Hume again contends against the immortality of the soul. He writes:

> Where any two objects are so closely connected that all altera-
> tions which we have ever seen in the one are attended with pro-
> portionable alterations in the other; we ought to conclude, by all
> the rules of analogy, that, when there are still greater alterations
> produced in the former, and it is totally dissolved, there follows a
> total dissolution of the latter. Sleep, a very small effect on the
> body, is attended with a temporary extinction, at least a great
> confusion in the soul. The weakness of the body and that of the
> mind in infancy are exactly proportioned; their vigor in manhood,
> their sympathetic disorder in sickness, their common gradual de-
> cay in old age. The step further seems unavoidable, the common
> gradual decay in old age. [*O*, 165]

Hume, of course, develops his analogy so as to support his conclusion. There are also disanalogies. A person's mind can be ill and his
body well; a person's mind can be well and her body ill. If one can
multiply similarity in conditions, one as easily can multiply dissimilarities. That there are a great many correlations between mental
states and physical states has long been known. A careful defender of
the claim that the soul or mind is immortal is aware of this and it is far
from clear that such correlations count against her view.

The questions Hume's argument raises are familiar ones to the
reader of the *Dialogues*. What are the *relevant* similarities, and the *relevant* dissimilarities, between the analogies? Have we an inductive argument, or a two-stage argument—one stage inductive and one stage
an argument from analogy—that establishes *the mind is mortal?* If so,
what is it? The argument quoted points out that there are certain similarities between a person's mind and that same person's body, and
that mind and body have causal impact on each other. Many things
bear such relations to one another without either, let alone each, depending for its existence on the other. Hume's argument does not tell
us that the mind-body relation is one of mutual causal influence and
also existential dependence. For all his argument shows, they may be
related (say) as two people riding a teeter-totter, each of whose move-
ments affects the other though either can leave whenever she wishes.
For all his argument shows, they may be related as a snake (analogous

to the mind) who enlivens a snakeskin (analogous to the body) so long as the snakeskin lives, and then shuffles it off and goes on its way.

Bishop Butler, in his *Analogy*, also reflected on the relations between mind and body. His argument is neither better nor worse than Hume's and it is to the opposite effect. He wrote:

> From our being born into the present world in the helpless, imperfect state of infancy, and having arrived from thence to mature age, we find it to be a general law of nature, in our own species, that the same creatures, the same individuals, should exist in degrees of life and perception, with capacities of action, of enjoyment and suffering, in one period of their being greatly different from those appointed them in another period of it. And in other creatures the same law holds. For the difference of their capacities and states of life at their birth (to go no higher) and in maturity; the change of worms into flies, and the vast enlargement of their locomotive powers by such change; and birds and insects bursting the shell, their habitation, and by this means entering into a new world, furnished with new accommodations for them, and finding a new sphere of action assigned them—these are instances of this general law of nature. Thus all the various and wonderful transformations of animals are to be taken into consideration here. But the states of life in which we ourselves existed formerly, in the womb and in our infancy, are almost as different from our present, in mature age, as it is possible to conceive any two states or degrees of life can be. Therefore, that we are to exist hereafter in a state as different (suppose) from our present as this is from our former, is but according to the analogy of nature; according to a natural order or appointment of the very same kind with what we have already experienced.[1]

Ethical Arguments

Hume adds some brief critiques of religious ethics in such pungent sentences as these:

> Why . . . eternal punishment for the temporal offenses of so frail a creature as man? [*O*, 164]

> Nature has rendered human infancy peculiarly frail and mortal, as it were on purpose to refute the notion of a probationary state; the half of mankind die before they are rational creatures. [*O*, 164]

It can be granted readily that various popular accounts of hell (for example, a literal everlasting barbecue for souls) do not represent an articulate theology; Hume's objections do not strike here at caricatures but at core considerations. In articulate theological perspectives of the more orthodox sort, there remains a heaven to gain and a hell to shun. Even in those versions in which a doctrine of purgatory offers an uncomfortable courtyard that must be traversed before entering a heavenly abode, and even when post-mortem choices are allowed, both heaven and hell typically are conceived as everlasting or as eternal. Hume queries whether everlasting or eternal punishment can be just recompense for any "temporal offense" of "so frail a creature" as a human.

"Temporal offense" is a pleonasm; all actions, including wrong ones, are done at some time or other. If this entails that an eternal being cannot act, then a God who acts must be everlasting rather than eternal. Hume's concern can be put this way: surely, at some point, no matter how horrendous the evil one knowingly, even gleefully, perpetrates, a just punishment will run its course.

Suppose that Andrew plans and carries out the murder of a father, the rape of a mother, and the torture to death of infant twins before the mother dies; then he tortures the mother to death. Andrew shows no remorse; rather, he is proud of his deed, performed freely as a way of defining the sort of person he is. Suppose he never repents but rather always glories in his wicked rampage, his only regret that he was unable to make and carry out similar plans for other victims.

On utilitarian moral theory, presumably one can quantify the evil that Andrew has wrought. Even had he carried out a lifetime of carnage, at some point the negative value of his evil would be balanced by some finite amount of quantifiable punishment.

Theistic ethics need not be utilitarian. For a theistic ethic that is non-utilitarian, an unrepentant Andrew is not an appropriate target for divine forgiveness. God does not take Andrew seriously as a moral agent or a person if He forgives Andrew for actions that Andrew exults in the memory of. Without repentance, Andrew retains guilt. Why, exactly, does he not merit hell? Even human institutions allow for death penalties and life imprisonment. In sum: Hume's claim of disproportionality rests on ethical assumptions that he has not established and that the theist need not share.

His remark concerning a probationary state is a response to the typical theistic view that 'this life' is a prologue to another, and that our fate then depends on our choices now. Hume tends to think of this in terms only of our moral choices, whereas theism itself focuses as well on religious or theological choices. In any case, Hume's objection is that if, as the author of Hebrews asserts, a human being "is destined to die once, and after that to face [final] judgment" (9:27, New International Version) then we must admit that some prologues are extremely short and hardly of such a character as to be genuine states of probation. "Half of mankind die before" they have become responsible moral agents. Hume's critique is forceful even if he exaggerates; reducing the infant mortality rate and raising life expectancy would not answer Hume's objection.

There are theistic responses. One is to deny that humans are persons before they become moral agents. Another is to say that the half who die in infancy are judged in accordance with the decisions that they would have made. A perhaps more promising reply contends that those who die before they reach an age of responsible choice are (in another life) allowed to become moral agents and are then judged on the choices they make. Still another is to hold that those who die in infancy are given a distinct status of their own that does not involve their being judged. The theistic answers operate under the constraint that "the judge of all this earth shall do rightly." Hume questions the epistemological status of the constraining assumption.

In the end, Hume's perspective and that of Christianity or Judaism, or any other traditional theism, differ as to whether revelation is a possible source of knowledge. The claim that there has been a revelation, and that it has yielded us knowledge of crucial information concerning our salvation that we would not have picked up on our own, need not be irrational or anti-rational. It may be accompanied by an insistence that what is revealed illuminate rather than contradict what is known from other sources—not that it need run counter to none of our assumptions (that is not even a constraint to put on new and non-revealed theories) but that it not be incompatible with what we rightly are surest of or that it not go utterly against the grain of our knowledge. Hume will have nothing to do with such a source of knowledge, even if it is not said to be self-illuminating or self-authenticating.

The theist, then, taking the justice of God to be a revealed truth, and thinking the content of that revelation to comport well with what we otherwise know, asks how to reconcile the fact of a high infant mortality rate with divine justice, and sees various ways of doing so without having any enormous confidence as to which is the correct one or even whether the correct one has been discovered. Hume, noting the rate and denying the revelation, finds the rate evidence against there being a just God. Hume argues, in effect, as follows:

(1) If there is a just God, then there will not be a high infant mortality rate.

(2) There is a high infant mortality rate.

So: (3) There is not a just God.

The theist, granting (2), wonders how Hume knows that (1) is true. She can suggest various circumstances in which God could be just and yet let an infant die; so (she contends) (1) is not a necessary truth. It is hardly an empirical generalization or the report of an introspective or sensory experience. How, then, does Hume know that (1) is true? None of his favored means of knowledge yield (1). Nor is it clear that some other means of knowledge leads us to it. The theist questions the epistemological status of Hume's claim about what follows from there being a just God, not by playing fast and loose with the notion of justice, but by noting that an omnicompetent being can allow things to occur without thereby becoming unjust that a non-omnicompetent being cannot allow without becoming unjust. So how does Hume know that if there is a just God then there will not be a high infant mortality rate?

The Pre-*Dialogues* Dialogue

In various places in his writings, other than in the *Natural History* and the *Dialogues*, Hume discusses the philosophy of religion. In Section XI of *An Enquiry Concerning Human Understanding*, "Of a Particular Providence and of a Future State," Hume offers a sort of practice *Dialogues*. I will briefly describe its main currents of argument.

"A friend who loves sceptical paradoxes" criticizes the argument from design and claims that morality requires no grounding in religion or metaphysics. Hume distances himself from this friend, whose views, he says, he "can by no means approve" though he discusses them because "they seem to be curious, and to bear some relation to the chain of reasoning carried on throughout this enquiry" (*O*, 132).

The friend's doctrines and criticisms coincide with those of the *Natural History* and the *Dialogues*. A central philosophical doctrine is that one must construct one's concept of God from the argument from design. Any property one ascribes to God must be a property that the cause of observed effects must have in order to be their cause. A properly constructed concept of God will contain concepts of only these

properties. The strategy of beginning with the view that God is omnicompetent and seeing how this view fares in the light of whatever
conceptual and empirical data may be relevant is ruled out as rationally arbitrary. It is one thing to point out that a proponent of
theism who has cast her fate on the success of the argument from design and proposed to accept nothing about God that that argument
does not sanction in all consistency cannot then go on to claim that
God is omnicompetent and derive consequences concerning God and
the world from that claim. It is another thing to rule out by sheer fiat
the thesis that God is omnicompetent—to claim that it is somehow
irrational to see what that hypothesis explains and whether anything
we know to be true is incompatible with its truth. Unfortunately, the
friend does both things.

The *Natural History* assumption that whatever is conceptually
complex must be historically late appears also in the *Enquiry*: "Specu-
lative dogmas of religion . . . could not possibly be conceived or admitted in the early stages of the world; when mankind, being wholly
illiterate, formed an idea of religion more suitable to their weak apprehension, and composed their sacred tenets of such tales chiefly as
were the objects of traditional belief, more than of argument or disputation" (*E*, 133).

There is the Humean analogue of the so-called presumption of
atheism—that if there is no proof that God exists, then the only reasonable assumption is that He does not. This presumption presumably has its roots either in a more general or a more specific thesis.
The more general thesis is that, for any existential proposition A, if
we have no reason to think A true, then we should think A false. The
more specific thesis is that, for any existential religious proposition, if
we have no reason to think it true, then we should think it false. I
know of no reason to suppose that the more specific thesis is true that
does not involve deducing it from the more general thesis. The more
general thesis is false; there is no rational prejudice in favor of negative existentials under conditions of evidential scarcity.

Consider the existential claims (E) *There is an elephant in the clearing*
and (D) *There is a dust mote in the clearing*. It seems not extravagant to
suggest that if the former is false, we will be able to discover its
falsehood by looking into the clearing, whereas if the latter is false,
we shall not be able to discover its falsehood by looking into the clearing. One can always quarrel with examples. If the clearing lies in a
dust storm, or in heavy fog, or in utter darkness or even a severe grey
dusk, then one might miss an elephant that nonetheless was there; so

let the clearing be light and atmospherically visually unencumbered; and suppose other similar cavils to have been answered, as they can be once they are raised. Then it is the case that if one observes no elephant in the clearing—if one has no reason to think (E) true—then no doubt it is reasonable to think (E) false. But if one sees no dust mote, that is no reason to think that there is none, and even if we have no reason to think (D) true that fact is not a reason to think (D) false. We might put the point this way: elephants, but not dust motes, have the feature that if they inhabit one's perceptual environment at all, it is likely that they will do so in such a manner that their presence will be perceptually detectable. Call those objects that resemble elephants rather than dust motes in this respect, *perceptually flagrant objects.* The more general thesis is true regarding perceptually flagrant objects, false concerning objects that are not perceptually flagrant.

Perhaps, strictly speaking, no objects are inherently perceptually flagrant or lacking in perceptual flagrancy. Perhaps *being perceptually flagrant* is a property an object has, or lacks, given certain conditions. Even an elephant will lack it in a dense forest and even a dust mote will have it within a well-lit artificial vacuum. Then the more general thesis will be true regarding existential propositions about objects under conditions in which they possess the property *being perceptually flagrant* and false regarding existential propositions about objects under conditions in which they lack this property.

The more general thesis, being universal, is false if it is false of any objects, or of any object under any condition. Since it is false of many objects, and of objects under many conditions, it is false. But then there is no presumption of atheism.

Even were one to accept the general claim that if we have no reason to accept an existential proposition, we should reject it, we will not get a presumption of atheism. Consider the proposition *this flower was not caused by God.* If we have no reason to accept this proposition, then we must reject it in the sense of thinking it false. But then (according to the general claim) we must think *this flower was created by God* is true, and so believe that God exists. So we can use the general claim as easily to create a presumption *against* atheism as to create one for it.

The "friend" insists on the principles that (P1) "When we infer any particular cause from an effect, we must proportion the one to the other, and can never be allowed to ascribe to the cause any qualities but what are sufficient to produce the effect" (*O*, 136) and (P2) "Nor can we, by any rules of just reasoning, return back from the cause, and infer other effects from it, beyond those by which alone it is known to us" (*O*, 136). It is not clear exactly what relationship is supposed to hold between (P1) and (P2)—whether they are supposed to be the same principle put in different words, or whether (P1) is supposed to entail (P2) but not conversely. They are not the same principle, put twice. If I argue that the potter who made my cup, since he knows how to make a cup, must be omniscient, I violate (P1) but not (P2). If I argue that the potter who made my cup, since he did produce it, must have produced my saucer as well, I violate (P2) but not (P1). If I can violate one principle without violating another, then the principles are two and not one.

Nor does (P1) entail (P2). Let a (perhaps complex) property that a cause must have in order for it to be the cause of its effect be its *causative* property. (P1) proscribes attributing to a cause its causative property to any greater degree than is necessary for it to yield its effect. Let the effect by which the existence of a cause is known be its *substantiating* effect. (P2) proscribes inferring from the fact that a cause has the causative property its has been inferred to possess to its being the cause of some effect other than its substantiating effect. That we should be maximally parsimonious in our attribution of causative properties to a cause does not entail that we should be maximally parsimonious in our ascription of effects to that cause; nor does the reverse entailment hold. Ascribing new effects to a cause *need* not increase our estimation of its causative property though it will increase our estimation of its exercise of that property.

(P1) and (P2), then, are not extensionally equivalent and they do not entail one another. But each does render more determinate the general principle "Ascribe to a cause only what experience of its substantiating effect justifies."

Hume offers a response to (P2). Upon finding one footprint in the sand, we can argue that its cause made others; upon finding a partially built house with new materials well stored, we can infer that its builder will complete the job. Both inferences violate (P2). The "friend's" response is that these inferences are allowable only because we have experience of human beings making more footprints than one and completing buildings that they have started. The causes, or at least causes of the same kind, have been experienced to have the sort of effect we infer to in our samples. "We comprehend . . . the *usual* figure and members of that species of animal, without which this method of argument must be considered as fallacious and sophistical" (*O*, 144).

Along similar lines, the "friend" embraces an early version of Logical Positivism when he asserts: "The experienced train of events is the great standard by which we all regulate our conduct. Nothing else can be appealed to in the field, or in the senate. Nothing else ought ever to be heard of in the school, or in the closet. In vain would our limited understanding break through those boundaries, which are too narrow for our fond imagination. While we argue from the course of nature, and infer a particular intelligent cause, which first bestowed, and still preserves order in the universe, we embrace a principle which is both uncertain and useless. It is uncertain; because the subject lies entirely beyond the reach of human experience. It is useless; because our knowledge of this cause being derived entirely from the course of nature, we can never, according to the rules of just reasoning, return back from the cause with any new inference, or making additions to the common and experienced course of nature, establish any new principles of conduct and behavior." (*O*, 142). Philosophical reflection is able to establish that we are unable to establish anything metaphysical; the epistemological principles of a radical empiricism can be rationally established, but no principles of any metaphysic. *How* the principles of radical empiricism are established is not revealed.

The "friend" also denies that morality requires any grounding in religion or metaphysics. The question is not whether a non-religious person can behave in a morally acceptable manner; that question is empirical and since some non-religious persons do so behave it has an affirmative answer. The question is whether behaving morally is rational only in a theistic world. This the "friend" denies: "I acknowledge that, in the present order of things, virtue is attended with more peace of mind than vice, and meets with a more favorable reception from the world. I am sensible that according to the past experience of mankind, friendship is the chief joy of human life and moderation the only source of tranquillity and happiness. I never balance between the virtuous and the vicious course of life; but am sensible that, to a well-disposed mind, every advantage is on the side of the former. And what can you say more, allowing all your suppositions and reasonings?" (*O*, 140) The argument seems to be this: (1) It is rational to so act as to bring to oneself peace of mind, tranquillity, happiness, and favorable reception from the world. (2) Acting morally better brings to oneself peace of mind, tranquillity, happiness, and favorable reception from the world. So: (3) It is rational to act morally.

This, of course, is no defense of the autonomy of morality. If tor-

turing infants and raping children brought peace of mind, then, given
(1–3), it would be rational to engage in them, perhaps provided that
one found onself in the society of those who favored such activities.
In (1–3) rationale for being moral is seen as prudential and psychological rather than as moral or as religious and/or metaphysical. This
is no defense of the autonomy of morality.

The "friend" also comments:

> *Are there marks of distributive justice in the world?* If you answer in
> the affirmative, I conclude that, since justice here exerts itself, it is
> satisfied. If you reply in the negative, I conclude that you have
> then no reason to ascribe justice, in our sense of it, to the gods. If
> you hold a medium between affirmation and negation, by saying
> that the justice of the gods, at present, exerts itself in part, but
> not in its full extent; I answer that you have no reason to give it
> any particular extent, but only so far as you see it, *at present*, exert
> itself. [*O*, 141–42]

Insofar as one's strategy is limited to inferring from what one observes
to what can be extrapolated from what one observes, this seems exactly right. There are philosophers, and others, who suppose that
empiricist inductivism is the only possibility in philosophy of religion. Hume, of course, is one of empiricist inductivism's profoundest
critics. There are criticisms as well that come from the side of the an-
gels, but that story goes beyond our concern here with Hume's philosophy of religion. The practice *Dialogues* serve as a brief indication
of what was to come. They do not contain much of interest that is not
more fully present in their more lengthy and complex successor.

CHAPTER 15

Miracles

What Is a Miracle?

R ICHARD SWINBURNE offers this definition: "To start with we may say very generally that a miracle is an event of an extraordinary kind, brought about by a god, and of religious significance."[1] As will become clear, and as is plain in any case, Hume's main concern is with alleged miracles whose occurrence is important to Christian belief and practice. It is *miracles as possible evidence for religious belief* that occupies his attention. So instead of "a god," I will simply talk about God—that omnicompetent, unembodied Spirit whom Judeo-Christian theology believes to be Creator, Providence, Judge, and Savior, and to have performed actions that no mere human could perform.

In the same spirit, instead of talking about "religious significance," let us say that no event is miraculous unless it is brought about by God in His creative, or providential, or judgmental, or redemptive, capacities.

Miracles and "Extraordinary" Events

This leaves "extraordinary," which is vague. Ford's pardon of Nixon was extraordinary, but not in a way relevant to being miraculous. But what is that way?

The standard answer is given by Swinburne: "Given talk of natural laws, an event which goes against them or 'violates' them would seem to be an event of 'an extraordinary kind,'"[2] and by Hume: "A miracle is a violation of the laws of nature" (*E*, 114).

The answer raises new questions. Notoriously, that L is at time T a law of some science does not entail that L will be at time $T + 1$ a law of any science at all. If an event violates L at T, and satisfies the other criteria, it is a miracle at T, provided L is at T a law of science. But if L at $T + 1$ ceases to be a law, the event ceases to be miraculous. And of course if L at $T + 2$ regains its place among the scientists, the event at $T + 2$ regains its prestige among the saints.

Faced with this inelegant circumstance, a natural move is to distinguish in the manner of:

(1) L is a *real* law of nature if and only if L is a law that is related to a set of phenomena such that (a) L describes and interprets the phenomena best, (b) L is not reducible to any other law, and (c) there is no law L' that supercedes L.

(2) L is an *apparent* law of nature if and only if L is accepted as a real law of nature by the scientific community, and at least one of the set (a, b, c) is false of L.

The distinction marked by (1) and (2) is of course roughly stated, and in fact a fair amount of philosophy of science would have to go into getting the distinction at which it is directed really sharply focused. But the *sort* of distinction (1) versus (2) makes should be clear enough for present purposes.

It seems logically possible, and even probable given the sort of argument that appeals to the stormy history of science as a reason for rehiring current laws on a yearly basis but never granting them tenure, that we shall never have legitimate confidence that any given law is real rather than only apparent.[3]

A real miracle, of course, violates a real law. An event that violates ever so many apparent laws, but nary a real one, be it ever so widely and prestigiously acclaimed a miracle, is only an apparent miracle, and so a sham miracle. Further, if we can never identify a real law, we can never identify a real miracle either. At this point an epistemic darkness descends.

Miracles and the Stormy History of Science

A currently popular view of the history and nature of science suggests an argument relevant to this darkness.[4]

(a) The probability favorable to any particular formulation of an alleged law of nature is not precisely or approximately one, but is low (less than .5) at any time past or present, given the stormy past history of science.

(b) The probability in favor of any actual formulation of a law of nature at any future time will not be close to one, but will be low, given the stormy history of science *up to then*.

(c) At any time t and for any law L, the probability in favor of L being, in its formulation at t, a real law of nature is low.

(d) Even if an event violates law L at t, the probability is low that the event is a real miracle (even if it satisfies the other criteria for being a miracle).

(e) Given the stormy past history of science, for any particular formulation of an alleged law of nature, the probability is high (at least .5) that a more precise (perhaps revolutionary) reformulation of this law will replace it in the future (at least in some restricted domain), even if the law in question is fundamental to some science.

(f) If L at t is fundamental to some science, the probability is high (at least .5) that there be a law L' at $t + 1$ such that L' is the successor of L, where:

Law L' at $t + 1$ is the *successor* of law L at t if and only if There is a domain that is included in the scope of both L and L', and some phenomenon x is an anomaly given L but not given L'.

(g) That x is a miracle at t entails that x is an anomaly with respect to some law L at t, but not conversely.[5]

(h) That x is an anomaly at t does not yield high (at least .5) probability that it will be an anomaly at $t + 1$.

Therefore:

(i) That x is a miracle at t does not yield high (at least .5) probability that it will be a miracle at $t + 1$.

Given (d), the probability is against any given accepted law being a real law. Even if it is a fact that a law that is basic among those currently accepted will have a successor, this does not guarantee that an event that violates such a law is a miracle. If anything, given (i), it makes probable the very opposite.

The argument just rehearsed contrasts with Hume's own perspective (insofar as he had one) on the philosophy of science. Hume seems to have supposed that the propositions accepted as laws of science in his day were (a) very nearly true and so (b) unlikely to need revision. The argument just rehearsed denies both (a) and (b) with regard to any propositions regarded as laws at any time. While Hume's own argument supposes that there is no great difficulty in discovering real laws of nature, the argument just rehearsed requires that the search for real laws be a never-ending and dubiously successful endeavor for closer and closer approximations to such laws. Further, when the argument is placed in the context of a certain view of the history (and future) of science—a view whose famous key category is 'paradigm shift'—insofar as a law itself is understood only in the context of a theory, insofar as a theory itself is understood only in the context of a paradigm, and insofar as paradigms themselves do not so much die as inevitably fade away, the result for miracles is obvious. In sum, the identification of a miracle is paradigm relative.[6] Since 'the true paradigm' is elusive—indeed, perhaps for a Kuhnian 'the true paradigm' is no more a coherent concept than 'the highest integer'—the distinction between real and apparent miracles is also elusive (if not incoherent).

It might, of course, be the case that some miracles are inevitably entrenched, where:

> Miracle M is *inevitably entrenched* if and only if Any plausible paradigm includes some theory which in turn includes some law that M violates.

If it is true of some miracle that it is *inevitably entrenched*, then some miracle is presumably—even for a Kuhnian—real. If one could discover some description D of an event E such that *D is true of E and E occurred* together with relevant truths about the current state of science[7] entailed *An inevitably entrenched miracle occurred*, then of course one could discover that an inevitably entrenched miracle had occurred by discovering that D was satisfied by some event. But, needless to say, all this is problematic. How exactly will D read?

In the absence of a successful "cashing in" of some such concepts as those noted above, the situation of a defender of the argument seems to be this. She could note that, given present evidence, a particular sort of event would be miraculous if it occurred. But she would have to add that this was no reliable evidence that, were this sort of event to occur, a real miracle would occur. For her perspective requires that she admit that it is not merely possible but highly likely that (a) on another paradigm, the occurrence of such an event would not be miraculous, and (b) another paradigm will soon (on a cosmic time scale anyway) arrive. She is in the strange position of having to report her experiences always on report forms which are even then in the process of being revoked by the Office of Paradigms. So the real-apparent miracle distinction (as paradigm-relative) is epistemic, not ontological.

Perhaps there is something of Humean skepticism in all this. Perhaps the paradigm-shift philosophy of science is Humeanism in one of its varieties, all sophisticated and in modern dress. Consider Humes' famed remark that:

> My natural propensity, and the course of my animal spirits and passions, reduce me to indolent belief in the general maxims of the world. . . . I must yield to the current of nature. . . . These are the sentiments of my spleen and indolence, and indeed I confess that philosophy has nothing to oppose them. . . . In all the incidents of life we ought still to preserve our scepticism. If we believe that fire warms, or water refreshes, it is only because it costs too much pains to think otherwise. [*T*, 269–270]

If this is so for Hume with respect to our belief even in particular laws of nature, perhaps we may also (with a little license) apply Hume's comments about religion to the more abstruse realms of scientific and metaphysical theory—and paradigms:

> Doubt, uncertainty, suspense of judgement appear the only result of our most accurate scrutiny concerning this subject. But such is the frailty of human reason, and such the irresistible contagion of opinion, that even this deliberate doubt could scarcely be upheld, did we not enlarge our view, and opposing one species of superstition to another set them a quarreling; while we ourselves, during their fury and contention happily make our escape into the calm, though obscure, regions of philosophy. [*N*, 98]

Given the sorts of creatures we are, we will adopt some system or other (*N*, 40). In science, there are alleged constraints. But it may be that for the sincere paradigm philosopher "correspondence with reality" is not among them. Or perhaps with regard to paradigms, talk of "correspondence" is incoherent. It played no role in appraising competing world models in the *Dialogues*. It is tempting to speculate how skeptical, and how Humean, a "paradigm shift philosophy of science" might be, but I exercise restraint.

It does seem clear that, given the perspective of the accepter of (3a–3c), miracles cannot be used as evidence for religious belief. For whenever we discover what is (on the current view) a miracle, we have better evidence than not that it is not a miracle on some soon-to-be-adopted view. Better, the real miracle–apparent miracle distinction has purchase only on paradigms, not on the world. As we shall see, this conclusion parallels Hume's own.

Miracles and Epistemology

Hume begins his *Enquiry* argument by referring to an argument by Dr. Tillotson which runs:

> (A) The evidence that the Eucharistic bread and wine literally becomes flesh and blood is at best that of Apostolic testimony.
> (B) The evidence that the Eucharistic bread and wine remain bread and wine is that of immediate sensory experience.
> (C) No one can rightly rest as much confidence in the evidence provided by testimony as in one's own immediate sensory experience.
> (D) "Were the doctrine that the Eucharistic bread and wine become real flesh and blood ever so clearly revealed in Scripture, it were directly contrary to the rules of just reasoning to give our assent to it" (*E*, 109).[8]

A further premise—"A weaker evidence can never destroy a stronger" (*E*, 109)—is expressible either respectively as an epistemic or a psychological claim:

> (E1) It is irrational to accept a claim as true if our evidence for it is weaker than our evidence against it.
> (E2) It is psychologically impossible that anyone know that the evidence for a claim is weaker than the evidence against it and yet accept it.[9]

In effect, Hume's own argument is an extrapolation from Tillotson's. This is a conceptual, not a causal, claim. Hume's philosophy surely has the resources requisite to this argument. It no doubt delighted Hume to find the thread of his own argument in an Anglican, just as he was on another occasion delighted to find something similar in a Jesuit. To the Reverend George Campbell on June 7, 1762, Hume wrote with some irony and considerable malice of forethought:

> It may perhaps amuse you to learn the first hint, which suggested to me that argument (against miracles) which you have so strenuously attacked (in *Dissertation on Miracles*, 1762). I was walking in the cloisters of the Jesuit's College of La Feche, a town

in which I passed two years of my youth, and engaged in a conversation with a Jesuit of some parts and learning, who was relating to me, and urging some nonsensical miracle performed in their own convent, when I was tempted to dispute against him, and as my head was full of the topics of my *Treatise of Human Nature*, which I was at that time composing, this argument immediately occurred to me, and I thought it very much graveled my companion, but at last he observed to me that it was impossible for that argument to have any solidity, because it operated equally against the Gospel as against the Catholic miracles;—which observation I thought proper to admit as a sufficient answer. I believe you will allow that the freedom at least of this reasoning makes it somewhat extraordinary to have been the produce of a convent of Jesuits, though perhaps you may think the sophistry of it savours plainly of the place of its birth.[10]

In any case, it is clear that a crucial portion of Hume's argument is captured in the following simple reasoning:

(1) If Al has never witnessed a miracle, Al's evidence (if any) that a miracle has occurred is testimonial evidence.

(2) Nothing is a miracle unless Al has sensory evidence against its occurrence.[11]

(3) Sensory evidence is always stronger than testimonial evidence.

(4) If Al has never witnessed a miracle, Al has better evidence that no miracle has occurred than Al has that some miracle has occurred.

Depending on whether one chooses to read (E) above as epistemic or psychological, one can continue the argument along the lines of either:

(5a) A rational person always believes in accord with stronger over weaker evidence.

(6a) If Al has never witnessed a miracle and is rational (or, *insofar as* Al is rational) Al does not believe that a miracle has occurred.

or else:

(5b) No one can in fact help but believe in accord with (what one [rightly] takes to be) stronger over weaker evidence.

(6b) If Al has never witnessed a miracle, Al does not believe that a miracle has occurred.

Thus for Hume if one has not witnessed a miracle, one ought not (cannot, if one is rational) and perhaps even cannot at all believe that a miracle has occurred.

Suppose, though, that Al witnesses a miracle. Can he then, in fact and even reasonably, believe that a miracle has occurred? For Hume at least, Al cannot so believe. For Hume sanctions this argument:

> (7) For any miracle that Al witnesses, it violates some law of nature, and so it occurs only if the law is false.
>
> (8) For any law of nature, Al has better evidence for it than against it.[12]
>
> (9) For any miracle that Al witnesses, he has better evidence that it did not occur than that the law is false (that is, that it did occur).

And to review a by-now-familiar alternative, one can complete the argument via either:

> (10a) A rational person always believes in accord with stronger over weaker evidence.
>
> (11a) If Al has witnessed a miracle and is rational, Al will believe that the miracle did not occur.

or else:

> (10b) No one in fact can help but believe in accord with (what one [rightly] takes to be) stronger over weaker evidence.
>
> (11b) If Al has witnessed a miracle, Al does not believe that a miracle has occurred.

There is, of course, a *lacunae* in both of the arguments that are supplemented by (5b). The (1–6b) argument requires Al (*rightly*) *takes his sensory evidence against a miracle to be greater than his testimonial evidence for a miracle* and the (7–11b) argument requires *Al* (*rightly*) *takes it that he has better evidence that a law is true than that a miracle has occurred*. But our concern is with:

> (4) If Al has never witnessed a miracle, Al has better evidence that no miracle has occurred than Al has that some miracle has occurred.

and:

> (9) For any miracle that Al witnesses, he has better evidence that it did not occur than that a law is false (that is, that it did occur).

Together, (4) and (9) amount in effect to *Hume's Barrier* (*HB*). Even if a miracle were to occur, we would always have better evidence that it has not occurred than that it has.

Our next task is to appraise the arguments for (*HB*).

Hume's Argument Appraised

The premises that stand out in Hume's arguments as stated above are these:

(2) Nothing is a miracle unless Al has sensory evidence against its occurrence.

(7) For any miracle that Al witnesses, it violates some law of nature, and so it occurs only if the law is false.

Why does Hume think these true? Concerning (2) Hume has an argument apparently worth immediate dismissal. He writes, "A miracle is a violation of the laws of nature; and as a firm and unalterable experience has established these laws, the proof against a miracle, from the very nature of the fact, is as entire as any argument from experience can possibly be imagined" [*E*, 114]. These words plainly suggest the following argument:

(1) *M* is a miracle if and only if there is a law *L* such that (a) *L* is a law of nature, (b) *M occurred* entails *L is false*.

(2) *L* is a law of nature if and only if *L* is confirmed by every *L*-relevant observation.

(3) *M* is a miracle if and only if *M* disconfirms a law *L* which is confirmed by every *L*-relevant observation.

If (1) and (2) are necessary truths, so is (3). (3) entails that no miracle can be observed. For if, per impossible, I were to observe a miracle, either it would not violate any law of nature (and so would not be miraculous) or would (and so couldn't be observed).[13]

In fact, (2) and (3) are ambiguous. Are we to understand "every *L*-relevant observation" to include "every *L*-relevant observation actually made" or "every *L*-relevant observation, whether made or not?" On the former reading (2) becomes:

(2') *L* is a law of nature if and only if *L* is confirmed by every *L*-relevant observation actually made.

(2') leaves it open that *L* be false. Then *L* is false or not. If not, presumably no reliable observation tells against it. If so, no observed event that tells against it is miraculous. On the latter reading, (2) becomes:

(2'') L is a law of nature if and only if L is confirmed by every L-relevant observation, whether made or not.

Then L is presumably true. So presumably no reliable observation tells against it. So no observed event tells against it. In sum, here at least, the ambiguity does not matter.

If Hume thus makes the observation (and so presumably the occurrence) of a miracle an *a priori* impossibility, is he not open to curt but legitimate dismissal? Not, I think, so obviously as is sometimes supposed. Hume's argument, interpreted here, is an argument for the incoherence of the concept 'miracle.' Conceivably, it succeeds.

But does it in fact succeed? It does not, if one can substitute for (1) some other and plausible definition of "miracle" or for (2) some other and plausible definition of "law of nature."

One alternative is to say that a miracle violates an "established" law of nature—one, that is, for which our evidence thus far is uniformly favorable.[14] But then everything rests on the degree to which my knowing a law is established renders me epistemically secure in supposing that it is a real law of nature. Epistemic security need not involve incorrigibility. On no doctrine of incorrigibility that I know of is *I have a head* incorrigible. Yet if I am rightly as confident that a law is a real law of nature as I am that *I have a head* is true, or anything very close to it, that is enough.

But is it right to read, on Hume's behalf, "law of nature" in Hume's definition as "established law?" Several points seem worth making in response to this query. First, that x is miraculous does not for Hume entail that x violates a known (or accepted) law. Hume notes that "a miracle may either be discoverable by men or not. This alters not its nature and essence" (*E*, 127). Second, and consequently, altering the right side of Hume's definition would seem to require altering the left, with this result:

x is accepted as a miracle if and only if x violates some established law of nature.

(Strictly, since other conditions must be met by miracles, the biconditional should be a conditional; but this is moot with respect to the present point.) Third, Hume's major concern is not to deny that miracles occur. Nor is it to deny that miracles ever may be observed. Instead, it is to deny that anyone ever has as good evidence for supposing a miracle to have occurred as one has for supposing the opposite. He makes an epistemic claim about real miracles (if any). His thesis requires that miracles be defined so as not to be relative to established laws. Only then can he argue as he wishes that "a miracle can never be proved, so as to be the foundation of a system of religion" (*E*, 127). But the major problem with the present suggestion is that it fits ill with Hume's own argument.

The same must be said, I think, for the view that Hume really intended to show that "miracle" is an incoherent concept. For one thing, Hume offers various subsidiary arguments in *Of Miracles*, Part Two. The arguments are intended to discredit testimonies that miracles have occurred. It is not contradictory to suppose Hume's strategy is: "first, prove 'miracle' is incoherent; then show testimony for miracles would be insufficient even if 'miracle' was coherent." But the addition of subsidiary arguments most naturally suggests that the conclusion of the subsidiary arguments does not suppose that the conclusion of the main argument is mistaken.

Again, Hume admits that "there may possibly be miracles, or violations of the usual course of nature, of such a kind as to admit of proof from human testimony" (*E*, 127). Further, Hume speaks of a variety of "contrariety of evidence" to the occurrence of miracles, each type of evidence being expressed in logically contingent claims. Testimonial evidence for miracles will be defective "when the witnesses contradict each other; when they are but few, or of a doubtful character; when they have an interest in what they affirm; when they deliver their testimony with hestitation, or on the contrary, with too violent asseveration" (*E*, 113). Further still, "there are many other particulars of the same kind" (*E*, 113). Yet again, when he distinguishes between *proof* of a law and *probability* of a law, the contrast is not between the inconsistent-to-deny and the consistently deniable, but rather between *constant* versus *positive but variable* confirming evidence (between *uniform* vs. *nearly uniform* confirmation) (*E*, 113). So Hume does not think the concept of a miracle is incoherent.

But what then *is* Hume's argument for *Hume's Barrier* in general, and for (2) and (7) in particular? Why, that is, did he think that even if a miracle were to occur, we would always have better evidence that it has not occurred than that it has occurred? It contains six elements. First there is a reminder that human testimony (and the memory it presupposes) is on the whole reliable, but only on the whole.

Were not the memory tenacious *to a certain degree*, had not men *commonly* an inclination to truth and a principle of probity; were they not sensible to shame, when detected in a falsehood; were not these, I say, discovered by *experience* to be qualities, inherent in human nature, we should never repose the least confidence in human testimony. [*E*, 112; my italics save the last]

Second, sensory experience is on the whole reliable, and is self-corrective.

> Though experience be our only guide in reasoning concerning matters of fact, it must be acknowledged that this guide is not altogether infallible, but in cases is apt to lead us into errors. . . . However, we may observe that, in such a case (of error, we) . . . have no cause to complain of experience, because it commonly informs us before hand of the uncertainty, by that contrariety of events which we may learn from a diligent observation. [*E*, 110]

Thirdly, sensory experience of the occurrence of an event is better evidence than testimony to its occurrence. Hume quotes what is in effect this dictum from Tillotson, apparently with approval (*E*, 109). So thus far we have what may be called the theses of general reliability of testimonial evidence, the general reliability of sensory evidence and the primacy of sensory over testimonial evidence, that is, that one is always or usually more reasonable to accept his own sensory evidence over the testimony of another, if they conflict, as well as the less problematic primacy involved in the fact that if an event is observable, Al is in a position to give non-inferential testimony that it occurred only if Al observed it.

Fourth, whenever testimony to a miracle is in question, one must consider the possibility that the relevant law-set has only probable (that is, non-uniform) support, and that one must balance competing evidences. For if *M* is a miracle candidate, *M occurs* violates some law of nature. If Al has testimonial but no sensory evidence that *M occurred* is true, and sensory evidence that the law is true and so that *M occurred* is false, Al must weigh competing evidence. Given the alleged primacy of sensory over testimonial evidence (that is, if Al is a Humean) Al's weighing process will be simple. If Al has sensory evidence that *M* occurred and also sensory evidence that the law is true, Al must weigh sensory evidence against sensory evidence.[15] Here, one engages in so-called probable reasoning.

> All probability . . . supposes an opposition of experiments and observations [not of experiments versus observations, but of experimental and/or other observations versus experimental and/or

still other observations], where one side is found to overbalance the other, and to produce a degree of evidence, proportioned to the superiority. [*E*, 111]

Fifth, if *L* is a law which has *proof* (uniform confirming evidence), there of course is no sensory evidence against *L*. If (1) (*Some miracle*) *M occurred* entails *L is false*, and (2) *L is a proved law* (that is, *Our experience uniformly supports L*), then (3) *No one has sensory evidence for 'M occurred.'* (1) *and* (2), *but not* (3) is a contradiction. But if *L* is a law which has *probability*, then there may be sensory evidence against *L*. For if (4) *M occurred* entails *L is false*, and (5) *L is a law supported by probability*, it does not follow that (6) *No one has sensory evidence for 'M occurred.'* Indeed, (5) entails (7) *There is some sensory evidence against L*, and while such evidence need not be miraculous, it may be.

Sixth, and finally, a *proved* law is presumably for Hume a *real* law of nature;[16] but so (if a little less assuredly) is a "probabilitied" law for Hume a real law of nature. Their credentials differ, but they are non-competing candidates for the same office, namely being part of the truth about the way the world really is.

Now we can see what (2) amounts to. Let *L* be a "probabilitied" law of nature. The bulk of sensory evidence relevant to *L* is hence pro-*L*. But there is some sensory evidence that is con-*L*. Suppose that among the con-*L* evidence is evidence that *M occurred*, where *M* is an event such that, if *M occurred* is true, *L* is false, and such that if *M occurred* is true, it is also true that *M* was caused by God, etc. There is then *some* evidence that *M occurred* is true, but better evidence that it is false. Nothing could be a miracle unless it violated some law of nature. Nothing is a serious candidate for being a miracle unless it is both true that if it occurred some law of nature would be false and that we have some evidence that it occurred. Given this last qualification, the perhaps-violated law must be a "probabilitied" law—a proved law will not be tainted by any contrary sensory evidence. But a "probabilitied" law loses its status as a law unless the preponderance of sensory evidence is in its favor. Hence where Al is any observationally informed person:

> (2) Nothing is a miracle unless Al has sensory evidence against its occurrence.

One question, then, is answered—namely, what is Hume's rationale for (2)?

The same discussion that answered that question also obviously answers the other—namely, what is his rationale for (7)? For given our discussion, it should be clear why Hume thinks that:

> (7) For any miracle that Al witnesses, it violates some law and so it occurs only if the law is false.

If we have a 'proof' of the law in question, all of our relevant sensory evidence favors the law. Even if it is a 'probabilified' law, the bulk of our evidence favors it. As a law, the proposition in question is a universal generalization. A Humean law of nature has the form *All x are y*, not *All x are probably y*. *Probably, all x are y* tells us that our evidence for *All x are y* is strong but mixed—that the evidence for the universal generalization falls short of 'proof.' That is the force of *Probably, all x are y* in a Humean setting. So we can have *some*, but never *adequate*, evidence that a miracle has occurred, since we can have *some*, but never *adequate*, evidence that a 'probabilified' genuine law is false. (We cannot have evidence against a 'proved' genuine law—or even a 'proved' non-genuine law.)

Yet another thing should now be clear. For if we can, given our discussion, see why Hume holds (2), we can also see why (provided his perspective on these matters is sound) he is entitled to the stronger:

> (2') Nothing is a miracle unless Al (any observationally informed person) has better sensory evidence against then for its occurrence.

Given (2'), we can see what motivates Hume toward:

> (7) Even if Al were to observe a miracle, Al would still have better evidence that it did not occur than that it did.

Still, there is a bit more to be said. As Hume notes, sometimes generalizations from particular experiences are both well-reasoned and false: "One who in our climate should expect better weather in any week of June than in one of December would reason justly, and conformably to experience; but it is certain that he may happen, in the event, to find himself mistaken" (*E*, 110). At other times, generalizations are premature. Suppose, having testimonial and sensory evidence that all A's are B, I apparently discover an A that is not. I apparently observe that what is before me is an A, and do not merely fail to observe that (or whether) A is a B, but apparently observe that A is not a B. Still, I can decide that what I observe is not an A after all, or that A is a B after all, or that *All A's are B's* is true—even having apparently observed an A that is not B.

Suppose, having apparently observed an *A* that is not *B*, one reasons: Sensory experience is, on the whole, reliable. My sensory experience, on the whole, is in favor of *All A's are B's*. So if I rely on my sensory experience I will accept *All A's are B's*.

This piece of reasoning is twice defective. First, my sensory experience is evidence that *Every A but one is a B*. Previously, my sensory evidence has supported *All observed A's have been B's* and so, together with some inductive axiom, supported *All A's are B's*. By rejecting *All A's are B's* I do not reject any sensory evidence. Indeed, by continuing to affirm it, having apparently experienced an *A* that is not *B*, I would (in the absence of special justification) *reject* my sensory evidence were I to continue to affirm *All A's are B's*. One who reasoned as above would disbelieve in black swans, albino elephants, and wealthy philosophers. In particular, taking my sensory experience to be on the whole reliable is not to accept stronger generalizations than such experience supports, or to reject all of its "minority reports."

Second, one who reasoned as above would need some special reason for not rejecting experience of grey elephants as well as albino. For that one observes white elephants less often by far than grey ones is not, by itself, a reason for supposing that observers of albino elephants are hallucinating. No *other* reason is offered. So one who reasons as above has as good reason for rejecting the "majority reports" of his senses as for rejecting their "minority reports."

Yet, while no doubt Hume in one sense knows all this, his talk of "subtraction" prevents him from seeing its relevance. Thus he writes:

> It is experience only, which gives authority to human testimony; and it is the same experience, which assures us of the laws of nature. When, therefore, these two kinds of experience are contrary, we have nothing to do but subtract the one from the other, and embrace an opinion, either on one side or the other, with that assurance which arises from the remainder. [*E*, 127]

It is difficult to see how Hume can justify (2) and (7) without some such fallacious reasoning as that noted above. The passage just quoted suggests that ascribing such reasoning to Hume is not arbitrary.[17]

There is one other point to be briefly made. Hume writes:

> When anyone tells me, that he saw a dead man restored to life, I immediately consider with myself, whether it be more probable, that this person should either deceive or be deceived, or that the fact, which he relates, should really have happened. I weigh the

one miracle against the other; and according to the superiority, which I discover, I pronounce my decision, and always reject the greater miracle. If the falsehood of this testimony would be more miraculous, than the event which he relates; then, and not till then, can he pretend to command my belief or opinion. [*E*, 116]

But suppose I myself have some such experience. I meet, alive, someone I know to have died. One crucial question, at least, is whether there is any plausible view of the world on which this might happen. If there is such a view, and I know of it and have no good reason to reject it, then no appeal to my sensory experience being reliable "on the whole" or to misleading "substraction models" will show my unusual experience to be unreliable. If not, it is *this* fact, no "subtraction," that counts most heavily against my unusual experience being also reliable.

Hume's Subsidiary Arguments

Part Two of "Of Miracles" begins:

In the foregoing reasoning, we have supposed that the testimony upon which a miracle is founded may possibly amount to an entire proof, and that the falsehood of that testimony would be a real prodigy: But it is easy to show that we have been a great deal too liberal in our concession, and that there never was a miraculous event established on so full an existence. [*E*, 116]

As Hume's last sentence suggests, he believes that what we might call "the maximum plausibility conditions" of testimony for a miracle have never been met. The conditions are stated, with something like the degree of precision of standard definitions of "the moral point of view," in the following passage:

First, there is not to be found, in all history, any miracle attested by a sufficient number of men, of such unquestioned good-sense, education, and learning, as to secure us against all delusion in themselves; of such undoubted integrity, as to place them beyond all suspicion of any design to deceive others; of such credit and reputation in the eyes of mankind, as to have a great deal to lose in case of their being detected in any falsehood; and at the same time, attesting facts performed in such a public manner and in so celebrated a part of the world, as to render the detection unavoidable: All which circumstances are requisite to give us a full assurance in the testimony of men. [*E*, 116–117]

To this Hume adds another consideration:

> *Secondly* . . . the passion of *surprise* and *wonder*, arising from miracles, being an agreeable emotion, gives a sensible tendency towards the belief of those events from which it is derived . . . if the spirit of religion join itself to the love of wonder, there is an end of common sense. [*E*, 117]

He then follows with another:

> *Thirdly*. It forms a strong presumption against all supernatural and miraculous relations, that they are observed chiefly to abound among ignorant and barbarous nations; or if a civilized people has ever given admission to any of them, that people will be found to have received them from ignorant and barbarous ancestors, who transmitted them with that inviolable sanction and authority, which always attend received opinions. [*E*, 119]

Such as they are, these are Hume's subsidiary and non-philosophical observations concerning miracles. I will comment briefly on them shortly. There is, however, a fourth and philosophical argument that deserves attention also.

Hume adds a further and importantly different sort of consideration. Suppose miracles $M1$ and $M2$ occur, and that $M1$ occurs "in" (Hume's preposition) religion $R1$ and $M2$ occurs in religion $R2$. But, as Hume puts it, "in matters of religion, whatever is different is contrary" (*E*, 121). If religion $R1$ is true, religion $R2$ is false, and conversely. Suppose, then, that $M1$'s occurrence supports $R1$ to just the degree that $M2$'s occurrence supports $R2$. Since $R1$ *and* $R2$ is false, *M1 occurred and M2 occurred* is probably false. For if *M1 occurred* fully supports $R1$ (proves $R1$ true), and likewise *M2 occurred* fully supports $R2$, that $R1$ *and* $R2$ is false entails that *M1 occurred and M2 occurred* is false. The greater the degree to which $M1$'s occurrence supports $R1$ *and* $M2$'s occurrence supports $R2$, the better reason the falsity of $R1$ *and* $R2$ is for rejecting *M1 occurred and M2 occurred*.

Consider, then, the "democracy of miracles" thesis:

> (DM) For every proposition of the form *Miracle M1 occurred (where M1 supports religion R1 to degree D)* for which there is testimony of degree A of plausibility, there is a proposition of the

form *Miracle M2 occurred (where M2 supports religion R2 to degree D)* for which there is testimony of degree *A* of plausibility (where, of course, [*M1* ≠ *M2*] and [*R1* ≠ *R2*].

If (DM) is true, and its Humean context correct, then for every case in which there is some reason to believe that a miracle has occurred, there is just that much reason to believe it has not occurred. Hume's assumption seems fairly clearly to be that, given the varieties of religious belief and of miracle reports, (DM) or something much like it is true.

Some Comments about the Subsidiary Arguments

The subsidiary arguments are clearly varied in type and value. The first is in effect an historical claim about the caliber of actual testimonies to miracles. No doubt it is true for much, probably most, of such testimony. That it is true for all is less clear; in fact, I think it is false of some. The indeterminacy of Hume's conditions for maximally plausible testimony restricts the degree of precision with which we can discern whether his conditions are met. Yet his statement of these conditions seems quite appropriate, and any substitute for his statement, I suspect, will have roughly the same degree of precision. It is not lack of precision that is most problematic, however. The crux of the matter is whether for Hume anyone *could* be of sufficiently "unquestioned good sense"—to go no further—and still believe that a miracle had occurred. It is clear that in order for the conditions to serve their function, the answer must be affirmative. It is less clear that the answer *is* affirmative so far as Hume is concerned. The same sort of consideration arises concerning Hume's "ignorant and barbarous nations" claims, on which I will not comment further.

The point that, so to say, people love prodigies is well taken. They love order, too, and hate being taken in. I suspect that one could explain the disbelief in miracles of a Hume as readily along the lines of fear of being superstitious as one could explain the belief in miracles of a Pascal along the lines of fear of damnation. When one starts explaining a person's beliefs by reference to his psychology, one assumes the person to be without, but in need of, good reasons. And this in turn is determined by what one supposes the truth to be.

If these brief comments are substantially correct, it is only the final subsidiary argument that might play a role not entirely dependent on the success of the argument of Part One. For a Christian, a person of good sense may believe Christ rose from the grave and his belief need not be merely psychologically explained; for (say) an atheist, perhaps, no person of good sense could so believe and anyone who did would have a belief in need of psychological explanation. Who is right? To this question, Hume's final subsidiary argument has some response. Consider the claims that: (a) one can never have sufficient reason to believe that a miracle occurred, and (b) one can never have sufficient reason to believe that a miracle's occurrence supported a religious belief. While (a) entails (b), Hume thinks he has reason for accepting (b) that is not dependent on (a).

I take it that for a miracle to be "in" a religion R, in Hume's sense, is for an event to (1) be interpreted in terms of the categories of R, (2) be an event whose occurrence provides evidence for some important tenets of R, while (3) being miraculous given both ordinary criteria and whatever criteria R includes for being miraculous.

Hume's argument is less impressive than it may seem. I note two relevant problems. Suppose there is equally good evidence for *M1 occurred* and *M2 occurred*. Suppose it is also true that *M1 occurred* supports *R1* and *M2 occurred* supports *R2*, and that it is clear that *R1 and R2* is false.[18] But suppose also that event *M1* is describable and interpretable (as miraculous or not) in terms of the categories of *R2*, and that once this is done *M1 (as re-described) occurred* supports *R2* (or at least does not support *R1* as against *R2*). And suppose that event *M2* is not so describable and interpretable in terms of the categories of *R1*. So long as there is no better reason to describe or interpret *M1 R1*-wise, *R2* seems (*contra* Hume) not negatively affected by *M1*'s occurrence while *R1* is negatively affected by the occurrence of *M2*.

The obvious reply is that under the circumstances just described, *M1 occurred* does not support *R1* as strongly as *M2 occurred* supports *R2*. This is true. That it is true underlines one factor to which Hume's argument is insufficiently sensitive. The ability of one religious system to describe and interpret events in a way at least not falsified by empirical features of what is being interpreted may be importantly different from that of another. For all Hume shows, these "elitism of miracles" principles may be true:

> (EM1) *M2*, whose occurrence supports *R2*, is *elitist* with respect to *M1* whose occurrence supports *R1* if and only if *M1* is describable and interpretable in *R2* so as not to support *R1* against *R2*, but *M2* is not describable and interpretable in *R1* so as not to support *R2* against *R1*.

(EM2) *M2*, whose occurrence supports *R2*, is *ultimately elitist* (where $M \neq M2$ and $R \neq R2$) if and only if For any miraculous event *M* whose occurrence supports religion *R*, *M2* is elitist with respect to *M*.

(EM3) There is exactly one miracle-set *S* and exactly one religion *R* such that *The members of S occurred* supports *R* and such that each member of *S* is ultimately elitist and supports only *R*.

Thus all genuine miracles, if any, for all Hume shows, might support but one religion; or some might support only one religion and the rest be so interpretable as to support that one as much as (on another interpretation, or under a not better description) they support another. A second matter deserves notice. Contrary to some of Hume's suggestions, and to put the point modestly, not all religions are equally implausible. Further, there can be evidence, either empirical or conceptual, that a religious claim (and so the system to which it is essential) is false.[19] For all Hume shows, these "elitism of religions" principles are true (where *R1* and *R2* are distinct religious conceptual schemes):

(ER1) *R2* is *elitist with respect to empirical or conceptual defect D* with regard to *R1* if and only if *D* is a defect of *R1* but not of *R2*.

(ER2) *R2* is *ultimately elitist* with respect to *R1* if and only if There is no empirical or conceptual defect *D* such that *R2* has *D* but *R1* does not and there is some defect *D* such that *R1* has *D* but *R2* does not.

(ER3) There is a religion *R* such that for any religion *R1* not identical to *R*, *R* is ultimately elitist with respect to *R1*.

Two brief comments are now in order. One is that there is, so to say, a reciprocity between an alleged miracle and its religious conceptual context. That God raise a person from the dead is not improbable if this world is as, say, Saint Paul conceived it. It is, if the world is as, say, David Hume conceived it. Given this reciprocity, if *R* is ultimately elitist, the miracles (if any) "native to *R*" are in an epistemically superior position with respect to those of any other religion. The other comment is that, as may be true for all Hume shows, the position of *R*'s favored miracles is much enhanced if:

(ER4) The religion *R* which is ultimately elitist with respect to all other religions has no defect *D* which renders it false.

It seems to me, then, that Hume's subsidiary arguments leave much to be desired. They much more presuppose than augment his

Enquiry case in Part One; and they presuppose a good deal else, much of which seems to me to be false or at least dubious. But to press this matter further would require leaving the abstract splendor of (DM) and (EM1–3) and (ER1–3) and coming to specific cases requiring, and criteria for, relevant rational appraisal.[20] Instead, I return to Hume's main arguments as presented in "On Miracles," Part One.

Hume's Main Position on Miracles

Hume is sometimes criticized[21] on the grounds that he assumed that the propositions accepted as laws of nature in his own day, being (at least presumably) supported by uniform (or nearly uniform) experience, had a probability of one (or very close to one), and that he thought that the only sort of evidence that could overturn a law favored by one set of uniform experiences was a larger set of uniform experiences in favor of some other law.[22] According to this critique the former assumption involves insensitivity to the continual reformulation of laws which the history of science has witnessed; the latter assumption involves, in effect, a claim that Hume was insufficiently sensitive to the possibility of "paradigm shifts."

I would not like to defend the view that Hume's philosophy has somewhere within it (implicitly if not explicitly) everything necessary for an adequate philosophy of science. Nor, in a chapter on Hume's view of miracles, do I propose to consider the degree to which Hume *has* a philosophy of science, or how adequate any philosophy of science he has might be. I wish instead to argue that Hume's views on miracles are not dependent on the views concerning the philosophy of science ascribed to Hume above. As to the matter of Hume holding those views, I make only two comments. First, as everyone knows, the first eight sections of the *Dialogues Concerning Natural Religion* contain a long and impressive discussion of some varieties of the design argument. Along the way, as we saw, Philo and Cleanthes propose various axioms of inductive inference in a way that comprises, given Hume's lack of symbolic machinery and the state of the inductive art in his day, a rather remarkable series of steps along the path toward, say, Plantinga's discussion of design and induction in *God and Other Minds*.[23] Statable as either axioms of inductive inference or (given appropriate alterations) conditions of meaningful assertion, they are part of Hume's "methodology." Any full-dress account of Hume's 'philosophy of science' would have to include them. Secondly, Philo (and so Hume, whether Philo or anyone "speaks for Hume" in the

Dialogues) is remarkably adept at constructing alternative models for interpreting the data to which the design arguer appeals. He produces root metaphors of world hypotheses, or alternative categorical commitments, or distinct paradigms, of different total interpretations, or clashing conceptual systems, or divergent world views, or varied theoretical frameworks, with profusion. That essentially the same range of phenomena can be viewed differently, and that one's reasons for taking one point of view rather than another need not to be new empirical information and need have no close (or far) relation to uniformity of experience—all this is evident in Hume's *Dialogues* discussion of alternative models for "reading" order in nature. It is, I think, true that Hume did not apply these features of his thought to the discussion of miracles.

Whether, on the other hand, Hume could have put these insights together into a philosophy of science both compatible with his major tenets and defensible in the context of contemporary philosophy of science is too large a topic to broach here.

It is not difficult, I think, to see how Hume might state his views concerning miracles in a manner not open to the "sceptical darkness" noted earlier. Indeed, it is so obvious it may seem scarcely worth mention. Still, the obvious is easily overlooked, and so perhaps I may be forgiven for asking for Hume's examples of these vaunted "laws of nature." He writes, "Why is it more than probable, that all men must die; that lead cannot, of itself, remain suspended in the air; that fire consumes wood, and is extinguished by water; unless it be, that these events are found agreeable to the laws of nature" (*E*, 114–115)? It is not lucidly clear whether Hume means that *All men must die, Fire consumes wood*, and so on are themselves laws of nature, or whether they are instances of such laws. His phrase "these events are found agreeable to the laws of nature" perhaps suggests the latter; yet if so Hume never offers us a single instance of a law of nature in "Of Miracles." I propose to sidestep the question as to which alternative Hume intends, and to simply call Hume's examples, and the vaguely delimited and large class they represent, "true garden-variety generalizations." True generalizations are not theoretical claims if theoretical claims contain reference to underlying entities, processes, or mechanisms which explain observable events, for Hume's generalizations are couched in terms descriptive of ordinary observable "middle sized objects." Such true generalizations seem unlikely to be revised in the light of progress in knowledge. However often particular types of theoretical entities postulated to explain observable events such as those Hume refers to may be replaced by yet other types, thus altering our *explicans*, the *explicandum* seems remarkably stable.

These generalizations, then, are little if any subject to revision in the light of paradigm shifts. Unless such shifts are purely arbitrary, there are criteria for appraising them. Unless such criteria are purely formal, appraisal will include reference to what some philosophers have called 'empirical fit.' Part of the empirical data to which theories must render their due—must "fit to," so to say—is just that which confirms such generalizations. Without supposing our knowledge of these generalizations, or of their conforming instances, is incorrigible or indubitable, or completely safe from revision, one can nonetheless hold it in high regard as part of the touchstone any theory must satisfy. Will appeal to these generalizations aid the cause of *Hume's Barrier?*

If so, it will presumably do so along some such lines as these. As we have said, such generalizations are little if at all affected by paradigm shifts. That a conceptual system require their rejection or revision is a significant mark against the system. Given the stability of such generalizations, perhaps we can say:

> (M) X is a real miracle if and only if the known truth of X *occurs* would require revision of a true, garden-variety generalization.

Still, (M) is subject to at least two defects. For one, the class of "true garden-variety generalizations" is obviously ill-defined. For another, such generalizations are eminently qualifiable. Iodine kills (without antidote); water quenches fire (except grease fires); and even when no known qualification is required, there remains the possibility that a qualification be made without destroying the generalization. Dead bodies stay so—except perhaps (in Hume's hypothetical case) for Queen Elizabeth's or the more famous instance which provides the model for Hume's hypothetical case. To be direct: suppose Jesus Christ died and then rose on the third day. The garden variety generalization that dead men remain dead would strictly be rendered false, but, since eminently qualifiable, could be easily itself resurrected as *On the whole, dead men remain dead* or *The bodies of non-divine persons remain dead*, or the like. A worldview whose sole parameters are set by garden-variety generalizations is plastic; its shape is alterable. This is why religious believers can accept garden variety generalizations and yet believe that miracles occur.[24]

A further point is worth noting. What renders garden-variety generalizations so secure is in part their eminent qualifiability. It is also their easy verification. If garden-variety generalizations are not verifiable and verified, then verification by appeal to sensory experience is a lost cause. The familiar particular cases that collectively support true garden-variety generalizations patently require "the reliability of the senses." If these cases do not yield knowledge, or at least reasonable belief, then meter readings and telescopic sightings are equally epistemically vacuous. Further, if these cases cannot be reliably described in common discourse, there is nothing for scientific theories to explain or interpret.

In any case, while Hume could retreat from theory-laden laws to true garden-variety generalizations, utilizing (M) or some similar thesis, it seems that knowledge of miracles is not thereby ruled out. For one thing, such generalizations are eminently qualifiable. For another, if sincere sensory reports can in principle and in fact confirm such generalizations, then sincere sensory reports can in principle and in fact lead to their qualification. Logically and philosophically, miracles may occur, and logically and philosophically nothing prevents us from knowingly observing them. What remains is the theological and historical question, "Have they occurred?"[25]

Suppose, then, that one appeals to: (M) X is a real miracle if and only if the known truth of *X occurs* would require revision of a true, garden-variety generalization, and adds the other relevant conditions noted in our earlier discussion of the definition of "miracle." Then, perhaps, one has a rough Humean criterion for separating the non-miraculous from the miraculous. Without some such criterion, *Hume's Barrier* is vacuous, for it supposes that talk of miracles occurring, and being observed, makes some sense. Even with it, *Hume's Barrier* is not justified. Neither appeal to the stormy history of science nor Hume's appeal to proof and probabilities establishes *Hume's Barrier*. Further, if some theistic religion R is maximally elitist and the elitism of miracles thesis true, it is presumably reasonable to believe that miracles occur. If the democracy of miracles thesis is true, and no theistic religion is maximally elitist, it is presumably not reasonable to believe that miracles occur. *Hume's Barrier*, then, seems false; at least, its supporting premises seem self-defeating in the sense that its non-vacuity requires some such criterion as (M). But given (M), plus the "axioms" offered concerning miracles and religions, *Hume's Barrier* seems false. It seems, then, that for all Hume's efforts "everything remains precisely as before" (*T*, 250–251)[26] though in this case such was not his intent. But no philosopher, however great, seems to realize all his intentions.[27]

CONCLUSION

Hume's philosophy of religion has been presented. The *Natural History* theory of religious belief caused by second-order propensities; the theory of human nature on which its core is comprised of original and universal propensities elicited by universal experiences yielding identical beliefs; the view of religious belief as a danger to fragile personal unity; the claim that all but the thinnest religion is poison to morality; the tension between two notions of what a person is; the extrapolation of Hume's theory of religious belief to religious experience; the question of the epistemic impact if Hume's explanation of religious belief and experience is correct: these topics filled Part One.

Hume seems correct in his view that much of human belief, religious or non-religious, fits lightly to evidence. Careful reflection, rigorous thought, even *concern* with evidence is not as common as sunlight. I doubt that it is less characteristic of religious belief than of belief of other sorts. If popular apologetics for religious belief is pretty bleak stuff, the same holds for popular apologetics against religious belief. The second worst lecture I ever heard was an attempt to prove that some religious beliefs were true; the worst lecture I ever heard was an attempt to prove the same beliefs false. Neither that fact, nor the intellectually tawdry state of most popular thought about religion (pro or con) that those lectures represent, would surprise Hume. Plato, no early Humean, claimed that what people believe, they mainly believe by chance (by which he meant without careful assessment of evidence or concern for assessment, not that their beliefs were inexplicable). Hume would agree, but he would lament less about the fact than would a Platonist. For the Platonist reason, and for Hume imagination, comprise the core of humanity. Not, of course, that saying that helps much—one needs to look carefully at Hume's doctrine of imagination more fully than has been possible here, and the relevant notion of reason as well, in order to see exactly what is at stake.

His views concerning religion and morality are discussed here, and found not to raise deeply, let alone answer, the hard questions that any really serious struggling with historical evidence concerning the behavior of religious devotees would require if one wanted to argue effectively that some substantial thesis about religious belief had been established.

I have argued that even if Hume's explanation of religious belief and experience is correct, nothing negative follows concerning religious belief or religious believers, or about religious experiences or experiencers. I sketched an alternative perspective on the propensities that Hume thinks lead to religious belief, but did not try to adjudicate between Hume's account and that alternative perspective. In part, the issue is empirical; one would have to look at a lot of data concerning various religious traditions to which Hume had little access and which would take us far afield. Of course, just having the relevant data would not settle the dispute; one would also have to look at various theoretical ways of shaping the data into an interpretation of the causes of religious belief and experience. By then, one would have a whole book on that topic.

Hume's overall epistemology, I argued, provides no way for Hume to justify his own theory of religious belief and experience. Nor have I argued, one way or another, about Hume's thesis that religious belief is a subtle threat to human stability. One problem with such disputes is that "stability" is likely to be defined by each party to the dispute in terms that reflect the side that she embraces. Thus the critic will find religion a crutch for the weak to lean on the believer will find antireligion a cloak to hide sin behind, and these perspectives will find their way into competing definitions of stability. Insofar as there is common ground about stability, there are plainly stable people on both sides of the religious fence, so that the dispute, insofar as it is realistic, tends to focus on the potential bad effects of religion or of areligion (*areligion*, of course, being religion's absence). One always can point to "crazy" people who are religious in their "craziness" and argue from there to the dangers of religious belief. One also could argue from the insect hallucinations of delirium tremens sufferers to the sophistical status of entomology. One always can point to people who have been brought back from the brink of mental collapse by religious faith. Both the argument *There are religious illnesses, so religion is false* and the argument *There are religious cures, so religion is true* exhibit fallacious reasoning. On the whole, I find the dispute often inelegant and in the end unprofitable.

Hume's evidentialism, his theory of meaning, his brilliant discussion of the argument from design, his less penetrating discussion of other theistic arguments, and his treatment of the problem of evil, all find their way into Part Two. Here, assessment matched one-to-one with presentation. Hume's evidentialism, carried through consistently and universally, like any evidentialism, simply given its own terms, is indefensible. Restricted to matters religious, it is arbitrary; structural beliefs, religious or not, are essential to theorizing, and theorizing is essential to understanding. Hume's theory of meaning, in its restrictive and potentially polemically effective version, bursts its own seams, or is meaningless on its own terms, or is hoist on its own petard, or whatever such expression you prefer for that which claims to legislate validly against other views in a way that demolishes its own validity. The discussions of the argument from design is articulate and thorough; for the sort of formulation that Cleanthes considers, it is negative and decisive. The discussions of the problems of evil are highly interesting and completely unsuccessful in establishing either the claim that *God exists and there is evil* is logically inconsistent or the claim *If evil exists then it is probable that God does not exist.*

Part Three canvasses Hume's more popular essays concerning philosophy of religion, and his infamous essay on miracles. The popular essays, whatever their literary merit and their influence, and independent of their date in Hume's career, philosophically are like the earlier and less glorious works of a great painter. By contrast, his great essay on miracles is subtle and philosophically fascinating. It argues that even if one observed a miracle, one would have better reason than not to think that one hadn't observed one. A great many issues are relevant to this essay—topics in the philosophy of science and epistemology on which Hume's discussion sheds interesting and controversial light. Still, his case is not made; his central theses are not established.

So the results, if I am right, are what one might expect. Hume is right about some things, wrong about others, but he touches no topic without making us his debtor for his having done so.

In general accord with the view of one of philosophers to whom this work is dedicated, but in sharp contrast to the view of the other, this work has argued that Hume's philosophy of religion is deeply flawed. Only his critique of Cleanthean arguments from design entirely succeeds. But such is the nature of philosophy that all three of us have claimed to learn from Hume's philosophy of religion. Those who can learn only from perspectives that are entirely without error will remain largely ignorant.

Notes, Bibliography, and Index

NOTES

Chapter 1

1. J. C. A. Gaskin, in *Hume's Philosophy of Religion* (London: Macmillan Press, 1978), offers an account of Hume's philosophy of religion; Gaskin is a devout Humean. Stanley Tweyman, in *Scepticism and Belief in Hume's Dialogues Concerning Natural Religion* (Dordrecht: Martinus Nijhoff, 1986), analyzes those portions of the *Dialogues* that deal with the argument from design, but sets those sections in a wider context as well.

Chapter 2

1. The interpretation offered in this volume expands that suggested in the present author's "Hume on Religious Belief," in Donald Livingston and James King, eds., *Hume: A Re-evaluation* (New York: Fordham University Press, 1976), pp. 109–25.

Chapter 3

1. Without at all trying to blame him for the errors of this volume, I do want to acknowledge its roots in Marvin Fox's masterful "Religion and Human Nature in the Philosophy of David Hume," in William L. Reese and Eugene Freeman, eds., *Process and Divinity* (LaSalle, Ill.: Open Court Publishing, 1964), pp. 561–77.

2. Norman Kemp Smith, *The Philosophy of David Hume* (1941; reprinted Macmillan, 1964), and his "The Naturalism of Hume," *Mind* 30, n.s. 14 (April 1905): 149–73, and (October 1905), pp. 335–47, are early and excellent expositions of Hume on natural belief.

Chapter 4

1. Robert Paul Wolff, "Hume's Theory of Mental Activity," *Philosophical Review* 69 (July 1960): 289–310, is an excellent account of the general role of propensities in Hume's account of the mind.

2. David Hume, *Abstract of a Treatise of Human Nature*, J. M. Keynes and Peter Sraffa, eds. (Cambridge: Cambridge University Press, 1938), p. 24.

Chapter 5

1. The *Natural History* in the Root edition covers 56 pages. Hume's main discussion of necessary causal connection occurs in the *Treatise* (Selby-Bigge edition), pp. 155–72; his main discussion of belief in external objects on pp. 187–218; and his main discussion of belief in an enduring self on pp. 232–63.

2. Analogously, "Of Miracles" could move from Section X of *An Enquiry Concerning Human Understanding* to, say, a position between *Dialogues* Nine and Ten. On Hume on miracles, see Ninian Smart, *Philosophers and Religious Truth* (London: SCM Press, 1964), chapter 2; Terrence Penelhum, *Religion and Rationality* (New York: Random House, 1971), chapter 19; and the present author's "Miracles, Epistemology, and Hume's Barrier," *International Journal for the Philosophy of Religion* (1976): 391–417, a revised version of which comprises Chapter 15.

3. This is not to sanction Hume's position, which is vitiated by the dispositional nature of most of the states so reported. It is but to note that Hume did take it that there exist cases of true and fully justified belief.

4. George Mavrodes, *Belief in God: A Study in the Epistemology of Religion* (New York: Random House, 1970), pp. 112–14. It should be mentioned that in this chapter I have given a statement of Hume's strategy only as complex as the present context requires.

5. I have explored these issues in "The Nonepistemic Explanation of Religious Belief," *International Journal for Philosophy of Religion* (forthcoming).

6. Isaiah 6:1 (King James Version).

7. *Bhagavad Gita*, chap. 11, sec. 24, trans. Juan Mascaro (Baltimore: Penguin Books, 1962).

8. Isaiah 6:2–5.

9. *Bhagavad Gita*, chap. 18, sec. 64, 65.

10. See Talcott Parsons, "Durkheim on Religion Revisited," in Charles Y. Glock and Phillip E. Hammond, eds., *Beyond the Classics? Essays in the Scientific Study of Religion*, pp. 158–60 (New York: Harper and Row, 1973). Parsons here describes Durkheim's views.

11. See Leonard Glick, "The Anthropology of Religion: Malinowski and Beyond," in Glock and Hammond, eds., *Beyond the Classics?*, p. 215. He is here discussing structuralism, and a proposition asserted by Ward Goodenough.

12. See Glick, "Anthropology," in Glock and Hammond, eds., *Beyond the Classics?*, p. 217. He is here discussing the view of Claude Lévi-Strauss.

Chapter 6

1. Bishop Joseph Butler, *The Analogy of Religion, Natural and Revealed, to the Constitution and Course of Nature* (London, 1736; reprinted New York: Eaton and Mains, and Cincinnati: Curt and Jennings, 1875), p. 33.
2. Ibid., 35.
3. Ibid., 34, 35.
4. Ibid., 36.
5. Ibid., 35.
6. Ibid., 36, 37.
7. Cited in John Orr, *English Deism: Its Roots and Its Fruits* (Grand Rapids, Mich.: Wm. B. Eerdmans, 1934), p. 160.
8. Ibid., 160, 161.

Chapter 7

1. Anthony Kenny, ed. and tr., *Descartes' Philosophical Letters* (London: Oxford, for Clarendon Press, 1970), p. 106.
2. Nicholas Malebranche, *Recherche de la Verité*, liv. 3, chapter 9 (Paris: Garnier Freres, Libraires-Editeurs, n.d.).
3. Compare the present author's "The Ineffability Theme," *International Journal for the Philosophy of Religion* 10, no. 4, (1979): 209–31; and "Some Varieties of Ineffability," *International Journal for the Philosophy of Religion* 6, no. 3 (1975): 167–79.
4. For those inclined to doubt this, an antidote can be found in William P. Alston, "Functionalism and Religious Language," in Thomas Morris, ed., *Divine and Human Action* (Ithaca: Cornell University Press, 1988), pp. 257–80.

Chapter 8

1. *Treatise*, Part Four, Section 2, "Of Scepticism with Regard to the Senses" (opening paragraph).
2. W. K. Clifford, "The Ethics of Belief," in Leslie Stephen and Frederick Pollock, eds., *Lectures and Essays* (London: Macmillan and Co., 1879), vol. II, p. 186.
3. More recent discussions of "proportioning belief to evidence" relevant to Hume's discussion have come from W. K. Clifford, William James, and George Mavrodes. See Keith E. Yandell, ed., *God, Man, and Religion* (New York: McGraw-Hill, 1973), pp. 505–41. See also Brand Blanshard, *Reason and Belief* (New Haven: Yale University Press, 1975), and Alvin Plantinga and

Nicholas Wolterstorff, eds., *Faith and Rationality* (Notre Dame: University of Notre Dame Press, 1984).

Chapter 9

1. See Richard Swinburne, *The Coherence of Theism* (London: Oxford University Press, 1977) and *The Existence of God* (London: Oxford University Press, 1979), for a recent exploration of this project.

2. For an alternative view of theory assessment not tied to giving an account of "best explanation," see the present author's *Christianity and Philosophy* (Grand Rapids, Mich.: W. B. Eerdmans, 1984), chapter 8.

Chapter 11

1. For discussions of the ontological argument, see Alvin Plantinga, *The Ontological Argument from St. Anselm to Contemporary Philosophers* (Garden City, N.Y.: Doubleday-Anchor, 1965); Plantinga, *God, Freedom, and Evil* (New York: Harper and Row, 1974); and Plantinga, *The Nature of Necessity* (Oxford: Oxford University Press, 1974). On the cosmological argument, see Donald R. Burill, ed., *The Cosmological Argument* (Garden City, N.Y.: Doubleday-Anchor, 1967), and William Rowe, *The Cosmological Argument* (Princeton: Princeton University Press, 1975).

2. See the present author's *Christianity and Philosophy* (Grand Rapids, Mich.: Wm. B. Eerdmans, 1984), p. 52.

3. Immanuel Kant, *Critique of Pure Reason*, beginning A603/B631. See Norman Kemp Smith's translation (New York: St. Martin's Press, 1963), pp. 507–18.

4. Leibniz, "That A Most Perfect Being Exists," in A. G. Langley, tr., *New Essays Concerning Human Understanding* (Chicago: University of Chicago Press, 1916), appendix.

Chapter 13

1. This chapter, and the preceding, discuss in brief scope some highly complex and controversial issues. the present author has defended various claims made here in other places as follows: "Ethics, Evils, and Theism," *Sophia* 8, no. 2 (July 1969): 18–28; "A Premature Farewell to Theism," *Religious Studies* 5, no. 4 (December 1969): 251–55; "Theism and Evil," *Sophia* 11, no. 2 (July 1972): 1–7; "Logic and the Problem of Evil," *God, Man, and Religion* (New York: McGraw-Hill, 1973), pp. 351–64; "The Greater Good Defense," *Sophia* 13, no. 3 (October 1974): 1–16; "The Problem of Evil," *Philosophical Topics* 12, no. 3 (1982): 7–38; "The Problem of Evil and the Content of Morality," *International Journal for Philosophy of Religion* 17 (1985): 139–65; "Divine Existence and Gratuitous Evil," *Religious Studies* (forthcoming); and the relevant

chapters in *Basic Issues in the Philosophy of Religion* and *Christianity and Philosophy*. Perhaps, at least, I cannot be accused of underestimating the complexity and controversiality of relevant issues.

2. For an early use of this strategy, see Alvin Plantinga, *God and Other Minds* (Ithaca: Cornell University Press, 1967).

Chapter 14

1. Bishop Joseph Butler, *The Analogy of Religion, Natural and Revealed, to the Constitution and Course of Nature* (London, 1736; reprinted New York: Eaton and Mains, and Cincinnati: Curt and Jennings, 1875), p. 44–45.

Chapter 15

1. Richard Swinburne, *The Concept of Miracle* (New York: St. Martins, 1970), p. 1.

2. Ibid., p. 3.

3. An argument of this sort was presented in an unpublished paper by Professor Joel Friedman, "Hume on Miracles: A Critique," at the Third Annual Hume Conference, Northern Illinois University, October 1974.

4. I have in mind, of course, Thomas Kuhn, *The Structure of Scientific Revolutions*, 2d ed. (Chicago: University of Chicago Press, 1970). The argument as stated here is indebted to Professor Friedman's paper, noted above. I do not ascribe it to him in the form it takes here.

5. Assuming the standard definition of "miracle" stated above, which is also true for (i) below.

6. See below for a different possibility that might, so to say, tenure a miracle.

7. For example, that L is included in a theory T entailed by any plausible paradigm, and that E violates (is an anomaly on) L.

8. The presentation of the Catholic doctrine of the Eucharist this critique presupposes is in fact inaccurate; for our purposes, we need only note this fact.

9. (E2), I take it, is clearly false.

10. *Letters of David Hume*, J. Y. T. Grieg, ed., 2 vols. (Oxford: Oxford University Press, 1932), vol. 1, p. 361.

11. Strictly, "has, *or can obtain*"; for sake of simplicity, I suppose S has obtained it. The backing of (4b) is that a miracle must violate a law of nature, and that a law of nature has the support of all (or most) sensory evidence that is relevant.

12. The caveat in note 15 applies here too. On the current interpretation, Hume's view entails, but is stronger than, that ascribed to him by, for example, M. J. Langford, "The Problem of the Meaning of 'Miracle,'" *Religious Studies* 7 (1971): 44, 46—namely, that no event could be regarded as a miracle

without there being independent theistic evidence. Compare Tan Tai Wei's reply in *Religious Studies* 8 (1972): 251–55.

13. On the problem of interpreting Hume in terms of *observed* or *occurrent-but-unobserved* events, compare Bruce Langtry, "Hume on Testimony to the Miraculous," *Sophia* 11, no. 1 (April 1972): 20–25.

14. Professor Friedman adopted this alternative in the paper referred to in note 3 above. Peter Caws, *The Philosophy of Science* (Princeton: Van Nostrand, 1965), p. 82, makes the same sort of move in an analogous context.

15. I will not deal with the complication that if Al sincerely reports to Ann that Al has observed *M*, and Ann has not observed *M* but has sensory evidence for law *L*, Ann in effect weights Al's sensory evidence against Ann's, and so on.

16. That is, *L* is true, and not merely "established," or accepted as true.

17. Lantry, "Hume on Testimony to the Miraculous," p. 21, makes other criticisms of the *E*, 127 passage. (I neglect, here and elsewhere, the complication that *S* may have observational evidence that an event occurred without having observed the event or having received testimony that the event occurred, for then the observational evidence will require some inference.)

18. I will not here investigate such other matters as whether the alleged miracles associated with various religions in fact have equally good historical credentials (a topic not unrelated to the views of history held by such religions) or to what degree one would or would not have to reject various types of evidence (sensory, historical, etc.) in order to accept the basic tenets of various 'Eastern' or 'Western' religions. Suffice it to say that I do not think all religions are in the very same boat concerning these matters.

19. Compare Ninian Smart, *Reasons and Faiths* (London: Routledge and Kegan Paul, 1958), and *A Dialogue on World Religions* (Baltimore: Penguin Books, 1966), and *Philosophers and Religious Truth* (London: SCM Press, 1964), and "Revelation, Reason and Religions," Ian Ramsey, ed., *Prospect for Metaphysics* (London: Allen and Unwin, 1956), and "The Relation Between Christianity and the Other Great Religions," Alec Vidler, ed., *Soundings* (London: Cambridge University Press, 1962); H. P. Owen, *Concepts of Deity* (New York: Herder and Herder, 1971); and William Christian, *Opposition of Religious Doctrines* (New York: Herder and Herder, 1972), for a sampling of relevant considerations.

20. A few things relevant to these matters can be found in the present writer's *Basic Issues in the Philosophy of Religion* (Boston: Allyn and Bacon, 1971), chapter 6; "Religious Experience and Rational Appraisal," *Religious Studies* 10, no. 2 (June 1974): 172–87.

21. For example, by Professor Friedman, in the paper mentioned in note 3, who holds that the probability in favor of any actual formulation of a law is low at any period in the history of science.

22. Compare Lantry, "Hume on Testimony to the Miraculous," p. 21.

23. Alvin Plantinga, *God and Other Minds* (Ithaca: Cornell University Press, 1969).

24. The degree of "plasticity" possessed by a world view whose parameters are set, at least in part, by law of nature and "physical possibility" is a different matter. One approach to it is through necessarily unrepeatable or *de facto* unrepeatable exceptions to such laws. Compare Ninian Smart, *Philosophers and Religious Truth*, chapter 2, and Richard Swinburne, *The Concept of Miracle*, p. 27. Another is through the variety of sufficient conditions conjoinable with such laws. Compare Robert Young, "Miracles and Physical Impossibility," *Sophia* 11, no. 3 (October 1972): 29–35.

25. Whether talk of "laws of nature" with all this implies—indeed, whether any of the various interpretations of what it does imply—is the best way of expressing a theistic view of natural order on the one hand and miracles on the other has not been discussed here. Those interested in this and similar topics might look at, for example, Dorothy Sayers, *The Mind of the Maker* (New York: Meridian Books, 1956) and C. S. Lewis, *Miracles* (London: Macmillan, 1957). Compare also the possibilities canvassed by Robert Young, "Miracles and Epistemology," *Religious Studies* 8, no. 2 (1972): 115–26 and Tan Tai Wei's further discussion in *Religious Studies* 10, no. 4 (1974): 333–37.

26. The full sentence is "If my philosophy, therefore, makes no addition to the arguments for religion, I have at least the satisfaction to think it takes nothing from them, but that everything remains precisely as before." He did not, of course, say this about "Of Miracles."

27. My concern has been with Hume's views on miracles. A rather different approach to the same topic is provided by Antony Flew, *Hume's Philosophy of Belief* (London: Routledge and Kegan Paul, 1961), chapter 8. Other aspects of the topic, beyond the scope of the present discussion are pursued by, for example, R. F. Holland, "The Miraculous," *American Philosophical Quarterly* 2, no. 1 (1965): 43–51; R. G. Swinburne, "Miracles," *Philosophical Quarterly* 18, no. 73 (October 1968): 320–28; R. C. Wallace, "Hume, Flew and the Miraculous," *Philosophical Quarterly* 20, no. 80 (July 1970): 230–43; Tan Tai Wei, "Recent Discussion on Miracles," *Sophia* 11, no. 3 (October 1972), among many others.

BIBLIOGRAPHY

Primary Sources

Abstract of a Treatise of Human Nature. Cambridge: Cambridge University Press, 1938. Edited by J. M. Keynes and Peter Sraffa.

Dialogues Concerning Natural Religion. 1779; reprinted Indianapolis: Bobbs-Merrill, 1962. Edited and with an Introduction by Norman Kemp Smith.

Enquiries Concerning Human Understanding and Concerning the Principles of Morals. 1748; reprinted Oxford: Clarendon Press, 1975. Introduction and Analytical Index by L. A. Selby-Bigge with text revised and notes by P. H. Nidditch.

Hume on Religion. 1757; reprinted New York: Meridian Books, 1963. Edited by Richard Wollheim (contains *The Natural History of Religion,* the *Dialogues,* and *My Own Life*).

Of the Standard of Taste and Other Essays. Indianapolis: Bobbs-Merrill, 1965. Edited by John W. Lenz.

A Treatise of Human Nature. 1739 and 1740; reprinted 1888; reprinted Oxford: Clarendon Press, 1978. Second ed. Analytical index by L. A. Selby-Bigge with text revised and notes by P. H. Nidditch.

Books

Butler, Bishop Joseph. *The Analogy of Religion, Natural and Revealed, to the Constitution and Course of Nature.* London, 1736; reprinted New York: Eaton and Mains, and Cincinnati; Curt and Jennings, 1875.

Calvin, John. *Institutes of the Christian Religion.* 1536; reprinted Grand Rapids, Mich.: Associated Publishers and Authors, n.d.

Gaskin, J. C. A. *Hume's Philosophy of Religion.* London: Macmillan Press, 1978.

Hendel, C. W. *Studies in the Philosophy of David Hume.* Indianapolis: Bobbs-Merrill, 1963.

Hurlbutt, R. H. *Hume, Newton, and the Design Argument*. Lincoln: University of Nebraska, 1965.

Orr, John. *English Deism: Its Roots and Fruits*. Grand Rapids, Mich.: Wm. B. Eerdmans, 1934.

Seth, James. *English Philosophers and Schools of Philosophy*. London: J. M. Dent and Sons, 1912.

Smith, Norman Kemp. *The Philosophy of David Hume*. 1941; reprint, New York: St. Martin's, 1966.

Sorley, W. R. *A History of English Philosophy*. New York: G. P. Putnam's Sons, 1921.

Tweyman, Stanley. *Scepticism and Belief in Hume's Dialogues Concerning Natural Religion*. Dordrecht: Martinus Nijhoff, 1986.

Articles

Andic, Martin. "Experiential Theism and Verbal Disputes in Hume's *Dialogues*." *Archiv für Geschichte der Philosophie* 56 (1974): 239–46.

Beanblossom, R. E. "A New Foundation for Humean Scepticism." *Philosophical Studies* 29 (1976): 73–95.

Bricke, John. "On the Interpretation of Hume's *Dialogues*." *Religious Studies* 11 (1975): 1–18.

Butler, R. J. "Natural Belief and the Enigma of Hume." *Archiv für Geschichte der Philosophie* 42 (1960): 73–100.

Capitan, William H. "Part X of Hume's *Dialogues*." In *Hume*, edited by V. C. Chappell, 387–96. New York: Doubleday, 1966.

Clarke, B. L. "The Argument from Design: A Piece of Abductive Reasoning." *International Journal for Philosophy of Religion* (1974): 65–78.

Clive, Geoffrey. "Hume's *Dialogues* Reconsidered." *Journal of Religion* 39 (1959): 110–19.

Doore, Gary. "The Argument from Design: Some Better Reasons for Agreeing with Hume." *Religious Studies* 16 (1980): 145–61.

Duerlinger, James. "The Verbal Dispute in Hume's *Dialogues*." *Archiv für Geschichte der Philosophie* 53 (1971): 22–34.

Fox, Marvin. "Religion and Human Nature in the Philosophy of David Hume," in *Process and Divinity*, edited by William L. Reese and Eugene Freeman, 561–77. LaSalle, Ill.: Open Court Publishing, 1964.

Franklin, James. "More on Part IX of Hume's *Dialogues*." *Philosophical Quarterly* 30 (1980): 69–71.

Gaskin, J. C. A. "The Design Argument: Hume's Critique of Poor Reason." *Religious Studies* 12 (1976): 331–45.

———. "God, Hume, and Natural Belief," *Philosophy* 49 (1974): 281–94.

———. "Hume's Critique of Religion." *Journal of the History of Philosophy* 14 (1976): 301–11.

———. "Hume's Criticism of the Argument from Design." *Revue Internationale de Philosophie* 30 (1976): 64–78.

Gawlick, Günter. "Hume and the Deists: A Reconsideration." In *David Hume: Bicentenary Papers*, edited by G. P. Morice, 128–38. Austin: University of Texas, 1977.

Harward, D. W. "Hume's *Dialogues* Revisited." *International Journal for Philosophy of Religion* 6 (1975): 33–42.

Henze, D. F. "On Some Alleged Humean Insights and Oversights." *Religious Studies* 6 (1970): 369–77.

Hurlbutt, R. H. "David Hume and Scientific Theism." *Journal of the History of Ideas* 17 (1956): 486–97.

Jacobson, N. P. "The Uses of Reason in Religion: A Note on David Hume." *Journal of Religion* 39 (1959): 103–9.

Jeffner, Anders. "Butler and Hume on Religion: A Comparative Analysis." *Philosophical Review* 77 (1966): 369–72.

Jones, Peter. "Hume's Two Concepts of God." *Philosophy* 47 (1972): 322–33.

Keen, C. N. "Reason in Hume's *Dialogues*." *Philosophical Papers* 5 (1976): 121–34.

Laing, B. M. "Hume's *Dialogues Concerning Natural Religion*." *Philosophy* 12 (1937): 175–90.

McPherson, Thomas. "The Argument from Design." *Philosophy* 32 (1957): 219–28.

Mossner, E. C., "The Enigma of Hume." *Mind* 45 (1936): 334–49.

———. "Hume and the Legacy of the *Dialogues*." In *David Hume: Bicentenary Papers*, edited by G. P. Morice, 1–22. Austin: University of Texas, 1977.

———. "Hume's *Dialogues Concerning Natural Religion*: An Answer to Dr. Laing." *Philosophy* 13 (1938): 84–86.

———. "The Religion of David Hume." *Journal of the History of Ideas* 39 (1978): 653–63.

Nathan, G. J. "The Existence and Nature of Hume's Theism." In *Hume: A Reevaluation*, edited by D. Livingston and J. King, 123–49. New York: Fordham University, 1976.

———. "Hume's Immanent God." In *Hume*, edited by V. C. Chappell, 396–423. New York: Doubleday, 1966.

Noxon, James. "Hume's Agnosticism." In *Hume*, edited by V. C. Chappell, 360–83. New York: Doubleday, 1966.

———. "In Defense of 'Hume's Agnosticism.'" *Journal of the History of Philosophy* 14 (1976): 469–73.

Parent, W. A. "An Interpretation of Hume's *Dialogues*." *Review of Metaphysics* 30 (1976): 96–114.

Pearl, Leon. "Hume's Criticism of the Design Argument." *The Monist* 54 (1970): 270–84.

Penelhum, Terence. "Hume's Scepticism and the *Dialogues*." In *McGill Hume Studies*, edited by D. F. Norton et al., 253–78. San Diego: Austin Hill Press, 1979.

Salmon, W. C. "Religion and Science: A New Look at Hume's *Dialogues*." *Philosophical Studies* 33 (1978): 143–76.

Stove, D. C. "Part IX of Hume's *Dialogues.*" *Philosophical Quarterly* 28 (1978): 199–212.

Taylor, A. E., Laird, J., and Jessop, T. E. "The Present Day Relevance of Hume's *Dialogues Concerning Natural Religion.*" *Aristotelian Society* suppl. vol. 18 (1939): 179–228.

Tweyman, Stanley. "Remarks on Wadia's 'Philo Confounded.'" *Hume Studies* April (1982): 19–42.

———. "The Vegetable Library and God." *Dialogue* 18 (1979): 512–27.

Wadia, P. S. "Philo Confounded." In *McGill Hume Studies,* edited by D. F. Norton et al., 279–90. San Diego: Austin Hill Press, 1979.

———. "Professor Pike on Part III of Hume's *Dialogues.*" *Religious Studies* 14 (1978): 325–42.

Yandell, K. E. "Hume on Religious Belief." In *Hume: A Re-evaluation,* edited by Donald Livingston and James King, 109–25. New York: Fordham University, 1976.

———. "Hume's Explanation of Religious Belief." *Hume Studies* 5 (1979): 94–109.

———. "Miracles, Epistemology, and Hume's Barrier." *International Journal for the Philosophy of Religion* 12 (1976): 391–417.

INDEX